ECONOMIC ISSUES, PROBLEMS AND PERSPECTIVES

STOCK MARKETS

EMERGENCE, MACROECONOMIC FACTORS AND RECENT DEVELOPMENTS

Economic Issues, Problems and Perspectives

Additional books in this series can be found on Nova's website under the Series tab.

Additional e-books in this series can be found on Nova's website under the e-book tab.

ECONOMIC ISSUES, PROBLEMS AND PERSPECTIVES

STOCK MARKETS

EMERGENCE, MACROECONOMIC FACTORS AND RECENT DEVELOPMENTS

FILIPPO PETRONI, Ph.D.
FLAVIO PRATTICO
AND
GUGLIELMO D'AMICO
EDITORS

nova publishers
New York

For permission to use material from this book please contact us:
Telephone 631-231-7269; Fax 631-231-8175
Web Site: http://www.novapublishers.com

Library of Congress Cataloging-in-Publication Data

ISBN: 978-1-62808-751-2

Published by Nova Science Publishers, Inc. † New York

CONTENTS

PREFACE

Much effort has gone into the study of financial markets and how prices vary with time. The usual approach of random walk is known to be inadequate to fully describe price dynamics. In this book, many different approaches are provided that use alternative and more adequate models.

Chapter 1 - Many previous studies report mean reversion phenomenon in stock returns, however, there are few studies devoted to detect the dynamics behind the process of mean reversion, or different driving forces responsible for the mean reversion phenomenon in the stock market. The major purpose of this chapter is to investigate dynamics of mean reversion in the U.S. stock market in four important sub-periods: World War I (1886-1919), World War II (1920-1946), Post war (1947-1985), and IT revolution (1986-2008).

Results of this study suggest four- and five-year mean reversion and aversion cycles in the first and second sub-periods: below-mean returns→ extremely positive returns→ (reduced returns→) near-mean returns→ below-mean returns. The cycles reflect two important phases, overreaction and correction, in the stock market. However, mean reversion lasts longer in the third sub-period and a delayed mean reversion is found in the fourth sub-period.

The behavior of the stock market after lowest negative returns is quite different. Results indicate that the mean reversion process takes place only in the second and fourth sub-periods and the sharp reversal process takes over mean reversion in the first and third sub-periods. The analysis of internal driving force of mean reversion process reveals a clear shift in the process of mean reversion between the first two sub-periods and last two sub-periods, sharp reversals in stock returns are replaced with gradual declines in stock returns after the stock market experiences extraordinary advances. On the other hand, after lowest negative stock returns, sharp return reversals push the extremely bearish stock market up to the historical accumulative mean and furthermore, their continuation push stock returns far beyond the accumulative mean in the first and third sub-periods. In these two sub-periods the reversal process completely overrides the mean reversion. However, in the second and fourth sub-periods that contain two most severe economic recessions, reversals are much milder. The driving force of reversals in different sub-periods is the continuing positive investor sentiment in the stock market.

Chapter 2 - Central and Eastern European stock markets were subject to two major events in the last ten years. In 2004 some of them became new members of the European Union. In 2008 global financial markets were shaken and the financial crisis substantially impacted

CEE markets. Several papers report these events have increased correlations among CEE stock market and vis-à-vis global markets. In this chapter the authors analyze time-varying conditional correlations for daily data of major index returns of six emerging stock markets of Central and Eastern Europe. As a proxy for global stock markets the authors select index returns for US, German, UK, and Japan stock exchanges. The authors apply methodology based on the Asymmetric Dynamic Conditional Correlations (ADCC) model extended in order to identify changes in the structure of correlations. Results indicate that the events studied had significant impact on the long-term mean of estimated models, while dynamics tended to change but insignificantly.

Chapter 3 - In this chapter, the author model financial markets with semi-Markov volatilities and price covariance and correlation swaps for this markets. Numerical evaluations of variance, volatility, covariance and correlations swaps with semi-Markov volatility are presented as well. The novelty of the chapter lies in pricing of volatility swaps in closed form, and pricing of covariance and correlation swaps in a market with two risky assets.

Chapter 4 - The renewal theory has great relevance in actuarial science. A simple actuarial model can be simulated well by means of this kind of stochastic process. The renewal process is strictly related to the Laplace transform theory. In a general case, solving the renewal equation is not a simple task and it is necessary to solve it numerically. Usually, in order to numerically solve the renewal equation the Laplace transform approach is used. There is a problem in that the inversion of the Laplace transform is not stable numerically thus implying that the results obtained in this way cannot be reliable.

In this chapter, a straightforward method is presented that deals directly with the numerical solution of the renewal equation. It is proved that any kind of renewal process can be solved by means of this approach. In conclusion, an application useful in the field of motorcar insurance is presented. By means of renewal equation, the mean number of car accidents that an insured person can have in one year, two years, three years and so on up to 37 years (maximum years number that is considered because of the available data) is computed The related distribution function was constructed with real data given by a primary insurance company.

Chapter 5 - Based on a theoretical model for opinion spreading on a network, through avalanches, the effect of external field is now considered, by using methods from non-equilibrium statistical mechanics. The original part contains the implementation that the avalanche is only triggered when a local variable (a so called awareness) reaches and goes above a threshold. The dynamical rules are constrained to be as simple as possible, in order to sort out the basic features, though more elaborated variants are proposed. Several results are obtained for a Erdos-Renyi network and interpreted through simple analytical laws, scale free or logistic map-like, i.e., (i) the sizes, durations, and number of avalanches, including the respective distributions, (ii) the number of times the external field is applied to one possible node before all nodes are found to be above the threshold, (iii) the number of nodes still below the threshold and the number of hot nodes (close to threshold) at each time step.

Chapter 6 - It is evident that the 2008-US sub-prime mortgage crisis broadly affected international financial markets. However, how the crisis's magnitude impacted on Asian financial markets has not had much attention. To fill this gap, this chapter examines changes in dependence structures between the US market and Asian financial markets before and after the crisis. The chapter uses two non-parametric methods of plotting, namely, Chi-plot and

Kendall-plot, and a copula analysis to characterize the changes. The results show that the dependence structure of the U.S. stock market and the stock markets of Hong Kong, Indonesia, Singapore and Thailand changed to a lower tail dependence after the crisis. In contrast, no changes in the dependence structure are found between the US market and the markets of Japan, Malaysia and the Philippines. The chapter's findings on the dependence changes, which have not previously been documented, provide important implications for risk management, hedging strategies and asset pricing.

Chapter 7 - The recent crisis poses serious doubts on the effectiveness of diversification to reduce draw-downs in balanced portfolios: "diversification failed when it was mostly needed" was the leitmotif of many institutional investors after 2008. Nevertheless, recent portfolio construction schemes, like risk parity and maximum diversification, make of diversification the kernel of asset allocation. While most approaches diversify on asset classes' level, the new challenge in asset allocation suggests diversifying on fundamental factors that are believed to be the main drivers of asset price dynamics.

In the present work the authors firstly review the main approaches to analyze portfolio concentration and diversification, and then the authors show how to get optimally diversified asset allocation from a practical point of view. Factors approach can be divided in statistical-based methods, mainly based on principal component analysis, and more fundamental approaches (economic scenario methods) which ex-ante identify factors in terms of macroeconomic and market stress indicators.

In this work the authors review main techniques:

- to evaluate portfolio risk concentration (Herfindahl index, Lorentz curves, Gini coefficient),
- to measure risk distribution within the asset-class space (marginal contribution to risk, and entropy-based diversification measure)
- and within the principal components' space.

Moreover the authors briefly review the economic scenario methods. The authors conclude discussing implications in terms of portfolio constructions focusing mainly on two diversification measures: (1) the entropy-based diversification metric of a scaled function of the marginal-contributions-to-risk, and (2) the difference between the weighted sum of volatilities of each position and the portfolio total volatility.

Chapter 8 - This article derives optimal fiscal rules within a stochastic model of Keynesian type in the context of Poole (1970) analysis. By using optimal control theory and applying the Hamilton-Jacoby-Bellman equation, the authors extend the original Poole results concerning the output stabilization properties of monetary policy to the case of fiscal policy. In particular, the authors look for the optimal setting of government expenditure and lump-sum taxation in the case that the fiscal authority wishes to keep the product close to a reference value and that the economy is assumed to be affected by stochastic disturbances of real and/or monetary type. According to the findings an expenditure rule is preferable to a taxation rule whatever the source of disturbances.

Chapter 9 - In this chapter the authors describe three stochastic models based on a semi-Markov chains approach and its generalizations to study the high frequency price dynamics of traded stocks. The three models are: a simple semi-Markov chain model, an indexed semi-Markov chain model and a weighted indexed semi-Markov chain model. The authors show, through Monte Carlo simulations, that the models are able to reproduce important stylized facts of financial time series as the persistence of volatility. In particular the authors analyzed high frequency data from the Italian stock market from first of January 2007 until end of December 2010 and the authors apply to it the semi-Markov chain model and the indexed semi-Markov chain model. The last model, instead, is applied to data from Italian and German stock market from 1 January 2007 until the end of December 2010.

Chapter 10 - A new multi-agent model of the stock market is formulated that contains four states in which the agents may be located. Next, the model is reformulated in the language of the functional integral containing fluctuations of prices and quantities of cash flows. It is shown that in the functional integral of that type description of the prices is given not by the real numbers as is made in many papers but the p-adic numbers. It is shown in the following simple examples extracted from the proposed theory that the p-adic description of prices gives good description of fractal behavior of the trends. The formula is given for the p-adic mapping of prices. Using this formula the authors obtain the main p-adic patterns which are the same as the patterns of Elliott wave theory, this fact allows them to give a rigorous mathematical proof of this theory. Their model is the only model that gives a strict point like description of the fractal behavior of prices. The developed approach opens the possibility to give the formulation of p-adic technical analysis of the stock market.

Chapter 11 - In the choices over the time between different sums the preference relation and the related indifference relation are of great interest in the development of the deterministic finance theory. In some previous paper the author showed how is possible to face this kind of problem in a stochastic environment by means of Semi-Markov processes. In this chapter they will enhance the previous results giving a larger weight to the non-homogeneous case that, in spite of the greatest difficulty, seems to be a more natural approach to the problem.

In the chapter will be also presented some new results on the numerical solution of this kind of processes. Furthermore an applicative example will be given.

In: Stock Markets
Editors: F. Petroni, F. Prattico and G. D'Amico

ISBN: 978-1-62808-751-2

Chapter 1

DYNAMICS OF MEAN REVERSION AFTER EXTREME STOCK RETURNS IN THE PAST 125 YEARS

Ling T. He*
Department of Economics and Finance,
University of Central Arkansas, Conway, Arkansas, US

ABSTRACT

Many previous studies reported mean reversion phenomenon in stock returns, however, there are few studies devoted to detect the dynamics behind the process of mean reversion, or driving forces responsible for the mean reversion phenomenon in the stock market. The major purpose of this chapter is to investigate dynamics of mean reversion in the U.S. stock market in four important sub-periods: World War I (1886-1919), World War II (1920-1946), Post war (1947-1985), and IT revolution (1986-2008).

Results of this study suggest four- and five-year mean reversion and aversion cycles in the first and second sub-periods: below-mean returns→ extremely positive returns→ (reduced returns→) near-mean returns→ below-mean returns. The cycles reflect two important phases, overreaction and correction, in the stock market. However, mean reversion lasts longer in the third sub-period and a delayed mean reversion is found in the fourth sub-period.

The behavior of the stock market after lowest negative returns is quite different. Results indicate that the mean reversion process takes place only in the second and fourth sub-periods and the sharp reversal process takes over mean reversion in the first and third sub-periods.

The analysis of internal driving force of mean reversion process reveals a clear shift in the process of mean reversion between the first two sub-periods and last two sub-periods, sharp reversals in stock returns are replaced with gradual declines in stock returns after the stock market experiences extraordinary advances. On the other hand, after lowest negative stock returns, sharp return reversals push the extremely bearish stock market up to the historical accumulative mean and furthermore, the long lasting momentum advances stock returns far beyond the accumulative mean in the first and

* Corresponding Author Email address: linghe@uca.edu

third sub-periods. In these two sub-periods the reversal process completely overrides the mean reversion. However, in the second and fourth sub-periods that contain two most severe economic recessions, reversals are much milder. The driving force of reversals in different sub-periods is the continuing positive investor sentiment in the stock market.

INTRODUCTION

Mean reversion is a statistical phenomenon that a nonrandom sample with extreme values, for purely statistical reasons, has a tendency to regress towards its population average. Francis Galton was the first to describe and explain this phenomenon in his experiments on the size of the seeds of successive generations of sweet peas in late 1860s (Bulmer, 2003). Later, Galton (1886) found that human characteristics also displayed a natural tendency of "regression towards mediocrity." Since then mean reversion has widely been observed or verified in many different areas and subjects, including economics and finance. For example, economists can effectively use mean reversion concept to explain business cycle. However, there is no consensus as to whether stock prices are mean reverting. By using various regression-based tests and the variance-ratio method, many economists, including Fama and French (1988a, 1988b) and Poterba and Summers (1988), report significant negative serial correlation in long-term stock returns. It implies that stock returns tend to revert to their mean in the long run. Nonetheless, Kim, Nelson and Startz (1991) discover that mean reversion only occurs before the World War II. Cochran and DeFina (1994) find mixed evidence from 18 country equity indexes over the period of 1969 to 1989 to support mean reversion phenomenon in long-term returns. Furthermore, in his study on extreme stock returns, Hirschey (2003) points out that those extreme returns do exhibit significant reversal adjustments, but not necessarily regression to the mean. He uses two nonrandom sample sets, extreme annual return series and their one-year forward-looking return series. His results suggest that the mean of forward-looking returns, after best historical S&P 500 returns, is close to the overall average, that is, it reverts to the population mean. On the other hand, the mean of forward-looking returns, after worst historical S&P 500 returns, does not revert to the population mean. In fact, the reversal far exceeds the population mean. The similar behavior is also found in Nasdaq returns.

In Hirschey's (2003) above analysis the population mean is based on his entire data set. In his paper on mean aversion and reversion in the stock market, He (2009) argues that this population mean may be problematic. In a time-series data set, for a particular observation, its population mean should cover a period which starts with this observation and extends back to the beginning of the data set. It means that regression to the mean implies the forward-looking returns, the one after extreme returns, leaning towards their past average. A population mean applied in the mean reversion analysis should not contain future observations. For example, in Hirschey's dataset (1950-2002) some worst returns occurred in 1974, it is not reasonable, based the mean reversion concept, to expect that reversals of extremely negative returns in 1975, one-year forward-looking returns, can partially "predict" future returns up to the end of his dataset (2002). In order to properly examine mean reversion phenomenon in S&P 500 returns, He (2009) proposes that accumulative means should serve as the population mean. For example, the accumulative mean for 1975 covers observations from the beginning of the dataset through 1975 only, consequently, each individual observation has its own corresponding accumulative mean. Using the accumulative mean to analyze the S&P 500 returns, He (2009) finds positive evidence for the mean reversion phenomenon over entire sample period of 1886-2008 and the time-varying nature of mean reversion.

Regardless previous mixed findings about mean reversion in stock returns, there are few studies devoted to detect the dynamics behind the process of mean reversion. Different driving forces can be responsible for the mean reversion phenomenon in the stock market. Extremely positive or negative stock returns may change their moving courses and directly head toward the historical means. This is a clear and simple reversion to mean process. However, extreme stock returns may completely reverse their courses, from positive to negative, or vice versa; or simply sustain the current courses in a much slower pace, for example, from an appreciation rate of 30% to 3%. If this is the case, mean reversion is merely the result of averaging of positive and negative returns or high and low returns. Thus, the dynamics of mean reversion may show actual patterns in volatile stock market fluctuations.

It is not arduous to understand a reversal of stock returns after the stock market reaches an extreme level; however, it is not so evident why positive stock returns might immediately follow some extremely positive returns. Previous findings, for instance, DeLong et al. (1991), indicate that stock investors are exuberant most times and reluctant to bid down stock prices even in the phase of forming equity bubbles. Furthermore, according to Abreu and Brunnermeier (2003) and Griffin et al. (2003), even rational traders typically bet with the bubble rather than against it, because the mispricing might increase further and bet against it implying losses. Therefore, information about different courses toward the historical mean in the post-periods of extreme stock returns is highly relevant to financial policy-making and risk management in precarious market conditions, such as a bust of equity bubble.

He (2009) points out that a complete long-term cycle of stock price changes consists of both overacting and correcting phases, as suggested by mean aversion and reversion. The two phases which shape the dynamics of stock prices divulge that investors cannot constantly be rational as implied in the Efficient Market Hypothesis or irrational as elaborated in Behavioral Finance. An effective research method should analyze both phases. However, the Efficient Market Hypothesis and Behavioral Finance tend to focus on one phase only, although both cast some useful insights into investor rational and irrational behaviors. In order to depict a full picture of long-term stock price changes, a thorough empirical analysis of the dynamics of stock prices is necessary and deserves serious attention from both academia and investment professionals.

The major purpose of this study is to investigate dynamics of mean reversion in several important periods in past 125 years, in order to uncover any meaningful changing patterns. Considering the time-varying nature of mean reversion, the entire 125-year sample period needs to be divided into some sub-periods based on significant historical events. Specifically, this study uses the following four sub-periods: World War I (1886-1919), World War II (1920-1946), Post war (1947-1985), and IT revolution (1986-2008).

DATA AND METHODOLOGY

A long time-series data set can provide us a clear picture about the time-varying nature of mean reversion. The S&P 500 Composite Index is the best to fit the need. The index can trace back as far as 1885. According to Standard & Poor's (1998), the monthly indexes for the period of 1885 through 1917 have been converted to the 1941-1943 base from the Cowles Commission Stock Price Indexes, the Cowles Commission Series P, that covers the period of 1871-1938. The Cowles Commission Series P used the weekly Standard Statistics Index (the predecessor of the Standard and Poor 500 Composite Index) to construct their indexes after 1917, in most cases without any adjustments (Cowles, 1939). In other words, starting in 1918, the Series P is simply the monthly averages of the weekly Standard Statistics Indexes. The only adjustment made by Cowles (1939) is the number of shares outstanding. Therefore, essentially, both the Series P of Cowles and the Standard Statistics Index employ the same method of index construction and contain the same companies as many as possible.

The data used in this analysis is the monthly S&P 500 Index starts with January of 1885 and extends to December of 2010 (1,500 observations). However, there are missing data for four months during World War I, August through November of 1914, and the index number for July of 1914 is applied to the four months.

Mean reversion phenomena after extremely positive and negative stock returns were reported in previous studies. However, the criteria used to determine extremely returns are arbitrary. He (2013) suggests a more rigorous method of determining extreme stock returns. An extreme stock return is defined as one that significantly deviates from its corresponding accumulative mean. Therefore, a simple test of equal mean can detect all extreme observations by testing the null hypothesis that a particular observation is equal to its corresponding accumulative mean. In order to uncover all extreme returns contained in a sample, He (2013) utilizes an equality-test loop. In a rigorous examination of mean reversion, the nonrandom sample set should include as many extreme observations as possible. Therefore, this study uses the ten percent significance level as the threshold in the equality test. Compared with the one or five percent significance levels, the ten percent level sets a higher standard for testing mean reversion, because it allows more returns to be qualified as extreme returns.

The following procedure is employed to building nonrandom samples. First, the whole sample set is divided into two subsample sets. One is a positive sample with a descending order and the other is a negative one with an ascending order. A loop is then set for the equality test for each of these two sample sets. Observations with significant (at the ten percent at the least) deviations from their corresponding accumulative means are included in the nonrandom samples. Finally, three more sample sets are built to attain one-, two-, and three-year forward-looking observations, respectively, for each initial nonrandom sample set. If a forward-looking sample has a mean which is insignificantly different from the average of accumulative means, a reversion to mean phenomenon is detected.

A further analysis of distribution of forward-looking returns that already demonstrated reversion to mean may shed insights on driving forces for mean reversion. The analysis can tell the exact number of returns that is insignificantly different from the corresponding accumulative mean, i.e., direct mean reversion; and how many observations are still significantly higher or lower than their corresponding accumulative means, i.e., indirect mean reversion- a consequence of the offset between these higher and lower returns. The results may reveal important information about stock market behavior. The forward-looking returns remaining positive after extremely positive returns indicate a buoyant market; while those turning into negative after extremely positive returns imply a market correction. The ratio of these two suggests the strength of exuberance of investors. The similar analysis can also be applied to forward-looking returns derived from the sample of extremely negative returns. In this case, a reversal indicates optimistic market momentum and the continuous negative forward-looking returns illustrate a distressed market.

EMPIRICAL RESULTS

There are 1,500 monthly rolling annual returns included in the 125-year sample period (1886-2010). Their average is 6.33% with a standard deviation of 19.16% (Table 1). In this return series positive returns greatly outnumber negative ones, 961 vs. 539 (1.78:1.00). It simply mirrors the long-term optimistic sentiment in the stock market. The average of positive returns is 17.34% with a maximum monthly return of 124.15%, while negative returns have a mean of -13.29% and a worst monthly return of -65.61%.

Table 1. Monthly Rolling Annual Returns and Averages of Their Corresponding Accumulative Means

	N	Mean	Std. Deviation	Maximum	Minimum
Return	1500	0.0633	0.1916	1.2415	-0.6561
Posireturn	961	0.1734	0.1294	1.2415	0.0000
Acumean	961	0.0503	0.0234	0.2264	-0.0025
Negareturn	539	-0.1329	0.1106	-0.0002	-0.6561
Acumean	539	0.0439	0.0173	0.1280	-0.0032

Return=monthly rolling annual return series of S&P 500 Stock Index (1886-2010).
Posireturn=positive monthly rolling annual returns.
Negareturn=negative monthly rolling annual returns.
Acumean=accumulative mean of monthly rolling annual returns corresponding to periods of Posireturn and Negareturn, respectively.
N=number of observations.

All possible highest positive returns (ReturnH) and their mean-reverting forward-looking returns are reported in Table 2. The nonrandom sample consists of 228 observations (ReturnH) that are selected from 961 positive returns through a loop of repeating equality test. The loop starts with the highest return to lower ones, therefore, the null hypothesis of equality between returns and the accumulative means is rejected at continuously declining significance levels, as lower returns are added into the sample. The cutoff point is the 10% significance level. The lowest return in ReturnH is 24.78% and the sample mean is 34.63%, in contrast to 4.80%, the average of accumulative means of the rolling annual returns corresponding to the periods of the 228 highest returns. The t-statistic for the equality test reaches 32.11. Evidently, the sample mean is significantly higher than the average of accumulative means.

After one year the average of the 228 returns (ReturnF1) reduces to 7.01% which is not substantially different from the average of corresponding accumulative means (5.12%) at the 10% significance level (Table 2). Statistically, this is a marginal case for mean reversion phenomenon. The mean return after two year further declines to 3.39% which is statistically

Table 2. 228 Highest Returns That Display Mean Reversion in the Following Year

	Mean	Std. Deviation	Maximum	Minimum
ReturnB	0.0201	0.2095	0.4860	-0.6561
AcumeanB	0.0445	0.0129	0.0673	0.0057
t-test	-1.76*			
ReturnH	0.3463	0.1208	1.2415	0.2478
AcumeanH	0.0480	0.0113	0.0687	0.0171
t-test	37.12***			
ReturnF1	0.0701	0.1750	0.4864	-0.3598
AcumeanF1	0.0512	0.0096	0.0692	0.0287
t-test	1.63			
ReturnF2	0.0339	0.2163	0.7669	-0.4307
AcumeanF2	0.0505	0.0103	0.0691	0.0241
t-test	-1.16			
ReturnF3	0.0241	0.2240	0.4610	-0.6561
AcumeanF3	0.0496	0.0114	0.0692	0.0251
t-test	-1.72*			
ReturnB	0.0201			
ReturnF1	0.0701			
t-test	2.76***			
ReturnB	0.0201			
	Mean	Std. Deviation	Maximum	Minimum
ReturnF2	0.0339			
t-test	0.69			
ReturnB	0.0201			
ReturnF3	0.0241			
t-test	0.19			

ReturnH= highest monthly rolling annual returns in the period of 1886-2008.
AcumeanH=accumulative means of the rolling annual returns corresponding to the periods of ReturnH.
ReturnB=returns one year prior to ReturnH.
AcumeanB=accumulative means of the rolling annual returns corresponding to the periods of ReturnB.
ReturnF1=returns one year after ReturnH.
AcumeanF1=accumulative means of the rolling annual returns corresponding to the periods of ReturnF1.
ReturnF2=returns two years after ReturnH.
AcumeanF2=accumulative means of the rolling annual returns corresponding to the periods of ReturnF2.
ReturnF3=returns three years after ReturnH.
AcumeanF3=accumulative means of the rolling annual returns corresponding to the periods of ReturnF3.
The t-test of equal means is not based on the assumption of equal variances.
* indicates the ten percent significance level.
** indicates the five percent significance level.
*** indicates the one percent significance level.

Table 3. Mean Reversions of ReturnH in Sub-Periods

	1886-1919	1920-1946	1947-1985	1986-2008
# of observations	33	82	62	51
ReturnB	-0.0899	0.0309	-0.0166	0.1185
AcumeanB	0.0280	0.0360	0.0510	0.0610
t-test	-4.78***	-0.19	-2.92***	2.53**
ReturnH	0.3209	0.3984	0.3267	0.3027
AcumeanH	0.0348	0.0406	0.0528	0.0626
t-test	31.37***	18.41***	34.00***	36.05***
ReturnF1	0.0532	0.0318	0.0824	0.1275
AcumeanF1	0.0423	0.0443	0.0546	0.0638
t-test	0.78	-0.50	1.59	3.16***
ReturnF2	-0.0672	-0.0045	0.0616	0.1273
AcumeanF2	0.0396	0.0432	0.0547	0.0644
t-test	-4.02***	-1.51	0.44	2.70***
ReturnF3	-0.0211	-0.0202	0.0663	0.0730
AcumeanF3	0.0347	0.0422	0.0548	0.0648
t-test	-2.09**	-1.86*	0.54	0.42
ReturnB	-0.0899	0.0309	-0.0166	0.1185
ReturnF1	0.0532	0.0318	0.0824	0.1275
t-test	-5.06***	-0.22	-3.41***	-0.30
ReturnB	-0.0899	0.0309	-0.0166	0.1185
ReturnF2	-0.0672	-0.0045	0.0616	0.1273
t-test	-0.63	0.85	-2.79***	-0.27
ReturnB	-0.0899	0.0309	-0.0166	0.1185
ReturnF3	-0.0211	-0.0202	0.0663	0.0730
t-test	-1.89**	1.18	-2.64***	1.51

ReturnH= highest monthly rolling annual returns in the period of 1886-2008.
AcumeanH=accumulative means of the rolling annual returns corresponding to the periods of ReturnH.
ReturnB=returns one year prior to ReturnH.
AcumeanB=accumulative means of the rolling annual returns corresponding to the periods of ReturnB.
ReturnF1=returns one year after ReturnH.
AcumeanF1=accumulative means of the rolling annual returns corresponding to the periods of ReturnF1.
ReturnF2=returns two years after ReturnH.
AcumeanF2=accumulative means of the rolling annual returns corresponding to the periods of ReturnF2.
ReturnF3=returns three years after ReturnH.
AcumeanF3=accumulative means of the rolling annual returns corresponding to the periods of ReturnF3.
The t-test of equal means is not based on the assumption of equal variances.
* indicates the ten percent significance level.
** indicates the five percent significance level.
*** indicates the one percent significance level.

indifferent from the corresponding accumulative mean of 5.05%, a clear case of mean reversion. After mean reversion, stock returns are expected to deviate from the corresponding accumulative means. The mean of ReturnH after three years (ReturnF3) is 2.41% which significantly below the accumulative mean of 4.96%. Both numbers are almost identical to that one year prior to the sample of ReturnH, the mean of ReturnB of 2.01% and the corresponding accumulative mean of 4.45%, as evidenced by a trivial t-value of 0.19 of the equality test. The results imply a five-year mean reversion and aversion cycle: below-mean returns→ extremely positive returns→ reduced returns→ near-mean returns→ below-mean returns. The cycle reflects two important phases, overreaction and correction, in the stock market.

However, results presented in Table 3 portray different mean reversion paths over time. During the period of 1886-1919 it takes only one year for stock returns reverting to the accumulative mean. The average of stock returns one year after the highest positive returns, ReturnH of 32.09%, is 5.32% which is insignificantly different from the accumulative mean of 4.23%. The downward trend quickly brings stock returns into the negative territory in the second (ReturnF2) and third year (ReturnF3) after ReturnH. Compared with their corresponding positive accumulative means, 3.96% and 3.47%, those negative stock returns obviously avert from the accumulative means. Nevertheless, ReturnF3 lessens the precipitous decline, evidenced with a mean of -2.11%, in contrast to -6.72% (ReturnF2) one year ago.

A similar one-year mean reversion process is also found in the second sub-period, 1920-1946. Stock returns abruptly drop from 39.84% to 3.18% which is even slightly below the accumulative mean of 4.43% (Table 3). The mean reversion process essentially extends into the second year after ReturnH as suggested by an insignificant t-value of -1.51 for the test of equal ReturnF2 and AcumeanF2, the accumulative mean. During the following two years stock returns keep sinking to -0.45% and -2.02%. There is no sign of reverse in the forward-looking stock returns (ReturnF3) in the second sub-period. The severe pessimistic sentiment in the stock market in the second sub-period may be the reflection of the great depression and World War II.

It seems that the mean reversion takes more time to reach in the post-war period of 1947-1985. Although stock returns drop from 32.67%, within one year, to 8.24%, compared with the accumulative mean of 5.46% (Table 3), it is just a marginal mean reversion. Stock returns continue to decline to 6.16% in the following year and remain at the similar level (6.63%) two years after ReturnH, and t-values indicate that the two levels are statistically equal to the corresponding accumulative means of about 5.5%. This enduring mean reversion process exhibits a remarkable course, in contrast to mean reversion processes in the first and second sub-periods. The decline in stock returns after the first plunge becomes mild and stable and never reaches the negative territory. The lasting post-war economic growth may be the crucial reason for resilient optimistic momentum in the stock market.

The positive momentum has a stronger demonstration during the information technology revolution period, 1986-2008. After stock returns reach the 30.27% level, the correction takes place. The stock returns tumble to 12.75% within one year and stay at the same level for another year and reduce to 7.3% in the third year (Table 3). This correction is much milder than that in the third sub-period. The stable declining of stock returns hinders the mean reversion process which is attained three years after ReturnH.

Results of equality test for forward-looking returns and corresponding accumulative means suggest four- and five-year mean reversion and aversion cycles in the first and second sub-periods: below-mean returns→ extremely positive returns→ (reduced returns→) near-mean returns→ below-mean returns. However, forward-looking returns are never lower than corresponding accumulative means in the third and fourth sub-periods in which buoyant investor sentiment dominates.

Table 4. Distribution of Returns in Mean Reversions of ReturnH in Following Years

	1886-1919	1920-1946	1947-1985	1986-2008
#ofPosi/Near/Nega	14/10/9	30/12/40	26/17/19	30/10/11
Posi-ReturnF1	0.1198	0.2842	0.2136	0.2317
Posi-AcumeanF1	0.0447	0.0462	0.0536	0.0646
Near-ReturnF1	0.0553	0.0457	0.0561	0.0652
Near-AcumeanF1	0.0444	0.0422	0.0551	0.0657
t-test	1.61	0.41	0.12	-0.57
Nega-ReturnF1	-0.0528	-0.1618	-0.0734	-0.1000
Nega-AcumeanF1	0.0361	0.0436	0.0554	0.0599
#ofPosi/Near/Nega	5/5/23	33/11/38	24/14/24	29/12/10
Posi-ReturnF2	0.2091	0.2783	0.1917	0.2409
Posi-AcumeanF2	0.0323	0.0400	0.0553	0.0647
Near-ReturnF2	0.0245	0.0278	0.0504	0.0810
Near-AcumeanF2	0.0425	0.04147	0.0541	0.0655
t-test	-0.94	-1.66	-0.46	1.56
Nega-ReturnF2	-0.1472	-0.2594	-0.0619	-0.1468
Nega-AcumeanF2	0.0406	0.0465	0.0544	0.0619
#ofPosi/Near/Nega	7/11/15	34/10/38	25/11/26	23/13/15
Posi-ReturnF3	0.1654	0.2664	0.2430	0.1924
Posi-AcumeanF3	0.0312	0.0432	0.0561	0.0639
Near-ReturnF3	0.0280	0.0478	0.0487	0.0755
Near-AcumeanF3	0.0383	0.0423	0.0537	0.0643
t-test	-0.87	0.59	-0.42	1.51
Nega-ReturnF3	-0.1442	-0.2945	-0.0962	-0.1121
Nega-AcumeanF3	0.034	0.0413	0.0539	0.0665

ReturnH= highest monthly rolling annual returns in the period of 1886-2008.
Posi=positive returns significantly exceed corresponding accumulative means.
Near=returns are statistically indifferent from corresponding accumulative means.
Nega=negative returns.
ReturnF1=returns one year after ReturnH.
AcumeanF1=accumulative means of the rolling annual returns corresponding to the periods of ReturnF1.
ReturnF2=returns two years after ReturnH.
AcumeanF2=accumulative means of the rolling annual returns corresponding to the periods of ReturnF2.
ReturnF3=returns three years after ReturnH.
AcumeanF3=accumulative means of the rolling annual returns corresponding to the periods of ReturnF3.
The t-test of equal means is not based on the assumption of equal variances.
* indicates the ten percent significance level.
** indicates the five percent significance level.
*** indicates the one percent significance level.

The exuberance in the stock market is evidently reflected in the driving forces of mean reversion in the fourth sub-period. In Table 4 forward-looking returns are classified into three categories: positive (larger than corresponding accumulative means), near accumulative means, and negative, in the four sub-periods, in order to better understand the process of mean reversion. In the fourth sub-period the composition of one-year forward-looking returns (ReturnF1) is as the following: 30 positive returns with a mean of 23.17%, 10 near-mean returns with a mean of 6.52%, and 11 negative ones with a mean of -10% (Table4). The positive/negative ratio is 2.73 (30/11).

Overall, the one-year forward-looking returns do not revert to the accumulative mean as indicated by the result in Table 3. The positive/negative ratio is 2.9 (29/10) for two-year forward-looking returns and reduces to 1.53 (23/15, Table 4) for ReturnF3 which reverts to the accumulative mean (Table 3). As discussed above, there is an enduring mean reversion in the third sub-period. The positive/negative ratio supplies evidence that tradeoffs between positive and negative forward-looking returns are the major cause for the lasting mean reversion. The ratio is 1.37 (26/19), 1.00 (24/24), and 0.96 (25/26) for the one-, two-, and three-year forward-looking returns, respectively.

In contrast, mean reversion in the second sub-period is mainly the result of sharp reversals, that is, 40 highest returns (ReturnH), out of 82, turn into negative in the following year. The reversals lead to a low positive/negative ratio of 0.75 (30/40) for ReturnF1 in the period of 1920-1946. The ratio remains at the similar levels, 0.87 (33/38) and 089 (34/38), for ReturnF2 and ReturnF3, respectively.

Although the positive/negative ratio of 1.56 (14/9) for ReturnF1 in the first sub-period (1886-1919) suggests that mean reversion is reached largely by declines in stock returns rather than sharp reversals one year after extremely high returns, the declines extend well into the negative territories. The positive/negative ratio is 0.22 (5/23) for ReturnF2 and 0.47 (7/15) for ReturnF3 (Table 4).

Results in Tables 3 and 4 demonstrate a clear shift in the process of mean reversion between the first two sub-periods and last two sub-periods, sharp reversals in stock returns are replaced with gradual declines in stock returns after the stock market experiences extraordinary advances. The shift reflects growing positive investor sentiments over time.

Table 5 reports 136 lowest negative returns (ReturnL) detected by the loop of repeating equality test at the 10% significance level from 539 negative returns. The mean of ReturnL is -27.36%, compared to the average of their corresponding accumulative means of 4.26%. ReturnL is significantly lower than the accumulative mean. One year later, the lowest negative returns reverse to a level which is statistically indifferent from the corresponding mean, 8.45% (ReturnF1) vs. 3.925 (AcumeanF1), with a t-value of 1.63 for the equality test. The momentum of reversal extends into the following year. ReturnF2 has a mean of 9.94% vs. the accumulative mean of 4.15%. The t-value reaches 2.63 indicating a significant aversion from mean. Overall, the results suggest a sharp reversal that leads the extremely bearish stock market to revert to the historical accumulative mean and the continuation of the reversal pushes stock returns far beyond the accumulative mean.

Results in Table 6 reveal that the power of reversal is time-varying. The reversals in the first and third sub-periods are so strong that ReturnF1 rebounds from about -23.7% (RetunL) to about 15% and stay at about 13% (ReturnF2) in the next year. The reversal process completely overrides the mean reversion. However, in the second and fourth sub-periods that contain two most severe economic recessions, reversals are much milder. ReturnF1 is 3.38%

in the second sub-period and 5.82% in the fourth sub-period and ReturnF2 moderately increases to 8.62% and 6.94%, respectively. The results show an enduring mean reversion process in the two sub-periods.

The strength of reversal is largely defined by its internal driving force measured by the positive/negative ratio. A high positive/negative ratio implies a strong reversal. The ratio, based on ReturnF1, is 3.28 (23/7) in the first sub-period and 4.00 (12/3) in the third sub-period, in contrast to 1.04 (29/28) in the second sub-period and 1.10 (11/10) in the fourth sub-period (Table 7). Similarly, the positive/negative ratios, based on ReturnF2, is 28 (28/1) in the first sub-period and 4.33 (13/3) in the third sub-period, compared to 0.78 (25/32) in the second sub-period and 2.67 (8/3) in the fourth sub-periods.

Table 5. 136 Lowest Returns That Display Mean Reversion in the Following Year

	Mean	Std. Deviation	Maximum	Minimum
ReturnB	0.0062	0.2303	0.8112	-0.5288
AcumeanB	0.0482	0.0119	0.0692	0.0028
t-test	2.12**			
ReturnL	-0.2736	0.1037	-0.1722	-0.6561
AcumeanL	0.0426	0.0148	0.0686	0.0016
t-test	-35.20***			
ReturnF1	0.0845	0.3250	1.2415	-0.6561
AcumeanF1	0.0392	0.0163	0.0666	-0.0007
t-test	1.63			
ReturnF2	0.0994	0.2561	1.2415	-0.6561
AcumeanF2	0.0415	0.0154	0.0653	0.0021
t-test	2.63***			
ReturnB	0.0062			
ReturnF1	0.0845			
t-test	-2.29**			
ReturnB	0.0062			
ReturnF2	0.0994			
t-test	-3.15***			

ReturnL= lowest monthly rolling annual returns in the period of 1886-2008.
AcumeanL=accumulative means of the rolling annual returns corresponding to the periods of ReturnL.
ReturnB=returns one year prior to ReturnL.
AcumeanB=accumulative means of the rolling annual returns corresponding to the periods of ReturnB.
ReturnF1=returns one year after ReturnL.
AcumeanF1=accumulative means of the rolling annual returns corresponding to the periods of ReturnF1.
ReturnF2=returns two years after ReturnL.
AcumeanF2=accumulative means of the rolling annual returns corresponding to the periods of ReturnF2.
The t-test of equal means is not based on the assumption of equal variances.
* indicates the ten percent significance level.
** indicates the five percent significance level.
*** indicates the one percent significance level.

Table 6. Mean Reversions of ReturnL in Sub-Periods

	1886-1919	1920-1946	1947-1985	1986-2008
# of observations	35	60	18	23
ReturnB	0.0397	-0.0232	0.0464	0.0005
AcumeanB	0.0384	0.0447	0.0547	0.0672
t-test	0.14	-1.65	-0.23	-2.09**
ReturnL	-0.2373	-0.3204	-0.2367	-0.2335
AcumeanL	0.0286	0.0388	0.0527	0.0656
t-test	-30.35***	-21.73***	-21.07***	-20.70***
ReturnF1	0.1518	0.0338	0.1567	0.0582
AcumeanF1	0.0235	0.0351	0.0516	0.0641
t-test	5.26***	-0.02	2.25**	-0.13
ReturnF2	0.1282	0.0862	0.1255	0.0694
AcumeanF2	0.0304	0.0359	0.0525	0.0643
t-test	6.10***	1.06	2.36**	0.22

ReturnL= lowest monthly rolling annual returns in the period of 1886-2008.
AcumeanL=accumulative means of the rolling annual returns corresponding to the periods of ReturnL.
ReturnB=returns one year prior to ReturnL.
AcumeanB=accumulative means of the rolling annual returns corresponding to the periods of ReturnB.
ReturnF1=returns one year after ReturnL.
AcumeanF1=accumulative means of the rolling annual returns corresponding to the periods of ReturnF1.
ReturnF2=returns two years after ReturnL.
AcumeanF2=accumulative means of the rolling annual returns corresponding to the periods of ReturnF2.
The t-test of equal means is not based on the assumption of equal variances.
* indicates the ten percent significance level.
** indicates the five percent significance level and *** indicates the one percent significance level.

Results of this study patently exhibit that the long-term optimistic market sentiment is manifested not only in the mean reversion or delayed mean reversion processes after extremely positive stock returns, the processes of lowering very high positive returns to positive historical averages; but also in the mean reversion or sharp reversal processes after extremely negative stock returns, the processes of turning negative returns to positive ones. In other words, all mean-reverting forward-looking returns, after extremely positive or negative stock returns, are positive. Nevertheless, the mean aversion processes two and three years after largest positive returns in the first and second sub-periods do pull stock returns down to negative levels (Table 3).

Table 7. Distribution of Returns in Mean Reversions of ReturnL in Following Years

	1886-1919	1920-1946	1947-1985	1986-2008
#ofPosi/Near/Nega	23/5/7	29/3/28	12/3/3	11/2/10
Posi-ReturnF1	0.2329	0.3953	0.2668	0.2471
Posi-AcumeanF1	0.0290	0.0351	0.0516	0.0634
Near-ReturnF1	0.0366	0.0590	0.0996	0.0914
Near-AcumeanF1	0.0172	0.0356	0.0487	0.0640
t-test	1.75	1.26	2.23	3.89
Nega-ReturnF1	-0.0234	-0.3434	-0.2268	-0.1562
Nega-AcumeanF1	0.0097	0.0350	0.0524	0.0649

	1886-1919	1920-1946	1947-1985	1986-2008
#ofPosi/Near/Nega	28/6/1	25/3/32	13/2/3	8/12/3
Posi-ReturnF2	0.1586	0.4161	0.1858	0.1485
Posi-AcumeanF2	0.0317	0.0351	0.0545	0.0643
Near-ReturnF2	0.0311	0.0795	0.0658	0.0766
Near-AcumeanF2	0.0246	0.0400	0.0552	0.0646
t-test	0.51	1.94	1.82	1.57
Nega-ReturnF2	-0.1401	-0.1709	-0.0958	-0.1705
Nega-AcumeanF2	0.0302	0.0361	0.0421	0.0631

ReturnL= lowest monthly rolling annual returns in the period of 1886-2008.
Posi=positive returns significantly exceed corresponding accumulative means.
Near=returns are statistically indifferent from corresponding accumulative means.
Nega=negative returns.
ReturnF1=returns one year after ReturnL.
AcumeanF1=accumulative means of the rolling annual returns corresponding to the periods of ReturnF1.
ReturnF2=returns two years after ReturnL.
AcumeanF2=accumulative means of the rolling annual returns corresponding to the periods of ReturnF2.
The t-test of equal means is not based on the assumption of equal variances.
* indicates the ten percent significance level.
** indicates the five percent significance level.
*** indicates the one percent significance level.

Results of this study patently exhibit that the long-term optimistic market sentiment is manifested not only in the mean reversion or delayed mean reversion processes after extremely positive stock returns, the processes of lowering very high positive returns to positive historical averages; but also in the mean reversion or sharp reversal processes after extremely negative stock returns, the processes of turning negative returns to positive ones. In other words, all mean-reverting forward-looking returns, after extremely positive or negative stock returns, are positive. Nevertheless, the mean aversion processes two and three years after largest positive returns in the first and second sub-periods do pull stock returns down to negative levels (Table 3).

CONCLUSION

The major purpose of this chapter is to investigate dynamics of mean reversion in the U.S. stock market proxied with the S&P 500 Stock Index in four important sub-periods: World War I (1886-1919), World War II (1920-1946), Post war (1947-1985), and IT revolution (1986-2008).

Results of equality test for forward-looking returns and corresponding accumulative means suggest the following four- and five-year mean reversion and aversion cycles in the first and second sub-periods: below-mean returns→ extremely positive returns→ (reduced returns→) near-mean returns→ below-mean returns. The cycles reflect two important phases, overreaction and correction, in the stock market. However, an enduring mean reversion is identified in the third sub-period and there is a delayed mean reversion in the fourth sub-period. The two unique mean reversion processes are caused by mild stock market corrections which are the result of dominance of buoyant investor sentiment in the third and fourth sub-periods.

The behavior of the stock market after lowest negative returns is quite different. Results of equality test indicate that the mean reversion process takes place only in the second and fourth sub-periods and the sharp reversal process takes over mean reversion in the first and third sub-periods. The swift reversal process after lowest negative returns provides additional evidence of long-term optimistic market sentiment.

The analysis of internal driving force of mean reversion process, denoted by the positive/negative ratio, detects that the tradeoffs between positive and negative forward-looking returns and return reversals are two major causes for the mean reversion after largest positive stock returns. The evidence of the positive/negative ratio suggests a clear shift in the process of mean reversion between the first two sub-periods and last two sub-periods, sharp reversals in stock returns are replaced with gradual declines in stock returns after the stock market experiences extraordinary advances. The shift reflects growing positive investor sentiments over time.

On the other hand, the evidence of the positive/negative ratio in the first and third sub-periods illustrate that sharp reversals regress the extremely bearish stock market to the historical accumulative mean and furthermore, their continuation pushes stock returns far beyond the accumulative mean. In these two sub-periods the reversal process completely overrides the mean reversion. However, in the second and fourth sub-periods that contain two most severe economic recessions, reversals are much milder. It is the mild reversals that lead to enduring mean reversion processes in the two sub-periods. Although the power of reversal differs in different sub-periods, the driving force of reversals remains the same, that is, the continuing positive investor sentiment in the stock market.

REFERENCES

Abreu, D., & Brunnermeier, M.K. (2003). "Bubbles and Crashes," Econometrica 71:1, pp. 173-204.

Bulmer, M. (2003). Francis Galton: Pioneer of Heredity and Biometry. Baltimore, MD: Johns Hopkins University Press.

Cochran, S. J., & DeFina, R.H. (1994). "International Evidence on Mean Reversion in Stock Prices." *Quarterly Journal of Business and Economics*, 33:2, pp. 79-85.

Cowles, Alfred, and Associates. (1939). Common Stock-Indexes, 2nd ed. Bloomington, IN: Principia Press.

DeLong, J.B., Shleifer A., Summers, L.H., & Waldmann, R.J. (1991). "The Survival of Noise Traders in Financial Markets," *Journal of Business,* 64:1, pp. 1-19.

Fama, E. F., & French, K.R. (1988a). "Permanent and Temporary Components of Stock Prices." *Journal of Political Economy*, 96, pp. 246-273.

Fama, E. F., & French, K.R. (1988b). "Dividend Yield and Expected Stock Returns." *Journal of Financial Economics*, 22, pp. 3-25.

Galton, Sir Francis. (1886) "Regression towards Mediocrity in Hereditary Stature." *Journal of the Anthropological Institute*, 15, pp. 246-263.

Griffin, J.M., Harris, J.H., & Topaloglu, S. (2003). "Investor Behavior over the rise and Fall of Nasdaq," Yale School of Management Working Paper, 431.

He, L. T. (2009). "What Can We Learn from 123 Years of Stock Market Fluctuation?" *Journal of Investing,* 18:4, pp. 57-71.

He, L. T. (2013). "Exuberance Embedded in the Process of Mean Reversion of Extreme Stock Returns." *Journal of Investing*, forthcoming.

Hirschey, M. (2003). "Extreme Return Reversal in the Stock Market." *Journal of Portfolio Management*, 29:3, pp. 78-90.

Kim, M. J., Nelson, C.R., & Startz, R. (1991). "Mean Reversion in Stock Prices? A Reappraisal of the Empirical Evidence." *Review of Economic Studies*, 58, pp. 515-528.

Poterba, J. M., & Summers, L.H. (1988). "Mean Reversion in Stock Prices: Evidence and Implications." *Journal of Financial Economics*, 22, pp. 27-59.

Standard and Poor's. (1986). Security Price Index Record. New York, NY: Standard and Poor's.

Summers, L.H. (1986) "Does the Stock Market Rationally Reflect Fundamental Values?" *Journal of Finance*, 41:3, pp. 591-601.

In: Stock Markets
Editors: F. Petroni, F. Prattico and G. D'Amico
ISBN: 978-1-62808-751-2

Chapter 2

RECENT CHANGES IN THE STRUCTURE OF CORRELATIONS BETWEEN CEE AND GLOBAL STOCK MARKETS

Jagric Timotej ***and Zunko Matjaz***[#]
Faculty of Economics and Business, University of Maribor, Slovenia

ABSTRACT

Central and Eastern European (CEE) stock markets were subjected to two major events over the last ten years: In 2004 some of them became members of the European Union and in 2008, global financial markets were shaken. The financial crisis substantially impacted CEE markets. Several papers have already examined how these events increased the correlations among CEE stock markets and, by comparison, global markets. In our research, we analyze time-varying conditional correlations for the daily data of major index returns of six emerging stock markets in Central and Eastern Europe. As a proxy for global stock markets we used index returns for stock exchanges in the US, Germany, UK, and Japan. Our methodology was based on the Asymmetric Dynamic Conditional Correlations (ADCC) model of Cappiello, Engle and Sheppard (2006), which we extended in order to identify changes in the structure of correlations. The results indicate that the events studied had a significant impact on the long-term mean of estimated models, while dynamics tended to change only insignificantly.

Keywords: structural break, asymmetric dynamic conditional correlation, multivariate GARCH, emerging European stock markets

* The paper "*Recent Changes in the Structure of Correlations between Cee and Global Stock Markets*" was produced within the framework of the operation entitled "Centre for Open Innovation and Research of the University of Maribor". The operation is co-funded by the European Regional Development Fund and conducted within the framework of the Operational Programme for Strengthening Regional Development Potentials for the period 2007 – 2013, development priority 1: "Competitiveness of companies and research excellence", priority axis 1.1: "Encouraging competitive potential of enterprises and research excellence".
# Corresponding Author address: Email: matjaz.zunko@uni-mb.si

INTRODUCTION

Since the introduction of the Autoregressive Conditional Heteroskedasticity (ARCH) model in the seminal paper of Engle (1982), the field of modeling volatility and correlations of financial time series has grown into an extended field of financial econometrics. Numerous variants of GARCH and the multivariate GARCH (MVGARCH) have been proposed (see, for example: Bauwens et. al. (2006) and Silvennoinen and Terasvirta (2008) for a review of MVGARCH literature).

The most commonly used model for modeling time varying correlations is the dynamic conditional correlations model (DCC) of Engle (2002). Its popularity arises from the simple formulation of the quasi-correlation model that is similar to the univariate GARCH equation. This enables the model to impose the positive definiteness of the covariance matrix, which is one of the major challenges of the MVGARCH models. It accounts for heteroskedasticity problems directly as it estimates the correlation coefficients of standardized residuals. The model is applicable on large data sets without increasing the number of model parameters as is the case with some other MVGARCH models. Irrespective of the size of the data, the model has two parameters for dynamic structure that are easy to interpret (Silvennoinen and Terasvirta 2008). Among others, Wang and Moore (2008), Büttner and Hayo (2010), Guidi and Gupta (2010), Kocenda and Egert (2011) and Syllignakis and Kouretas (2011) used the DCC model in their analysis of stock market correlations between the CEE and developed countries.

Several papers have demonstrated that stock market volatility and correlations increase more after a negative shock than after a positive shock of the same size (see, for example: Engle and Ng 1993, and Cappiello et al. 2006). Cappiello et al. (2006) extended the DCC model of Engle with an additional parameter that permits conditional asymmetries in correlation dynamics. They proposed the asymmetric dynamic conditional correlations (ADCC) model. Baumohl (2013) found a significant asymmetric parameter in his application of the ADCC model on CEE and G7 stock market data.

As documented by Andreou and Ghysels (2002, 2008) and Hillebrand (2005), there is strong evidence for the occurrence of structural breaks in financial time series. If a structural break occurs during the sample period, ignoring a change in parameters can lead to an unsuitable model and can result in incorrect statistical inferences (Hansen 2001). For this reason, we should be careful in the analysis of higher moments of financial time series, particularly those that span over longer periods of time, if there was a major event during the sample period that could introduce a structural break into the MVGARCH model. When working with the data of CEE countries, there were at least two such major events in the last decade that need to be considered. One was the enlargement of the EU into the CEE countries in 2004 and the second was the beginning of the global financial crisis in 2008.

Most researchers include structural breaks in their ADCC correlation analysis with the methodology proposed by Cappiello et al. (2006). They use a dummy variable in the dynamic conditional correlation model equation for the distinction of intercept terms or for the model as a whole. With this approach, the researcher is only limited to a likelihood ratio testing procedure for exploring the significance of a structural break. Zunko and Jagric (2013) have proposed an extension of this methodology, which in addition to statistical testing, also enables the conceptual interpretation of the parameter difference. They extended dynamic conditional correlation model equations with differential parameters, combined with dummy variables. These differential parameters indicate directly by how much the parameters in the period after the structural break differ from the parameters before the structural break. As every ADCC model parameter has its own special meaning, difference in them indicate changes in the structure of the correlations as well.

In this chapter, we employ the methodology for a structural break in the ADCC model proposed by Zunko and Jagric (2013) to analyze how major events influenced the structure of correlations between CEE and global stock markets. We analyze the impact of joining the EU and the impact of the global financial crisis on the stock markets correlations of these countries.

The results indicate that the long-term mean changed significantly in both of the research events. The CEE market correlations tended to be more persistent after these countries joined the EU and less persistent again in the period of the global financial crisis. Surprisingly, the asymmetric parameter tended to decrease after the Lehman Brothers bankruptcy. Since the parameter α tend to increase in approximately the same magnitude as γ tend to decrease, this means that correlations become more volatile with both positive and negative shocks. These changes in the dynamic part of the models are mostly insignificant, except that the models estimated on the data panels consisted of six CEE markets and the DAX30 or SP500 as a proxy, with an allowance of a structural break in the spread of the global financial crisis.

The rest of this chapter is organized as follows: In the next section we carry out a literature review of the dynamic conditional correlations models on CEE stock market data and about a general structural break in such models. Then we present a methodology for the allowance of a structural break in the ADCC model. Thereafter is a section about sample data and research questions. The results are presented and analyzed and the chapter concludes with summarizing words.

Literature Review

Papers concerning the dynamic correlations between Central European, Eastern European and global stock markets use a different range of countries and a variety of MVGARCH models. Kasch-Haroutonian and Price (2001) used CCC and BEKK models in their investigation of interdependence among four CEE stock markets between 1994 and 1998. They found significant conditional correlations between two pairs of countries: Hungary and Poland, as well as Hungary and the Czech Republic. They detected return volatility spillovers from Hungary to Poland, but no such effect in the opposite direction.

Scheiher (2001) used a vector autoregression (VAR)-CCC model on the data of the stock markets of the Czech Republic, Poland and Hungary from 1995 to 1997. He only reported a limited influence of Western financial markets, since in returns he identified both regional and global shocks, whereas with volatilities, innovations have a primarily regional character. But his data sample covers the period prior to the full financial liberalization of these markets.

Wang and Moore (2008) investigated the co-movements of the Czech, Polish and Hungarian markets with the aggregate Eurozone market by using the DCC model, using a sample period from 1994 to 2006. They found a significant increase in correlations between these emerging markets and the euro area market after EU accession and in the aftermath of the global financial crisis.

Savva and Aslanidis (2010) used the smooth transition conditional correlation GARCH (STCC-GARCH) and CCC models to investigate stock market integration between five CEEs (Hungary, the Czech Republic, Slovakia, Slovenia and Poland) and the Eurozone. The sample consisted of weekly data that spanned from 1997 to 2008. They reported the strongest regional interconnection between the Czech Republic, Poland and Hungary. Slovenia and Slovakia exhibited smaller correlations with the Eurozone than the largest CEE markets. The correlation between the Czech, Slovenian and Polish stock markets and those of the Eurozone increased substantially from 1997 to 2008. They reported that this increase was mainly driven by EU-related developments.

Guidi and Gupta (2010) investigated the long-term relationship between German and CEE (the Czech Republic, Hungary and Poland) stock markets. Among methods for cointegration they used the BEKK-GARCH and the DCC model on daily data from 1999 to 2009. They reported a large increase in correlation coefficients after CEE countries joined the European Union and "a dramatic rise" during 2008.

Büttner and Hayo (2010) investigate comovements for foreign exchange markets, short-term money markets and the stock markets of the Czech Republic, Hungary and Poland. They employed the DCC model to construct time-varying correlations for daily data between 2004 and 2006. The foreign exchange and stock markets were at their most interconnected level during this period, especially between Hungary and Poland, whereas interbank money markets were more isolated. They examined the effect of news on correlations and for their sample period (which does not include any major shocks) they observed some influence from local news but no broad effects from international news.

Syllignakis and Kouretas (2011) applied the DCC model to investigate the time-varying conditional correlations between seven emerging stock markets of Central and Eastern Europe (the Czech Republic, Estonia, Hungary, Poland, Romania, Slovakia and Slovenia) and the stock markets of the US, Germany and Russia. They presented evidence for contagion effects originating in the herd behavior of investors in these markets. Conditional correlations between the US and the Garman stock returns and the CEE stock returns increased significantly during the 2007–2009 financial crises. They attributed this to a greater degree of financial openness, particularly after the accession of the CEE countries to the EU in 2004, which increased the participation of foreign investors in their markets.

Horvath and Petrovski (2012) used the BEKK-GARCH model to examine the international stock market comovements between Western Europe vis-à-vis Central (the Czech Republic, Hungary and Poland) and South Eastern Europe (Croatia, Macedonia and Serbia) in the period from 2006–2011. They reported a much higher degree of comovements for the CEE group than for the SEE group.

Kocenda and Egert (2011) applied the DCC model on intraday data to examine comovements between Western European (France, Germany and United Kingdom) and CEE (the Czech Republic, Poland and Hungary) stock markets. With 5-minute tick intraday stock price data from June 2003 to January 2006, they found very low correlations among the emerging markets and between emerging markets and developed ones. They observed a small increase in the interconnectedness of CEE markets after joining the European Union.

Literature about the ADCC model applied on CEE stock markets data is rather sparse. Gjika and Horvath (2013) used the ADCC model on daily data from 2001 to 2011 to examine time-varying correlations among the Czech, Polish, Hungarian and European (STOXX50) stock markets. In their pairwise analysis they surprisingly found asymmetry in conditional correlations for only one pair: the Czech Republic and Poland, but not in other pairs. They reported increasing correlations between the CEE markets and the euro area with an evident boost after these countries entered the European Union and a continuation at high levels during the financial crisis.

Baumohl (2013) used the ADCC model to study the integration of CEE and G7 stock markets. His dataset for the Czech Republic, Hungary, Poland, Slovakia and G7 countries spans from 1998 to 2012. He reported significant asymmetric parameter in the ADCC model for the whole panel. A strengthening relationship between the CEE and G7 markets was found.

In summary, previous literature suggests that the correlations between CEE and global stock markets have increased over time and that this increase was mostly evident after EU-related developments and after the global financial crisis. But to our knowledge, none of them investigated whether these had such a huge impact on the correlations process that it led to a structural break in the dynamic correlations model. This could have an effect on both the empirical results and on their subsequent interpretation.

The theoretical as well as empirical consequences of structural breaks in models of univariate conditional volatility are better studied than in models of time-varying correlations. It has been demonstrated that ignoring structural breaks can yield spurious persistence in conditional volatility GARCH models, reporting an abundance of long-memory effects in a financial time series (Diebold 1986, Lastrapes 1989, Lamoureux and Lastrapes 1990, Hillebrand 2005). Hamilton and Susmel (1994) and Gray (1996) obtained lower persistence estimates by extending the volatility models with Markov-switching or the regime-switching approach.

The inclusion of structural breaks in empirical studies of time-varying correlations has only started recently (Kalotychou et al. 2009). Studies that include a structural break in the DCC or ADCC model mostly follow a procedure proposed by Cappiello et al. (2006). The authors of this article present the asymmetric version of the DCC model and employ it on the data of international equities and government bonds. But since the sample period includes the introduction of the new currency (the euro) they tested if that would introduce a structural break in their model. Their results indicate a significant difference in the mean, but not in the dynamics, of time-varying correlations at international equities and government bonds after fixing the exchange rates. This has motivated several other researches to include a structural break in the mean of their dynamic conditional correlations models.

One such paper is by Kearney and Potì (2006) who confirmed a structural break in the mean around the time of the introduction of the euro in their research of correlation dynamics in the European equity market. Hyde et al. (2007) reported that the Asian crisis acted as a structural break in their data of equity markets in the Asian-pacific region, Europe and US, with correlations increasing markedly for the crisis countries. Frank et al. (2008) found a structural break in the long-run mean of the conditional correlations between the liquidity and other financial market variables in the US during the 2007 subprime crisis. Li (2008, 2010) mostly found significant evidence of a structural break in his research of exchange rate correlations since the European Monetary System in the European Union was replaced with Economic and Monetary Union.

The model of dynamic conditional correlation proposed by Cappiello et al. (2006) uses a dummy variable in the model equation for the distinction of intercept terms or for the model as a whole. Zunko and Jagric (2013) proposed an extension of the model equation with differential parameters, combined with dummy variables, for every parameter. This enables a wider range of testing opportunities, while in the empirical part of the paper they show that the new common European currency brought a significant structural break in both the long-run mean and the dynamic part of the dynamic conditional correlations of major European stock indices.

METHODOLOGY

We analyzed recent changes in the structure of correlations between CEE and global stock markets with the methodology proposed by Zunko and Jagric (2013). They extended the ADCC model of Cappiello et al. (2006) with differential parameters in the period after a possible structural break. The general ADCC model assumes that returns from k assets are conditionally multivariate normal with zero expected value and covariance matrix H_t (Cappiello et al. 2006):

$$r_t|\mathfrak{I}_{t-1} \sim N(0, H_t), \tag{1}$$

where $\mathfrak{I}_{t-1}$ is the information set available at time $t-1$. The variance-covariance matrix H_t can be decomposed into variance and correlation parts as (Cappiello et al. 2006):

$$H_t = D_t R_t D_t, \tag{2}$$

where D_t is the diagonal matrix of time-varying standard deviations from univariate GARCH models with $\sqrt{h_{it}}$ on the i-th diagonal, and R_t is the time varying correlation matrix.

The estimation is done in two stages. In the first stage, the univariate volatility model is fitted to each of the assets to estimate their standard deviations $\sqrt{h_{it}}$, that are then used to construct standardized residuals or volatility-adjusted returns $\varepsilon_{it} = r_{it}/\sqrt{h_{it}}$ (Engle 2009). Different GARCH-type models are possible for different assets. Cappiello et al. (2006) state that for this de-garching part of the estimation any univariate GARCH process that is covariance stationary and assumes normally distributed errors can be used, as long as we assume that volatility models are correctly specified. If this assumption does not hold, the correlation estimates will not be consistent (Cappiello et al. 2006). To minimize the risk that the univariate volatility model will lead to inconsistent correlation estimates they estimated several GARCH models and then selected the best one using the Bayesian information criterion (BIC). We used a similar approach by applying the following models on every asset (all with one lag of volatility, one lag of innovation and if the model includes it, one lag of negative innovation):

1. AGARCH (Engle 1990)
2. AVGARCH (Taylor 1986)
3. EGARCH (Nelson 1991)

4. GARCH (Bollerslev 1986)
5. GJR-GARCH (Glosten et al. 1993)
6. NAGARCH (Engle and Ng 1993)
7. TGARCH (Zakoian 1994)
8. VGARCH (Engle and Ng 1993).

The exact specification of these models can be found in the appendix.

In the second stage, the parameters of the dynamic conditional correlations are estimated. Cappiello et al. (2006) in the ADCC model, similarly to Engle (2002) in his DCC model, used the correlation targeting approach to estimate the intercept parameters of the conditional correlation process. Engle (2009) states that this procedure is only an approximation but that the estimator is consistent and it substantially reduces the number of remaining unknown parameters. For correlation targeting, the unconditional covariance $\bar{R}$ of the volatility-adjusted returns ε_{it} and the negative part of the unconditional covariance $\bar{N}$ of the specific volatility-adjusted returns $n_{it} = \min(\varepsilon_{it}, 0)$ in the ADCC model are computed before the second stage. The structure of quasi-correlation for the scalar ADCC model is (Cappiello et al. 2006):

$$Q_t = (1 - \alpha - \beta)\bar{R} - \gamma\bar{N} + \alpha\varepsilon_{t-1}\varepsilon'_{t-1} + \gamma n_{t-1}n'_{t-1} + \beta Q_{t-1}, \tag{3}$$

Since the quasi-correlation matrix Q_t is not necessarily the correlation matrix, we must rescale it as

$$R_t = Q_t^{*-1} Q_t Q_t^{*-1}, \tag{4}$$

where Q_t^* is a diagonal matrix with the square root of the i-th diagonal element of Q_t on its i-th diagonal position.

In the presence of a structural break the model parameters in equation (3) can be misleading. They may be different before and after a major event which could have an impact on the structure of the dynamic conditional correlations.

Let D_t be a dummy variable which takes the value of 1 in the period after the structural break ($t \geq \tau$, where τ is the first time point after the structural break), and 0 in the period before the structural break.

The breakdate is assumed to be known *a priori* and so is exogenously set at some time point of the data. Zunko and Jagric (2013) proposed extending the equation (3) in a way that the parameters after the break date α_2, β_2 and γ_2 are sums of the parameters from the first period and the differential parameters:

$$\alpha_2 = \alpha_1 + \alpha_D, \beta_2 = \beta_1 + \beta_D, \gamma_2 = \gamma_1 + \gamma_D. \tag{5}$$

These differential parameters indicate to us by how much parameters in the period after the structural break differ from parameters before the structural break. They allow us to test directly if the differential parameters are statistically different from zero when we are interested in testing the parameter change from one period to another. The joint inclusion of differential parameters and dummy variable D_t rearranges equation (3) into

$$Q_t = [(1-\alpha_1-\beta_1)\bar{R}_1 - \gamma_1\bar{N}_1](1-D_t) + [(1-(\alpha_1+\alpha_D)-(\beta_1+\beta_D))\bar{R}_2 - (\gamma_1+\gamma_D)\bar{N}_2]D_t + (\alpha_1+D_t\alpha_D)\varepsilon_{t-1}\varepsilon'_{t-1} + (\gamma_1+D_t\gamma_D)n_{t-1}n'_{t-1} + (\beta_1+D_tB_D)Q_{t-1}, \quad (6)$$

where the separate estimates of both the full covariance matrix of volatility-adjusted returns and the negative part of it are needed before and after the break in the correlation targeting of intercept parameters. Dummy variable D_t in equation (6) provides the calculation without or with differential parameters depending on the period before or after the structural break.

On the other hand, we are not always interested in a structural break in all of the parameters but maybe only in some of them. For these purposes we can write a general form of ADCC model with dummy variables specific to every parameter that take part in the quasi-correlation structure:

$$Q_t = [(1-\alpha_1-\beta_1)\bar{R}_1 - \gamma_1\bar{N}_1](1-D_{intr,t}) + [(1-(\alpha_1+D_{\alpha,t}\alpha_D)-(\beta_1+D_{\beta,t}\beta_D))\bar{R}_2 - (\gamma_1+D_{\gamma,t}\gamma_D)\bar{N}_2]D_{intr,t} + (\alpha_1+D_{\alpha,t}\alpha_D)\varepsilon_{t-1}\varepsilon'_{t-1} + (\gamma_1+D_{\gamma,t}\gamma_D)n_{t-1}n'_{t-1} + (\beta_1+D_{\beta,t}\beta_D)Q_{t-1}, \quad (7)$$

where $D_{intr,t}$ is 1 for $t \geq \tau$ at the assumption that the intercept part can change and 0 otherwise, $D_{\alpha,t}$ is 1 for $t \geq \tau$ at the assumption that parameter α can change and 0 otherwise, $D_{\beta,t}$ is 1 for $t \geq \tau$ at the assumption that parameter β can change and 0 otherwise and $D_{\gamma,t}$ is 1 for $t \geq \tau$ at the assumption that parameter γ can change and 0 otherwise. With these parameter specific dummy variables we have a necessary condition that to allow for a structural break in any of the parameters α, β or γ, we must allow for a structural break in the intercept, since as soon as we have any of these dynamic parameters different in two periods, we also have different correlation targeting estimates in two periods. An advantage of this model is that although we assume that a structural break occurred during the period of interest, we still use one model on the whole data and thus are likely to have high relative precision of the estimated parameters.

Cappiello et al. (2006) state that necessary and sufficient conditions for Q_t to be positive definite in the scalar ADCC model beside positive values of dynamic parameters α, β and γ is that $\alpha + \beta + \delta\gamma < 1$, where δ is the maximum eigenvalue of the matrix $\bar{R}^{-1/2}\bar{N}\bar{R}^{-1/2}$. We must take this into account during the estimation of model (7) for both periods, that is for basic parameters and for the parameters with differential parts added. In the implementation of the estimation process we used the quasi-maximum likelihood (QML) sandwich estimators and the outer product of gradients (OPG) estimators for the covariance matrix of parameter estimates (see Engle and Sheppard 2001).

With an appropriate choice of assumptions for which dynamic parameters can change, we have a class of nested models included in the formulation of the quasi-correlation structure (7), from an ordinary ADCC model to the ADCC model that allows for a structural break in the intercept part and all of the dynamic parameters. Because of this nesting property we can use different testing procedures for a variety of hypotheses about a structural break. This enables us to not only answer the question of whether the model as a whole has changed after the structural break but can also pinpoint the source of the difference.

Namely, with only one estimation of the unrestricted model, we have parameters estimates and an estimate of their asymptotic covariance so we are able to test a hypothesis of the stability for the dynamic part of the model as a whole

$$H_0: \alpha_D = \beta_D = \gamma_D = 0 \tag{8}$$

with the Wald statistic

$$W = (\alpha_D, \beta_D, \gamma_D)\text{Est. Asy. Var}[(\alpha_D, \beta_D, \gamma_D)](\alpha_D, \beta_D, \gamma_D)', \tag{9}$$

that has a chi-squared distribution with 3 degrees of freedom. Beside this, we can look at the *t*-test statistics on individual difference parameters to gain knowledge about explicitly which of the coefficients have changed. We can focus on the results of the asymmetric parameter only. Following the procedure of a Wald test, other sets of hypotheses for a function of parameters $H_0: c(\psi_0) = q$ can also be done. At hypothesis testing, which includes statements about the intercept terms, we are restricted with regard to the likelihood ratio testing procedure since asymptotic covariances of intercept estimates are not directly observable.

Zunko and Jagric (2013) made an extensive Monte Carlo simulation experiment of the methodology described above. They found that this kind of testing procedure has favorable small sample properties. Since a major event in the data sample could impact univariate volatilities as well as correlations, they investigated if an inclusion of a structural break in the de-garching models in a similar fashion as in the ADCC model makes any difference. It turns out that the methodology is quite robust at repeating simulations and the complication of GARCH models is redundant. Distributional assumption turns out to be relevant for choosing among QML sandwich and OPG covariance estimation procedures and subsequent inference, since Monte Carlo experiments confirm the statement of Hafner and Herwartz (2008) that QML based P-values should be preferred over OPG counterparts only if diagnostic tests indicate the non-normality of de-garched data that enters the correlation part of the estimation.

DATA AND RESEARCH QUESTIONS

We analyzed time-varying conditional correlations for six emerging stock markets of Central and Eastern Europe. We collected daily closing prices of the main stock indices for the Czech Republic (PX), Hungary (BUX), Poland (WIG20), Slovenia (SBI20 and SBITOP), Bulgaria (SOFIX) and Romania (BET). Detailed market characteristics and the course of market development for these countries can be found in Syllignakis and Kouretas (2011) and Dvorak and Podpiera (2006). As a proxy for global stock markets we selected stock indices for the USA (SP500), Germany (DAX30), UK (FTSE100), and Japan (NIKKEI225). Although Russia remains an influential regional and political power, with important trade and investment links in the CEE countries, we did not include the Russian stock market among the benchmarks since Syllignakis and Kouretas (2011), using a similar data sample, discovered that it only had limited stock market influence. The source of the data is Bloomberg's database.

The selected stock markets do not entirely overlap in trading days as they have various market closure dates due to public holidays. A correlation analysis requires synchronized data. We balanced the sample in a way that we selected only days when data for every stock market was available and suspended data on other days. We think this synchronization is more relevant for preserving information in data than others, e.g. adding missing data as the last known price – this generates zero returns. The issue of intraday non-synchronous data due to different stock market closing hours remains open.

To overcome this deficiency we used different proxy indices to achieve more robust results. A synchronized panel of price series is then transformed into log returns by taking the log first-difference $r_t = \log(P_t/P_{t-1})$.

The synchronization technique described above can lower the number of data points substantially since missing data in only one series affects the whole panel. To preserve original data as much as possible, we formed different data panels, according to the research question. The first panel consisted of countries that joined the European Union in 2004: the Czech Republic, Hungary, Poland and Slovenia (SBI20), with one of the benchmark indices as a proxy. From a synchronization standpoint, it is better to include only one benchmark at once. This gives us four different versions of the panel one (and similarly for panels two and three). The data spans from May 1, 2000 to July 31, 2007. At the beginning of the new millennium these countries had markets that were open to foreign investors, since most capital restrictions were lifted between 1996 and 1999 (Dvorak and Podpiera 2006, Syllignakis and Kouretas 2011). They became members of the European Union on the 1st of May 2004 and experienced a relatively stable period of stock index growth, reaching all time highs in the second half of 2007. During that period, the first signs of the world's financial fragility appeared as the subprime crisis in USA started to spill beyond its borders. The loan spreads suddenly skyrocketed in August 2007 as a result of consumer defaults on subprime mortgages (Duchin et al. 2010, Longstaff 2010). CEE countries were hit dramatically by the events that followed since their stock markets lost over half of their value and their currencies were under devaluation pressure in subsequent years (Syllignakis and Kouretas 2011). By ending the period of the first panel before the ignition of the financial crisis, we have a sample with only one major event for selected countries: becoming new member states of the European Union. A comparison of the correlation structure before and after EU expansion can therefore account for a potential difference mainly as a consequence of this event.

The second data panel consists of CEE countries that mainly appear in similar studies – the Czech Republic, Hungary and Poland, with an addition of one of the benchmarks. The beginning of the data is May 4, 2004, the first joint trading day after EU enlargement. The data terminates at the end of 2012 (December 28, 2012). This period has two different characteristics: the bull markets in the first part and distress of financial markets after the expansion of the global financial crisis. Such a sample allows us to analyze the impact that the global financial crisis has had on the correlations structure of the CEE stock markets. There are several events on the global crisis timeline but only one has special importance – the bankruptcy of the Lehman Brothers investment bank on the 15th of September 2008. We used this date as a structural break date in panel two.

The third data panel addresses a similar research question as the second data panel but uses all six of the developing countries' stock indices along with one of the benchmarks. The data spans over the same period as data panel two. Slovenia started to calculate its new blue-chip stock market index SBITOP in April 2006 and after some months terminated the calculation of its prior main index, the SBI20. Since data for the SBITOP is available up to May 2004, we used this index for Slovenia in the third panel, in contrast with panel one, where we used the SBI20.

The third panel has seven assets. Thus, a benchmark index has a low weight in the model calculation, whereas the ADCC parameters represent dynamic conditional correlations for the whole panel. We could perform an analysis with a bivariate approach but this would substantially increase the number of estimated models and resulting parameters. The results would be less stable, and with lower statistical power, since the estimation of the model on smaller data panels can have numerical calculation obstacles. Therefore, an analysis on large data panels is, in our opinion, more suitable despite a smaller benchmark weight in the data.

Table 1. The number of data points in data panels, depending on a benchmark index

panel version	I – DAX30	I – FTSE100	I - NIKKEI225	I – SP500
n	1785	1763	1702	1738

panel version	II – DAX30	II – FTSE100	II - NIKKEI225	II – SP500
n	2092	2056	1980	2039

panel version	III – DAX30	III – FTSE100	III - NIKKEI225	III – SP500
n	1959	1935	1860	1877

Note: The version of the data panel is labeled with numbers I – III.

The summary statistics for the returns of data panels described above are presented in Tables 1, 2, 3 and 4. Since the number of series in all combinations of panels, and their versions, is too large for a transparent display, we reported the results for panels using only the DAX30 as a benchmark. Table 1 provides information about the number of data points in all of the combinations. They vary because of differences in dates at the synchronization procedure. Statistical properties reveal that daily index return series for emerging stock markets were highly leptokurtic and mostly negatively skewed, indicating that they are not normally distributed. The Jarque-Bera test statistic confirms non-normality. The null hypothesis of a unit root is rejected at the 5% significance level for all return series.

Table 2. Descriptive statistics of the return series in the first panel, with the DAX30 as a benchmark index

index	BUX	PX	SBI20	WIG20	DAX30
mean	6.95E-04	7.32E-04	1.04E-03	4.16E-04	8.62E-04
st. dev.	0.0144	0.0129	0.0074	0.0162	0.0163
skewness	-0.02	-0.45	0.86	0.11	0.05
kurtosis	4.56	6.15	15.60	4.72	6.18
JB	181.82*	797.10*	12033*	224.72*	752.88*
ADF	-40.51*	-39.93*	-32.32*	-41.19*	-42.90*

Notes: JB denotes the Jarque-Bera statistic for the null of normality; ADF denotes the Augmented Dickey-Fuller statistic for the null of a unit root. (*) denotes statistical significance at the 5% critical level.

Table 3. Descriptive statistics of the return series in the second panel, with the DAX30 as a benchmark index

index	BUX	PX	WIG20	DAX30
mean	2.37E-04	1.14E-04	1.84E-04	3.09E-04
st. dev.	0.0183	0.0169	0.0165	0.0149
skewness	0.42	-1.14	-0.10	-0.07
kurtosis	17.08	22.70	7.07	9.73
JB	17342*	34299*	1444*	3948*
ADF	-44.52*	-44.41*	-45.13*	-46.36*

Notes: JB denotes the Jarque-Bera statistic for the null of normality; ADF denotes the Augmented Dickey-Fuller statistic for the null of a unit root. (*) denotes statistical significance at the 5% critical level.

Table 4. Descriptive statistics of the return series in the third panel, with the DAX30 as a benchmark index

index	BET	BUX	PX	SBITOP	SOFIX	WIG20	DAX30
mean	3.28E-04	2.53E-04	1.22E-04	-1.75E-04	-1.59E-04	1.97E-04	3.30E-04
st. dev.	0.0200	0.0187	0.0176	0.0126	0.0148	0.0171	0.0151
skewness	-1.11	0.35	-1.01	-0.83	-1.93	-0.07	0.00
kurtosis	15.52	16.21	21.75	15.08	26.00	6.93	9.66
JB	13204*	14288*	29045*	12145*	44406*	1259*	3623*
ADF	-42.52*	-43.31*	-43.64*	-38.91*	-38.81*	-44.35*	-45.40*

Notes: JB denotes the Jarque-Bera statistic for the null of normality; ADF denotes the Augmented Dickey-Fuller statistic for the null of a unit root. (*) denotes statistical significance at the 5% critical level.

RESULTS

We employed the methodology for testing a structural break in the ADCC model described in the methodological part of the chapter on every data panel described above. Altogether there are 12 models estimated and the results are presented in Tables 5 – 10.

For every data panel, we first reported results for the de-garching part of the model estimation. There are differences in the selected GARCH model between different versions of the same panel, although panels do not change much from one version to another. The reason for this is that there are small differences in the estimated log-likelihood function values for several GARCH models. Asymmetric models especially tend to be similarly suitable. A small difference in the data can therefore make a different ranking in the BIC criterion, leading to a change in the selected model. Because these changes are between similar models we assume that they do not have much of an impact on the following dynamic conditional correlation analysis.

Tables 6, 8 and 10 report the results of the ADCC model parameters estimation and two test statistics on which we subsequently make statistical inferences about the research questions.

Table 5. The GARCH models selected with BIC in the de-garching part of the ADCC model estimation for the first panel

	BUX	PX	SBI20	WIG20	BMRK
I - D	NAGARCH	TGARCH	GARCH	GARCH	NAGARCH
I - F	NAGARCH	TGARCH	AVGARCH	GARCH	NAGARCH
I - N	NAGARCH	TGARCH	EGARCH	AVGARCH	NAGARCH
I - S	NAGARCH	TGARCH	AVGARCH	AVGARCH	NAGARCH

Notes: The version of the data panel is denoted in the first column: D denotes a panel with the DAX30, F denotes a panel with the FTSE100, N denotes a panel with the NIKKEI225 and S denotes a panel with the SP500 as a benchmark index, respectively. BMRK denotes a corresponding benchmark index. The exact specification of the GARCH models can be found in the appendix.

Table 6. The results of the ADCC model with allowance for a structural break on the 1st of May 2004 for the first panel

	α_1	β_1	γ_1	α_D	β_D	γ_D	W	LRT
I - D	0.0086	0.9224**	0.0150	-0.0056	0.0483	0.0057	1.17	37.81**
I - F	0.0041	0.8967**	0.0431**	-0.0038	0.0744	-0.0224	1.41	63.47**
I - N	0.0067	0.8500**	0.0131	-0.0067	0.0905	0.0147	0.35	43.63**
I - S	0.0012	0.8831**	0.0363*	-0.0008	0.0938	-0.0208	0.26	35.05**

Notes: The numbers in this table represent the estimated value of parameters or the value of test statistic – W stands for the Wald test statistic for the stability of the dynamic part of the model as a whole, while LRT stands for the likelihood ratio test for the stability of the intercept. (*) and (**) denote statistical significance at the 5% and 1% critical level, respectively. The version of the data panel is denoted in the first column: D denotes a panel with the DAX30, F denotes a panel with the FTSE100, N denotes a panel with the NIKKEI225 and S denotes the panel with the SP500 as a benchmark index, respectively.

Table 5 indicates asymmetric volatilities in the BUX, PX and benchmark indices before the financial crisis. The SBI20 and WIG20 show no such properties, since there are mostly GARCH and AVGARCH models selected as the most suitable.

From the ADCC model results in the first panel we can see that dynamic conditional correlations between Central European emerging markets in the first period were subject to asymmetric shocks. The weight for new information α_1 was lower than the asymmetric parameter γ_1 which was significant with the FTSE100 or SP500 as a proxy. Correlations in this period were moderately persistent with β_1 around 0.9. After these countries joined the European Union, the parameter α even tended to decrease and β tended to increase, leading to more persistent models where correlations change gradually. The parameter γ tended to decrease with the FTSE100 or SP500 as a proxy and slightly increase with other proxies where it was low in the first period. But all these changes were insignificant, which is confirmed with the insignificant Wald test statistic for the stability of the dynamic part of the model. What did change significantly in the research period is the long-term mean, as the LRT test statistics for the stability of the intercept shows. Changes in intercept parameters led to a higher long-term mean in correlations after the selected break date. This confirms the results reported in Wang and Moore (2008), Savva and Aslanidis (2010), Guidi and Gupta (2010), Gjika and Horvath (2013) and Baumohl (2013) that CEE countries, as new EU members, became more intercorrelated and more correlated with Western markets.

Table 7. The GARCH models selected with BIC in the de-garching part of the ADCC model estimation for the second panel

	BUX	PX	WIG20	BMRK
III - D	NAGARCH	TGARCH	TGARCH	NAGARCH
III - F	NAGARCH	TGARCH	NAGARCH	EGARCH
III - N	NAGARCH	NAGARCH	TGARCH	NAGARCH
III - S	NAGARCH	TGARCH	TGARCH	NAGARCH

Notes: The version of the data panel is denoted in the first column: D denotes a panel with the DAX30, F denotes a panel with the FTSE100, N denotes a panel with the NIKKEI225 and S denotes a panel with the SP500 as a benchmark index, respectively. BMRK denotes the corresponding benchmark index. The exact specification of the GARCH models can be found in the appendix.

Table 8. The results of the ADCC model, with an allowance for a structural break on the 15th of September 2008 for the second panel

	α_1	β_1	γ_1	α_D	β_D	γ_D	W	LRT
II - D	0.0080*	0.9708**	0.0247**	0.0115	-0.0669	-0.0098	1.04	3.04
II - F	0.0043	0.9613**	0.0358**	0.0224	-0.0746	-0.0251	0.21	14.72*
II - N	0.0084*	0.9512**	0.0229*	-0.0082	-0.0089	0.0133	1.31	11.06*
II - S	0.0049	0.9690**	0.0217*	0.0174	-0.0894	-0.0217	2.83	14.35*

Notes: The numbers in table represent the estimated value of the parameters or the value of the test statistic – W stands for the Wald test statistic for the stability of the dynamic part of the model as a whole, while LRT stands for the likelihood ratio test for the stability of the intercept. (*) and (**) denote statistical significance at the 5% and 1% critical level, respectively. The version of the data panel is denoted in the first column: D denotes a panel with the DAX30, F denotes a panel with the FTSE100, N denotes a panel with the NIKKEI225 and S denotes a panel with the SP500 as a benchmark index, respectively.

All univariate volatility models in the de-garching procedure for the second panel are from the group of asymmetric GARCH models.

In the stable period from 2004 to the spread of the global financial crisis, the stock market dynamic conditional correlations of CEE countries had a highly persistent structure with β_1 from 0.95 to 0.97, depending on the proxy. Asymmetric parameter γ_1 ranged from 0.02 to 0.036 and was significant, indicating that the correlations in that period were strongly affected by the joint bad news. After the Lehman Brothers event, the correlations structure became less persistent (β_D negative). Surprisingly, the asymmetric parameter γ tended to decrease in the second period. Since the parameter α tended to increase in approximately the same magnitude as γ tended to decrease, this means that correlations became more volatile on both positive and negative shocks. An exception is the version of the data panel, where the NIKKEI225 is used as a proxy. The ADCC model in the second period for this data set preserved a similar level of persistence and increased the asymmetric parameter.

The Wald test statistic for the stability of the dynamic part of the model reported insignificant values. The indicated changes in the ADCC model parameters were confirmed to be insignificant by individual *t*-tests. LRT test statistics for the stability of the intercept showed a change in the long-term mean for the FTSE100, NIKKEI225 and SP500 as a proxy but not for the DAX30 as a proxy. Deeper analysis of the intercept parameters indicated that the long-term mean increased in the period of financial distress, leading to higher correlation coefficients.

Table 9. The GARCH models selected with BIC in the de-garching part of the ADCC model estimation for the third panel

	I - D	I - F	I - N	I - S
BET	AVGARCH	AVGARCH	GARCH	AVGARCH
BUX	NAGARCH	NAGARCH	NAGARCH	TGARCH
PX	TGARCH	TGARCH	NAGARCH	NAGARCH
SBITOP	NAGARCH	NAGARCH	NAGARCH	NAGARCH
SOFIX	EGARCH	EGARCH	EGARCH	EGARCH
WIG20	TGARCH	NAGARCH	GJR-GARCH	GJR-GARCH
BMRK	NAGARCH	NAGARCH	NAGARCH	NAGARCH

Notes: The version of the data panel is denoted in the first column: D denotes a panel with the DAX30, F denotes a panel with the FTSE100, N denotes a panel with the NIKKEI225 and S denotes a panel with the SP500 as a benchmark index, respectively. BMRK denotes the corresponding benchmark index. The exact specification of the GARCH models can be found in the appendix.

Table 10. The results of the ADCC model, with an allowance for a structural break on the 15th of September 2008 for the third panel

	α_1	β_1	γ_1	α_D	β_D	γ_D	W	LRT
III - D	0.0037*	0.9756**	0.0174**	0.0032	-0.0449*	-0.0038	9.20*	46.04**
III - F	0.0020	0.9668**	0.0238**	0.0072	-0.0342	-0.0099	4.98	59.52**
III - N	0.0036	0.9386**	0.0292**	0.0039	-0.0083	-0.0116	1.71	77.80**
III - S	0.0009	0.9749**	0.0183**	0.0099*	-0.0502*	-0.0135	9.68*	75.88**

Notes: The numbers in this table represent the estimated value of the parameters or the value of test statistic – W stands for the Wald test statistic for the stability of the dynamic part of the model as a whole, while LRT stands for the likelihood ratio test for the stability of the intercept. (*) and (**) denote statistical significance at the 5% and 1% critical level, respectively. The version of the data panel is denoted in the first column: D denotes a panel with the DAX30, F denotes a panel with the FTSE100, N denotes a panel with the NIKKEI225 and S denotes a panel with the SP500 as a benchmark index, respectively.

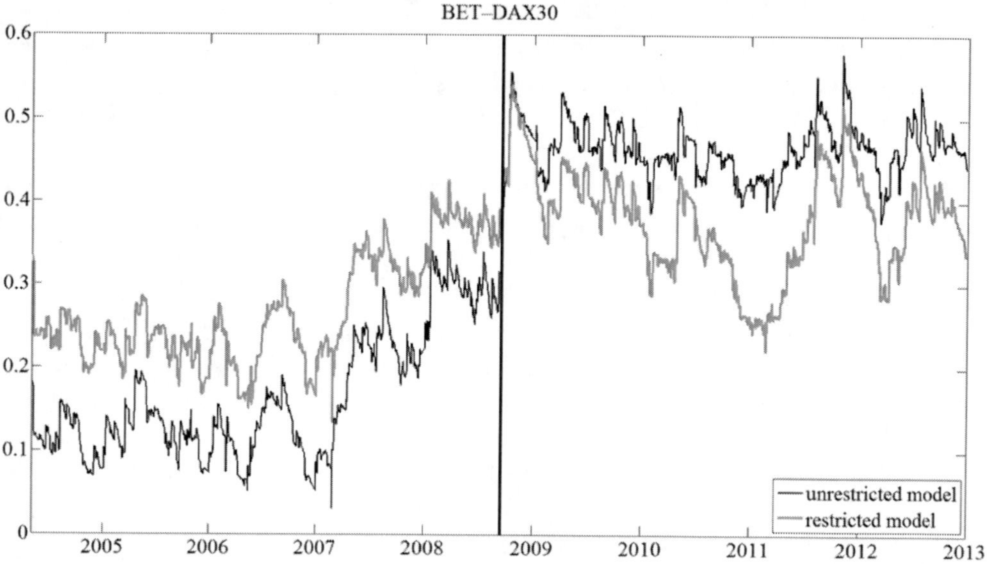

Figure 1. Dynamic correlations of the ADCC model with constant parameters (restricted model) and of the ADCC model with an allowance for a structural break on the 15th of September 2008 (unrestricted model) between the Romanian and German stock markets.

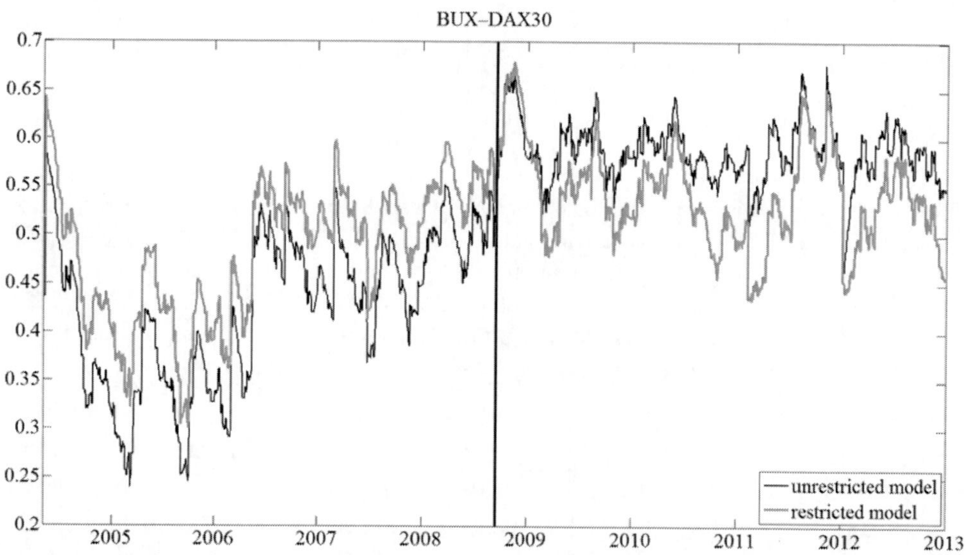

Figure 2. Dynamic correlations of the ADCC model with constant parameters (restricted model) and of the ADCC model with an allowance for a structural break on the 15th of September 2008 (unrestricted model) between the Hungarian and German stock markets.

In the de-garching part of the ADCC model estimation for the third panel, all indices except BET exhibit asymmetry in the volatility.

The ADCC model parameters in the period before the Lehman Brothers bankruptcy on the third data panel were similar to those in the inclusive second data panel. After the structural break date, the parameter α increased while β and γ decreased. Some of these changes were so substantial that they were reflected in significant test statistics. The Wald test statistic for the stability of the dynamic part of the model indicated a significant change at DAX30 and SP500 as a proxy.

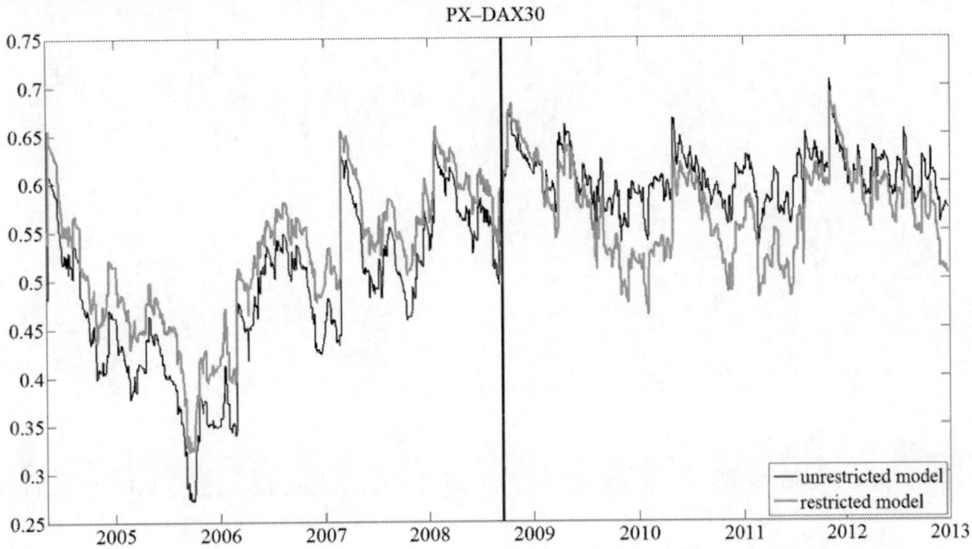

Figure 3. Dynamic correlations of the ADCC model with constant parameters (restricted model) and of the ADCC model with an allowance for a structural break on the 15th of September 2008 (unrestricted model) between the Czech and German stock markets.

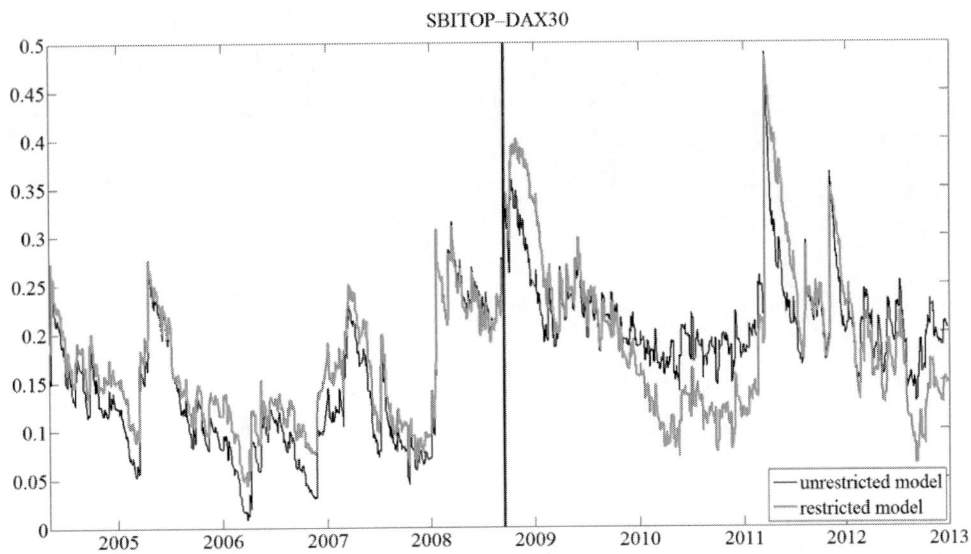

Figure 4. Dynamic correlations of the ADCC model with constant parameters (restricted model) and of the ADCC model with an allowance for a structural break on the 15th of September 2008 (unrestricted model) between the Slovenian and German stock markets.

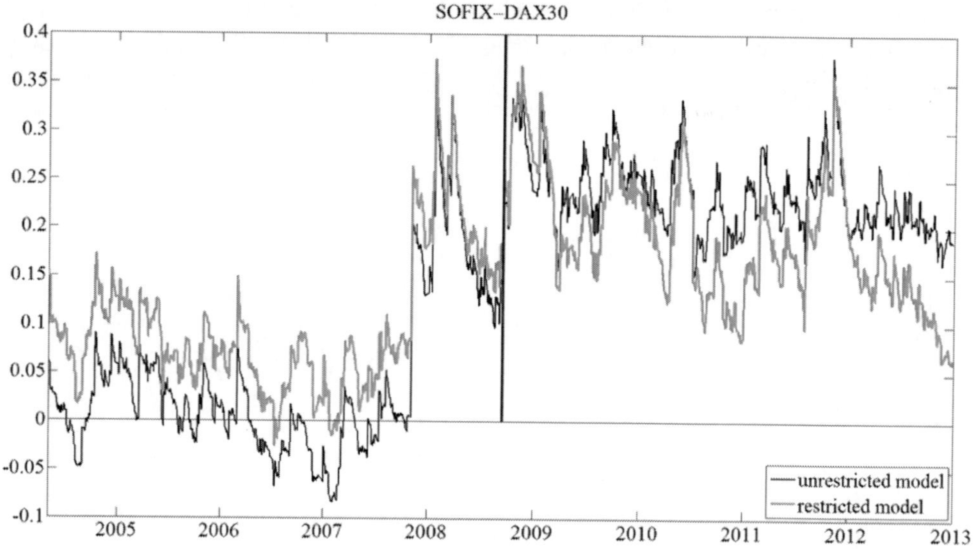

Figure 5. Dynamic correlations of the ADCC model with constant parameters (restricted model) and of the ADCC model with an allowance for a structural break on the 15th of September 2008 (unrestricted model) between the Bulgarian and German stock markets.

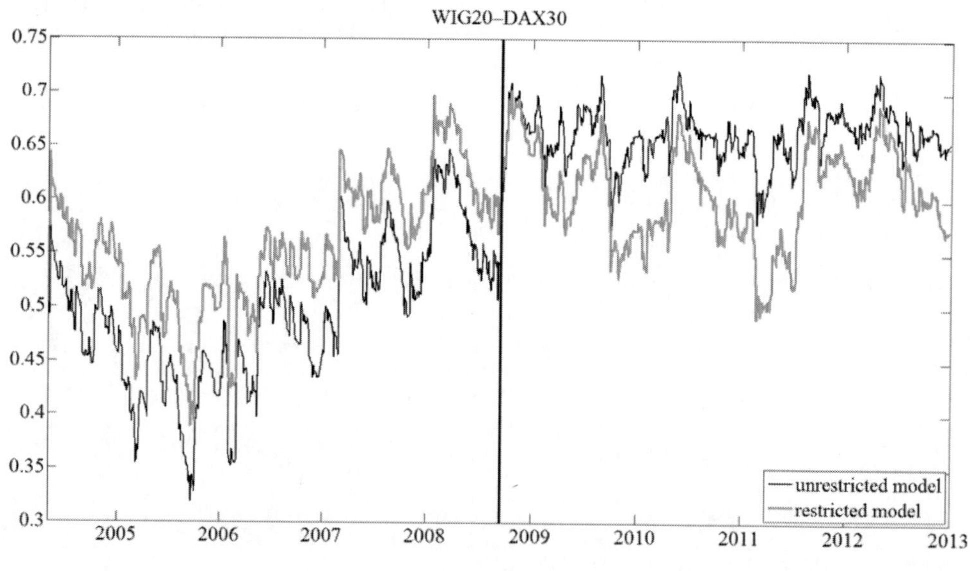

Figure 6. Dynamic correlations of the ADCC model with constant parameters (restricted model) and of the ADCC model with an allowance for a structural break on the 15th of September 2008 (unrestricted model) between the Polish and German stock markets.

In the first case, the parameter β decreased significantly while in the second case the parameter α increased and β decreased significantly. Changes in persistence were smaller than in the inclusive second data panel. The intercept parameters changed significantly as evidenced by LRT test statistics and the direction of the long-term mean difference was upward for all combinations.

Since the results in the third data panel reported at most significant differences before and after the structural break, we present correlation coefficients based on the ordinary ADCC model with constant parameters through the whole data period (restricted model) and those based on the ADCC model reported in Table 10 (unrestricted model). The number of all pairwise combinations in this data panel is too large, so we present dynamic conditional correlation coefficients only for pairs where the DAX30 appears. From Figures 1 – 6 we can see that the difference between coefficients calculated by different models can be large, leading to false subsequent interpretations.

CONCLUSION

This chapter contributes to the literature regarding an application of an asymmetric dynamic conditional correlations (ADCC) model on the Central and Eastern European (CEE) markets. We applied an extension of the ADCC model that allows for a possible structural break in the model on the primary stock market indices of the Czech Republic, Hungary, Poland, Slovenia, Bulgaria and Romania. As a proxy for global stock markets we used stock indices for the USA (SP500), Germany (DAX30), the UK (FTSE100), and Japan (NIKKEI225). The data spans from the year 2000 to the year 2012. In this period there were two major events that affected the stock markets of CEE countries. In the year 2004 some of them became members of an enlarged European Union. In 2008, the financial crisis quickly spread all around the world and substantially impacted CEE markets.

Some papers have reported that these two events increased correlations between CEE markets and with global stock markets. This chapter addresses the research question of whether these events impacted the correlation structure as well. We tested how the ADCC model parameters differ from one period to another and compare dynamic correlation coefficients estimated with an ordinary ADCC model and those estimated with a model that allows them to change at a break date. Research was conducted on three data panels, depending on the research question.

Correlations among CEE markets and vis-à-vis global markets appear to have an asymmetric effect, which was the highest before the EU enlargement with the FTSE100 and the SP500 as a proxy and it fell during the process of market integration and even in the period of the global financial crisis. After the Lehman Brothers bankruptcy, the decrease in the asymmetric parameter was compensated by the increase of the general shock parameter, meaning that correlations became more volatile with both positive and negative shocks. After joining the EU, CEE market correlation structure became more persistent with gradual development. The persistence lowered during the period of the global financial crisis, again becoming more affected by shocks.

These changes in the dynamic parameters of the ADCC model were mostly insignificant. Wald test statistics for the stability of the dynamic part of the model were inconclusive with regard to a structural break with EU enlargement and at the spread of the crisis for the panel consisting of the Czech Republic, Hungary, Poland and a benchmark. The second break date impacted correlation dynamics significantly for the panel of six CEE countries and the DAX30 or SP500 as a proxy. This was mostly reflected in the persistence parameter.

The results indicate that besides weak evidence of a change in dynamics, the intercept parameters changed significantly at both break dates. A deeper investigation showed that they updated in a way that the long-term mean of the models increased, leading to higher average correlation coefficients. This confirms results reported in similar studies that CEE market correlations increased after joining the EU in 2004 and in the period of the global financial crisis. An exception is the data panel consisting of the Czech Republic, Hungary, Poland and Germany, where a change in the intercept parameters appeared to be insignificant. This may be due to the already high intercorrelations before the crisis.

An appearance of a structural break in the model that is present mostly at events with major consequences, can have a large impact on the subsequent interpretation. This chapter shows that a structural break should be taken into account when modeling CEE stock markets during the enlargement of the EU into CEE countries and for the spread of the global financial crisis in 2008. Global financial markets are evolving continuously and the next major event involving a structural break could happen at any time or may have even already taken place.

APPENDIX

List of GARCH models used in the de-garching stage of the model estimation (all with one lag of volatility, one lag of innovation, and if a model includes it, one lag of negative innovation).

AGARCH (Engle 1990)

$$h_t = \omega + \alpha(\varepsilon_{t-1} - \gamma)^2 + \beta h_{t-1} \tag{A1}$$

AVGARCH (Taylor 1986)

$$h_t^{1/2} = \omega + \alpha|\varepsilon_{t-1}| + \beta h_{t-1}^{1/2} \tag{A2}$$

EGARCH (Nelson 1991)

$$\ln(h_t) = \omega + \alpha\left(\frac{|\varepsilon_{t-1}|}{\sqrt{h_{t-1}}} - E\left(\frac{|\varepsilon_{t-1}|}{\sqrt{h_{t-1}}}\right)\right) + \gamma\frac{\varepsilon_{t-1}}{\sqrt{h_{t-1}}} + \beta\ln(h_{t-1}) \tag{A3}$$

GARCH (Bollerslev 1986)

$$h_t = \omega + \alpha\varepsilon_{t-1}{}^2 + \beta h_{t-1} \tag{A4}$$

GJR-GARCH (Glosten et al. 1993)

$$h_t = \omega + \alpha\varepsilon_{t-1}{}^2 + \gamma I[\varepsilon_{t-1} < 0]\varepsilon_{t-1}{}^2 + \beta h_{t-1} \tag{A5}$$

NAGARCH (Engle and Ng 1993)

$$h_t = \omega + \alpha\left(\varepsilon_{t-1} - \gamma\sqrt{h_{t-1}}\right)^2 + \beta h_{t-1} \quad \text{(A6)}$$

TGARCH (Zakoian 1994)

$$h_t^{1/2} = \omega + \alpha|\varepsilon_{t-1}| + \gamma I[\varepsilon_{t-1} < 0]|\varepsilon_{t-1}| + \beta h_{t-1}^{1/2} \quad \text{(A7)}$$

VGARCH (Engle and Ng 1993)

$$h_t = \omega + \alpha\left(\frac{\varepsilon_{t-1}}{\sqrt{h_{t-1}}} - \gamma\right)^2 + \beta h_{t-1} \quad \text{(A8)}$$

REFERENCES

Andreou, E. and Ghysels, E. (2002). Detecting multiple breaks in financial market volatility dynamics. *Journal of Applied Econometrics* 17, 579–600.

Andreou, E. and Ghysels, E. (2008). Structural breaks in financial time series. In T. G. Anderson, R. A. Davis, J.-P. Kreiss, & T. Mikosch (Eds.), *Handbook of financial time series* (p. 839–866). Berlin: Springer.

Baumöhl, E. (2013). Stock market integration between the CEE-4 and the G7 markets : Asymmetric DCC and smooth transition approach. MPRA Paper 43834, University Library of Munich, Germany.

Bauwens, L., Laurent S., and Rombouts J. V. K. (2006): Multivariate GARCH models: A survey, *Journal of Applied Econometrics*, 21, 79–109.

Bollerslev, T. (1986). Generalized Autoregressive Conditional Heteroskedasticity, *Journal of Econometrics*, 31, 307-327.

Büttner, D. and Hayo, B. (2010). News and correlations of CEEC-3 financial markets. *Economic Modelling*, 27(5), 915–922.

Cappiello, L., R. F. Engle, and K. Sheppard (2006). Asymmetric dynamics in the correlations of global equity and bond returns, *Journal of Financial Econometrics*, 4, 537–572.

Diebold, F.X. (1986). Modeling the persistence of conditional variances: a comment. *Econometric Reviews* 5, 51–56.

Duchin, R., Oguzhan Ozbas and Berk A. Sensoy. (2010). Costly external finance, corporate investment, and the subprime mortgage credit crisis, *Journal of Financial Economics*, 97(3), 418–435.

Dvorak, T., and Podpiera, R. (2006). European Union enlargement and equity markets in accession countries. *Emerging Markets Review*, 7, 129−146.

Engle, R. F. (1982). Autoregressive Conditional Heteroscedasticity with Estimates of the Variance of United Kingdom Inflation. *Econometrica* 50, 987–1007.

Engle, R.F. (1990), Discussion: Stock Market Volatility and the Crash of '87, *Review of Financial Studies*, 3, 103–106.

Engle, R. F. (2002). Dynamic conditional correlation: A simple class of multivariate generalized autoregressive conditional heteroskedasticity models. *Journal of Business and Economic Statistics* 20, 339–350.

Engle, R. (2009). *Anticipating correlations: a new paradigm for risk management.* Princeton University Press.

Engle, R. and Ng, V. (1993). Measuring and testing the impact of news on volatility. *Journal of Finance* 48, 1749–1778.

Engle, R. F., and K. Sheppard. (2001). Theoretical and Empirical Properties of Dynamic Conditional Correlation MVGARCH. *Working Paper No. 2001–15*, University of California, San Diego.

Frank, N., Gonzalez-Hermosillo, B. and Hesse, H. (2008). Transmission of Liquidity Shocks: Evidence from the 2007 Subprime Crisis, *IMF Working Paper, n. 08/200*, International Monetary Fund, Washington (DC).

Gjika, D. and Horváth, R. (2013). Stock market comovements in Central Europe: Evidence from the asymmetric DCC model. *Economic Modelling*, 33, 55–64.

Glosten, L., R. Jagannathan, and D. Runke (1993). Relationship between the expected value and the volatility of the nominal excess return on stocks, *Journal of Finance* 48, 1779–1801.

Gray, S.F. (1996). Modeling the conditional distribution of interest rates as a regime-switching process, *Journal of Financial Economics* 42, 27–62.

Guidi, F. and Gupta, R. (2010). Cointegration and conditional correlations among German and Eastern Europe equity markets. *MPRA Paper 21732*, University Library of Munich, Germany.

Hafner, C. M., and Herwartz, H. (2008). Analytical quasi maximum likelihood inference in multivariate volatility models, *Metrika*, 67, 219–239.

Hamilton, J.D., Susmel, R. (1994). Autoregressive conditional heteroskedasticity and changes in regime, *Journal of Econometrics* 64, 307–333.

Hansen, B. E. (2001). The New Econometrics of Structural Change: Dating Breaks in U.S. Labor Productivity, *The Journal of Economic Perspectives* , Vol. 15, No. 4 (Autumn), pp. 117-128.

Hillebrand, E. (2005). Neglecting parameter changes in GARCH models, *Journal of Econometrics* 129, 121–138.

Horvath, R. and Petrovski, D. (2013). International stock market integration: Central and South Eastern Europe compared. *Economic Systems*, 37(1), 81–91.

Hyde, S., Bredin, D., Nguyen, N. (2007). Correlation Dynamics between Asia-Pacific, EU and US Stock Returns. In: Kim S. J., McKenzie M. (Eds.), Asia-Pacific Financial Markets: Integration, Innovation and Challenges, International Finance Review, Vol. 8, 39–61.

Kalotychou, E., Staikouras, S. K. and Zhao, G. (2009). On the dynamics of asset correlations: What matters to portfolio managers, Cass Business School.

Kasch-Haroutounian, M. and Price, S. (2001). Volatility in the Transition Markets of Central Europe. *Applied Financial Economic*, 11(1), 93–105.

Kearney, C. and Potì, V. (2006). Correlation dynamics in European equity markets, *Research in International Business and Finance*, Volume 20, Issue 3, 305–321.

Kocenda, E. and Egert, B. (2011). Time-Varying Synchronization of European Stock Markets. *Empirical Economics*, 40(2), 393–407.

Lamoureux, C. and Lastrapes, W. (1990). Persistence in variance, structural GARCH model. *Journal of Business and Economic Statistics* 8, 225–234.

Lastrapes,W. D. (1989). Exchange Rate Volatility and U. S. Monetary Policy: An ARCH Application, *Journal of Money, Credit, and Banking*, 21, 66–77.

Li, X-M, (2008). From the EMS to EMU: Has There Been Any Change in the Behaviour of Exchange Rate Correlation?, *Quantitative Economic Policy. Advances in Computational Economics*, Volume 20, Part 4, 261–273.

Li, X-M, (2010). How do exchange rates co-move? A study on the currencies of five inflation-targeting countries. *Journal of Banking and Finance* 35, 418–429.

Longstaff, F. A. (2010). The subprime credit crisis and contagion in financial markets, *Journal of Financial Economics*, 97(3), 436–450.

Nelson, D. (1991). Conditional heteroskedasticity in asset returns: A new approach. *Econometrica* 59, 347–370.

Savva, C. S. and Aslanidis, C. (2010). Stock Market Integration between New EU Member States and the Eurozone. *Empirical Economics*, 39(2), 337–351.

Scheicher, M. (2001). The Comovements of Stock Markets in Hungary, Poland and the Czech Republic. *International Journal of Finance & Economics*, 6(1), 27–39.

Silvennoinen, A., and Terasvirta, T. (2008). Multivariate GARCH models, *Handbook of Financial Time Series*, ed. by T. Andersen, R. Davis, J. Kreiss, and T. Mikosch. Springer.

Syllignakis, M. N. and Kouretas, G. P. (2011). Dynamic Correlation Analysis of Financial Contagion: Evidence from the Central and Eastern European Markets. *International Review of Economics and Finance*, 20(4), 717–732.

Taylor, S. (1986). *Modelling Financial Time Series*. New York: Wiley.

Wang, P. and Moore, T. (2008). Stock Market Integration for the Transition Economies: Time-varying Conditional Correlation Approach. *The Manchester School*, 76, 116–133.

Zakoian, J.-M. (1994). Threshold heteroskedastic models. *Journal of Economic Dynamics and Control* 18, 931–955.

Zunko, M. and Jagric, T. (2013). Testing for a structural break in dynamic conditional correlation models, *Quantitative finance*, under review.

In: Stock Markets
Editors: F. Petroni, F. Prattico and G. D'Amico
ISBN: 978-1-62808-751-2

Chapter 3

MODELING AND PRICING OF COVARIANCE AND CORRELATION SWAPS FOR FINANCIAL MARKETS WITH SEMI-MARKOV VOLATILITIES

Giovanni Salvi[1,*] *and Anatoliy V. Swishchuk*[2,†]
[1]Department of Methods and Models for Economics, Territory and Finance MEMOTEF, 'Sapienza' University of Rome, Rome, Italy
[2]Department of Mathematics and Statistics, University of Calgary, Calgary, Alberta, Canada

Abstract

In this paper, we model financial markets with semi-Markov volatilities and price covariance and correlation swaps for these markets. Numerical evaluations of variance, volatility, covariance and correlations swaps with semi-Markov volatility are presented as well. The novelty of the paper lies in pricing of volatility swaps in closed form, and pricing of covariance and correlation swaps in a market with two risky assets.

Keywords: semi-Markov-modulated volatility; covariance and correlation swaps

1. Introduction

One of the recent and new financial products is variance and volatility swaps, which are useful for volatility hedging and speculation. The market for variance and volatility swaps has been growing, and many investment banks and other financial institutions are now actively quoting volatility swaps on various assets: stock indexes, currencies, as well as commodities. A stock's volatility is the simplest measure of its riskiness or uncertainty. Formally, the volatility σ_R is the annualized standard deviation of the stock's returns during the period of interest, where the subscript R denotes the observed or 'realized' volatility. Why trade volatility or variance? As mentioned in M. Broadie and A. Jain [5], 'just as stock investors

*E-mail address: giovanni.salvi@uniroma1.i
†E-mail address: aswish@ucalgary.ca

think they know something about the direction of the stock market so we may think we have insight into the level of future volatility. If we think current volatility is low, for the right price we might want to take a position that profits if volatility increases'.

In this paper, we model financial markets with semi-Markov volatilities and price covariance and correlation swaps for these markets. Numerical evaluations of variance, volatility, covariance and correlations swaps with semi-Markov volatility are presented as well.

Volatility swaps are forward contracts on future realized stock volatility, variance swaps are similar contract on variance, the square of the future volatility, both these instruments provide an easy way for investors to gain exposure to the future level of volatility. A stock's volatility is the simplest measure of its risk less or uncertainty. Formally, the volatility σ_R is the annualized standard deviation of the stock's returns during the period of interest, where the subscript R denotes the observed or "realized" volatility.

The easy way to trade volatility is to use volatility swaps, sometimes called realized volatility forward contracts, because they provide pure exposure to volatility (and only to volatility).

A stock *volatility swap* is a forward contract on the annualized volatility. Its payoff at expiration is equal to

$$N(\sigma_R(S) - K_{vol}),$$

where $\sigma_R(S)$ is the realized stock volatility (quoted in annual terms) over the life of contract,

$$\sigma_R(S) := \sqrt{\frac{1}{T}\int_0^T \sigma_s^2 ds}\ ,$$

σ_t is a stochastic stock volatility, K_{vol} is the annualized volatility delivery price, and N is the notional amount of the swap in dollar per annualized volatility point. The holder of a volatility swap at expiration receives N dollars for every point by which the stock's realized volatility σ_R has exceeded the volatility delivery price K_{vol}. The holder is swapping a fixed volatility K_{vol} for the actual (floating) future volatility σ_R. We note that usually $N = \alpha I$, where α is a converting parameter such as 1 per volatility-square, and I is a long-short index ($+1$ for long and -1 for short).

Although options market participants talk of volatility, it is its variance, or volatility squared, that has more fundamental significance (see Demeterfi *et al* [11]).

A variance swap is a forward contract on annualized variance, the square of the realized volatility. Its payoff at expiration is equal to

$$N(\sigma_R^2(S) - K_{var}),$$

where $\sigma_R^2(S)$ is the realized stock variance(quoted in annual terms) over the life of the contract,

$$\sigma_R^2(S) := \frac{1}{T}\int_0^T \sigma_s^2 ds\ ,$$

K_{var} is the delivery price for variance, and N is the notional amount of the swap in dollars per annualized volatility point squared. The holder of variance swap at expiration receives N dollars for every point by which the stock's realized variance $\sigma_R^2(S)$ has exceeded the variance delivery price K_{var}.

Therefore, pricing the variance swap reduces to calculating the realized volatility square.

Valuing a variance forward contract or swap is no different from valuing any other derivative security. The value of a forward contract P on future realized variance with strike price K_{var} is the expected present value of the future payoff in the risk-neutral world:

$$P = E\{e^{-rT}(\sigma_R^2(S) - K_{var})\} ,$$

where r is the risk-free discount rate corresponding to the expiration date T, and E denotes the expectation.

Thus, for calculating variance swaps we need to know only $E\{\sigma_R^2(S)\}$, namely, the mean value of the underlying variance.

To calculate volatility swaps we need more. From Brockhaus and Long [6] approximation (which is used the second order Taylor expansion for function $\sqrt{x}$) we have (see also Javaheri *et al* [17]):

$$E\{\sqrt{\sigma_R^2(S)}\} \approx \sqrt{E\{V\}} - \frac{Var\{V\}}{8E\{V\}^{3/2}} ,$$

where $V := \sigma_R^2(S)$ and $\frac{Var\{V\}}{8E\{V\}^{3/2}}$ is the convexity adjustment.

Thus, to calculate volatility swaps we need both $E\{V\}$ and $Var\{V\}$.

The realized continuously sampled variance is defined in the following way:

$$V := Var(S) := \frac{1}{T}\int_0^T \sigma_t^2 dt .$$

Realized continuously sampled volatility is defined as follows:

$$Vol(S) := \sqrt{Var(S)} = \sqrt{V} .$$

Options dependent on exchange rate movements, such as those paying in a currency different from the underlying currency, have an exposure to movements of the correlation between the asset and the exchange rate. This risk may be eliminated by using covariance swap. Variance and volatility swaps have been studied by Swishchuk [20]. The novelty of this paper with respect to Swishchuk [20] is that we calculate the volatility swap price explicitly; moreover we price covariance and correlation swap in a two risky assets market model.

A *covariance swap* is a covariance forward contact of the underlying rates S^1 and S^2 which payoff at expiration is equal to

$$N(Cov_R(S^1, S^2) - K_{cov}) ,$$

where K_{cov} is a strike price, N is the notional amount, $Cov_R(S^1, S^2)$ is a covariance between two assets S^1 and S^2.

Logically, a *correlation swap* is a correlation forward contract of two underlying rates S^1 and S^2 which payoff at expiration is equal to:

$$N(Corr_R(S^1, S^2) - K_{corr}) ,$$

where $Corr(S^1, S^2)$ is a realized correlation of two underlying assets S^1 and S^2, K_{corr} is a strike price, N is the notional amount.

Pricing covariance swap, from a theoretical point of view, is similar to pricing variance swaps, since

$$Cov_R(S^1, S^2) = 1/4\{\sigma_R^2(S^1S^2) - \sigma_R^2(S^1/S^2)\} ,$$

where S^1 and S^2 are two given assets, $\sigma_R^2(S)$ is a variance swap for underlying assets, $Cov_R(S^1, S^2)$ is a realized covariance of the two underlying assets.

Thus, we need to know variances for S^1S^2 and for S^1/S^2. Correlation $Corr_R(S^1, S^2)$ is defined as follows:

$$Corr_R(S^1, S^2) = \frac{Cov_R(S^1, S^2)}{\sqrt{\sigma_R^2(S^1)}\sqrt{\sigma_R^2(S^2)}} ,$$

where $Cov_R(S^1, S^2)$ is defined above.

Given two assets S_t^1 and S_t^2 with $t \in [0, T]$, sampled on days $t_0 = 0 < t_1 < t_2 < ... < t_n = T$ between today and maturity T, the log-return of each asset is: $R_i^j := \log(\frac{S_{t_i}^j}{S_{t_{i-1}}^j}), \quad i = 1, 2, ..., n, \quad j = 1, 2.$

Covariance and correlation can be approximated by

$$Cov_n(S^1, S^2) = \frac{n}{(n-1)T} \sum_{i=1}^{n} R_i^1 R_i^2 ,$$

and

$$Corr_n(S^1, S^2) = \frac{Cov_n(S^1, S^2)}{\sqrt{Var_n(S^1)}\sqrt{Var_n(S^2)}} ,$$

respectively.

The literature devoted to the volatility derivatives is growing. We give here a short overview of the latest development in this area. The Non-Gaussian Ornstein-Uhlenbeck stochastic volatility model was used by Benth *et al.* [1] to study volatility and variance swaps. M. Broadie and A. Jain [4] evaluated price and hedging strategy for volatility derivatives in the Heston square root stochastic volatility model and in M. Broadie and A. Jain [5] they compare result from various model in order to investigate the effect of jumps and discrete sampling on variance and volatility swaps. Pure jump process with independent increments return models were used by Carr *et al.* [7] to price derivatives written on realized variance, and subsequent development by Carr and Lee [8]. We also refer to Carr and Lee [9] for a good survey on volatility derivatives. Da Fonseca *et al.* [10] analyzed the influence of variance and covariance swap in a market by solving a portfolio optimization problem in a market with risky assets and volatility derivatives. Correlation swap price has been investigated by Bossu [2, 3] for component of an equity index using statistical method. Drissien *et al.* [12] discusses the price of correlation risk for equity options. Pricing volatility swaps under Heston's model with regime-switching and pricing options under a generalized Markov-modulated jump-diffusion model are discussed in and Elliott *et al.* [13, 14], respectively. Howison *et al.* [16] considers the pricing of a range of volatility derivatives, including volatility and variance swaps and swaptions. The pricing options on realized variance in the Heston model with jumps in returns and volatility is studied in Sepp [19]. An analytical closed-forms pricing of pseudo-variance, pseudo-volatility, pseudo-covariance and pseudo-correlation swaps is studied in Swishchuk *et al.* [21]. Windcliff *et al.* [22] investigates the behavior and hedging of discretely observed volatility derivatives.

The rest of the paper is organized as follows. Section 1 is devoted to the study of semi-Markov volatilites and their martingale characterization. Section 2 deals with pricing of variance and volatility swaps and numerical evaluation of them for markets with semi-Markov volatilities. Section 3 studies the pricing of covarinace and correlation swaps for a two risky assets in financial markets with semi-Markov volatilities. We also give here a numerical evaluation of these derivatives. Appendix presents a first order correction for a realized correlation.

2. Martingale Representation of Semi-Markov Processes

Let $(\Omega, \mathscr{F}, (\mathscr{F}_t)_{t\in\mathbb{R}_+}, \mathbb{P})$ be a filtered probability space, with a right-continuous filtration $(\mathscr{F}_t)_{t\in\mathbb{R}_+}$ and probability $\mathbb{P}$.

Let $(X, \mathscr{X})$ be a measurable space and

$$Q_{SM}(x, B, t) := P(x, B)G_x(t) \qquad \text{for } x \in X, B \in \mathscr{X}, t \in \mathbb{R}_+ , \tag{1}$$

be a semi-Markov kernel. Let $(x_n, \tau_n; n \in \mathbb{N})$ be a $(X \times \mathbb{R}_+, \mathscr{X} \otimes \mathscr{B}_+)$-valued Markov renewal process with Q_{SM} the associated kernel, that is

$$\mathbb{P}(x_{n+1} \in B, \tau_{n+1} - \tau_n \le t \mid \mathscr{F}_n) = Q_{SM}(x_n, B, t) . \tag{2}$$

Let us define the process

$$\nu_t := sup\{n \in \mathbb{N} : \tau_n \le t\} , \tag{3}$$

that gives the number of jumps of the Markov renewal process in the time interval $(0, t]$ and

$$\theta_n := \tau_n - \tau_{n-1} , \tag{4}$$

that gives the sojourn time of the Markov renewal process in the n-th visited state. The semi-Markov process, associated with the Markov renewal process $(x_n, \tau_n)_{n\in\mathbb{N}}$, is defined by

$$x_t := x_{\nu(t)} \qquad \text{for } t \in \mathbb{R}_+ . \tag{5}$$

Associated with the semi-Markov process, it is possible to define some auxiliaries processes. We are interested in the backward recurrence time (or life-time) process defined by

$$\gamma(t) := t - \tau_{\nu(t)} \qquad \text{for } t \in \mathbb{R}_+ . \tag{6}$$

The next result characterizes backward recurrence time process (*cf.* Swishchuk [20]), we give the proof for completeness.

Proposition 1. *The backward recurrence time $(\gamma(t))_t$ is a Markov process with generator*

$$Q_\gamma f(t) = f'(t) + \lambda(t)[f(0) - f(t)]\,, \tag{7}$$

where $\lambda(t) = -\frac{\overline{G_x}'(t)}{\overline{G_x}(t)}$, $\overline{G_x}(t) = 1 - G_x(t)$ *and* $Domain(Q_\gamma) = C^1(\mathbb{R}_+)$.

Proof. Let t be the present time such that $\gamma(t) = t$, without loss of generality we can assume that $t < \tau_1$, then for $T > t$ we have

$$\mathbb{E}_t\{f(\gamma(T))\} = \mathbb{E}_t\{f(\gamma(T))\mathbb{I}_{\theta_1>T}\} + \mathbb{E}_t\{f(\gamma(T))\mathbb{I}_{\theta_1\leq T}\}\,. \tag{8}$$

Using the properties of conditional expectation we obtain

$$\begin{aligned}\mathbb{E}_t\{f(\gamma(T))\} =& f(T)\frac{\overline{G}_x(T)}{\overline{G}_x(t)} + \frac{1}{\overline{G}_x(t)}\mathbb{E}\{f(\gamma(T))\mathbb{I}_{t<\theta_1\leq T}\} \\ =& f(T)\frac{\overline{G}_x(T)}{\overline{G}_x(t)} + \frac{1}{\overline{G}_x(t)}\int_t^T f(T-u)G_x'(u)du\,.\end{aligned} \tag{9}$$

By adding and subtracting $f(t)$ in the integrand we get

$$\mathbb{E}_t\{f(\gamma(T))\} = f(T)\frac{\overline{G}_x(T)}{\overline{G}_x(t)} + \frac{1}{\overline{G}_x(t)}\int_t^T (f(T-u) - f(t))G_x'(u)du + f(t)\frac{\overline{G}_x(t) - \overline{G}_x(T)}{\overline{G}_x(t)}\,,$$

then

$$\mathbb{E}_t\{f(\gamma(T))\} - f(t) = (f(T) - f(t))\frac{\overline{G}_x(T)}{\overline{G}_x(t)} + \frac{1}{\overline{G}_x(t)}\int_t^T (f(T-u) - f(t))G_x'(u)du. \tag{10}$$

Recalling the definition of the generator and using the above equation we have

$$Q_\gamma f(t) = \lim_{T\to t}\frac{\mathbb{E}_t\{f(\gamma(T))\} - f(t)}{T-t} = f'(t) - \frac{\overline{G_x}'(t)}{\overline{G_x}(t)}[f(0) - f(t)]\,, \tag{11}$$

this concludes the proof. □

Remark 1. *As well known, semi-Markov processes preserve the lost-memories property only at transition times, then* $(x_t)_{t\in\mathbb{R}_+}$ *is not Markov. However, if we consider the joint process* $(x_t, \gamma(t))_{t\in\mathbb{R}_+}$*, and we record at any instant the time already spent by the semi-Markov process in the present state, then it result that* $(x_t, \gamma(t))_{t\in\mathbb{R}_+}$ *is a Markov process.*

The following result allow us to associate a martingale to any Markov process we refer to Swishchuk [20], Elliott and Swishchuk [15] for details.

Proposition 2. *Let* $(x_t)_{t\in\mathbb{R}_+}$ *be a Markov process with generator* Q *and* $f \in Domain\,(Q)$*, then*

$$m_t^f := f(x_t) - f(x_0) - \int_0^t Qf(x_s)ds \tag{12}$$

is a zero-mean martingale with respect to $\mathscr{F}_t := \sigma\{y(s); 0 \leq s \leq t\}$.

Let us evaluate the quadratic variation of this martingale (see Swishchuk [20], Elliott and Swishchuk [15]).

Proposition 3. *Let* $(x_t)_{t\in\mathbb{R}_+}$ *be a Markov process with generator* Q, $f \in$ *Domain* (Q) *and* $(m_t^f)_{t\in\mathbb{R}_+}$ *its associated martingale, then*

$$\langle m^f \rangle_t := \int_0^t [Qf^2(x_s) - 2f(x_s)Qf(x_s)]ds \tag{13}$$

is the quadratic variation of m^f.

The next result concern the evaluation of the quadratic covariation, for details and proof we refer to Salvi and Swishchuk [18].

Proposition 4. *Let* $(x_t)_{t\in\mathbb{R}_+}$ *be a Markov process with generator* Q, $f, g \in$ *Domain* (Q) *such that* $fg \in$ *Domain* (Q). *Denote by* $(m_t^f)_{t\in\mathbb{R}_+}$, $(m_t^g)_{t\in\mathbb{R}_+}$ *their associated martingale. Then*

$$\langle f(x.), g(x.)\rangle_t := \int_0^t \{Q(f(x_s)g(x_s)) - [g(x_s)Qf(x_s) + f(x_s)Qg(x_s)]\}ds \tag{14}$$

is the quadratic covariation of f *and* g.

We would like to study the martingale associated to the Markov process $(x_t, \gamma(t))_{t\in\mathbb{R}_+}$ and its generator. The following statement concerns this task, and is a direct application of Proposition 2.

Lemma 1. *(Swishchuk [20])*
Let $(x_t)_{t\in\mathbb{R}_+}$ *be a semi-Markov process with kernel* Q_{SM} *defined in Eq. (1). Then, the process*

$$m_t^f := f(x_t, \gamma(t)) - \int_0^t Qf(x_s, \gamma(s))ds\,, \tag{15}$$

is a martingale with respect to the filtration $\mathscr{F}_t := \sigma\{x_s, \nu_s; 0 \le s \le t\}$, *where* Q *is the generator of the Markov process* $(x_t, \gamma(t))_{t\in\mathbb{R}_+}$ *given by*

$$Qf(x,t) = \frac{df}{dt}(x,t) + \frac{g_x(t)}{\bar{G}_x(t)}\int_X P(x,dy)[f(y,0) - f(x,t)]\,, \tag{16}$$

here $g_x(t) = \frac{dG_x(t)}{dt}$.

The following statement follows directly from Proposition 3 and it allows us to evaluate the quadratic variation of the martingale associated with $(x_t, \gamma(t))_{t\in\mathbb{R}_+}$.

Lemma 2. *Let* $(x_t)_{t\in\mathbb{R}_+}$ *be a semi-Markov process with kernel* Q_{SM}, $(x_t, \gamma(t))_{t\in\mathbb{R}_+}$ *is a Markov process with generator* Q, $f \in$ *Domain* (Q) *and* $(m_t^f)_{t\in\mathbb{R}_+}$ *its associated martingale, then*

$$\langle m^f \rangle_t := \int_0^t [Qf^2(x_s, \gamma(s)) - 2f(x_s, \gamma(s))Qf(x_s, \gamma(s))]ds\,, \tag{17}$$

is the quadratic variation of m^f.

3. Variance and Volatility Swaps for Financial Markets with Semi-Markov Stochastic Volatilities

Let us consider a Market model with only two securities, the risk free bond and the stock. Let us suppose that the stock price $(S_t)_{t\in\mathbb{R}_+}$ satisfies the following stochastic differential equation

$$\begin{cases} dB_t = B_t r(x_t, \gamma(t))dt \\ dS_t = S_t(\mu(x_t, \gamma(t))dt + \sigma(x_t, \gamma(t))dw_t) \end{cases}, \tag{18}$$

where w is a standard Wiener process independent of (x, γ). We are interested in studying the property of the volatility $\sigma(x, \gamma)$. Salvi and Swishchuk [18] have studied properties of volatility modulated by a Markov process. Here we would like to generalize their work to the semi-Markov case. First of all we study the second moment of the volatility.

Proposition 5. *(Swishchuk [20])*
Suppose that $\sigma \in$ Domain (Q). Then

$$\mathbb{E}\{\sigma^2(x_t, \gamma(t))|\mathscr{F}_u\} = \sigma^2(x_u, \gamma(u)) + \int_u^t Q\mathbb{E}\{\sigma^2(x_s, \gamma(s))|\mathscr{F}_u\}ds\,, \tag{19}$$

for any $0 \le u \le t$.

Remark 2. *From Proposition 5, we can directly solve the equation for $\mathbb{E}\{\sigma^2(x_t, \gamma(t))|\mathscr{F}_u\}$ and we obtain*

$$\mathbb{E}\{\sigma^2(x_t, \gamma(t))|\mathscr{F}_u\} = e^{(t-u)Q}\sigma^2(x_u, \gamma(u))\,, \tag{20}$$

for any $0 \le u \le t$.

In this semi-Markov modulated model we are able to evaluate high order moment of volatility, e.g next result concern the fourth moment.

Proposition 6. *Suppose that $\sigma^2 \in$ Domain (Q).*

$$\mathbb{E}\{\sigma^4(x_t, \gamma(t))\} = e^{tQ}\sigma^4(x, 0) \qquad \text{for } t \in \mathbb{R}_+. \tag{21}$$

Proof. If $\sigma^2 \in$ Domain (Q), then from Proposition 2 we have that

$$m_t^{\sigma^2} := \sigma^2(x_t, \gamma(t)) - \sigma^2(x, 0) - \int_0^t Q\sigma^2(x_s, \gamma(s))ds \tag{22}$$

is a zero-mean martingale with respect to $\mathscr{F}_t := \sigma\{x_s, \gamma(s); 0 \le s \le t\}$, where Q is the infinitesimal generator of the Markov process $(x_t, \gamma(t))_{t\in[0,T]}$ (cf. lemma 1). Then σ^2 satisfies the following stochastic differential equation

$$d\sigma^2(x_t, \gamma(t)) = Q\sigma^2(x_t, \gamma(t))dt + dm_t^{\sigma^2}. \tag{23}$$

By applying the Ito's Lemma we obtain

$$d\sigma^4(x_t, \gamma(t)) = 2\sigma^2(x_t, \gamma(t))d\sigma^2(x_t, \gamma(t)) + d\langle m_\cdot^{\sigma^2}\rangle_t. \tag{24}$$

We note that, the quadrating variation of m^{σ^2} is (see Propositon 3) given by

$$\langle m^{\sigma^2}\rangle_t := \int_0^t [Q\sigma^4(x_s,\gamma(s)) - 2\sigma^2(x_s,\gamma(s))Q\sigma^2(x_s,\gamma(s))]ds. \tag{25}$$

Substituting the expression for the quadratic variation $\langle m^{\sigma^2}\rangle$ and for σ^2, we obtain that σ^4 satisfies the following stochastic differential equation

$$d\sigma^4(x_t,\gamma(t)) = Q\sigma^4(x_t,\gamma(t))dt + 2\sigma^2(x_t,\gamma(t))dm_t^{\sigma^2}. \tag{26}$$

By tacking the expectation of both side of these equation we obtain

$$\mathbb{E}\{\sigma^4(x_t,\gamma(t))\} = \sigma^4(x,0) + \int_0^t Q\mathbb{E}\{\sigma^4(x_s,\gamma(s))\}ds. \tag{27}$$

Solving this differential equation we finally get

$$\mathbb{E}\{\sigma^4(x_t,\gamma(t))\} = e^{tQ}\sigma^4(x,0). \tag{28}$$

□

It is known that the market model with semi-Markov stochastic volatility is incomplete, see Swishchuk [20]. In order to price the future contracts we will use the minimal martingale measure, we refer to Swishchuk [20] for the details.

3.1. Pricing of Variance Swaps

Let us start from the more straightforward variance swap. Variance swaps are forward contracts on future realized level of variance. The payoff of a variance swap with expiration date T is given by

$$N(\sigma_R^2(x) - K_{var}), \tag{29}$$

where $\sigma_R^2(x)$ is the realized stock variance over the life of the contract

$$\sigma_R^2(x) := \frac{1}{T}\int_0^T \sigma^2(x_s,\gamma(s))ds, \tag{30}$$

K_{var} is the strike price for variance and N is the notional amounts of dollars per annualized variance point, we will assume that $N = 1$ just for sake of simplicity. The price of the variance swap is the expected present value of the payoff in the risk-neutral world

$$P_{var}(x) = \mathbb{E}\{e^{-rT}(\sigma_R^2(x) - K_{var})\}. \tag{31}$$

The following result concerns the evaluation of a variance swap in this semi-Markov volatility model. We refer to Swishchuk [20] for details and proof.

Theorem 1. *(Swishchuk [20])*
The present value of a variance swap for semi-Markov stochastic volatility is

$$P_{var}(x) = e^{-rT}\left\{\frac{1}{T}\int_0^T (e^{tQ}\sigma^2(x,\gamma) - K_{var})dt\right\}, \tag{32}$$

where Q is the generator of $(x_t,\gamma(t))_t$, that is

$$Qf(x,t) = \frac{df}{dt}(x,t) + \frac{g_x(t)}{\bar{G}_x(t)}\int_X P(x,dy)[f(y,0) - f(x,t)]. \tag{33}$$

3.2. Pricing of Volatility Swaps

Volatility swaps are forward contract on future realized level of volatility. The payoff of a volatility swap with maturity T is given by

$$N(\sigma_R(x) - K_{vol}) , \tag{34}$$

where $\sigma_R(x)$ is the realized stock volatility over the life of the contract

$$\sigma_R(x) := \sqrt{\frac{1}{T}\int_0^T \sigma^2(x_s, \gamma(s))ds} , \tag{35}$$

K_{vol} is the strike price for volatility and N is the notional amounts of dollars per annualized volatility point, as before we will assume that $N = 1$. The price of the volatility swap is the expected present value of the payoff in the risk-neutral world

$$P_{vol}(x) = \mathbb{E}\{e^{-rT}(\sigma_R(x) - K_{vol})\} . \tag{36}$$

In order to evaluate the volatility swaps we need to know the expected value of the square root of the variance, but unfortunately, in general we are not able to evaluate analytically this expected value. Then in order to obtain a close formula for the price of volatility swaps we have to make an approximation. Using the same approach of the Markov case (see also Brockhaus and Long [6] and Javaheri *at al.* [17]), from the second order Taylor expansion we have

$$\mathbb{E}\{\sqrt{\sigma_R^2(x)}\} \approx \sqrt{\mathbb{E}\{\sigma_R^2(x)\}} - \frac{Var\{\sigma_R^2(x)\}}{8\mathbb{E}\{\sigma_R^2(x)\}^{3/2}} . \tag{37}$$

Then, to evaluate the volatility swap price we have to know both expectation and variance of $\sigma_R^2(x)$. The next result gives an explicit representation of the price of a volatility swap approximated to the second order for this semi-Markov volatility model.

Theorem 2. *The value of a volatility swap for semi-Markov stochastic volatility is*

$$P_{vol}(x) \approx \; e^{-rT}\left\{\sqrt{\tfrac{1}{T}\int_0^T e^{tQ}\sigma^2(x,\gamma)dt} - \frac{Var\{\sigma_R^2(x)\}}{8\left(\frac{1}{T}\int_0^T e^{tQ}\sigma^2(x,\gamma)dt\right)^{3/2}} - K_{vol}\right\},$$

where the variance is given by

$$Var\{\sigma_R^2(x)\} = \frac{2}{T^2}\int_0^T\int_0^t \left\{e^{sQ}\left[\sigma^2(x,\gamma)e^{(t-s)Q}\sigma^2(x,\gamma)\right] - \left[e^{tQ}\sigma^2(x,\gamma)\right]\left[e^{sQ}\sigma^2(x,\gamma)\right]\right\} dsdt ,$$

and Q is the generator of $(x_t, \gamma(t))_t$, that is

$$Qf(x,t) = \frac{df}{dt}(x,t) + \frac{g_x(t)}{\overline{G}_x(t)}\int_X P(x,dy)[f(y,0) - f(x,t)] . \tag{38}$$

Proof. We have already obtained the expectation of the realized variance,

$$\mathbb{E}\{\sigma_R^2(x)\} = \frac{1}{T}\int_0^T e^{tQ}\sigma^2(x,\gamma)dt , \tag{39}$$

then it remains to prove that

$$Var\{\sigma_R^2(x)\} = \frac{2}{T^2}\int_0^T\int_0^t \{e^{sQ}\left[\sigma^2(x,\gamma)e^{tQ}\sigma^2(x,\gamma)\right] - \left[e^{tQ}\sigma^2(x,\gamma)\right]\left[e^{sQ}\sigma^2(x,\gamma)\right]\}\, dsdt\,.$$

The variance is, from the definition, given by

$$Var\{\sigma_R^2(x)\} = \mathbb{E}\{[\sigma_R^2(x) - \mathbb{E}\{\sigma_R^2(x)\}]^2\}\,, \tag{40}$$

Using the definition of realized variance, and Fubini theorem, we have

$$Var\{\sigma_R^2(x)\} = \mathbb{E}\left\{\left[\frac{1}{T}\int_0^T \sigma^2(x_t,\gamma(t))dt - \frac{1}{T}\int_0^T \mathbb{E}\{\sigma^2(x_t,\gamma(t))\}dt\right]^2\right\}$$

$$= \mathbb{E}\left\{\left[\frac{1}{T}\int_0^T \left(\sigma^2(x_t,\gamma(t)) - \mathbb{E}\{\sigma^2(x_t,\gamma(t))\}\right)dt\right]^2\right\} \tag{41}$$

$$= \frac{1}{T^2}\int_0^T\int_0^T \mathbb{E}\left\{[\sigma^2(x_t,\gamma(t)) - \mathbb{E}\{\sigma^2(x_t,\gamma(t))\}][\sigma^2(x_s,\gamma(s)) - \mathbb{E}\{\sigma^2(x_s,\gamma(s))\}]\right\} dsdt\,.$$

We note that the integrand is symmetric in the exchange of s and t. We can divide the integration on the plan in two areas above and below the graph of $t = s$, thanks to the symmetry the contribution on the two parts is the same. Then we obtain

$$\begin{aligned} Var\{\sigma_R^2(x)\} =& \tfrac{2}{T^2}\textstyle\int_0^T\int_0^t \mathbb{E}\{[\sigma^2(x_t,\gamma(t)) - \mathbb{E}\{\sigma^2(x_t,\gamma(t))\}][\sigma^2(x_s,\gamma(s)) - \mathbb{E}\{\sigma^2(x_s,\gamma(s))\}]\}dsdt \\ =& \tfrac{2}{T^2}\textstyle\int_0^T\int_0^t \left[\mathbb{E}\{\sigma^2(x_t,\gamma(t))\sigma^2(x_s,\gamma(s))\} - \mathbb{E}\{\sigma^2(x_t,\gamma(t))\}\mathbb{E}\{\sigma^2(x_s,\gamma(s))\}\right] dsdt\,. \end{aligned} \tag{42}$$

We would like to stress that, in this representation, the integration set is such that the inequality $s \le t$ holds true. Using the property of conditional expectation and Proposition 5, we have

$$Var\{\sigma_R^2(x)\} = \frac{2}{T^2}\int_0^T\int_0^t \left[\mathbb{E}\{\sigma^2(x_s,\gamma(s))\mathbb{E}\{\sigma^2(x_t,\gamma(t))|\mathscr{F}_s\}\} - \left(e^{tQ}\sigma^2(x,\gamma)\right)\left(e^{sQ}\sigma^2(x,\gamma)\right)\right] dsdt\,.$$

The process $(x_t,\gamma(t))_t$ is Markovian, then using Remark 2 the conditional expected value in the integrand, can be expressed as

$$\mathbb{E}\{\sigma^2(x_t,\gamma(t))|\mathscr{F}_s\} = e^{(t-s)Q}\sigma^2(x_s,\gamma(s)) =: g(x_s,\gamma(s))\,. \tag{43}$$

Thus, the variance becomes

$$Var\{\sigma_R^2(x)\} = \frac{2}{T^2}\int_0^T\int_0^t \left[\mathbb{E}\{\sigma^2(x_s,\gamma(s))g(x_s,\gamma(s))\} - \left(e^{tQ}\sigma^2(x,\gamma)\right)\left(e^{sQ}\sigma^2(x,\gamma)\right)\right] dsdt\,.$$

Solving the expectation on the r.h.s we obtain

$$Var\{\sigma_R^2(x)\} = \frac{2}{T^2}\int_0^T\int_0^t \left[e^{sQ}\left(\sigma^2(x,\gamma)g(x,\gamma)\right) - \left(e^{tQ}\sigma^2(x,\gamma)\right)\left(e^{sQ}\sigma^2(x,\gamma)\right)\right] dsdt\,.$$

We notice that function g evaluated in (x,γ) is simply given by

$$g(x,\gamma) = e^{(t-s)Q}\sigma^2(x,\gamma)\,, \tag{44}$$

then substituting in the previous formula the variance finally becomes

$$Var\{\sigma_R^2(x)\} = \frac{2}{T^2}\int_0^T\int_0^t \left\{e^{sQ}\left[\sigma^2(x,\gamma)e^{(t-s)Q}\sigma^2(x,\gamma)\right] - \left[e^{tQ}\sigma^2(x,\gamma)\right]\left[e^{sQ}\sigma^2(x,\gamma)\right]\right\} dsdt\,.$$

□

3.3. Numerical Evaluation of Variance and Volatility Swaps with Semi-Markov Volatility

When we attempt to evaluate the price of a variance or a volatility swaps we have to deal with numerical problems. The family of exponential operators $(e^{tQ})_t$ involved in Theorems 1 and 2 for the semi-Markov stochastic volatility model is usually difficult to evaluate from a numerical point of view. To solve this problem, we first look to the following identity

$$e^{tQ}f(\cdot) = \sum_{n=0}^{\infty} \frac{(tQ)^n}{n!} f(\cdot) \,, \tag{45}$$

for any function $f \in Domain(Q)$. This identity allows us to obtain the operator $(e^{tQ})_t$ at any order of approximation. For example, for $n = 1$, we obtain

$$e^{tQ}f(\cdot) \approx (I + tQ)f(\cdot) \,, \tag{46}$$

where I is an identity operator. At this order of approximation we allow semi-Markov process to make at most one transition during the life time of contract. If we think to semi-Markov process as a macroeconomic factor this can be plausible. However we can always evaluate the error in this approximation using the subsequent orders. Using the first order approximation the variance swap price becomes

$$\begin{aligned} P_{var}(x) \approx & e^{-rT}\left\{\frac{1}{T}\int_0^T (I + tQ)\sigma^2(x,\gamma)dt - K_{var}\right\} \\ = & e^{-rT}\left\{\sigma^2(x,\gamma) + \frac{T}{2}Q\sigma^2(x,\gamma) - K_{var}\right\}. \end{aligned} \tag{47}$$

Using the same approximation the volatility swap price can be expressed as

$$\begin{aligned} P_{vol}(x) \approx & e^{-rT}\left\{\sqrt{\frac{1}{T}\int_0^T (I+tQ)\sigma^2(x,\gamma)dt} - \frac{Var\{\sigma_R^2(x)\}}{8\left(\frac{1}{T}\int_0^T (I+tQ)\sigma^2(x,\gamma)dt\right)^{3/2}} - K_{vol}\right\} \\ = & e^{-rT}\left\{\sqrt{\sigma^2(x,\gamma) + \frac{T}{2}Q\sigma^2(x,\gamma)} - \frac{Var\{\sigma_R^2(x)\}}{8\left(\sigma^2(x,\gamma) + \frac{T}{2}Q\sigma^2(x,\gamma)\right)^{3/2}} - K_{vol}\right\}. \end{aligned}$$

Here, the variance of realized volatility is given by

$$\begin{aligned} Var\{\sigma_R^2(x)\} \approx & \frac{2}{T^2}\int_0^T\int_0^t \{(I+sQ)[\sigma^2(x,\gamma)(I+(t-s)Q)\sigma^2(x,\gamma)] \\ & - [(I+tQ)\sigma^2(x,\gamma)][(I+sQ)\sigma^2(x,\gamma)]\}\, dsdt \,. \end{aligned} \tag{48}$$

Solving the product and keeping only the terms up to the first order in Q, we obtain

$$\begin{aligned} Var\{\sigma_R^2(x)\} \approx & \frac{2}{T^2}\int_0^T\int_0^t \{sQ\sigma^4(x,\gamma) - 2\sigma^2(x,\gamma)sQ\sigma^2(x,\gamma)\}dsdt \\ = & \frac{T}{3}\left\{Q\sigma^4(x,\gamma) - 2\sigma^2(x,\gamma)Q\sigma^2(x,\gamma)\right\} \,. \end{aligned} \tag{49}$$

Finally, to first order of approximation in Q the volatility swap price becomes

$$P_{vol}(x) \approx e^{-rT}\left\{\sqrt{\sigma^2(x,\gamma) + \frac{T}{2}Q\sigma^2(x,\gamma)} - \frac{T[Q\sigma^4(x,\gamma) - 2\sigma^2(x,\gamma)Q\sigma^2(x,\gamma)]}{24\left(\sigma^2(x,\gamma) + \frac{T}{2}Q\sigma^2(x,\gamma)\right)^{3/2}} - K_{vol}\right\}.$$

4. Covariance and Correlation Swaps for a Two Risky Assets in Financial Markets with Semi-Markov Stochastic Volatilities

Let's consider now a market model with two risky assets and one risk free bond. Let's assume that the risky assets are satisfying the following stochastic differential equations

$$\begin{cases} dS_t^{(1)} = S_t^{(1)}(\mu_t^{(1)}dt + \sigma^{(1)}(x_t, \gamma(t))dw_t^{(1)}) \\ dS_t^{(2)} = S_t^{(2)}(\mu_t^{(2)}dt + \sigma^{(2)}(x_t, \gamma(t))dw_t^{(2)}) \end{cases}, \tag{50}$$

where $\mu^{(1)}$, $\mu^{(2)}$ are deterministic functions of time, $(w_t^{(1)})_t$ and $(w_t^{(2)})_t$ are standard Wiener processes with quadratic covariance given by

$$d[w_t^{(1)}, w_t^{(2)}] = \rho_t dt\,. \tag{51}$$

Here ρ_t is a deterministic function and $(w_t^{(1)})_t$, $(w_t^{(2)})_t$ are independent of (x, γ).
In this model it is worth to study the covariance and the correlation swaps between the two risky assets.

4.1. Pricing of Covariance Swaps

A covariance swap is a covariance forward contract on the underlying assets $S^{(1)}$ and $S^{(2)}$ which payoff at maturity is equal to

$$N(Cov_R(S^{(1)}, S^{(2)}) - K_{cov})\,, \tag{52}$$

where K_{cov} is a strike reference value, N is the notional amount and $Cov_R(S^{(1)}, S^{(2)})$ is the realized covariance of the two assets $S^{(1)}$ and $S^{(2)}$ given by

$$Cov_R(S^{(1)}, S^{(2)}) = \frac{1}{T}[\ln S_T^{(1)}, \ln S_T^{(2)}] = \frac{1}{T}\int_0^T \rho_t \sigma^{(1)}(x_t, \gamma(t))\sigma^{(2)}(x_t, \gamma(t))dt\,. \tag{53}$$

The price of the covariance swap is the expected present value of the payoff in the risk neutral world

$$P_{cov}(x) = \mathbb{E}\{e^{-rT}(Cov_R(S^{(1)}, S^{(2)}) - K_{cov})\}\,, \tag{54}$$

here we set $N = 1$. The next result provides an explicit representation of the covariance swap price.

Theorem 3. *The value of a covariance swap for semi-Markov stochastic volatility is*

$$P_{cov}(x) = e^{-rT}\left\{\frac{1}{T}\int_0^T \rho_t e^{tQ}[\sigma^{(1)}(x,\gamma)\sigma^{(2)}(x,\gamma)]dt - K_{cov}\right\}, \tag{55}$$

where Q is the generator of $(x_t, \gamma(t))_t$, that is

$$Qf(x,t) = \frac{df}{dt}(x,t) + \frac{g_x(t)}{\overline{G}_x(t)}\int_X P(x,dy)[f(y,0) - f(x,t)]\,. \tag{56}$$

Proof. To evaluate the price of covariance swap we need to know

$$\mathbb{E}\{Cov_R(S^{(1)}, S^{(2)})\} = \frac{1}{T}\int_0^T \rho_t \mathbb{E}\{\sigma^{(1)}(x_t,\gamma(t))\sigma^{(2)}(x_t,\gamma(t))\}dt\,. \tag{57}$$

It remains to prove that

$$\mathbb{E}\{\sigma^{(1)}(x_t,\gamma(t))\sigma^{(2)}(x_t,\gamma(t))\} = e^{tQ}[\sigma^{(1)}(x,\gamma)\sigma^{(2)}(x,\gamma)]\,. \tag{58}$$

By applying Ito's lemma we have

$$\begin{aligned} d(\sigma^{(1)}(x_t,\gamma(t))\sigma^{(2)}(x_t,\gamma(t))) =& \sigma^{(1)}(x_t,\gamma(t))d\sigma^{(2)}(x_t,\gamma(t)) + \sigma^{(2)}(x_t,\gamma(t))d\sigma^{(1)}(x_t,\gamma(t)) \\ &+ d\langle\sigma^{(1)}(x_\cdot,\gamma(\cdot)),\sigma^{(2)}(x_\cdot,\gamma(\cdot))\rangle_t\,. \end{aligned} \tag{59}$$

Using Proposition 4 we obtain

$$\begin{aligned} d\langle\sigma^{(1)}(x_\cdot,\gamma(\cdot)),\sigma^{(2)}(x_\cdot,\gamma(\cdot))\rangle_t =& Q(\sigma^{(1)}(x_t,\gamma(t))\sigma^{(2)}(x_t,\gamma(t)))dt \\ &- [\sigma^{(1)}(x_t,\gamma(t))Q\sigma^{(2)}(x_t,\gamma(t)) + \sigma^{(2)}(x_t,\gamma(t))Q\sigma^{(1)}(x_t,\gamma(t))]dt\,. \end{aligned} \tag{60}$$

Furthermore we have

$$d\sigma^{(i)}(x_t,\gamma(t)) = Q\sigma^{(i)}(x_t,\gamma(t))dt + dm^{\sigma^{(i)}} \qquad i = 1,2\,. \tag{61}$$

Substituting (60) and (61) in equation (59) we get

$$\begin{aligned} d(\sigma^{(1)}(x_t,\gamma(t))\sigma^{(2)}(x_t,\gamma(t))) =& Q(\sigma^{(1)}(x_t,\gamma(t))\sigma^{(2)}(x_t,\gamma(t)))dt \\ &+ \sigma^{(1)}(x_t,\gamma(t))dm^{\sigma^{(2)}} + \sigma^{(2)}(x_t,\gamma(t))dm^{\sigma^{(1)}}. \end{aligned} \tag{62}$$

Taking the expectation on both side we can rewrite the above equation as

$$\begin{aligned} \mathbb{E}\{\sigma^{(1)}(x_t,\gamma(t))\sigma^{(2)}(x_t,\gamma(t))\} =& \sigma^{(1)}(x,\gamma)\sigma^{(2)}(x,\gamma) \\ &+ \int_0^t Q\mathbb{E}\{\sigma^{(1)}(x_s,\gamma(s))\sigma^{(2)}(x_s,\gamma(s))\}dt\,. \end{aligned} \tag{63}$$

Solving this differential equation we obtain

$$\mathbb{E}\{\sigma^{(1)}(x_t,\gamma(t))\sigma^{(2)}(x_t,\gamma(t))\} = e^{tQ}[\sigma^{(1)}(x,\gamma)\sigma^{(2)}(x,\gamma)]\,, \tag{64}$$

this conclude the proof. □

4.2. Pricing of Correlation Swaps

A correlation swap is a forward contract on the correlation between the underlying assets S^1 and S^2 which payoff at maturity is equal to

$$N(Corr_R(S^1,S^2) - K_{corr})\,, \tag{65}$$

where K_{corr} is a strike reference level, N is the notional amount and $Corr_R(S^1,S^2)$ is the realized correlation defined by

$$Corr_R(S^1,S^2) = \frac{Cov_R(S^1,S^2)}{\sqrt{\sigma_R^{(1)^2}(x)}\sqrt{\sigma_R^{(2)^2}(x)}}\,, \tag{66}$$

here the realized variance is given by

$$\sigma_R^{(i)^2}(x) = \frac{1}{T}\int_0^T (\sigma^{(i)}(x_t, \gamma(t)))^2 dt \qquad i = 1, 2\,. \tag{67}$$

The price of the correlation swap is the expected present value of the payoff in the risk neutral world, that is

$$P_{corr}(x) = \mathbb{E}\{e^{-rT}(Corr_R(S^1, S^2) - K_{corr})\}\,, \tag{68}$$

where we set $N = 1$ for simplicity. Unfortunately the expected value of $Corr_R(S^1, S^2)$ is not known analytically. Thus, in order to obtain an explicit formula for the correlation swap price, we have to make some approximation.

4.3. Correlation Swaps Made Simple

First of all, let us introduce the following notations

$$\begin{aligned} X =& Cov_R(S^1, S^2) \\ Y =& \sigma_R^{(1)^2}(x) \\ Z =& \sigma_R^{(2)^2}(x)\,, \end{aligned} \tag{69}$$

and with the subscript 0 we will denote the expected value of the above random variables. Following the approach frequently used for the volatility swap, we would like to approximate the square root of Y and Z to the first order as follows

$$\begin{aligned} \sqrt{Y} \approx& \sqrt{Y_0} + \frac{Y - Y_0}{2\sqrt{Y_0}} \\ \sqrt{Z} \approx& \sqrt{Z_0} + \frac{Z - Z_0}{2\sqrt{Z_0}}\,. \end{aligned} \tag{70}$$

The realized correlation can now be approximated by

$$Corr_R(S^1, S^2) \approx \frac{X}{\left(\sqrt{Y_0} + \frac{Y-Y_0}{2\sqrt{Y_0}}\right)\left(\sqrt{Z_0} + \frac{Z-Z_0}{2\sqrt{Z_0}}\right)} = \frac{\frac{X}{\sqrt{Y_0}\sqrt{Z_0}}}{\left(1 + \frac{Y-Y_0}{2Y_0}\right)\left(1 + \frac{Z-Z_0}{2Z_0}\right)}\,. \tag{71}$$

Solving the product in the denominator of the last term on the r.h.s and keeping only the terms up to the first order in the increment, we have

$$Corr_R(S^1, S^2) \approx \frac{\frac{X}{\sqrt{Y_0}\sqrt{Z_0}}}{1 + \left(\frac{Y-Y_0}{2Y_0} + \frac{Z-Z_0}{2Z_0}\right)} \approx \frac{X}{\sqrt{Y_0}\sqrt{Z_0}}\left[1 - \left(\frac{Y - Y_0}{2Y_0} + \frac{Z - Z_0}{2Z_0}\right)\right]. \tag{72}$$

In what follows, we will consider only the zeroth order of approximation. The first order correction will be discuss in the next section.

Here, we are going to approximate the realized correlation as

$$Corr_R(S^1, S^2) \approx \frac{X}{\sqrt{Y_0}\sqrt{Z_0}}\,, \tag{73}$$

Substituting X, Y and Z we obtain

$$Corr_R(S^1, S^2) \approx \frac{1}{\sqrt{\mathbb{E}\{\sigma_R^{(1)^2}(x)\}}\sqrt{\mathbb{E}\{\sigma_{2R}^{(2)^2}(x)\}}} \frac{1}{T}\int_0^T \rho_t \sigma^{(1)}(x_t, \gamma(t))\sigma^{(2)}(x_t, \gamma(t))dt\,, \tag{74}$$

where (*cf.* Teorem 1), we have

$$\mathbb{E}\left\{\sigma_R^{(i)^2}(x)\right\} = \mathbb{E}\left\{\frac{1}{T}\int_0^T (\sigma^{(i)}(x_t, \gamma(t)))^2 dt\right\} = \frac{1}{T}\int_0^T e^{tQ}(\sigma^{(i)}(x, \gamma))^2 dt\,, \tag{75}$$

for $i = 1, 2$. In order to price a correlation swap we have to be able to evaluate the expectation of both side of Eq. (74), the expectation of the r.h.s becomes

$$\mathbb{E}\left\{\sigma^{(1)}(x_t, \gamma(t))\sigma^{(2)}(x_t, \gamma(t))\right\} = e^{tQ}\sigma^{(1)}(x, \gamma)\sigma^{(2)}(x, \gamma)\,. \tag{76}$$

We can summarize the previous result in the following statement.

Theorem 4. *The value of a correlation swap for semi-Markov stochastic volatility is*

$$P_{corr}(x) \approx e^{-rT}\left\{\frac{\int_0^T \rho_t e^{tQ}[\sigma^{(1)}(x, \gamma)\sigma^{(2)}(x, \gamma)]dt}{\sqrt{\int_0^T e^{tQ}(\sigma^{(1)}(x, \gamma))^2 dt}\sqrt{\int_0^T e^{tQ}(\sigma^{(2)}(x, \gamma))^2 dt}} - K_{corr}\right\}, \tag{77}$$

where Q is the generator of $(x_t, \gamma(t))_t$, that is

$$Qf(x, t) = \frac{df}{dt}(x, t) + \frac{g_x(t)}{\bar{G}_x(t)}\int_X P(x, dy)[f(y, 0) - f(x, t)]. \tag{78}$$

5. Numerical Evaluation of Covariance and Correlation Swaps with Semi-Markov Stochastic Volatility

In order to obtain a more handy expression for the price of covariance and correlation swaps to use in the application, we will introduce here an approximation for the family of operators $(e^{tQ})_{t\in\mathbb{R}_+}$. Following the approach used for the variance and volatility case, we are going to approximate the operators at the first order in Q as

$$e^{tQ}f(\cdot) \approx (I + tQ)f(\cdot)\,. \tag{79}$$

Using this approximation the covariance swap price becomes

$$\begin{aligned} P_{cov}(x) \approx& e^{-rT}\left\{\frac{1}{T}\int_0^T \rho_t(I + tQ)[\sigma^{(1)}(x, \gamma)\sigma^{(2)}(x, \gamma)]dt - K_{cov}\right\} \\ =& e^{-rT}\left\{\sigma^{(1)}(x, \gamma)\sigma^{(2)}(x, \gamma)\int_0^T \rho_t dt + Q[\sigma^{(1)}(x, \gamma)\sigma^{(2)}(x, \gamma)]\int_0^T t\rho_t dt - K_{cov}\right\}. \end{aligned} \tag{80}$$

The same approximation allow us to express the zeroth order approximation of correlation swap price as

$$\begin{aligned} P_{corr}(x) \approx& e^{-rT}\left\{\frac{\int_0^T \rho_t(I + tQ)[\sigma^{(1)}(x, \gamma)\sigma^{(2)}(x, \gamma)]dt}{\sqrt{\int_0^T (I + tQ)(\sigma^{(1)}(x, \gamma))^2 dt}\sqrt{\int_0^T (I + tQ)(\sigma^{(2)}(x, \gamma))^2 dt}} - K_{corr}\right\} \\ =& e^{-rT}\left\{\frac{\sigma^{(1)}(x, \gamma)\sigma^{(2)}(x, \gamma)\int_0^T \rho_t dt + Q[\sigma^{(1)}(x, \gamma)\sigma^{(2)}(x, \gamma)]\int_0^T t\rho_t dt}{\sqrt{(\sigma^{(1)}(x, \gamma))^2 + \frac{T}{2}Q(\sigma^{(1)}(x, \gamma))^2}\sqrt{(\sigma^{(2)}(x, \gamma))^2 + \frac{T}{2}Q(\sigma^{(2)}(x, \gamma))^2}} - K_{corr}\right\}. \end{aligned} \tag{81}$$

Appendix

1. Correlation Swaps: First Order Correction

We would like to obtain a first-order approximation for the realized correlation between two risky assets

$$Corr_R(S^1,S^2) = \frac{Cov_R(S^1,S^2)}{\sqrt{\sigma_R^{(1)^2}(x)}\sqrt{\sigma_R^{(2)^2}(x)}} \,. \tag{82}$$

In section 4.3 we have already obtained the following approximated expression

$$Corr_R(S^1,S^2) \approx \frac{\frac{X}{\sqrt{Y_0}\sqrt{Z_0}}}{1+\left(\frac{Y-Y_0}{2Y_0}+\frac{Z-Z_0}{2Z_0}\right)} \approx \frac{X}{\sqrt{Y_0}\sqrt{Z_0}}\left[1-\left(\frac{Y-Y_0}{2Y_0}+\frac{Z-Z_0}{2Z_0}\right)\right]. \tag{83}$$

where

$$\begin{aligned} X =& Cov_R(S^1,S^2) \\ Y =& \sigma_R^{(1)^2}(x) \\ Z =& \sigma_R^{(2)^2}(x) \,, \end{aligned} \tag{84}$$

and with the pedix 0 we have denoted the expected values. We have already evaluated the expectation of the zeroth order approximation, now we would like to evaluate the first-order. Substituting X, Y and Z in Eq. (83) we obtain

$$\begin{aligned} Corr_R(S^1,S^2) \approx & \frac{1}{\sqrt{\mathbb{E}\{\sigma_R^{(1)^2}(x)\}}\sqrt{\mathbb{E}\{\sigma_{2R}^{(2)^2}(x)\}}}\frac{1}{T}\int_0^T \rho_t\sigma^{(1)}(x_t,\gamma(t))\sigma^{(2)}(x_t,\gamma(t))dt \\ & - \frac{1}{2T^2(\mathbb{E}\{\sigma_R^{(1)^2}(x)\})^{3/2}(\mathbb{E}\{\sigma_R^{(2)^2}(x)\})^{3/2}}\int_0^T \rho_t\sigma^{(1)}(x_t,\gamma(t))\sigma^{(2)}(x_t,\gamma(t))dt \\ & \times\left\{\mathbb{E}\{\sigma_R^{(2)^2}(x)\}\int_0^T[(\sigma^{(1)}(x_s,\gamma(s)))^2-\mathbb{E}\{(\sigma^{(1)}(x_s,\gamma(s)))^2\}]ds\right. \\ & \left.+\,\mathbb{E}\{\sigma_R^{(1)^2}(x)\}\int_0^T[(\sigma^{(2)}(x_u,\gamma(u)))^2-\mathbb{E}\{(\sigma^{(2)}(x_u,\gamma(u)))^2\}]du\right\}, \end{aligned} \tag{85}$$

where

$$\mathbb{E}\left\{\sigma^2_{(i)R}(x)\right\} = \mathbb{E}\left\{\frac{1}{T}\int_0^T(\sigma^{(i)}(x_t,\gamma(t)))^2dt\right\} = \frac{1}{T}\int_0^T e^{tQ}(\sigma^{(i)}(x,\gamma))^2dt \,, \tag{86}$$

for $i = 1, 2$. We have to evaluate the expectation of the r.h.s of equation (85). We already calculated the expectation of the first term, which is the zero order approximation for the realized correlation. Then we will focus now on the other terms. First of all, let us rewrite them as follows

$$\begin{aligned} \int_0^T\int_0^T & \rho_t\sigma^{(1)}(x_t,\gamma(t))\sigma^{(2)}(x_t,\gamma(t))\left(\mathbb{E}\{\sigma_R^{(2)^2}(x)\}[(\sigma^{(1)}(x_s,\gamma(s)))^2-\mathbb{E}\{(\sigma^{(1)}(x_s,\gamma(s)))^2\}]\right. \\ & \left.+\,\mathbb{E}\{\sigma_R^{(1)^2}(x)\}[(\sigma^{(2)}(x_s,\gamma(s)))^2-\mathbb{E}\{(\sigma^{(2)}(x_s,\gamma(s)))^2\}]\right)dsdt \,, \end{aligned} \tag{87}$$

we have four different contributions in the integrals, the expectation of the terms

$$\int_0^T \int_0^T \rho_t \sigma^{(1)}(x_t, \gamma(t))\sigma^{(2)}(x_t, \gamma(t))\mathbb{E}\{\sigma^{(i)^2}(x_s, \gamma(s))\}\mathbb{E}\{\sigma^{(-i)^2}(x_s, \gamma(s))\}dsdt\,, \quad (88)$$

for $i = 1, 2$, can be evaluate using Theorem 3. Then, in order to evaluate the expectation of the approximated realized correlation, it only remains to calculate

$$\mathbb{E}\left\{\int_0^T \int_0^T \rho_t \sigma^{(1)}(x_t, \gamma(t))\sigma^{(2)}(x_t, \gamma(t))\sigma^{(i)^2}(x_s, \gamma(s))dsdt\right\} \qquad i = 1, 2\,, \quad (89)$$

To this end, let's first divide the range of integration in two intervals as follows

$$\begin{aligned}\mathbb{E}\Bigg\{&\int_0^T \int_0^t \rho_t \sigma^{(1)}(x_t, \gamma(t))\sigma^{(2)}(x_t, \gamma(t))\sigma^{(i)^2}(x_s, \gamma(s))dsdt \\ &+ \int_0^T \int_t^T \rho_t \sigma^{(1)}(x_t, \gamma(t))\sigma^{(2)}(x_t, \gamma(t))\sigma^{(i)^2}(x_s, \gamma(s))dsdt\Bigg\}\,,\end{aligned} \quad (90)$$

for $i = 1, 2$. We notice that the first integral set is such that $t > s$ while the second has $t < s$. We can now use the property of conditional expectation to obtain

$$\begin{aligned}\mathbb{E}\Bigg\{&\int_0^T \int_0^t \rho_t \mathbb{E}\{\sigma^{(1)}(x_t, \gamma(t))\sigma^{(2)}(x_t, \gamma(t))|\mathscr{F}_s\}\sigma^{(i)^2}(x_s, \gamma(s))dsdt \\ &+ \int_0^T \int_t^T \rho_t \sigma^{(1)}(x_t, \gamma(t))\sigma^{(2)}(x_t, \gamma(t))\mathbb{E}\{\sigma^{(i)^2}(x_s, \gamma(s))|\mathscr{F}_t\}dsdt\Bigg\}\,.\end{aligned} \quad (91)$$

We notice that $(x_t, \gamma(t))_t$ is a Markov process, then using the Markov property, we can express the conditional expectations as

$$\mathbb{E}\{\sigma^{(1)}(x_t, \gamma(t))\sigma^{(2)}(x_t, \gamma(t))|\mathscr{F}_s\} = e^{(t-s)Q}\sigma^{(1)}(x_s, \gamma(s))\sigma^{(2)}(x_s, \gamma(s)) =: h(x_s, \gamma(s))\,,$$

for $t > s$, and

$$\mathbb{E}\{\sigma^{(i)^2}(x_s, \gamma(s))|\mathscr{F}_t\} = e^{(s-t)Q}\sigma^{(i)^2}(x_t, \gamma(t)) =: g^{(i)}(x_t, \gamma(t))\,,$$

for $s > t$. Therefore, the first term of Eq. (91) can be expressed as

$$\mathbb{E}\left\{\int_0^T \int_0^t \rho_t h(x_s, \gamma(s))\sigma^{(i)^2}(x_s, \gamma(s))dsdt\right\} = \int_0^T \int_0^t \rho_t e^{sQ}[h(x, \gamma)\sigma^{(i)^2}(x, \gamma)]dsdt\,, \quad (92)$$

while the second as

$$\begin{aligned}\mathbb{E}&\left\{\int_0^T \int_t^T \rho_t \sigma^{(1)}(x_t, \gamma(t))\sigma^{(2)}(x_t, \gamma(t))g^{(i)}(x_t, \gamma(t))dsdt\right\} \\ &= \int_0^T \int_t^T \rho_t e^{tQ}[\sigma^{(1)}(x, \gamma)\sigma^{(2)}(x, \gamma)g^{(i)}(x, \gamma)]dsdt\,.\end{aligned} \quad (93)$$

Now, we can evaluate the functions h and g at x obtaining

$$h(x, \gamma) = e^{(t-s)Q}[\sigma^{(1)}(x, \gamma)\sigma^{(2)}(x, \gamma)] \quad (94)$$

and

$$g^{(i)}(x,\gamma) = e^{(s-t)Q}[\sigma^{(i)^2}(x,\gamma)]. \tag{95}$$

We can summarize the previous result in the following statement which gives the correlation swap price up to the first-order of approximation.

Theorem 5. *The value of the correlation swap for a semi-Markov volatility is*

$$P_{corr}(x) = e^{-rT}\left(\mathbb{E}\{Corr_R(S^1,S^2)\} - K_{corr}\right), \tag{96}$$

where the realized correlation can be approximated by

$$\mathbb{E}\{Corr_R(S^1,S^2)\} \approx \frac{2\int_0^T \rho_t e^{tQ}\sigma^{(1)}(x,\gamma)\sigma^{(2)}(x,\gamma)dt}{\sqrt{\int_0^T e^{tQ}(\sigma^{(1)}(x,\gamma))^2 dt}\sqrt{\int_0^T e^{tQ}(\sigma^{(2)}(x,\gamma))^2 dt}} \tag{97}$$

$$-\frac{\int_0^T \rho_t(\int_0^t e^{sQ}\{e^{tQ}[\sigma^{(1)}(x,\gamma)\sigma^{(2)}(x,\gamma)]\sigma^{(1)^2}(x,\gamma)\}ds+\int_t^T e^{tQ}\{\sigma^{(1)}(x,\gamma)\sigma^{(2)}(x,\gamma)e^{uQ}[\sigma^{(1)^2}(x,\gamma)]\}du)dt}{2\left(\int_0^T e^{tQ}(\sigma^{(1)}(x,\gamma))^2 dt\right)^{3/2}\left(\int_0^T e^{tQ}(\sigma^{(2)}(x,\gamma))^2 dt\right)^{1/2}} \tag{98}$$

$$-\frac{\int_0^T \rho_t(\int_0^t e^{sQ}\{e^{tQ}[\sigma^{(1)}(x,\gamma)\sigma^{(2)}(x,\gamma)]\sigma^{(2)^2}(x,\gamma)\}ds+\int_t^T e^{tQ}\{\sigma^{(1)}(x,\gamma)\sigma^{(2)}(x,\gamma)e^{uQ}[\sigma^{(2)^2}(x,\gamma)]\}du)dt}{2\left(\int_0^T e^{tQ}(\sigma^{(1)}(x,\gamma))^2 dt\right)^{1/2}\left(\int_0^T e^{tQ}(\sigma^{(2)}(x,\gamma))^2 dt\right)^{3/2}}, \tag{99}$$

here Q is the generator of the Markov process $(x_t,\gamma(t))_{t\in\mathbb{R}_+}$ given by

$$Qf(x,t) = \frac{df}{dt}(x,t) + \frac{g_x(t)}{G_x(t)}\int_X P(x,dy)[f(y,0)-f(x,t)]. \tag{100}$$

References

[1] F. E. Benth, M. Groth and R. Kufakunesu. Valuing Volatility and Variance Swaps for a Non-Gaussian Ornstein-Uhlenbeck Stochastic Volatility Model. *Applied Mathematical Finance*, Vol. 14, No. 4, 347-363, (September 2007).

[2] S. Bossu. Arbitrage Pricing of Equity Correlation Waps. *JPMorgan Equity Derivatives, Working paper* (2005).

[3] S. Bossu. A New Approach For Modelling and Pricing Correlation Swaps. *Equity Structuring - ECD London, Working paper* (2007).

[4] M. Broadie and A. Jain. Pricing and Hedging Volatility Derivatives. *The Journal of Derivatives*, Vol. 15, No. 3, pp. 7-24 (2008).

[5] M. Broadie and A. Jain. The Effect of Jumps and Discrete Sampling on Volatility and Variance Swaps. *International Journal of Theoretical and Applied Finance*, Vol.11, No.8. pp. 761-797 (2008).

[6] O. Brockhaus and D. Long. Volatility swap made simple. *Risk*, January, 92-96 (2000).

[7] P. Carr, H. Geman, D. B. Madan and M. Yor. Pricing options on realized variance. *Finance Stochast.* 9, 453-475 (2005).

[8] P. Carr and R. Lee. *Realized volatility and variance: Options via swaps*. Bloomberg LP and University of Chicago, (2007). Available at: http://math.uchicago.edu/~rl/OVSwithAppendices.pdf.

[9] P. Carr and R. Lee. Volatility Derivatives. *Annu. Rev. Financ. Econ.*, Vol.1, pag. 319-39 (2009).

[10] J. Da Fonseca, F. Ielpo and M. Grasselli. *Hedging (Co)Variance Risk with Variance Swaps*. Available at SSRN: http://ssrn.com/abstract=1341811 (2009).

[11] K. Demeterfi, E. Derman, M. Kamal and J. Zou. A Guide to Volatility and Variance Swaps. *The Journal of Derivatives* (1999).

[12] J. Drissien, P. J. Maenhout and G. Vilkov. The price of Correlation Risk: Evidence from Equity Options. *The Journal of Finance*, Vol. 64, Issue 3, pages 1377-1406 (2009).

[13] R. J. Elliott, T. K.n Siu and L. Chan. Pricing Volatility Swaps Under Heston's Stochastic Volatility Model with Regime Switching. *Applied Mathematical Finance*, Volume 14, Issue 1, (2007).

[14] R. J. Elliott, T. K.n Siu and L. Chan. *Pricing Options Under a Generalized Markov-Modulated Jump-Diffusion Model. Stochastic Analysis and Applications*, 25: 821-843, (2007).

[15] R. Elliott and A. V. Swishchuk. Pricing Options and Variance Swaps in Markov-Modulated Brownian Markets. In: *'Hidden Markov Model in Finance'*, Eds. R. Mamon and R. Elliott, Springer (2007).

[16] S. Howison, A. Rafailidis and Henrik Rasmussen. On the pricing and hedging of volatility derivatives. *Applied Mathematical Finance* 11, 317-346 (December, 2004).

[17] A. Javaheri, P. Wilmott and E. Haug. GARCH and volatility swaps. *Wilmott Technical Article*, January, 17p (2002).

[18] G. Salvi and A. V. Swishchuk. *Pricing of Variance, Volatility, Covariance and Correlation Swaps in a Markov-modulated Volatility Model*. Preprint (2012).

[19] A. Sepp. Pricing Options on Realized Variance in the Heston Model with Jumps in Returns and Volatility. *Journal of Computational Finance*, 2008, 11(4), 33-70.

[20] A. V. Swishchuk. Pricing of Variance and Volatility Swaps with semi-Markov volatilities. *Canadian Applied Mathematics Quarterly*. Vol. 18, Nu. 4, Winter (2010).

[21] A. V. Swishchuk, R. Cheng, S. Lawi, A. Badescu, H. B. Mekki, A. F. Gashaw, Y. Hua, M. Molyboga, T. Neocleous and Y. Petrachenko. Price Pseudo-Variance, Pseudo-Covariance, Pseudo-Volatility, and Pseudo-Correlation Swaps-In Analytical Closed-Forms. *Proceedings of the Sixth PIMS Industrial Problems Solving Workshop, PIMS IPSW* 6, University of British Columbia, Vancouver, Canada, May 27-31, 2002, pp. 45-55 (2002).

[22] H. Windcliff, P.A. Forsyth and K.R. Vetzal. Pricing methods and hedging strategies for volatility derivatives. *Journal of Banking & Finance* 30 (2006) 409-431.

In: Stock Markets
Editors: F. Petroni, F. Prattico and G. D'Amico
ISBN: 978-1-62808-751-2

Chapter 4

MEAN ANNUAL NUMBER OF MOTORCAR ACCIDENTS: A RENEWAL APPROACH

G. Di Biase[1], R. Manca[*], G. Ventura[2] and J. Janssen[3]

[1]Dipartimento di Farmacia, Università "G. D'Annunzio" di Chieti-Pescara. Chieti, Italy

[2]Università "La Sapienza", Dipartimento di Metodi e Modelli per l'Economia, la Finanza ed il Territorio, Roma, Italy

[3]CADEPS, Université Libre de Bruxelles, Solvay Business School and Department of Mathematics - Actuarial Section, Brussels, Belgium

ABSTRACT

The renewal theory has great relevance in actuarial science. A simple actuarial model can be simulated well by means of this kind of stochastic process. The renewal process is strictly related to the Laplace transform theory. In a general case, solving the renewal equation is not a simple task and it is necessary to solve it numerically. Usually, in order to numerically solve the renewal equation the Laplace transform approach is used. There is a problem in that the inversion of the Laplace transform is not stable numerically thus implying that the results obtained in this way cannot be reliable.

In this paper, a straightforward method is presented that deals directly with the numerical solution of the renewal equation. It is proved that any kind of renewal process can be solved by means of this approach. In conclusion, an application useful in the field of motorcar insurance is presented. By means of renewal equation, the mean number of car accidents that an insured person can have in one year, two years, three years and so on up to 37 years (maximum years number that is considered because of the available data) is computed The related distribution function was constructed with real data given by a primary insurance company.

Keywords: Renewal processes, Motorcar Insurance, Numerical solution, Approximation

---

[*] Corresponding Author's Email address: raimondo.manca@uniroma1.it

INTRODUCTION

Renewal theory has great relevance in actuarial science. When the studied phenomenon is verified then the system is renewed and the system can restart with the same initial characteristics. It is clear that a simple actuarial model can be simulated well by this kind of stochastic process.

The renewal process is strictly related to the Laplace transform theory [2]. Usually, the renewal equation is solved by applying the Laplace transform apparatus.

If the increasing distribution function (d.f.) of the renewal process is of a negative exponential type, then the renewal process becomes a Poisson process and the related integral equation can be solved easily [3]. This is a very particular case. In a more general case, the renewal equation cannot be solved analytically and it is necessary to solve the equation numerically.

Usually, in order to solve the renewal equation numerically the Laplace transform approach is used. There is a problem in that the inversion of the Laplace transform is not numerically stable [2] and [5]. This fact implies that the results obtained in this way cannot be reliable.

In this light, this paper presents a straightforward method that deals directly with the numerical solution of the renewal equation.

It is proved that any kind of renewal process can be solved by means of this approach. It is also proved that, in a very particular case of the general numerical solution, (general because the d.f. is not specified), the related discrete time renewal equation is obtained.

This approach was presented in [10] without any theoretical justification and also in [13] in which the so called "midpoint" formula was given with neither a general introduction nor a theoretical justification. Many other papers treat the problem of discretization of the renewal equation or of the Markov renewal equation; see for example [6], [7] but, as far as the authors know, none of these papers state that it is possible to obtain the discrete time renewal equation from the continuous one and the continuous from the discrete.

In this paper, all the results are proved and are given in a general environment. A similar approach was presented in [11] for the non-homogeneous semi-Markov processes and in [4] for the homogeneous case. The results obtained in these two papers will be used to obtain some of the results given in this paper.

Once the strong relation between the continuous and discrete time renewal processes is proved, it is possible to work with a general discrete time d.f.. In this light, it is possible to think of constructing the discrete time d.f. directly from the observed data. This approach leads to giving as d.f. that constituted by the cumulative frequencies obtained by the observed data. In this way, the model to be applied needs only raw data derived from observations.

The results derive directly from the data. The so called "physical measure" is applied. In our opinion, this comes near to the way in which actuaries usually face the problems. The results are a direct function of the observed data but without strong theoretical restrictions. In our opinion, this last observation is the main finding of the paper.

An application useful to motor car insurance is presented in the last paragraph. By means of the renewal equation, the mean number of accidents that an insured person can have within one year, two years, three years and so on up to 37 years (37 years being the longest time interval in the observed data between two subsequent accidents) is computed. Firstly, without taking in account the sex of insured people and after giving the same results but dividing the data in function of the sex.

Applications of Poisson processes and their generalizations with regards to motorcar insurance can be found in [12].

The author uses these processes in order to find the distribution of the number of accidents in one year. The application of the renewal process given in this paper shows how to construct the mean number of accidents by an insured person had annually during his driving life.

The d.f. put into the renewal function were constructed with real data given by a primary insurance company.

MAIN DEFINITIONS

In this part, the main definitions of renewal theory as given in [3] are reported. Let $(X_n, \ n \geq 1)$ be a sequence of non-negative, independent and identically distributed random variables defined on the probability space (Ω, F, P).

Definition 2.1. The random sequence $(T_n, \ n \geq 0)$, where:

$$T_0 = 0 \text{ a.s., and } T_n = X_1 + \cdots + X_n, \qquad n \geq 1, \tag{1}$$

is called a *renewal sequence* or *renewal process.* □

The random variables (r.v.) $T_n, \ n \geq 0$ are called *renewal times* and the r.v. $X_n, \ n \geq 1$ are called *interarrival times.*

Definition 2.2. With each renewal sequence, the following stochastic process, continuous in time, can be associated with values in N :

$$(N(t), \quad t \geq 0), \tag{2}$$

where

$$N(t) > n-1 \Leftrightarrow T_n \leq t, \qquad n \in \mathbb{N}_0. \tag{3}$$

This process is called the *associated counting process* or the *renewal counting process.* □

$N(t)$ represents the total number of "renewals" on $(0,t]$.

Definition 2.3. The *renewal function* is defined as

$$H(t) = \mathrm{E}[N(t)] \tag{4}$$

provided the expectation is finite. □

The integral equation of renewal theory or simply the *renewal equation* can be written as follows:

$$H(t) = F(t) + \int_0^t F(t-x)dH(x). \tag{5}$$

Or:

$$F * H(t) = H * F(t), \tag{6}$$

$$H(t) = F(t) + \int_0^t H(t-x)dF(x). \tag{7}$$

In the particular case where the density function f of F exists, the last integral equation becomes

$$H(t) = F(t) + \int_0^t H(t-x)f(x)dx. \tag{8}$$

Numerical Aspects

The renewal equation (7) can be solved directly in some very special cases or by means of the Laplace or Laplace-Stieltjes transforms in other cases. In this way, the analytical solution of the integral equation (7) can be obtained. In most real life applications, however, the equation that is obtained by the model can't be solved by analytical methods even if, from a theoretical point of view, the solution exists. In these cases, it is necessary to use a numerical approach in order to obtain the solution to the general renewal equation (7) in a bounded horizon time.One way of dealing with the problem could be by transforming the renewal equation by means of the Laplace transform. The problem that arises is due to the fact that, in order to obtain the solution to the equation, it is necessary to make use of the inverse Laplace transform that, as is well known [2] and [5], is not numerically stable.

The idea, therefore, is to solve the (7) using numerical methods for integral equations without using the Laplace transform apparatus.

General Quadrature Methods

It is assumed that the density function of f of F exists. So, the integral equation given by (8) has to be solved.Each generic quadrature formula can be written in the following way see [8]:

$$\int_0^{kh} f(t)dt \cong \sum_{l=0}^{k} w_{k,l} f(lh), \tag{9}$$

where h is the step length, $k \le N,\quad k, N \in \mathbb{N},\quad w_{k,l}$ are the weights related to the quadrature formula (9); they are functions of:

i) the end point,
ii) the point in which we compute the function value.

Furthermore, the number N is such that $hk = t,\quad hN = Y$ and $0 \le t \le Y$, Y representing the horizon time length. General quadrature method means that the value of weights $w_{k,l}$ depends on the polynomial that was used to approximate the integrand function.

The following relation approximates the solution of (8) that can be obtained using (9)

$$\hat{H}(kh) = F(kh) + \sum_{l=0}^{k} w_{k,l} \hat{H}(kh - lh) f(lh), \quad k = 1, \dots, N, \tag{10}$$

where $\hat{H}$ represents an approximate value of the function H .

In this way, the following linear system is obtained:

(11)

$$\begin{array}{llllll}
\hat{H}(h) - w_{1,0}\hat{H}(h)f(0) & & w_{1,1}\hat{H}(0)f(h) + F(h) & & & \\
-w_{2,1}\hat{H}(h)f(h) & \hat{H}(2h) - w_{2,0}\hat{H}(2h)f(0) & & w_{2,2}\hat{H}(0)f(2h) + F(2h) & & \\
\vdots & \ddots & \ddots & \ddots & \ddots & \ddots \\
w_{k,k-1}\hat{H}(h)f((k-1)h) & \cdots & w_{k,1}\hat{H}((k-1)h)f(h) & \cdots & \hat{H}(kh) - w_{k,0}\hat{H}(kh)f(0) & w_{k,k}\hat{H}(0)f(kh) + F(kh) \\
\vdots & \vdots & \vdots & \ddots & \vdots & \ddots \; \ddots
\end{array}$$

It is trivial to say that the system (11) admits solution if

$$1 - w_{k,0} f(0) \neq 0, \quad k = 1, \dots, N. \tag{12}$$

There is a theorem given in [1] that gives the condition for which if $h \to 0$ then $\hat{H} \to H$. This result is reported here. Before stating the theorem it is necessary to give two lemmas that hold for real numbers and which are proved in [1].

Lemma 3.1. *If*

$$|\xi_r| \le A \sum_{i=0}^{r-1} |\xi_i| + B, \quad r = q,\ q+1, \dots\ , \quad q \ge 1, \tag{13}$$

where $A > 0,\ B > 0,$ *and* $\sum_{i=0}^{q-1} |\xi_i| \le \xi,$ *then*:

$$|\xi_r| \leq (A\xi + B)(1+A)^{r-q}, \quad r = q, \ q+1, \dots \quad q \geq 1. \ \square \tag{14}$$

Lemma 3.2. *Suppose that*:

$$A = h\widehat{L} \leq 0 \text{ and } ph = x \geq 0. \tag{15}$$

then

$$(1+A)^{p-q} \leq e^{\widehat{L}x} \text{ if } p \geq q. \tag{16}$$

Remark 3.1. From lemmas 3.1 and 3.2 results:

$$|\xi_r| \leq (A\xi + B)(1+A)^{r-q} \leq (A\xi + B)e^{\widehat{L}x} = (h\widehat{L}\xi + B)e^{\widehat{L}rh} \tag{17}$$

Theorem 3.1. *Let*

$$F : [0, Y] \to \mathbb{R}, \qquad H : [0, Y] \to \mathbb{R} \tag{18}$$

Let $q \in \{1, \dots, \ N\}$ $\quad N \in \mathbb{N}$, *such that* $Nh \leq Y$. *Let*

$$\xi^k(h) = \hat{H}(kh) - H(kh), \qquad k = 0, \ 1 \ , 2, \dots, \ N, \tag{19}$$

where $H(kh)$ *is a solution of* (7) and $\hat{H}(kh)$ *is a solution of* (11).

We define:

$$\eta^k(h) = \left|\xi^k(h)\right|. \tag{20}$$

Furthermore, let:

$$w = w_N = \max_{0 \leq u \leq k \leq N} \frac{|w_{ku}|}{h} < \infty \tag{21}$$

$$t^k(h) = \int_0^{kh} H(kh - \tau) f(\tau) d\tau - \sum_{u=0}^{k} w_{ku} \hat{H}(kh - uh) f(uh) \tag{22}$$

$$\sigma^k(h) = \left|t^k(h)\right|, \tag{23}$$

$$\tau(h) = \tau_N(h) = \max_{q \leq k \leq N} \sigma^k(h), \tag{24}$$

$$\xi(h) = \sum_{u=0}^{n-1} \eta^u(h). \tag{25}$$

Suppose, finally, that $|f(t)| \le c_1$ *for* $t \in [0,Y]$.
Then

$$\eta^k(h) \le \frac{\tau(h) + mhw_N c_1 \xi(h)}{1 - mhw_N c_1} e^{\frac{mc_1 w_N kh}{1 - mhw_N c_1}} \quad , \quad k = q,\ q+1, \ldots,\ N \tag{26}$$

given that $mhw_N c_1 < 1$.

For the proof of the theorem see [1]. □

Remark 3.2. It follows that if $\tau_N(h) = o(h^p)$, $h \to 0$ with fixed Nh (so $N \to \infty$), $\xi(h) = o\left(h^{p-1}\right)$ and $\lim_{N\to\infty} w_N < \infty$, then

$$\eta^h(h) = o\left(h^p\right). \; \square \tag{27}$$

By means of these lemmas and this theorem, it results that the equation (8) can be discretized by means of a general quadrature formula and that the error given by the discretization process goes to 0 as the h, discretization step, tends to 0.

Some Particular Formulas

In this part, some formulas of the numerical solution of the renewal equation will be given. The formula (10) will be related to particular generalized Newton-Cotes formulas.

Simpson quadrature method gives the following equations:

$$\begin{aligned} \hat{H}(kh) = F(kh) + \frac{h}{3}\hat{H}(kh)f(0) + \frac{4h}{3}\sum_{\tau=1}^{\frac{k}{2}} \hat{H}\left(kh - (2\tau-1)h\right) f\left((2\tau-1)h\right) + \\ \frac{2h}{3}\sum_{\tau=1}^{\frac{k}{2}-1} \hat{H}\left(kh - 2\tau h\right) f\left(2\tau h\right) + \frac{h}{3}\hat{H}(0)f(kh). \end{aligned} \tag{28}$$

Using Bezout formula the s:

$$\begin{aligned} \hat{H}(kh) = F(kh) + \frac{h}{2}\hat{H}(kh)f(0) + h\sum_{\tau=1}^{k-1} \hat{H}\left(kh - \tau h\right) f\left(\tau h\right) + \\ \frac{h}{2}\hat{H}(0)f(kh). \end{aligned} \tag{29}$$

Finally, if the most simple quadrature method (rectangle formulas) is applied then it is possible to obtain two different formulas, one obtaining the value of the integrating function at the beginning of the interval and the other at the end of the interval. In this way, the following formulas are obtained:

$$\hat{H}(kh) = F(kh) + h\sum_{\tau=1}^{k} \hat{H}(kh - \tau h) f(\tau h). \tag{30}$$

$$\hat{H}(kh) = F(kh) + h\sum_{\tau=0}^{k-1} \hat{H}(kh - \tau h) f(\tau h). \tag{31}$$

Substituting the differential by means of the difference it respectively results:

$$\hat{H}(kh) \cong F(kh) + \sum_{\tau=1}^{k} \hat{H}(kh - \tau h)(F(\tau h) - F((\tau - 1)h)). \tag{32}$$

$$\hat{H}(kh) \cong F(kh) + \sum_{\tau=0}^{k-1} \hat{H}(kh - \tau h)(F((\tau + 1)h) - F((\tau)h)). \tag{33}$$

Posing $h = 1$ in (32)

$$\hat{H}(k) \cong F(k) + \sum_{\tau=1}^{k} \hat{H}(k - \tau)(F(\tau) - F(\tau - 1)). \tag{34}$$

Furthermore, putting:

$$v(\tau) = \begin{cases} F(\tau) & \tau = 0, \\ F(\tau) - F(\tau - 1) & \tau > 0, \end{cases} \tag{35}$$

the following is obtained:

$$H(k) = F(k) + \sum_{\tau=1}^{k} H(k - \tau)v(\tau), \tag{36}$$

that is the discrete time renewal equation [9] pag 330.

Now let H be a continuous time renewal function and $\{T_n\}$ the related renewal process. If the following is set:

$$T_n^h = \left\lfloor \frac{T_n}{h} \right\rfloor h \tag{37}$$

and

$$N^h(t) = n \text{ if } T_n^h \le t < T_{n+1}^h, \tag{38}$$

then the related discrete time renewal function is given by:

$$H^h(kh) = F^h(kh) + \sum_{\tau=1}^{k} H^h((k-\tau)h)v^h(\tau h). \tag{39}$$

The renewal process T_n^h is defined in the same probability space (Ω, F, P) of T_n. Given $\omega \in \Omega$ the following result holds a.s..

Theorem 3.2. *The* T_n^h *process converges to* T_n *for* $h \to 0$.

Proof. From the definitions given in the section 2 and the (38) it results:

$$P\left[\underset{h\to 0}{N^h(t) = n}\right] = P\left[N(t) = n\right] \quad \forall n. \tag{40}$$

The formula (40) implies:

$$\underset{h\to 0}{T_n^h} \xrightarrow{a.s.} T_n. \qquad \square \tag{41}$$

At the end of theoretical part the following remarks should be made:

1) The theorem can be considered a very special case of the Theorem 4.5 proved in [4]. But in this paper, the proof can be obtained by means of very simple tools.
2) The results obtained show that it is possible to obtain the discrete time renewal equation by means of the discretization of the related continuous time and that starting from the discrete time it is also possible to obtain the continuous time.
3) In Freiberger and Grenanders' book [10] there is a similar approach to the renewal equation numerical solution but there is no justification of the method. Many other papers (see the introduction) deal with the same problem but, as far as the authors know, no one has justified the relations between the discrete time and continuous time renewal process as is done in this paper.

A Real Application of Motor Accidents

The Data Description

In this section, the renewal equation is applied to a real actuarial data application. It is demonstrated that the renewal process can be applied in a very general case utilising data from statistical observations. The formula that we will use in this case is the (36).

The renewal process will be applied in the case of motor car accidents.

In a motor car insurance contract, each time that the insured has an accident the insurance company will pay for the damage. It is possible to think that once the insured car is repaired all the conditions are renewed as at beginning of the contract and the renewal theory can be applied.

Table 1.

# years	1-2	2-3	1-2 + 2-3
1	153	88	241
2	695	126	821
3	1 576	226	1 802
4	1 549	224	1 773
5	1 344	172	1 516
6	928	176	1 104
7	619	138	757
8	386	107	493
9	278	86	364
10	189	69	258
11	139	61	200
12	101	33	134
13	77	21	98
14	40	15	55
15	36	16	52
16	15	7	22
17	11	3	14
18	11	4	15
19	10	3	13
20	7	2	9
21	14	1	15
22	6		6
23	8		8
24	7		7
25	7		7
26	2		2
27	-		-
28	4		4
29	3		3
30	5		5
31	3		3
32	2		2
33	1		1
34	-		-
35	1		1
36	-		-
37	1		1
Total	8228	1578	9 806

We have the raw data regarding accidents that an insurance company collected during a period of about 50 years.

It is possible to construct the discrete time d.f. of the renewal time of the motorcar accident from this data.

The data concerning a total of 156,428 insured people is available and 22,395 had at least one accident.

Data concerning the insurance premiums and dates of individual contracts were not available.

Two vectors are constructed. In the first, the number of insured persons that had a second accidents in 1 year, in 2 years,..., in n years from the first is counted. In the second, the number of insured persons that had a third accident in 1 year, in 2 years,..., in n years from the second is counted.

More precisely, at the beginning, all the elements of the vectors equal to 0 were included. 1 is added to the n-th element of the first vector when the second accident is verified after n-1 and before n years by the first one.

In the same way, 1 at the n-th element is added to the second vector when the third accident is verified after n-1 and before n years by the second one.

At the end of this process in the n-th element of vectors there will be the number of accidents during the n-th years from the previous one, respectively the second after the first and the third after the second.

The results obtained in this way are reported in Table 1. For example 1,576 in the third row of this table represents the number of second accidents that occurred after two years and before the third year since the first accident. The number 226 represents the number of third accidents that occurred after two years and before the third year by the second accident.

In Table 2 the year mean number and the variance related to the three distributions of Table 1 are reported. In Table 3 the distributions of the frequencies of the three vectors given in Table 1 are reported. The columns are obtained dividing the number of each column by the total number of considered accidents in the vector. The three histograms that can be obtained by Table 3 have a shape similar to that of a Poisson process.

Observing the data, it is possible to consider the following:

i. all the three distributions have the same shape,
ii. these distributions have the Poisson shape but the variance is the double of the mean,
iii. the mean and the variance of the first two columns of Table 1 are similar.

In this light, it can be said that the renewal hypothesis is acceptable because of the similar shape and the parameters of the first two distributions. It is possible to suppose that after an accident the process is renewed and the behaviour of the insured people will be the same.

In order to get more reliable data it was decided to combine the observations of the first and second distributions thereby obtaining the third column of each table.

The Results Description

Now the frequencies of the last column of the Table 3 will be considered as the "probability" that a new accident will be verified after n-1 and before n years from the previous one. The n-th result can be considered as an evaluation of the "probability" that there will be an accident between the n-1-th and the n-th year, given that at least one accident occurred. As already mentioned, the dates of first contract premiums aren't available in the data.

Table 2.

	1-2	2-3	1-2 + 2-3
mean	5.3453	5.8676	5.4293
variance	10.8680	11.7207	11.0421

Table 3.

# years	1-2	2-3	1-2 + 2-3
1	0.018595	0.055767	0.02457679
2	0.084468	0.079848	0.08372425
3	0.191541	0.143219	0.183765042
4	0.188260	0.141952	0.180807669
5	0.163345	0.108999	0.154599225
6	0.112786	0.111534	0.112584132
7	0.075231	0.087452	0.077197634
8	0.046913	0.067807	0.050275342
9	0.033787	0.054499	0.037120131
10	0.022970	0.043726	0.026310422
11	0.016894	0.038657	0.020395676
12	0.012275	0.020913	0.013665103
13	0.009358	0.013308	0.009993881
14	0.004861	0.009506	0.005608811
15	0.004375	0.010139	0.005302876
16	0.001823	0.004436	0.002243524
17	0.001337	0.001901	0.001427697
18	0.001337	0.002535	0.001529676
19	0.001215	0.001901	0.001325719
20	0.000851	0.001267	0.000917805
21	0.001702	0.000634	0.001529676
22	0.000729		0.00061187
23	0.000972		0.000815827
24	0.000851		0.000713849
25	0.000851		0.000713849
26	0.000243		0.000203957
27	0		0
28	0.000486		0.000407914
29	0.000365		0.000305935
30	0.000608		0.000509892
31	0.000365		0.000305935
32	0.000243		0.000203957
33	0.000122		0.000101978
34	0		0
35	0.000122		0.000101978
36	0		0
37	0.000122		0.000101978

Table 4.

year	Cond. Freq	Frequencies	Cum. Freq	mean numb.
1	0,024577	0.003519	0.003519	0.003519
2	0,083724	0.011986	0.015505	0.01551738
3	0,183765	0.026309	0.041814	0.04191078
4	0,180808	0.025885	0.067699	0.06812506
5	0,154599	0.022133	0.089832	0.09107341
6	0,112584	0.016118	0.10595	0.10866922
7	0,077198	0.011052	0.117002	0.12175334
8	0,050275	0.007198	0.1242	0.13130704
9	0,03712	0.005314	0.129514	0.13903198
10	0,02631	0.003767	0.133281	0.14506757
11	0,020396	0.00292	0.136201	0.15000748
12	0,013665	0.001956	0.138157	0.15371498
13	0,009994	0.001431	0.139588	0.15663962
14	0,005609	0.000803	0.140391	0.15870604
15	0,005303	0.000759	0.14115	0.16051876
16	0,002244	0.000321	0.141471	0.16170875
17	0,001428	0.000204	0.141676	0.16261899
18	0,00153	0.000219	0.141895	0.16340732
19	0,001326	0.00019	0.142085	0.16404851
20	0,000918	0.000131	0.142216	0.16453603
21	0,00153	0.000219	0.142435	0.16503802
22	0,000612	8.76E-05	0.142523	0.16535298
23	0,000816	0.000117	0.142639	0.16565263
24	0,000714	0.000102	0.142742	0.16590744
25	0,000714	0.000102	0.142844	0.16613383
26	0,000204	2.92E-05	0.142873	0.16626641
27	0	0.0	0.142873	0.16635287
28	0,000408	5.84E-05	0.142931	0.16648298
29	0,000306	4.38E-05	0.142975	0.16658543
30	0,00051	7.3E-05	0.143048	0.16670596
31	0,000306	4.38E-05	0.143092	0.16679003
32	0,000204	2.92E-05	0.143121	0.16685396
33	0,000102	1.46E-05	0.143136	0.16690042
34	0	0.0	0.143136	0.16692826
35	0,000102	1.46E-05	0.14315	0.16696609
36	0	0.0	0.14315	0.16698588
37	0,000102	1.46E-05	0.143165	0.16701685

The time interval between two subsequent accidents is used. Values shown in the second column are “conditional probabilities” of having at least one accident as described before.

To apply the renewal model it is necessary to construct the d.f that gives the probability of having an accident within n years. The “probability” of having at least one accident is obtained from the raw data. It is obtained by dividing the number of people that had at least an accident (22,395) by the total number of the insured people (156,428).

9,806 accidents are considered to represent the number of accidents that occurred after a previous accident.

The following events for an insured person are defined:

A = have at least two accidents during the observed period

B_n = have another accident after the n-1-th and before the n-th year from the previous one

C = have at least one accident during all the subscription time: 22,395/156,428 (=0.14316).

The authors would like to estimate the following probabilities for the inter-arrival time for successive accidents:

D_n = have an accident after the n-1-th and before the n-th year from the contract premium or from the previous one.

The n-th element of the second column the Table 4 that is equal to the fourth of the Table 3 gives the following value:

$$P[B_n / A], \tag{42}$$

but more interesting is:

$$P[D_n / C]. \tag{43}$$

In the data, as already specified, the contract subscription date is not available. Knowing the probabilities $P[D_n]$ is more interesting. If it is supposed that (42) is an evaluation of (43) that means:

$$P[B_n / A] \cong P[D_n / C].$$

Then, by means of Bayes' theorem, it is possible to reconstruct the "probabilities" $P[D_n]$ of having the first accident after one year, two years and so on. These results are reported in the third column of Table 4.

In the fourth column of the table, the "increasing d.f." obtained by the elements of the third column is reported. In this case the n-th element represents the "probability" of having the first accident within n years.

This data represents the d.f that was needed in the discrete time renewal equation in order to evaluate the mean number of accidents that an insured person will have within 1, 2,…, n, years. These results are obtained by solving the discrete time renewal equation (36) and are reported in the last column of the Table 4.

In the obtained results, it can be seen that the mean number of accidents seems low. Real data obtained from an insurance company.

If any reader feels that the results are too low the authors will be glad to receive other data and to evaluate them by means of the same model.

Data Comparison by Sex

Once having obtained general results and given that the data indicates the sex of each insured person, the simple probability of a man and or woman having an accident during their driving life was computed.

The related results are reported in the Table 5.

Usually, insurance companies say that women are better drivers than men but our result contradicted this "axiom".

With this in mind, it was decided to apply all the methodology applied previously to the two sexes. The results reported in the following tables were obtained.

Table 6 for men, and Table 10 for women, correspond to the Table 1. For example, the second column reports, respectively, the number of men and women that had second accidents after the first in n years, where n is given in the first column.

For men, accidents after 33 years were not considered. So the related data stop at 33 years.

In the Table 7 and 11 the year mean number and the related variance of the men and women are reported.

The results are similar to those of the general data but it can be seen that men tend to have more accidents at a younger age than women.

In Table 8 and 12 the frequencies distributions respectively of men and women are reported.

Finally, tables 9 and 13 correspond to table 4. It is noteworthy that, in this case, because of the reconstruction of the "probabilities" by means of Bayes theorem, the mean number of accidents for males is always lower than that for females. On the other hand, in the first years of driving, the results should be higher for men and later on should become higher for women. This fact depends on the probability of having an accident during in one's life that is, as we noted before, higher for women than for men.

Knowing the complete history of each insured person, the Bayes theorem step will not be necessary and this kind of discrepancy will disappear.

Table 5.

	insured	at least 1 acc	probability
women	49988	7 986	0.159758
men	106440	14 409	0.135372

Table 6.

# years	1-2	2-3	1-2 + 2-3
1	104	58	162
2	469	83	552
3	1 076	168	1 244
4	1 012	151	1 163
5	908	112	1 020
6	591	129	720
7	395	79	474

Table 6. (Continued)

# years	1-2	2-3	1-2 + 2-3
8	261	81	342
9	163	55	218
10	115	52	167
11	92	40	132
12	54	23	77
13	44	13	57
14	24	10	34
15	21	11	32
16	10	5	15
17	7	3	10
18	6	3	9
19	7	1	8
20	6	2	8
21	7		7
22	4		4
23	7		7
24	7		7
25	4		4
26	2		2
27	-		-
28	4		4
29	1		1
30	4		4
31	2		2
32	1		1
33	1		1
total	5 409	1 079	6 488

Table 7.

	1-2	2-3	1-2 + 2-3
mean	5.269181	5.853568	5.366369
variance	10.69811	11.64492	10.90292

Table 8.

# years	1-2	2-3	1-2 + 2-3
1	0.019227	0.053753	0.024969
2	0.086707	0.076923	0.08508
3	0.198928	0.155700	0.191739
4	0.187096	0.139944	0.179254
5	0.167868	0.103800	0.157213
6	0.109262	0.119555	0.110974
7	0.073026	0.073216	0.073058
8	0.048253	0.075070	0.052713

# years	1-2	2-3	1-2 + 2-3
9	0.030135	0.050973	0.0336
10	0.021261	0.048193	0.02574
11	0.017009	0.037071	0.020345
12	0.009983	0.021316	0.011868
13	0.008135	0.012048	0.008785
14	0.004437	0.009268	0.00524
15	0.003882	0.010195	0.004932
16	0.001849	0.004634	0.002312
17	0.001294	0.002780	0.001541
18	0.001109	0.002780	0.001387
19	0.001294	0.000927	0.001233
20	0.001109	0.001854	0.001233
21	0.001294	0.000634	0.001079
22	0.00074		0.000617
23	0.001294		0.001079
24	0.001294		0.001079
25	0.00074		0.000617
26	0.00037		0.000308
27	0		0
28	0.00074		0.000617
29	0.000185		0.000154
30	0.00074		0.000617
31	0.00037		0.000308
32	0.000185		0.000154
33	0.000185		0.000154

Table 9.

year	Cond. Freq	Frequencies	Cum. Freq	mean numb.
1	0.024969	0.00338	0.00338	0.00338
2	0.08508	0.011517	0.014898	0.014909
3	0.191739	0.025956	0.040854	0.040943
4	0.179254	0.024266	0.06512	0.065517
5	0.157213	0.021282	0.086402	0.0875639
6	0.110974	0.015023	0.101425	0.1039717
7	0.073058	0.00989	0.111315	0.1157368
8	0.052713	0.007136	0.118451	0.125030
9	0.0336	0.004549	0.122999	0.131759
10	0.02574	0.003484	0.126484	0.1372705
11	0.020345	0.002754	0.129238	0.1418210
12	0.011868	0.001607	0.130844	0.1449648
13	0.008785	0.001189	0.132034	0.1474572
14	0.00524	0.000709	0.132743	0.1492595
15	0.004932	0.000668	0.133411	0.1508254
16	0.002312	0.000313	0.133724	0.1518702

Table 9. (Continued)

year	Cond. Freq	Frequencies	Cum. Freq	mean numb.
17	0.001541	0.000209	0.133932	0.1526658
18	0.001387	0.000188	0.13412	0.1533243
19	0.001233	0.000167	0.134287	0.1538629
20	0.001233	0.000167	0.134454	0.1543223
21	0.001079	0.000146	0.1346	0.1546998
22	0.000617	8.35E-05	0.134683	0.1549680
23	0.001079	0.000146	0.13483	0.1552638
24	0.001079	0.000146	0.134976	0.1555322
25	0.000617	8.35E-05	0.135059	0.1557166
26	0.000308	4.17E-05	0.135101	0.1558445
27	0	0	0.135101	0.1559182
28	0.000617	8.35E-05	0.135184	0.1560636
29	0.000154	2.09E-05	0.135205	0.1561355
30	0.000617	8.35E-05	0.135289	0.1562604
31	0.000308	4.17E-05	0.13533	0.1563379
32	0.000154	2.09E-05	0.135351	0.1563896
33	0.000154	2.09E-05	0.135372	0.1564387

Table 10.

# years	1-2	2-3	1-2 + 2-3
1	49	30	79
2	226	43	269
3	500	58	558
4	537	73	610
5	436	60	496
6	337	47	384
7	224	59	283
8	125	26	151
9	115	31	146
10	74	17	91
11	47	21	68
12	47	10	57
13	33	8	41
14	16	5	21
15	15	5	20
16	5	2	7
17	4	0	4
18	5	1	6
19	3	2	5
20	1	0	1
21	7	1	8
22	2		2

# years	1-2	2-3	1-2 + 2-3
23	1		1
24	0		0
25	3		3
26	0		0
27	0		0
28	0		0
29	2		2
30	1		1
31	1		1
32	1		1
33	0		0
34	0		0
35	1		1
36	0		0
37	1		1
total	2 819	499	3 318

Table 11.

	1-2	2-3	1-2 + 2-3
mean	5.491309	5.897796	5.552441
variance	11.1616	11.88334	11.29125

Table 12.

# years	1-2	2-3	1-2 + 2-3
1	0.017382	0.06012	0.02381
2	0.08017	0.086172	0.081073
3	0.177368	0.116232	0.168174
4	0.190493	0.146293	0.183846
5	0.154665	0.12024	0.149488
6	0.119546	0.094188	0.115732
7	0.079461	0.118236	0.085292
8	0.044342	0.052104	0.045509
9	0.040795	0.062124	0.044002
10	0.02625	0.034068	0.027426
11	0.016673	0.042084	0.020494
12	0.016673	0.02004	0.017179
13	0.011706	0.016032	0.012357
14	0.005676	0.01002	0.006329
15	0.005321	0.01002	0.006028
16	0.001774	0.004008	0.00211
17	0.001419	0	0.001206

Table 12. (Continued)

# years	1-2	2-3	1-2 + 2-3
18	0.001774	0.002004	0.001808
19	0.001064	0.004008	0.001507
20	0.000355	0	0.000301
21	0.002483	0.002004	0.002411
22	0.000709		0.000603
23	0.000355		0.000301
24	0		0
25	0.001064		0.000904
26	0		0
27	0		0
28	0		0
29	0.000709		0.000603
30	0.000355		0.000301
31	0.000355		0.000301
32	0.000355		0.000301
33	0		0
34	0		0
35	0.000355		0.000301
36	0		0
37	0.000355		0.000301

Table 13.

year	Cond. Freq	Frequencies	Cum. Freq	mean numb.
1	0.02381	0.003804	0.003804	0.003804
2	0.081073	0.012952	0.016756	0.01677
3	0.168174	0.026867	0.043623	0.043736
4	0.183846	0.029371	0.072994	0.07348
5	0.149488	0.023882	0.096876	0.098284
6	0.115732	0.018489	0.115365	0.118449
7	0.085292	0.013626	0.128991	0.134444
8	0.045509	0.00727	0.136262	0.144512
9	0.044002	0.00703	0.143291	0.154471
10	0.027426	0.004382	0.147673	0.161674
11	0.020494	0.003274	0.150947	0.167494
12	0.017179	0.002744	0.153692	0.172485
13	0.012357	0.001974	0.155666	0.176411
14	0.006329	0.001011	0.156677	0.179094
15	0.006028	0.000963	0.15764	0.181484
16	0.00211	0.000337	0.157977	0.183032
17	0.001206	0.000193	0.158169	0.184221
18	0.001808	0.000289	0.158458	0.185327
19	0.001507	0.000241	0.158699	0.186223

year	Cond. Freq	Frequencies	Cum. Freq	mean numb.
20	0.000301	4.81E-05	0.158747	0.186792
21	0.002411	0.000385	0.159132	0.187594
22	0.000603	9.63E-05	0.159229	0.188028
23	0.000301	4.81E-05	0.159277	0.188349
24	0	0	0.159277	0.188579
25	0.000904	0.000144	0.159421	0.188912
26	0	0	0.159421	0.189062
27	0	0	0.159421	0.189184
28	0	0	0.159421	0.189284
29	0.000603	9.63E-05	0.159518	0.189459
30	0.000301	4.81E-05	0.159566	0.189571
31	0.000301	4.81E-05	0.159614	0.189672
32	0.000301	4.81E-05	0.159662	0.189766
33	0	0	0.159662	0.189806
34	0	0	0.159662	0.189842
35	0.000301	4.81E-05	0.15971	0.189921
36	0	0	0.15971	0.189947
37	0.000301	4.81E-05	0.159758	0.190016

CONCLUSION

In the authors' opinion the main results of this paper are:

The possibility of working with discrete time renewal processes instead of continuous ones given the strict relation between the two kinds of stochastic processes,

2. The possibility, within the renewal equation, of using the d.f. constructed directly from the observed data.

These results can be considered as particular cases of the results obtained by two of the authors in previous papers on semi-Markov processes.

The proposed application in the field of automobile insurance could be interesting for insurance companies since, by being able to predict the mean number of accidents that a person could have during his driving life, the companies can judge as to whether an insured person is a good or a bad driver.

The subdivision between the sexes was carried out in order to demonstrate that sometimes, by observing data, some facts that most consider to be true can be denied. Clearly we don't have the cost of each accidents and this fact could diversify the results.

ACKNOWLEDGMENTS

This research was supported by a MIUR-PRIN and University "La Sapienza" grants. The authors are grateful to the doctor Cardinaletti of the Winterthur Insurance Company that gave the data that were used to construct the example and to the colleague and friend Nikolaos Limnios for his very useful suggestions.

REFERENCES

[1] C.T.H. Baker, *The Numerical Treatment of Integral Equations.* Clarendon Press, New York (1977).

[2] R. Bellman, R. E. Kalaba and R. S. Roth, *Numerical Inversion of the Laplace Transform: Applications to Biology, Economics, Engineering and Physics.* Elsevier New York (1966).

[3] E. Cinlar, *Introduction to Stochastic Processes.* Prentice Hall, New York (1975).

[4] G. Corradi, J. Janssen and R. Manca, *Numerical treatment of homogeneous semi-Markov processes in transient case - a straightforward approach.* To be published on Methodology and Computing in Applied Probability.

[5] Csenki, *Dependability for Systems with a Partizioned State Space (Markov and Semi-Markov Theory and Computational Implementation).* Springer Verlag, Berlin (1994).

[6] F. De Vylder, E. Marceau, The numerical solution of the Schimitter problems: Theory. Insurance Mathematics & Economics. *Elsevier,* 19, 1-18, (1996).

[7] D.A. Elkins, M.A. Wortman, On numerical solution of the Markov renewal equation: tight upper and lower kernel bounds. *Methodology and Computing in Applied Probability*. Kluwer, 3 239-253, (2001).

[8] G. Evans, *Practical Numerical Integration.* Wiley, London (1993).

[9] W. Feller, *An Introduction to Probability Theory and Its Applications, Volume I, Second Edition*, Wiley, New York (1957).

[10] W. Freiberger and U. Grenander, *A Short Course in Computational Probability and Statistics*. Springer Verlag, Berlin (1971).

[11] J. Janssen and R. Manca, *Numerical solution of non homogeneous semi-Markov processes in transient case. Methodology and Computing in Applied Probability.* Kluwer, 3, 271-293, (2001).

[12] J. Lemaire, *Bonus Malus Systems in Automobile Insurance*, Kluwer, (1995).

[13] M. Xie, On the solution of renewal-type integral equations, Commun. *Statist. –Simula.*, 18, 281-293 (1989).

In: Stock Markets
Editors: F. Petroni, F. Prattico and G. D'Amico
ISBN: 978-1-62808-751-2

Chapter 5

THRESHOLD MODEL FOR TRIGGERED AVALANCHES ON NETWORKS

M. Ausloos[1,2,*] ***and F. Petroni***[3,†]
[1]GRAPES, SUPRATECS, Université de Liège, Liège, Euroland
[2]eHumanities group, Royal Netherlands Academy of Arts and Sciences, Joan Muyskenweg 25, 1096 CJ Amsterdam, Netherlands
[3]Dipartimento di Scienze Economiche ed Aziendali, Università degli studi di Cagliari, Cagliari, Italy

Abstract

Based on a theoretical model for opinion spreading on a network, through avalanches, the effect of external field is now considered, by using methods from non-equilibrium statistical mechanics. The original part contains the implementation that the avalanche is only triggered when a local variable (a so called *awareness*) reaches and goes above a threshold. The dynamical rules are constrained to be as simple as possible, in order to sort out the basic features, though more elaborated variants are proposed. Several results are obtained for a Erdös-Rényi network and interpreted through simple analytical laws, i.e. Weibull distribution, sometimes reduced to a mere exponential, or logistic function, i.e., (i) the sizes, durations, and number of avalanches, including the respective distributions, (ii) the number of times the external field is applied to one possible node before all nodes are found to be above the threshold, (iii) the number of nodes still below the threshold and the number of hot nodes (close to threshold) at each time step.

PACS: 89.75.Fb, 89.75.Hc, 87.23.Ge

1. Introduction

From a statistical physics point of view, opinion formation is similar to epidemic or forest fire spreading, landslide, crystal growth, fracture, percolation and pertains to the abundant

*E-mail address: marcel.ausloos@ulg.ac.be
†E-mail address: fpetroni@unica.it

literature on phase transition studies. The modeling of such phenomena, i.e. for reproducing stylized features, is highly important in order to connect statistical physics with the socio-economic world. Some conceptual difficulty has been resolved due to the abandon of (Bravais or random) lattice based concepts in favor of studies of cases on more elaborate networks in which the statistical characteristics, like the number of sites, neighbors, distances, weights and directivity of links are not trivial.

Euler invented network theory [1], for the Königsberg (or Kaliningrad) bridge crossing problem, in the 1780s, but this subject remained a form of abstract mathematics. Graph Theory was born later to study similar problems, including molecular bonding [2, 3]. An increased interest in the topics can be registered during the last decade, particularly due to their potential for an apparently quite unbounded area of applications. Indeed, the inter-disciplinary (or rather trans-disciplinary) concept of "network" is frequently met in all scientific research areas [4, 5, 6], its covering field spanning from computer science to medicine and social psychology, e.g. see some work in classical random graph study [7], non-equilibrium growing networks [8], WWW and Internet structure properties [5, 9, 10, 11, 12, 13], social networks of scientific collaborations [10, 11, 12, 13, 14, 15], paper citations [15, 16], collective listening habits and music genres [17, 18], language [19], and even finance [20, 21, 22]. Relevant questions pertain to the critical dynamics of properties, not only on the network, but also about the network structure itself. Recent results on the dynamics of social networks [23, 24] suggest the occurrence of phase transitions in a large class of models [25]. This is similar to percolation and nucleation-growth problems.

As a paradigm for large-scale networks, colleagues often consider co-authorship or citation networks [10, 11, 12, 13, 14, 15], namely networks where nodes represent scientists, and where a link is drawn between them if they co-authored a common paper or cite some paper. Other examples, where a system (nodes) has an evolution between two phases on a network, are those implying a unanimity rule on random networks [26, 27, 28, 29, 30, 31, 32]. Lattice based cases for social evolutions are on the contrary quite numerous: see those studied within prey-predator hypotheses [33].

Let us stress that the identification of the mechanisms responsible for diffusion and, possibly leading to scientific avalanches [34] is primordial in a very general sense in order to understand the scientific response to external political decisions, and to develop efficient policy recommendations. It is important to point that science spreading is usually modeled by master equations with auto-catalytic processes [35], or by epidemic spreading models on static networks [36, 37, 38, 39]. In this article, however, we present a novel approach where the opinion formation and spreading is controlled by a triggering field and occurs only if a threshold is reached. Without going into comparative details, the model can be thought to be connected to epidemic [36] and forest fire spreading [40, 41, 42, 43, 44], and landslide [45, 46, 47, 48] models. However, the process as discussed here below occurring on a network seems to be novel and of crucial interest and differs from already known models like the Galam [28, 29] and/or Sznajd [30, 31, 32] model and their extensions. We focus on the development of neighboring (scientific or not) "opinions" in the course of time, thereby eyeing the spreading of ideas in the scientific community. We will indicate the possibility of variants.

For our present framework, let us recall that two decades ago people looked at forest fires [41, 42] in particular in the case when a tree is ignited only if a neighboring tree burns long enough. This fact that wet wood does not yet burn corresponds to our awareness below the threshold ϕ. We also agree that avalanche problems are similar to epidemic spreading with threshold, see a recent paper [37], when there is some self-organized information propagation, restricted to realistic "social" constraints. Finally,no need to repeat that most of the ideas here below developed can encompass many networks, not only those formed by scientists.

2. Avalanche on Networks

2.1. Modelisation

Let a network be given and statistically characterized by a number N of nodes (also called sites) and a number L of links; as usual one call k_i the degree of the node i, i.e. the number of links attached to the node i. The network considered below is chosen to be a so called Erdös-Rényi network, i.e. each node i $(i = 1, \ldots, N)$ has a probability equal to p to be connected to another node j $(j \neq i, j = 1, \ldots, N)$. Studies on other networks are opened to further investigations.

Each site i can be considered to be an agent, e.g. a scientist or not, which has an $awareness$ a_i about an opinion; a_i is hereby taken from a uniform distribution between 0 and 1 at time t_0; this can be modified in further studies, so is the number of opinions

Suppose that there is a predefined threshold of opinion ϕ at time t_0, ($\phi = 1$, here to reduce the number of parameters in the model; this can be modified in further papers as well). When some a_i is above the threshold we consider that the site/agent spreads its *awareness* over its neighbors, as should be intuitively the case practically. Notice that in view of the hypothesis on the initial distribution of a_i 's here above, no spontaneous spreading occurs at t_0, in this paper. Some triggering is needed. Consider that due to some cause, at time t_1, a randomly chosen site has an increase of awareness such that $a_i(t_1) = a_i(t_0) + \nu$. The initial *increase of awareness* value ν could be chosen in many various ways, i.e. i and t dependent; let it be a forever constant in the present discussion. We consider that the spreading dynamics of the awareness could be restricted to a (to be decided in later variants) number n_i of nodes which have necessarily an awareness below the threshold. In the following we let n_i be all nearest neighbor nodes which are not yet aware. Some of these n_i neighbors, due to the incoming information a_i/n_i from i, may reach the awareness threshold ϕ; next, these, newly fully aware sites (agents) also spread $information$, during the same time step, again to their own neighbors which have an awareness below threshold. The process can go one and lasts until none of the newly aware neighbor sites goes above the threshold; consequently, this avalanche stops.

We define the $size$ of the (first) $avalanche$ as the number of nodes (here N_1) which have been reached by the $information$ spreading; the $duration$ of the avalanche is the number of "levels", away from the original site, i.e. n_{T_1} which has been encountered in order to reach this stop during the time step. Sometimes this avalanche size is the number of nodes N in the network; in such a case the time duration of the avalanche is T_1.

However, it is possible that the process stops even though not all nodes have been "infected" by the spreading opinion, but there is a new awareness value distribution in the network; these are new "initial conditions". We let the dynamical process repeat itself, under the same rules: one arbitrary but a *not fully aware* node i' is picked up; its awareness is increased $a_{i'}(t_{h,1}) = a_{i'}(t_{h,0}) + \nu$, for simplicity through the same ν value which led to the first triggering; we insist that we consider that the same ν value is used in order to reduce the number of parameters, but this can also be modified in further studies.

Since there is a new time origin for the subsequent process, it is useful to introduce a notation h labeling the number of times a triggering has been activated; the value $h = 2$ indicates the second sequence in time (t_2) for which there is an external (or not) $field$ (implying a ν) which modifies the opinion awareness of some site, here i'.

Thereafter, the spreading goes on again with the same rules as above up to the network is so called *fully aware*, i.e. when all nodes have $a_i \geq \phi$. In so doing one can measure for a given N, ν and p (and for this ϕ)

1. the size of each avalanche
2. the time duration of each avalanche
3. the number of times the external field is applied to one possible node before all nodes are found to be above the threshold
4. which is equivalent to ... the number of avalanches N_A before all nodes are above the threshold
5. the number of times the external field is added before an avalanche starts
6. the number of nodes still below the threshold at each time step
7. the number of hot nodes (close to threshold) at each time step.

3. Results

In order to implement the above dynamics, we have here below chosen to examine the case of a finite and fixed size random network composed of N nodes, and a connection probability p varying between 0.10 and 1.0. We have examined cases of N less than 500; it was found that the size of the system can be reduced for answering the above questions, thus allowing some shortening of the computation time. Therefore we report results for $N = 100$. We let ν varying between 0.01 and 0.15; however for reasons which will become evident, here we show only results for two cases $\nu = 0.01$ and $\nu = 0.10$. In all cases, the displayed results are obtained after averaging over 100 simulations.

In Figs. 1 and 2, we show the cumulative distribution functions (cdf) for the avalanche size, normalized to the number of links L, for each p and for two values of the external field $\nu = 0.01$ and $\nu = 0.10$. Each cdf is fitted with the corresponding cdf of a Weibull distribution that can be written

$$F(x) = 1 - e^{-(x/\alpha)^{\beta}} \tag{1}$$

The behavior of the parameters α and β as function of the connection probability p is shown in Fig. 3 for both field values. One can notice that the parameters do not depend

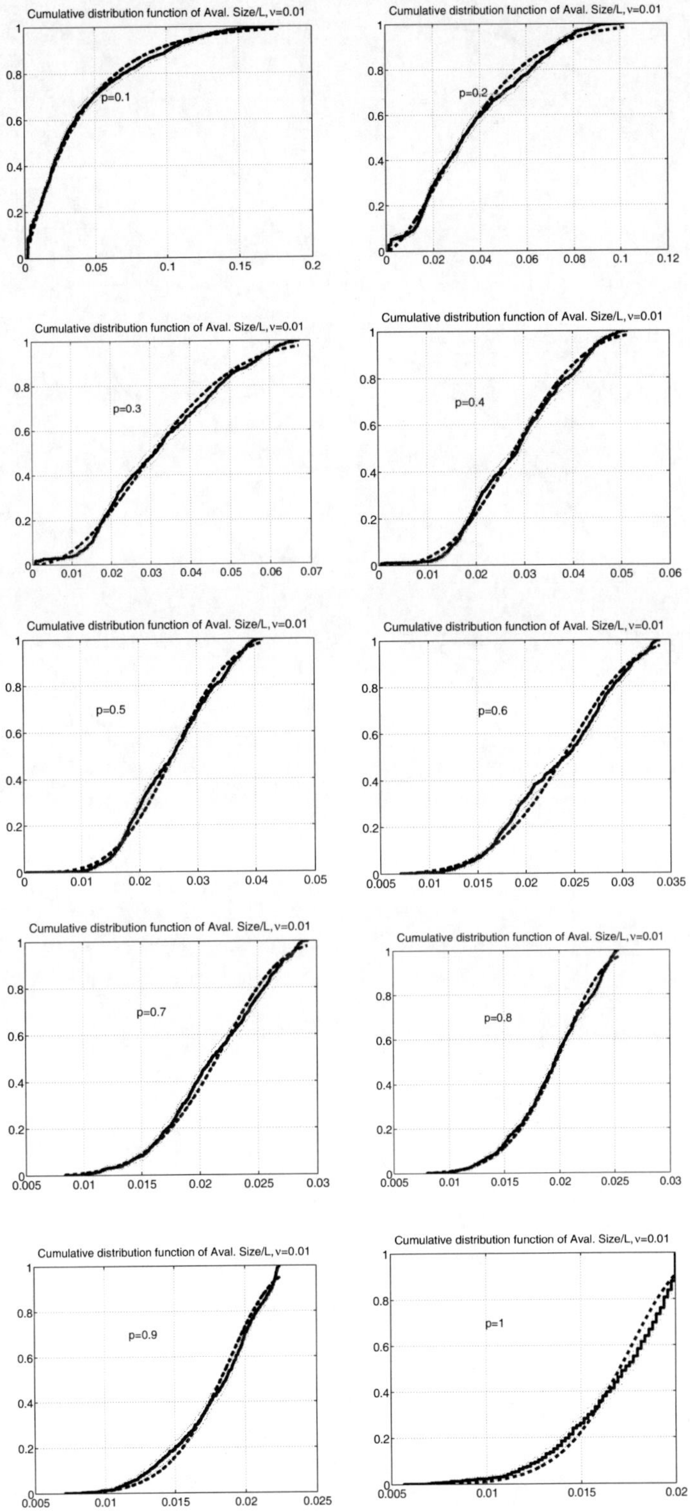

Figure 1. Cumulative distribution function of the avalanche size fitted with a Weibull distribution. In all plots $\nu = 0.01$ and for each plot the value of the connection probability p is indicated.

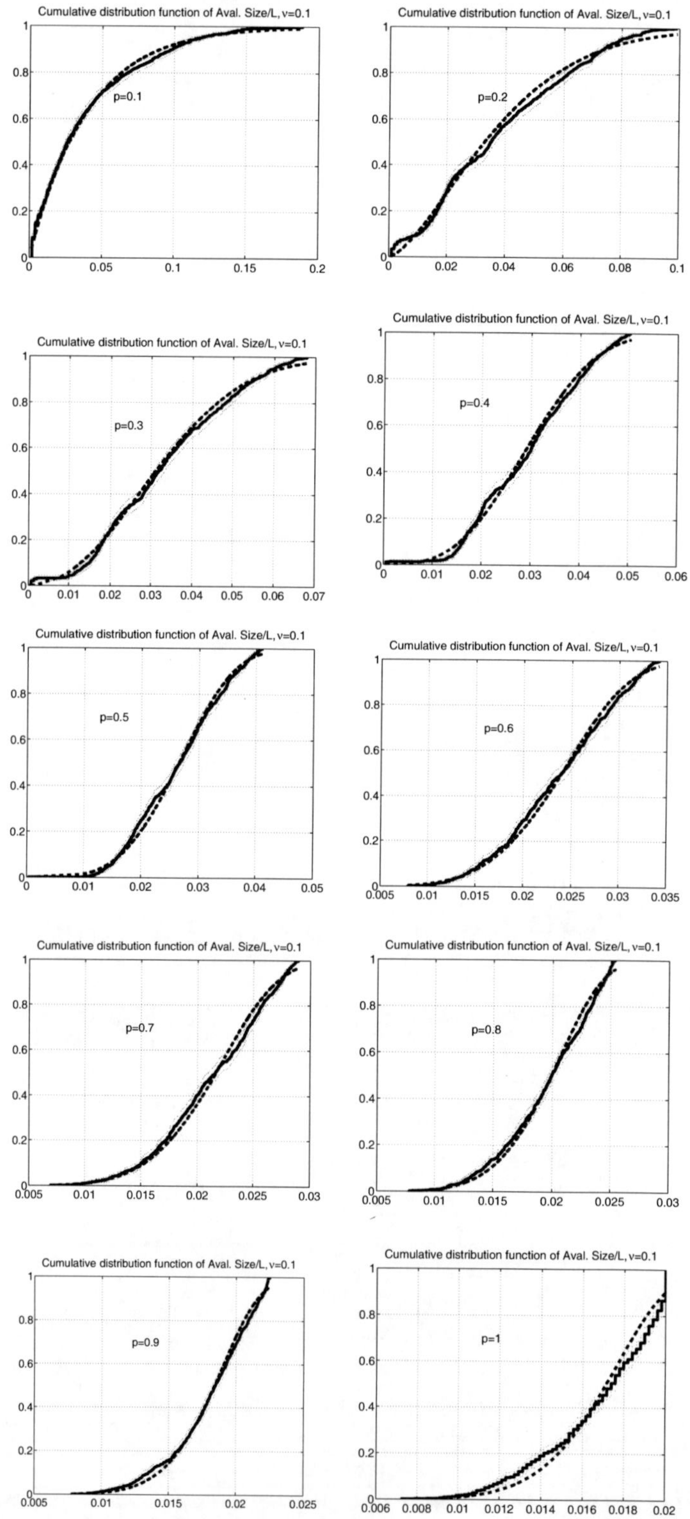

Figure 2. Cumulative distribution function of the avalanche size fitted with a Weibull distribution. In all plots $\nu = 0.10$ and for each plot the value of the connection probability p is indicated.

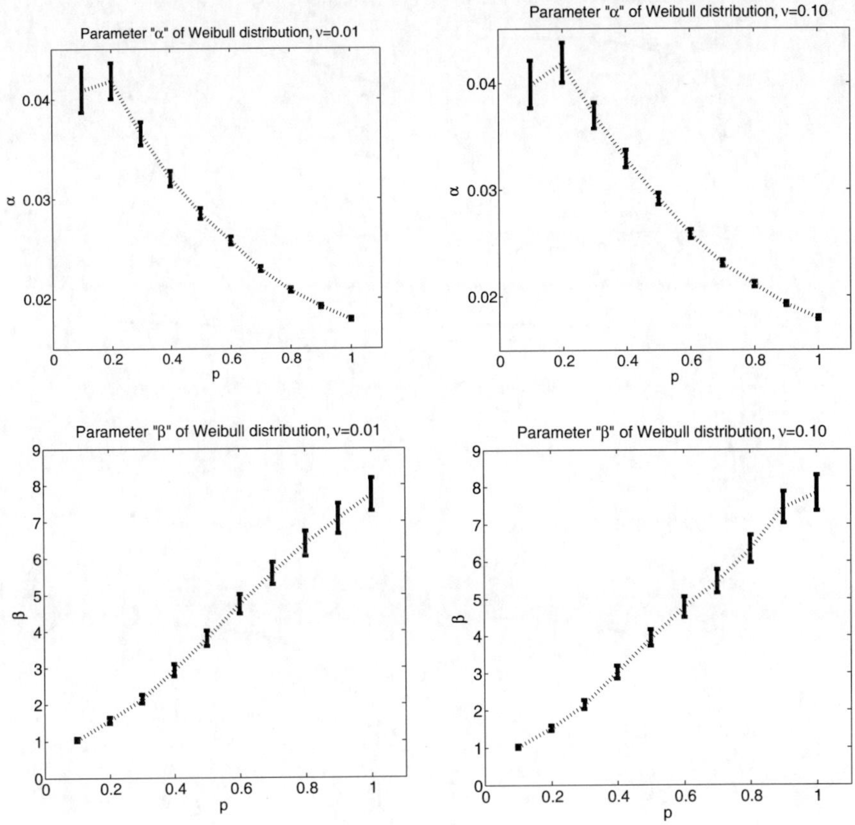

Figure 3. (a) Parameter α of the Weibull fit as a function of p for $\nu = 0.01$, (b) parameter α of the Weibull fit as a function of p for $\nu = 0.10$, (c) parameter β of the Weibull fit as a function of p for $\nu = 0.10$, (d) Parameter β of the Weibull fit as a function of p for $\nu = 0.10$; the line between data points serves only to emphasize some tendency.

on the external field value ν but only on the probability p. The percolation transition of a Erdös-Rényi network, i.e. when a connected network occurs [49] is adequately seen near $p_0 = (1/N)ln(N) \sim 0.05$.

In Figs. 4 and 5, we show the cdf of the time duration of the avalanches. Also in this case, we show the cdf for each studied p and for two values of $\nu = 0.01$ and $\nu = 0.10$. In this case, each cdf is fitted with an exponential cdf written as

$$G(x) = 1 - e^{-x/\mu}. \tag{2}$$

The behavior of the parameter μ as a function of p and for both values of ν is shown in figure 6. Also in this case there is no field dependence of the parameter μ and the dependence on p is not strong.

Furthermore, in Fig. 7, the number of avalanches N_A before all nodes are fully aware is shown as a function of p for $\nu = 0.01$ and for $\nu = 0.10$. One finds independently of ν: $N_A \simeq 8 + 0.1\ p^2$. Moreover, in order to see how long it takes before a network is fully aware it is of interest to display the number N_h of sequences (h) before all nodes

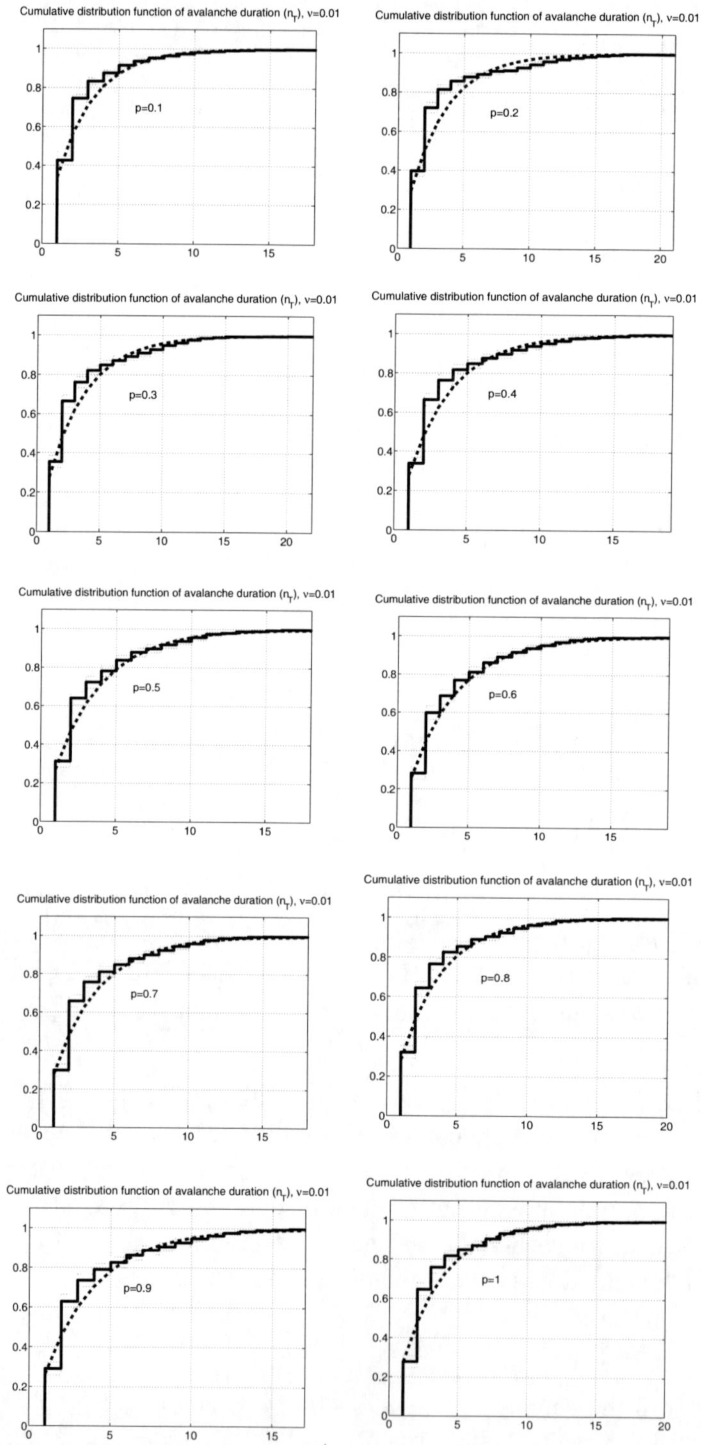

Figure 4. Cumulative distribution function of the avalanche time duration fitted with an Exponential distribution. In all plots $\nu = 0.01$ and for each plot the value of the connection probability p is indicated.

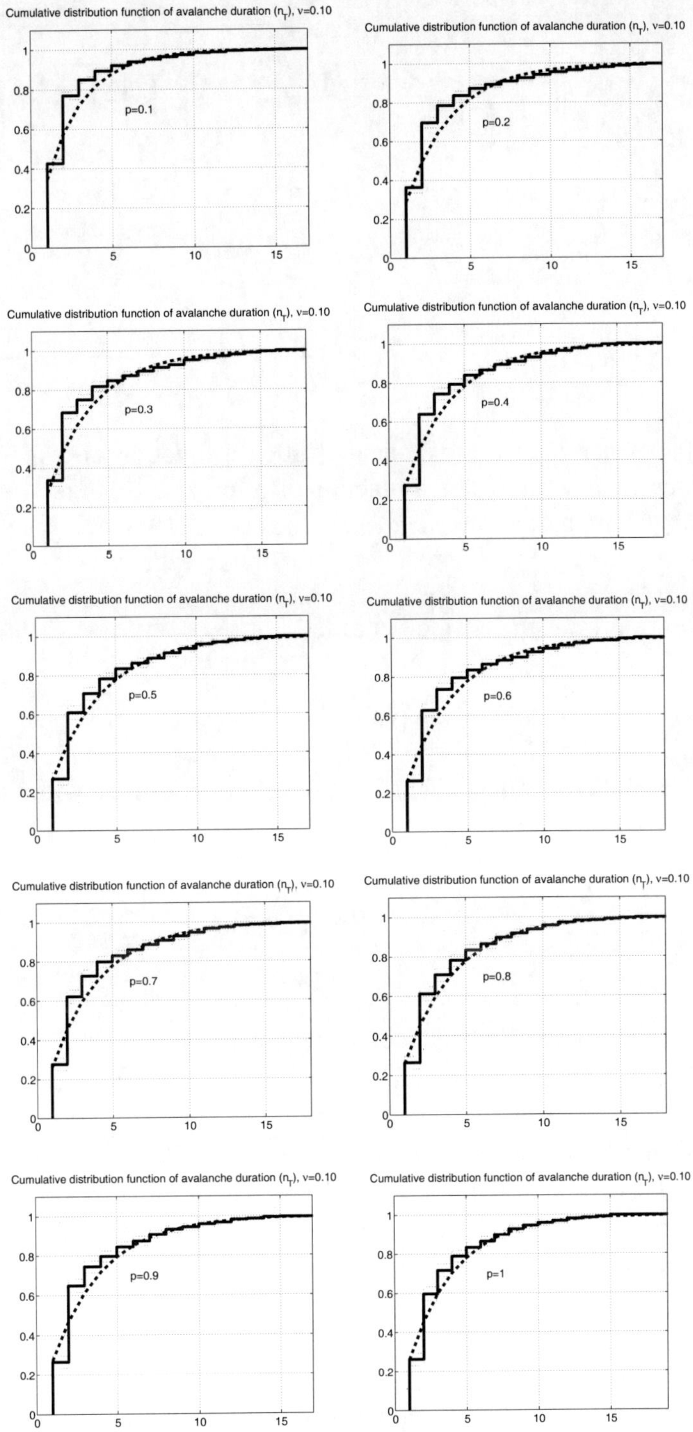

Figure 5. Cumulative distribution function of the avalanche time duration fitted with an Exponential distribution. In all plots $\nu = 0.10$ and for each plot the value of the connection probability p is indicated.

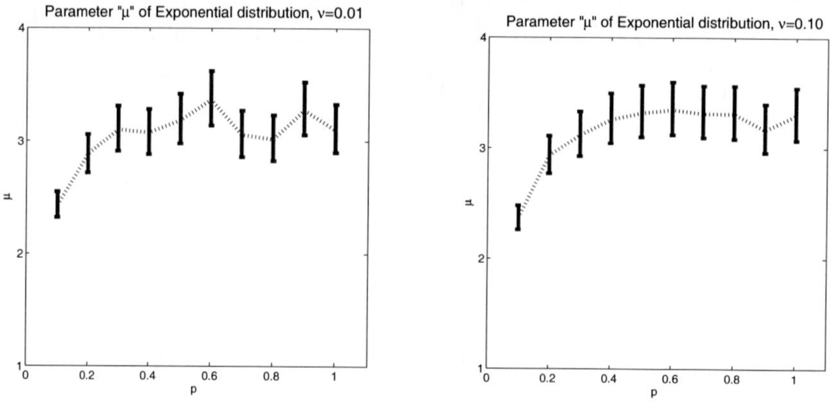

Figure 6. (a) Parameter μ of the Exponential fit as a function of p for $\nu = 0.01$; (b) parameter μ of the Exponential fit as a function of p for $\nu = 0.10$; the line between data points serves only to emphasize some tendency.

are aware as function of p; this is shown in Fig. 8 for $\nu = 0.01$ and $= 0.10$. One finds $N_h \simeq (1/\nu)(6 + 0.02p^{-5/2})$.

The number of *hot* nodes, for example with a between $\phi - 0.10\phi$ and ϕ as displayed in Figs. 9-10 as a function of h for $\nu = 0.01$ and $\nu = 0.10$ respectively. In each plot the value of the connection probability p is indicated. The curve is fitted with a three parameter logistic function written as

$$f(h) = \frac{A}{1 + B\, e^{Kh}}. \tag{3}$$

The parameters A and B are used for the fit of the logistic function. Their values (e.g. $A \sim 10$; $B \sim 0.025$) are easily understood, in view of the type of studied network.

It is interesting, as a complement to the above, to calculate the number of nodes with a still below ϕ as function of h. This is shown for both ν values In Figs. 11-12; for each plot the value of the connection probability p is indicated. The data can be fitted with a three parameter logistic function; the same K value, i.e. $K \cong 0.005$ when $\nu = 0.01$ and $K \cong 0.05$ when $\nu = 0.10$, are found for the number of hot nodes and for the number of not yet fully aware nodes. However the parameters A and B are increased by a numerical factor, i.e. to become $A \sim 100$; $B \sim 0.065$.

From the preceding illustrations, Figs. (9-12), one also observes that the (x-) "time" scale has now a different order of magnitude, as easily understood, due to the value of ν, while the y-axis scale for the number of hot nodes is an order of magnitude smaller than for the total number of not yet fully aware nodes, due to the assumed initial conditions on the a_i distribution, the type of network and the model dynamics. The important parameter for the model is K, playing the role of an inverse relaxation time, more exactly here a growth rate; we emphasize that K does not depend on the value of p, but one has a universal relation: $K = \nu/2$.

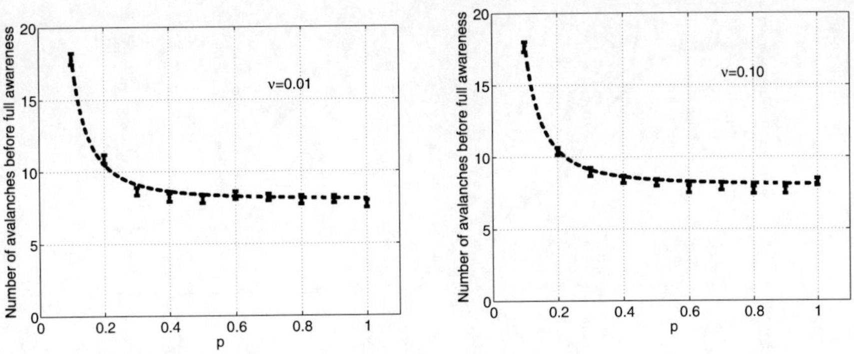

Figure 7. Number of avalanches before all nodes are aware as function of p : (a) for $\nu = 0.01$, (b) for $\nu = 0.10$; the line between data points has an analytical form given in the main text.

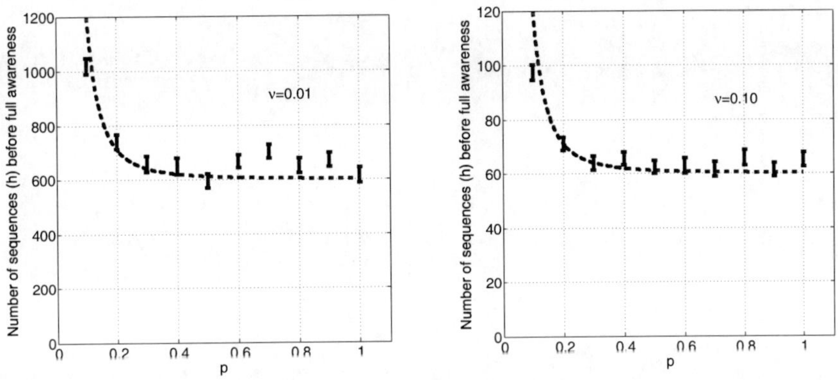

Figure 8. Number of sequences (h) before all nodes are aware as function of p: (a) for $\nu = 0.01$, (b) for $\nu = 0.10$; the line between data points has an analytical form given in the main text.

4. Discussion

According to [50], catastrophic events share characteristic nonlinear behaviors that are often generated by cross-scale interactions and feedbacks among system elements. These events result in surprises that cannot easily be predicted based on information obtained at a single scale [50]. Progress on studying catastrophic events has mainly focused on one of the following two themes or approximations: (i) nonlinear dynamics of the events through their time evolution, but without an explicit consideration of spatial connectivity [51] or (ii) spatial connectivity and the spread of contagious processes, without a consideration of cross-scale interactions and feedbacks [52].

However, is there a need to stress that the process dynamics should be correlated with the local and global structures of the network? These should result into (if possible) simple analytic laws for describing features, or through the exponents characterizing the network, if the latter belongs to the scale free category.

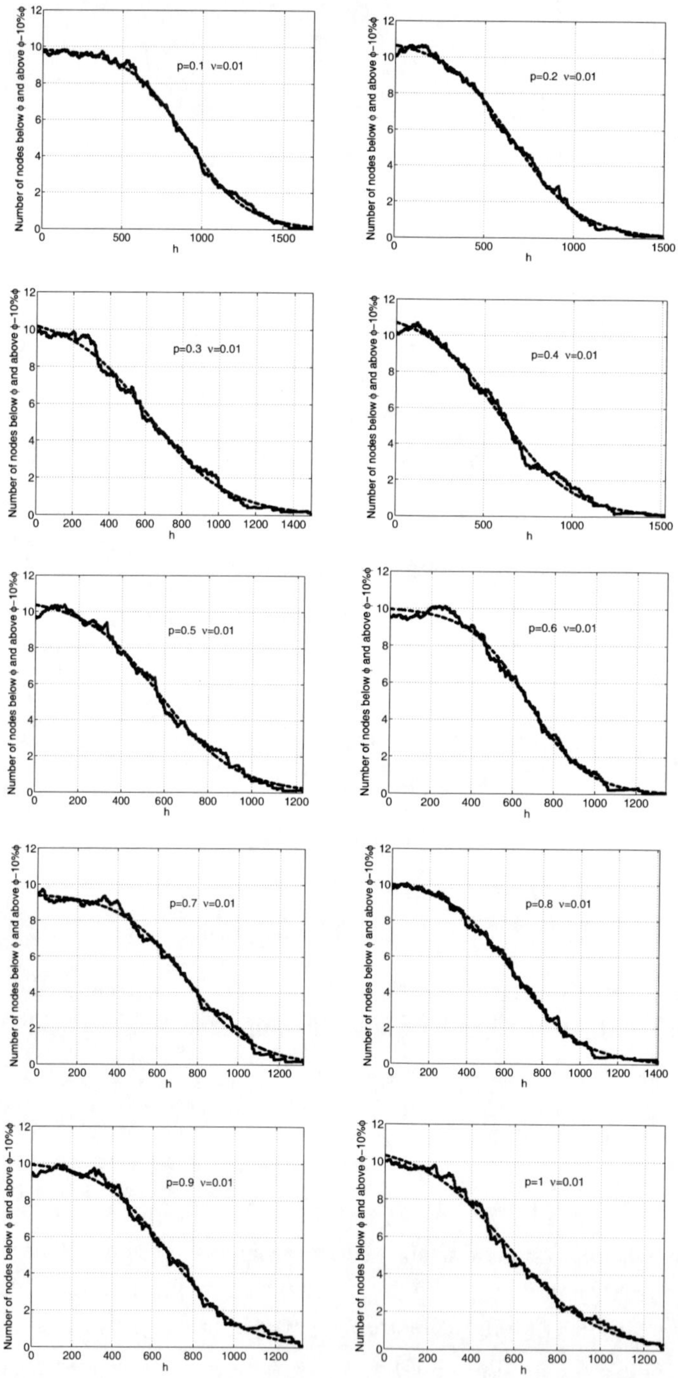

Figure 9. Number of nodes with a between $\phi - 0.10\phi$ and ϕ as function of h. In all plots $\nu = 0.01$ and for each plot the value of the connection probability p is indicated. The curve is fitted with a logistic function as explained in the text.

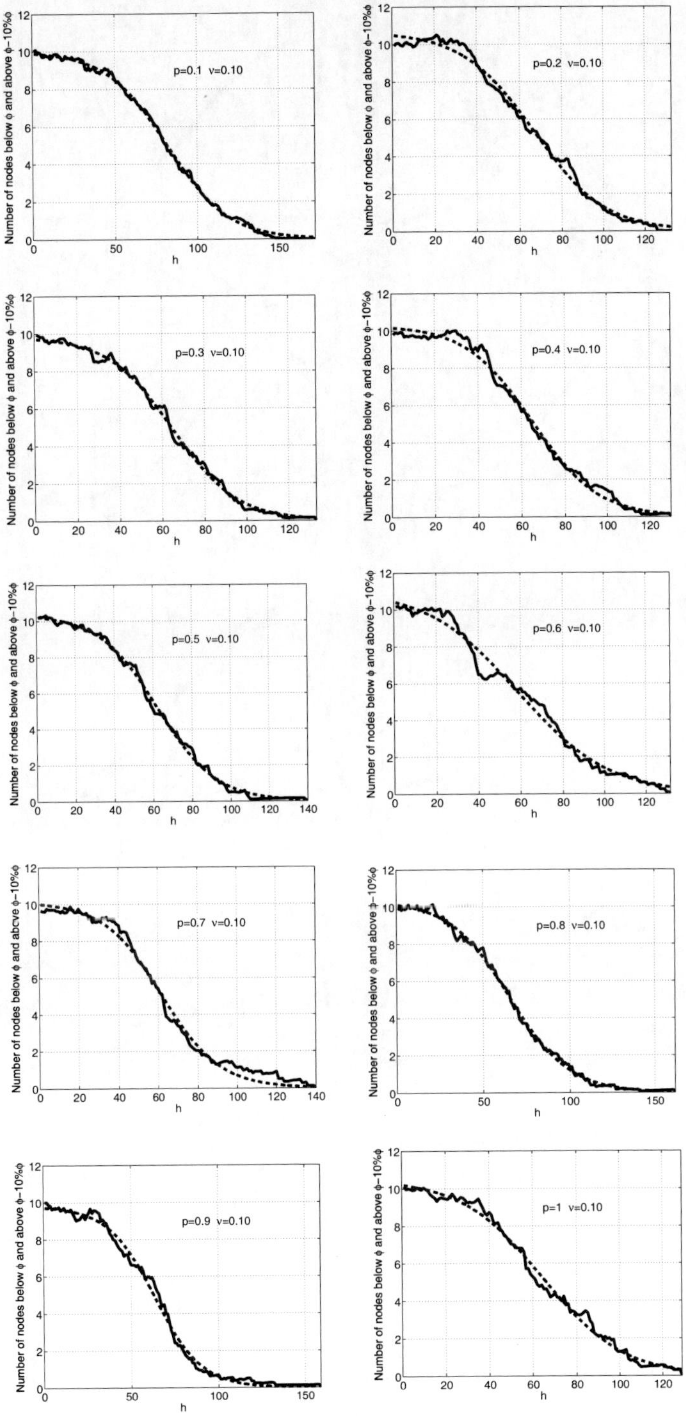

Figure 10. Number of nodes with a between $\phi - 0.10\phi$ and ϕ as function of h. In all plots $\nu = 0.10$ and for each plot the value of the connection probability p is indicated. The curve is fitted with a logistic function as explained in the text.

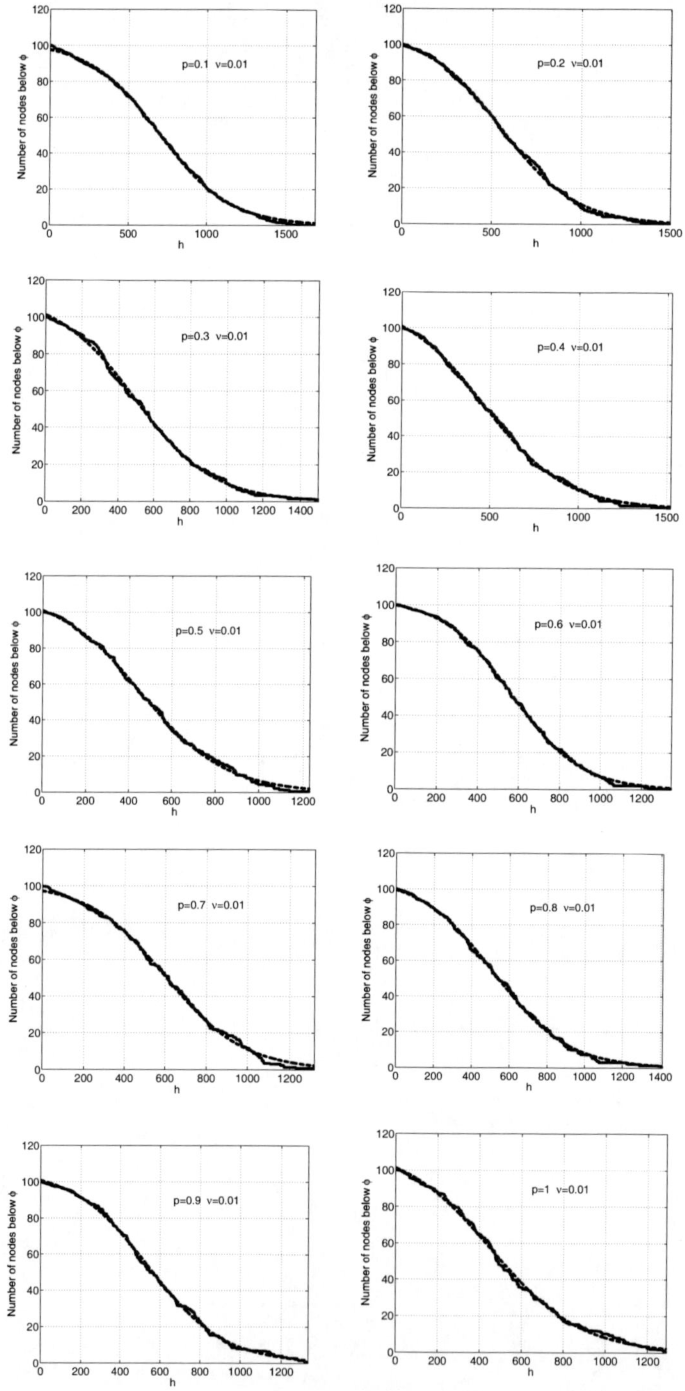

Figure 11. Number of nodes with a below ϕ as function of h. In all plots $\nu = 0.01$ and for each plot the value of the connection probability p is indicated. The curve is fitted with a logistic function as explained in the text.

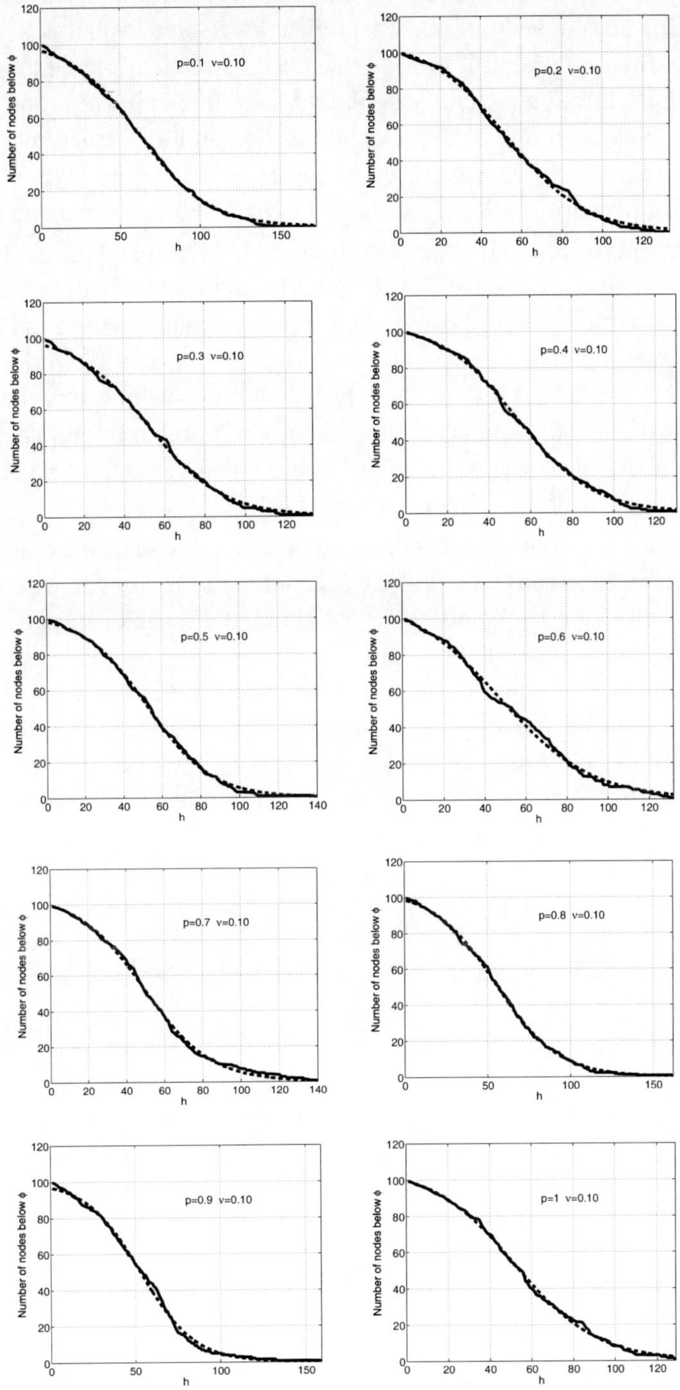

Figure 12. Number of nodes with a below ϕ as function of h. In all plots $\nu = 0.10$ and for each plot the value of the connection probability p is indicated. The curve is fitted with a logistic function as explained in the text.

In this paper, we have concentrated on a network of (scientific or more generally opinion) communication and looked into the phenomena of related avalanches. It is intuitively known that (opinions like scientific) ones occur as a avalanches spreading out of (fashion, paradigm) topics through (scientific) communities, in use of tools and instruments in scientific communities or in the sudden increase in cooperation structures (co-authorship, conferences) [17, 18]. Here, we have presented an original model implying some spreading of information after triggering and excitation of some node over an awareness threshold.

This should be put in line with considerations on driven threshold systems which are now used to model sand piles, earthquakes, magnetic depining transitions and driven foams [53], etc. usually on lattices. Indeed the model is reminiscent of the original BTW sand pile model [54, 55] as applied in recent papers on a lattice [56] or on a network [24] though the present pile toppling conditions differs from the usual ones, - which are related to the number of neighbors, usually a fixed integer. Here, the node "number of grains" is a continuous function, there is no toppling but some effect occurs when the height of the pile reaches a threshold *independent* of the number of neighbors.

On the other hand, the connectivity of a landscape can influence the dynamics of disturbances, e.g. in internet (or neural or biological) epidemics and/or fire extension problems [44]. Thus, networks indeed should be investigated. A question raised often concerns whether the spatial pattern rather than the disturbance dynamics (ordinarily) determines the total extent of a single disturbance event. We have shown that, for a Erdös-Rényi network, a fixed *a priori* disturbance perfectly scales the evolution process, in time *and* in space. We have found (non-scale free) evolution laws similar, though with different numerical exponent values, to those found in other problems, e.g. even in earthquake dynamics [53]. As an example recall, the frequency of spinodal fluctuations $n(A)$ of area A, which are realized here as clusters of excited nodes above a threshold, given by the Fisher-Stauffer relation [57],

$$n(A, \delta t) = \frac{n_0}{A^\zeta}\, exp\left[-k[K_L V \delta t]^{1/\sigma_s} A\right]. \qquad (4)$$

where the interesting exponent σ_s is the surface exponent. The exponent ζ is either τ or $\tau - 1$, in terms of the Fisher-Stauffer exponent τ which characterizes the fluctuations about the spinodal or describes the frequency of "arrested" nucleation events, respectively. Here above we find $\sigma_s = 1$, $\zeta = 0$, - somewhat unspectacular results, because of the type of network being studied [49]. We emphasize that the sequence of avalanches much varies from one simulation case to another. However the *global* dependence on p disappears following case averaging, and only the ν dependence remains in a scaling way.

Another aspect which might be also theoretically interesting is the relation between dynamic changes of the network and dynamics on the network. In science, and in many other interacting agent communities, diffusion of ideas is linked to the emergence of coalitions [58]. What predictions complex network theory can make for the coupling between epidemics, in a wide sense, on networks and the evolution of networks themselves is clearly of interest! The main challenge after this will be to make use of the various qualitative descriptions science and technology studies have produced describing such phenomena and to re-consider them in the light of complex network research, - through the parameters and variants that we have indicated. At this time, the results seem qualitatively sound.

Acknowledgments

The authors would like to thank European Commission Project CREEN FP6-2003-NEST-Path-012864 (CREEN: Critical Events on Evolving Networks) and European Commission Project E2C2 FP6-2003-NEST-Path-012975 (E2C2: Extreme Events: Causes and Consequences) for support. MA contribution is also part of scientific activities in COST Action TD1210, Analyzing the dynamics of information and knowledge landscapes - KNOWeSCAPE. Comments by D. Stauffer are also much recognized.

References

[1] L. Euler, Solutio problematis ad geometriam situs pertinentis, *Commetarii Academiae Scientiarum Imperialis Petropolitanae* 8, 128 (1736).

[2] N. L. Biggs, E. K. Lloyd, and R. J. Wilson, *Graph Theory* 1736-1936. (Oxford University Press, Oxford, 1976).

[3] $http://www.math.fau.edu/locke/GRAPHTHE.HTM$.

[4] A.-L. Barabási, *Linked: How Everything Is Connected to Everything Else and What It Means* (Perseus, Cambridge, 2002).

[5] R. Pastor-Satorras and A. Vespignani, *Evolution and Structure of the Internet: A Statistical Physics Approach*, (Cambridge University Press, Cambridge, 2004).

[6] R. Pastor-Satorras, M. Rubi, and A. Diaz-Guilera, *Statistical Mechanics of Complex Networks*, in *Lect. Notes Phys.*, Vol. 625 (Springer, Berlin, 2003).

[7] P. Erdös and A. Rényi *Publications Mathematicae* 6, 290 (1959).

[8] R. Albert and A.-L. Barabási, *Rev. Mod. Phys.* 74, 47 (2002).

[9] B. A. Huberman and L. A. Adamic, *Nature* 401, 131 (1999).

[10] M. E. J. Newman, *Proc. Natl. Acad. Sci. USA*, 98, 404 (2001).

[11] M. E. J. Newman, *Phys. Rev. E* 64, 016131 (2001).

[12] M. E. J. Newman, *Phys. Rev. E* 64, 016132 (2001).

[13] M. E. J. Newman, *SIAM Review* 45, 167 (2003).

[14] A.-L. Barabási, H. Jeog, Z. Néda, E. Ravasz, A. Schubert, and T. Vicsek, *Physica A* 311, 590 (2002).

[15] I. Hellsten, R. Lambiotte, A. Scharnhorst, and M. Ausloos, *Scientometrics* 72, 469 (2007).

[16] S. Redner, *Eur. Phys. J. B* 4, 131 (1998).

[17] R. Lambiotte and M. Ausloos, *Phys. Rev. E* 72, 066117 (2005).

[18] R. Lambiotte and M. Ausloos, *Eur. Phys. J. B* 50, 183 (2006).

[19] A. P. Masucci and G. J. Rodgers, *Phys. Rev. E* 74, 026102 (2006).

[20] M. Gligor and M. Ausloos, *Eur. Phys. J. B* 57, 139 (2007).

[21] M. Ausloos and R. Lambiotte, *Physica A* 382, 16 (2007).

[22] T. Di Matteo, T. Aste, and M. Gallegati, *Eur. Phys. J. B* 47, 459 (2005).

[23] P. Fronczak, A. Fronczak, and J. A. Hołyst, *Eur. Phys. J. B* 59, 133 (2007).

[24] P. Fronczak, A. Fronczak, and J. A. Hołyst, *Phys. Rev. E* 73, 046117 (2006).

[25] R. Lambiotte and M. Ausloos, *Phys. Rev. E* 72, 066117 (2005).

[26] S. Galam, *Eur. Phys. J. B* 25, 403 (2002).

[27] S. Galam, *Europhys. Lett.* 70, 705 (2005).

[28] S. Galam, *Int. J. Mod. Phys. C* 19, 409 (2008).

[29] S. Galam, *Sociophysics: a physicist's modeling of psycho-political phenomena*, (Springer, Berlin-Heidelberg, 2012).

[30] K. Sznajd-Weron and J. Sznajd, *Int. J. Mod. Phys. C* 11, 1157 (2000).

[31] D. Stauffer, *J. Artif. Soc. Soc. Simul.* 5, No.1, paper 4 (2002) = $http://jasss.soc.surrey.ac.uk/5/1/4.html$.

[32] D. Stauffer, *Comp. Phys. Comm.* 146, 93 (2001).

[33] A. Pekalski, *Comput. Sci. Eng.* 6, 62 (2004).

[34] G. Bianconi and M. Marsili, *Phys. Rev. E* 70, 035105(R) (2004).

[35] E. Bruckner, W. Ebeling, and A. Scharnhorst, *Scientometrics* 18, 21 (1990).

[36] R. Pastor-Satorras and A. Vespignani, *Phys. Rev. Lett.* 86, 3200 (2001).

[37] M. Boguna and R. Pastor-Satorras, *Phys. Rev. E* 66, 047104 (2002).

[38] M. Boguna, R. Pastor-Satorras, and A. Vespignani, *Phys. Rev. Lett.* 90, 028701 (2003).

[39] J. A. Hołyst, K. Kacperski, and F. Schweitzer, *Ann. Rev. Comput. Phys.* 9, 253 (2001).

[40] D. Chowdhury and D. Stauffer, *Principles of Equilibrium Statistical Mechanics*, (Wilkey-VCH, Weinheim, 2000).

[41] J. A. M. S. Duarte, in *Ann. Rev. Comput. Phys.*, (ed. by D. Stauffer, World Scientific Singapore), V, 1 (1997).

[42] G. L. W. Perry, *Progr. Phys. Geogr.* 22, 222 (1998).

[43] D. L. Turcotte, B. D. Malamud, F. Guzzetti, and P. Reichenbach, *Proc. Natl. Acad. Sci. U.S.A* 99, 2530 (2002).

[44] C. Miller and D. L. Urban, *Landscape Ecology* 15, 145 (2000).

[45] B. D. Malamud, D. L. Turcotte, F. Guzzettic, and P. Reichenbach, *Earth Planet. Sci. Lett.* 229, 45 (2004).

[46] B. D. Malamud, D. L. Turcotte, F. Guzzetti, and P. Reichenbach, *Earth Surf. Process. Landf.* 29, 687 (2004).

[47] E. Piegari, V. Cataudella, R. Di Maio, L. Milano, and M. Nicodemi, *Geophys. Res. Lett.* 33, L01403 (2006).

[48] E. Piegari, V. Cataudella, R. Di Maio, L. Milano, and M. Nicodemi, *Phys. Rev. E* 73, 026123 (2006).

[49] T. Luczac, *Random Struct. Algor.* 1, 287 (1990).

[50] D. P. C. Peters, R. A. Pielke, Sr., B. T. Bestelmeyer, C. D. Allen, S. Munson-McGee, and K. M. Havstad, *Proc. Natl. Acad. Sci. U.S.A* 101, 15130 (2004).

[51] C. S. Holling, *Ecol. Monogr.* 62, 447(1992).

[52] N. Zeng, J. D. Neeling, L. M. Lau, and C. J. Tucker, *Science* 286, 1537 (1999).

[53] J. B. Rundle, W. Klein, S. Gross, and C. D. Ferguson, *Phys. Rev. E* 56, 293 (1997).

[54] P. Bak, C. Tang, and K. Wiesenfeld, *Phys. Rev. Lett.* 59, 381 (1987).

[55] P. Bak, C. Tang, and K. Wiesenfeld, *Phys. Rev. A* 38, 364 (1988).

[56] Z. Koza and M. Ausloos, *Physica A* 375, 199 (2007).

[57] D. Stauffer and A. Aharony, *Introduction to Percolation Theory* (Taylor and Francis, London, 1991).

[58] M. Ausloos and R. Lambiotte, *Eur. Phys. J. B* 57, 89 (2007).

In: Stock Markets
Editors: F. Petroni, F. Prattico and G. D'Amico

ISBN: 978-1-62808-751-2

Chapter 6

INTERNATIONAL DEPENDENCE STRUCTURE: EVIDENCE FROM ASIA AMID THE US MORTGAGE CRISIS

***Cuong Nguyen*[1,*], *Thang Nguyen*[2], *Baiding Hu*[1] *and Christopher Gan*[1]**

[1]Department of Accounting, Economics and Finance,
Lincoln University, New Zealand
[2]Faculty of Economics, National Economics University
of Vietnam, Vietnam

ABSTRACT

It is evident that the 2008-US sub-prime mortgage crisis broadly affected international financial markets. However, how the crisis's magnitude impacted on Asian financial markets has not had much attention. To fill this gap, this chapter examines changes in dependence structures between the US market and Asian financial markets before and after the crisis. The chapter uses two non-parametric methods of plotting, namely, Chi-plot and Kendall-plot, and a copula analysis to characterise the changes. The results show that the dependence structure of the U.S. stock market and the stock markets of Hong Kong, Indonesia, Singapore and Thailand changed to the left tail dependence after the crisis. In contrast, no changes in the dependence structure are found between the US market and the markets of Japan, Malaysia and the Philippines.The chapter's findings on the dependence changes, which have not previously been documented, provide important implications for risk management, hedging strategies and asset pricing.

Keywords: copula, Chi-plot, financial crisis, K-plot, Stock market

---

* Corresponding author's Email: Cuong.Nguyen@lincoln.ac.nz, Ph: +64 3 4230245

INTRODUCTION

It is evident that the 2008-US sub-prime mortgage crisis broadly affected international financial markets. However, how the crisis's magnitude impacted on Asian financial markets has had much attention. To fill this gap in literature, this chapter examines changes in dependence structures between the US market and Asian financial markets before and after the crisis.

There are several methods to detect co-movement between variables, such as the cointegration test or Dynamic Conditional Correlation-Generalised Autoregressive Conditional Heteroscedasticity (DCC-GARCH) models. However, with our interest in dependence structures, we use two non-parametric methods of plotting, namely, the K-plot and Chi-plot, and a copula analysis to characterise the changes in dependence between stock markets. Dependence structure will tell us whether two markets are likely to crash or boom together, which is left tail or right tail dependence, respectively.

Using the copula method has several advantages in modelling dependence. First, copula functions are very flexible in modelling dependence since they are able to separate model marginals and the corresponding dependence structure. Second, copula functions enable us to directly model tail dependence and tell us not only the degree but also the structure of the dependence. Third, copula functions are invariant under transformations of the data but linear correlation is not. The plot methods will act as detection methods for capturing the dependence structure between markets. The non-parametric methods of plotting also visualize the dependence, especially the tail dependence.Therefore, the flexibility in model specification allows us to fully detect and characterise changes in dependence between international financial markets.

The remainder of this chapter is organized as follows. The next section contains a literature review of co-movement between stock markets, followed by a section on the methods used, Chi-plot, K-plot and copula. The data and results are then presented and the conclusion ends the chapter.

LITERATURE REVIEW

The aim of the review is to provide an overview of modelling techniques used to characterise and measure co-movements and dependence structures while summarising related empirical evidence.

Co-movements among international financial markets have attracted a lot of attention since the US subprime housing loans led to a worldwide financial crisis in 2008. Various analytical tools have been employed to characterise financial market co-movements and dependence. These tools include cointegration tests, Granger causality tests, Dynamic Conditional Correlation-Generalised Autoregressive Conditional Heteroscedasticity (DCC-GARCH) models, copula and waverlet functions, and factor and principal component analyses. Because of the variety of the analytical tools used, the meaning of co-movements and dependence varies between studies.

Cointegration analysis aims to detect a long-run equilibrium relationship between two markets. In other words, the two markets are deemed to move together in the long-run if their stock indices never drift too far apart. Clearly, cointegrated stock markets imply dependence between them. The work of Gupta and Guidi (2012) employed three types of cointegration tests, namely, the Engle-Granger test, the Johassen test and the Gregory and Hansen test to measure co-movements and dependence between Indian and Asian developed markets using daily data from 31 August 1999 to 17 June 2009. Pairwise, they found that there was no evidence of cointegration between the Indian and any of the other stock markets, suggesting that, in the long-run, stock returns in the Indian market are independent of the returns in the developed markets. The authors argued that such evidence offered investors the information that a diversification of investment could be achieved by splitting the investment between the Indian market and the developed markets. The cointegration testing approach was also used to examine co-movements between the Shanghai Composite Index (SCI) and daily exchange rate of RMB/USD in Liu and Wan (2012). The result was a lack of evidence of co-movement between the two markets.

Testing a co-integration relationship based on a contemporaneous relationship between the time series is considered traditional co-integration analysis. The study by Nieh et al. (2012) was prompted by evidence produced by traditional co-integration analysis that there was no co-movement between the U.S. and Asian markets and China and the Asian markets. The authors found it hard to reconcile the lack of co-movement evidence with the correlation analysis of return and correlation analysis of volatility of return, all of which pointed to an increase in the correlation coefficients of return and correlation coefficients of volatility of returns for those markets. Recognising the possibility of market co-integration asymmetrically, that is, one market co-moves asynchronously with another, Nieh et al. (2012) applied the Enders-Siklos asymmetric threshold co-integration model to a sample of daily data from 2 January 2004 through 31 March 2010, and found co-integration relationships existed between the markets. More specifically, they found that there were significant increases in correlation coefficients of returns between U.S. and Asian markets and between China and the Asian markets. There were asymmetric co-integration relationships between U.S. and Asian markets (except the China market) before the crisis but China had no co-integration relationship with the Asian markets. During the crisis, the asymmetric co-integration relationship between U.S. and Asian markets increased and an asymmetric co-integration relationship between China and the Asian markets appeared.

Though the notion of co-integration has been used to capture co-movement, the "close-ness" between co-integrated stock returns had seemed unattended until the study by Lee et al. (2012). The "close-ness" of a co-integration relationship is measured by the variance of the residual series or the linear combination of the co-integrated series. Such a measure provides extra information enabling differentiation between co-integration relationships rather than just the dichotomy of either co-integration or not. Their findings suggest that although the common impressions of investors were that the stock markets of the U.S. and Taiwan were strongly linked, there existed a closer relationship between Taiwan and Hong Kong than between Taiwan and other countries for the sample period 1 January 1992 to 31 December 2007, covering the 1997 Asian Financial Crisis.

Another way to assess the varying extent of co-movement is presented by Lin (2012) who examined the co-movement between exchange rates, stock prices, interest rates and foreign reserves in six Asian emerging countries, India, Indonesia, Korea, the Philippines, Taiwan and Thailand from January 1986 to December 2010. The study found that co-integration between the exchange rates, stock prices, interest rates and foreign was significant in four and one of the six countries during the Asian financial crisis and the recent global financial crisis, respectively. This compares with no significant relationship during other or tranquil periods. The evidence based on co-integration analysis is also supported by the results of Granger causality tests in thatthe more significant outcomes of testing were during the crises.

Though co-integration analysis and Granger causality tests shed light on market co-movements, they are limited in indicating how likely the markets, typically stock markets, are going to boom or crash together. A measure of this particular type of market dependence is the copula of the stock returns, which is a distribution function of the individual distribution functions of the stock returns. Specifically, the copula measures the correlation between two series by giving different weights to different parts of the joint distribution depending on the degree of variation. For example, it gives unequal weights to positive and negative returns as well as large and small realizations. This contrasts with conventional correlation coefficients, such as the Pearson correlation coefficient, which gives the same weight to every part of the joint distribution since it relies only on the marginal distributions. Sklar's theorem shows that the joint probability distribution of random variables can be expressed as a copula, which is a function of the marginal distributions of the random variables. A number of functional forms have been used for the copula, for example, Gaussian, Clayton, Gumbel, and symmetrized Joe-Clayton, to name a few.

Fitting five different copulas to stock return data from several countries, Luo et al. (2011) investigate the effect of the open policy introduced in 2002 to allow foreigners to invest in the Chinese 'A' share market in the Chinese domestic capital market, especially on the dependence between the financial index returns of the 'A' shares and those of some emerging markets, specifically Hong Kong, Singapore, Thailand, Korea and Taiwan, as well as the developed markets U.S., Japan and Australia. Like model selection, the authors used the information criteria, AIC and BIC, to select the best copula functional form for each market pair, which resulted in three different copulas selected with the Clayton copula suitable for most market pairs. The copula modelling results are consistent with those of nonparametric plots in that evidence of weak dependence in these markets before the introduction of the open policy, except for the U.S. and Japan, and the tail dependence is non-significant for all country pairs. These dependence structures are adequately captured by Clayton and normal copula models. On the other hand, in the period 2002–2009, there is significant dependence in all but the Korean market, as indicated by the symmetric Joe-Clayton, Clayton and rotated Gumbel copula models. Further, a significant lower tail dependence of the 'A' shares with other markets was found, except for the U.S., Japan and Korea, which indicates that the financial sectors returns in these five paired markets move downwards together. These findings have implications for international portfolio diversification and financial market participants.

Wang et al. (2013) develop a dependence-switching copula model based on the switching regime incorporating a two-state Markov chain variable in the copula density function. The study examined dependence and tail dependence for four different market statuses, namely, rising-stocks/appreciating-currency, falling-stocks/depreciating-currency, rising-stocks/depreciating-currency, and falling-stocks/appreciating-currency. The model was applied to daily stock and foreign-exchange returns for six major industrial countries from 1990–2010. The dependence and tail dependence among the above four market statuses were asymmetric; for most countries, in the negative correlation regime, but symmetric in the positive correlation regime. These results suggest that analyzing cross-market dependence based on a time-invariant copula may not provide the whole picture.

Chang and Hsueh (2013) examined the dynamic dependence between real estate and stock markets of six emerging countries in Asia, Taiwan, India, Indonesia, Thailand, Malaysia, and Philippines. They considered four different copulas, namely, Gaussian, Clayton, Gumbel and symmetrized Joe-Clayton (SJC) copulas to identify the types of dependency structures between real estate and stock markets. Their main finding is the existence of extreme co-movements and tail dependence between the real estate and stock markets. The extreme co-movements are symmetric, implying both markets boom and crash together in Indonesia, Malaysia, the Philippines, Thailand and Taiwan. In India, the real estate and stock markets are under high downturn risk exposure because the lower tail dependence is much higher than the upper tail dependence. The dynamic dependence between real estate and stock markets is crucial in identifying the optimal portfolio for investors. Of the four copulas, the Gaussian copula can capture the dependence between real estate and stock markets in Indonesia, Malaysia, the Philippines and Taiwan very well both under constant and time-varying conditions. The SJC copula is the best fitting dependence structure for the series pairs in Thailand and the U.S. both under constant and time-varying conditions, and for the series pair in India under constant conditions. The Clayton copula is the best fitting dependence structure for the series pair in India under time-varying conditions.

A non-parametric alternative to the parametric methods is wavelet analysis. With wavelet analysis, a non-stationary time-series can be decomposed into frequency components; the Fourier analysis is capable only of decomposing and representing a stationary time-series. Wavelets conserve the time-localized information and, therefore, enable the measurement of co-movement in the time-frequency space, which provides a richer analysis of co-movement. Once the wavelets are constructed, one can calculate the wavelet squared coherency, analogous to R-squared in linear regression models, to measure co-movements. Applying wavelet squared coherency methodology to examine the co-movement of stock markets is advantageous since it offers a refinement in analysis. That is, it allows for both time and frequency domains to be simultaneously considered in a single framework to examine the co-movement of financial time series. The methodology concurrently enables the assessment of the impact of investment horizon. From a risk management viewpoint, short term (long-term) investors are more interested in return fluctuations at higher (lower) frequencies.

Rua and Nunes (2009) focused on financial market co-movements among Germany, Japan, UK and U.S.; the analysis was done at both aggregate and sectorial levels. The data cover January 1973 to December 2007, comprising 420 monthly observations. A finding of that paper is that the strength of the co-movement of international stock returns depends on the frequency; co-movement between markets was stronger at lower frequencies suggesting that the benefits from international diversification may be relatively less important in the long-term than in the short-term. It also found stronger co-movement at higher frequencies between the U.S. and UK markets around the 1987 crash and the end-of-the-century technological bubble, which are clearly of a distinct transitory nature.

Kiviaho et al. (2012) examine the co-movement of European frontier stock markets with the U.S. and developed markets in Europe. Based on the computed wavelet squared coherency, they found that the strength of co-movement varied considerably across frontier markets, at different frequencies (time horizons) and over time. Co-movement was relatively weaker for the frontier markets of Central and Southeastern Europe than in the Baltic region.

Of the markets examined, Slovakia, in particular, showed low dependence, whereas Lithuania seemed the most dependent market. Co-movement was stronger at lower frequencies (longer horizons) and increased during the turbulent period of the global financial crisis of 2008/2009. This particular finding suggests that the benefits of international portfolio diversification in the European frontier markets may be more significant in the short-term than the long-term.

A larger scale study on the co-movement between establishing markets and the U.S. market can be found in Graham et al. (2012), which investigates the integration of 22 emerging stock markets with the U.S. market. They found a high degree of co-movement at relatively lower frequencies between the U.S. and the 22 individual emerging markets. The results showed that the strength of co-movement, however, differed by country. For example, a high degree of co-movement between the U.S. and Brazil, Mexico and Korea was found, but a low co-movement for Egypt and Morocco. The results also revealed a change in the general pattern of the market relationship after 2006;co-movements at relatively higher frequencies emerged. Co-movement at the highest frequencies was, however, weak for fluctuations with aduration less than a year, which implies that investing selectively in emerging markets may provide significant diversification benefits. A recommendation for U.S. investors was that it would be beneficial for them to invest in emerging markets, especially for short-term investment horizons. Although some recent studies suggest that co-movement in global equity markets may have increased over time, some short-term diversification benefits were still apparent. A study by Graham et al. (2013) examines the co-movement of selected Middle East and North African (MENA) stock markets with the U.S. stock market and the regional co-movement among these markets from June 2002 to June 2010. They applied the analysis of wavelet squared coherency with simulated confidence bounds. The methodology enabled simultaneous assessment of short and long term stock market co-movement and detecteda change in market relationships over time. The evidence suggests a modest degree of co-movement of stock returns between the S&P 500 and MENA stock markets at higher frequencies, implying enhanced short term diversification gains. Dependencies on the U.S. stock market intensify toward the end of the stock return series, supporting the increasing trend toward international capital market co-movement. The evidence also shows a relatively high degree of co-movement among stock markets in the MENA region at lower frequencies across the entire sample; these dependencies increased toward the end of the sample period.

Apart from the discussed modelling techniques, it is worth mentioning that graphical methods, dynamic conditional correlation coefficients coupled with GARCH, and factor analysis were also used by analysts to investigate market co-movements. For example, in the study by Luo et al. (2011) both the Chi-plot and Kendall-plot were used to supplement the copula modelling exercises. The study by Arouri et al. (2010) analyzed the time variations in the co-movements of Latin American stock markets. Conditional correlations were estimated from the dynamic conditional correlation GARCH model. They concluded that the degree of cross-market co-movements changed over time and significantly increased since 1994. However, room for international diversification still remains largely possible. Second, co-movements are subjected to various regime shifts, essentially due to major economic events. Finally, stock markets move much more together in crises.

Harrison and Moore (2010) investigate co-movement in five Caribbean stock markets (Barbados, Jamaica and Trinidad and Tobago, The Bahamas and Guyana) using common factor analysis. The common factors were obtained using principal component analysis and, therefore, accounted for the maximum portion of the variance present in the stock exchanges investigated. The authors break the analysisdown and test for co-movement in different periods to ascertain any changes that have taken place from one period to the next. In particular they examine 10-year, 5-year and 3-year periods. In addition, they also specified a vector autoregressive model to test for co-movement between the five markets during 1990-2008 through examining the impulse response functions. Both types of test failed to find any evidence of co-movement between the exchanges over the sample period. However, some evidence of periodic co-movement, particularly between exchanges in Barbados, Jamaica and Trinidad and Tobago emerged.

No study has examined changes in dependence structure between the U.S. stock market and Asian stock markets using the up-to-date copula method. Hence, the aim of this chapter is to investigate whether dependence changes after the U.S. sub-mortgage crisis in 2008. The chapter divides the data into two sub-groups, before and after the crisis. The non-parametric methods of plotting are used to visualize the dependence structure and copula functions are applied to capture the structure changes between stock markets, if any. The results present significant implications for risk managers, investors or hedging strategists in making international investment decisions.

METHODS

We use the non-parametric methods of Chi-plots and Kendall (K)-plots to find the dependence structure between markets. Three copulas, Gumbel, Clayton and Normal, will be used to assessthe structure. The brief theory is as follows.

1. Non-Parametric Methods

Chi-Plot

The chi-plot proposed by Fisher and Switzer (1985, 2001) can be used to detect the presence and the pattern of dependence between two variables, if any exists. Let $(x_1; y_1)$, …, $(x_n; y_n)$ be a random sample from H (Equation (1) below), the joint continuous distribution function for a pair of random variables (X,Y), and let I(A) be the indicator function of the event A. For each data point $(x_i; y_i)$, then:

$$H_i = \sum_{j \neq i} I(x_j \leq x_i, y_j \leq y_i)/(n-1)$$
$$F_i = \sum_{j \neq i} I(x_j \leq x_i)/(n-1), G_i = \sum_{j \neq i} I(y_j \leq y_i)/(n-1), \quad (1)$$

where the indicator function I(.) is defined as 1 if the event A occurs and 0 otherwise, and

$$S_i = sign\{(F_i - \frac{1}{2})(G_i - \frac{1}{2})\}$$

and

$$\chi_i = (H_i - F_i.G_i) / \{F_i(1 - F_i)G_i(1 - G_i)\}^{1/2}$$

$$\lambda_i = 4S_i \max\{(F_i - \frac{1}{2})^2 (G_i - \frac{1}{2})^2\}$$

The Chi-plot is a scatter plot of the pairs (λ_i, χ_i) within the rectangle [-1,1]x[-1,1]. The Chi-plot is uniquely determined by the copula of the joint distribution. However, it is helpful to introduce the Chi-plot with a pseudo-confidence limit base at $\chi = \pm c_p / n^{1/2}$, where c_p is determined by Monte Carlo simulations in such a way that approximately p x 100% of the pairs (λ_i, χ_i) lie between the lines. In this way, if there is no relationship between the variables, approximately 95% of the χ_i values should be plotted between the two control lines, and when the association is increased, values of χ_i move away towards the bivariate median.

Kendall-Plot

The Kendall-plot (K-plot), originally proposed by Genest and Boies (2003), can be used to detect dependence between variables. It is an alternative rank-based procedure that adopts the concept of a probability plot (a Q-Q plot). The resulting graph is known as the K-plot. The form of the bivariate distribution K_o is constructed as follows:

$$K(\omega) = K_0(\omega) = \Pr\{UV \le \omega\} = \omega - \log(\omega), 0 \le \omega \le 1,$$

where U and V are independent uniform random variables within the interval [0,1]. $W_{(i:n)}$, as defined by Genest and Boies (2003), is formed as follows:

$$W_{(i:n)} = n \binom{n-1}{i-1} \int_0^1 \omega \{K_0(\omega)\}^{i-1} \{1 - K_0(\omega)\}^{n-1} dK_0(\omega)$$

The amount of curvature in the proposed graph is a characteristic of the degree of association in the data; a lack of linearity is a sign of non-normality in a standard Q-Q plot. In other words, the closer the K-plot is to the 45 degree line, the less the association between the random variables.

2. The Copula Method

Theoretically, we can use multiple dimension copulas, but in this chapter,two-dimensional copulas of Gumbel, Clayton and Normal will be used. Therefore, the bivariate copula will be summarized as follows. As introduced in Nelsen 2006, if F(x,y) is a joint density function with margin F_X and F_Y, then there exists a copula for all $x, y \in [-\infty, \infty]$:

$$F(x, y) = C(F_X(x), F_Y(y)), \tag{2}$$

Note that the copula C is unique whenever X and Y are continuous random variables. The copula C of X and Y is invariant strictly increasing transformations of the margins F_X and F_Y. This property is useful for figuring measures of dependence.

Gumbel Copula

Generator $\phi(t) = (-\ln t)^{\theta}$, where $\theta \geq 1$, and the function is as follows:

$$C_\theta(u, v) = e^{-\left[(-\ln u)^{\theta}+(-\ln v)^{\theta}\right]^{1/\theta}},$$

with tail dependence: $\lambda_L = 0$, $\lambda_U = 2-2^{1/\theta}$.

It is able to capture the upper tail dependence;a tail index of λ_U is the upper tail dependence.

Clayton Copula

Generator $\phi(t) = \dfrac{t^{-\theta}-1}{\theta}$, where $\theta > 0$, and the function is:

$$C_\theta(u, v) = \left(u^{-\theta}+v^{-\theta}-1\right)^{-1/\theta} \quad \text{and } C_0(u, v) = \Pi = u\,v,$$

with tail dependence: $\lambda_L = 2^{-1/\theta}$, $\lambda_U = 0$.

It is able to capture the lower tail dependence;a tail index of λ_L is the lower tail dependence

Normal Copula

The most frequently used copula is the normal copula. It does not display either lower or upper tail dependence and its parameter is in the interval of $0 \leq \theta \leq 1$:

$$C_\theta(u,v) = \int_{-\infty}^{\Phi^{-1}(u)} dx \int_{-\infty}^{\Phi^{-1}(v)} dy \frac{1}{2\pi\sqrt{1-\theta^2}} \exp\left\{-\frac{x^2-2\theta xy+y^2}{2(1-\theta^2)}\right\}$$

We will use the maximum pseudo likelihood method to estimate copula parameters. First, data are filtered out using GARCH (1,1), then the marginal distributions are estimated using the empirical distribution. Secondly, the maximum likelihood estimation method is used to estimate the copula parameter. This method involves maximizing a rank-based log-likelihood of the form:

$$L(\theta) = \sum_{i=1}^{n} ln\left(c_\theta \left(\frac{R_i}{n+1}; \frac{S_i}{n+1} \right) \right), \tag{3}$$

where n is the sample size and $\boldsymbol{\theta}$ is vector of parameters in the model. Note that arguments $\frac{R_i}{n+1}, \frac{S_i}{n+1}$ equal to corresponding values of empirical marginal distributional functions of random variables X and Y.

To compare the goodness of fit of our estimated model, we apply the log-likelihood approach in which the largest value of log-likelihood will show the best fitted copula. All copulas are tested for goodness-of-fit using Prokhorov method (2008), becauseunder the hypothesis of proper specification the statistics $\sqrt{n}\hat{\boldsymbol{D}}_\theta$ has asymptotical distribution N (0, $\boldsymbol{V}$), where $\boldsymbol{V}$ can be estimated by:

$$\hat{\boldsymbol{V}} = \frac{1}{n-1} \sum \boldsymbol{d}_i'(\theta).\boldsymbol{d}_i(\theta).$$

Therefore $\chi^2 = n.\hat{\boldsymbol{D}}_\theta'.\hat{\boldsymbol{V}}_\theta^{-1}.\hat{\boldsymbol{D}}_\theta$ (4)

is asymptotically as $\chi^2_{k(k+1)/2}$.If the p-value, computed from (4), is greater than alpha (level of significance), then the estimated copula is similar to the empirical copula and can be used to represent the dependence structure.

DATA AND EMPIRICAL RESULTS

1. Data

The data include the stock market indices of Hong Kong, Indonesia, Japan, Malaysia, Singapore, the Philippines, Thailand and the U.S. from January 2003 to November 2011. The daily data total of 2276 observations for each country were taken from DataStream and the returns computed accordingly. Table 1 provides the summary statistics for returns from the sample stock market indices. As commonly observed, in most cases, the percentage means of the daily stock index returns are close to zero. The average daily return is highest for the Indonesia market, followed by the Philippines and Thailand markets. The U.S. and Japan stock markets show relatively poor performance, as evidenced by their low stock returns. The skewness of almost all of the series is different from zero, skewing to the left; the Hong Kong market skewed to the right.All the return series show excess kurtosis, ranging from 5.19 to 13.9, with the Malaysia stock market displaying the highest kurtosis.

Table 1. Descriptive statistics of the daily data from various countries' stock markets from January 2003 to November 2011

	Hong Kong	Indonesia	Japan	Malaysia	Singapore	Philippines	Thailand	US
Mean	0.000293	0.000981	0.000018	0.000339	0.000339	0.000603	0.000398	0.000162
SE	0.000339	0.000311	0.000325	0.000168	0.000264	0.000283	0.000298	0.000278
Median	0.000003	0.000757	0.000000	0.000214	0.000364	0.000000	0.000000	0.000577
Mode	0.000000	0.000000	0.000000	0.000000	0.000000	0.000000	0.000000	0.000000
SD	0.016185	0.014855	0.015497	0.007997	0.012592	0.013508	0.014219	0.013254
Kurtosis	9.728595	6.894972	9.376494	13.900581	5.191080	7.864251	13.045218	10.741367
Skewness	0.033246	-0.688719	-0.589703	-1.105328	-0.203959	-0.611264	-0.916368	-0.317914
Range	0.269888	0.185771	0.253456	0.142372	0.162265	0.224540	0.266403	0.204267
Minimum	-0.135820	-0.109540	-0.121110	-0.099785	-0.086960	-0.130887	-0.160633	-0.094695
Maximum	0.134068	0.076231	0.132346	0.042587	0.075305	0.093653	0.105770	0.109572
Count	2276	2276	2276	2276	2276	2276	2276	2276

Notes: SE is standard error, SD is standard deviation.

Table 2. Correlations for countries' stock markets with the US stock market from January 2003 to November 2011

Country	Before	After	Whole
Hong Kong	0.077	0.562	0.227
Indonesia	0.065	0.177	0.126
Japan	0.077	0.119	0.114
Malaysia	0.038	0.161	0.100
Singapore	0.135	0.293	0.258
Philippines	0.016	0.000	0.023
Thailand	0.058	0.184	0.192

Notes: Before and after are for before and after the 2008 US crisis, respectively. Whole is for the whole period.

Figure 1 shows the trends of all data series during the examined period. As can be seen, all examined markets exhibited a downturn during the sub-prime mortgage crisis, late 2008 to early 2009. Therefore, we divide our data set into two sub-groups, before the crisis and after the crisis. The crisis period, August 2008 to April 2009, which marked the fall of Lehman Brothers, was not taken into consideration for the sub-groups since all markets show the same movement.

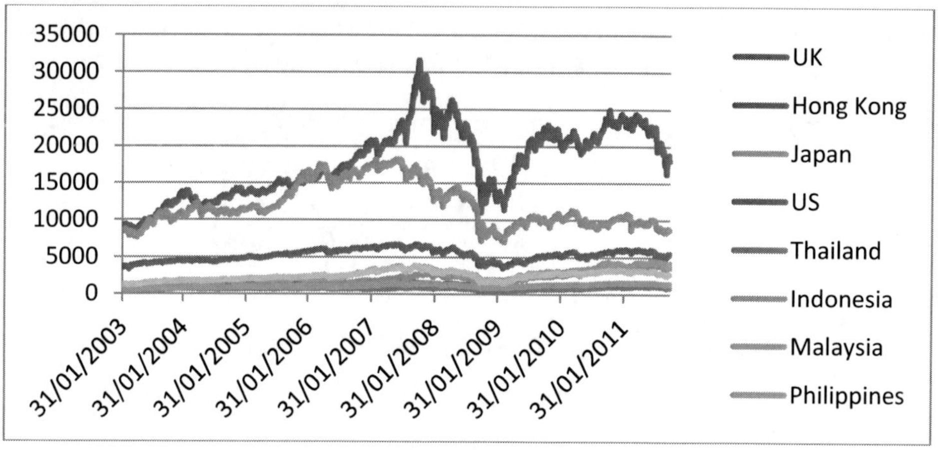

Figure 1. Trends in various countries' stock markets from January 2003 to November 2011.

Table 2 showsthe linear correlations between the U.S. market and the other stock marketsin two sub-groups and the whole sample. For the whole sample, all correlations are relatively weak, with the highest correlation between Singapore and the U.S. of 0.258 and the lowest correlation between the Philippines and the U.S. of 0.023. Interestingly, the correlations change dramatically from before to after the crisis. The highest increase is the correlation between the Hong Kong and the U.S. markets, from 0.077 before the crisis to 0.562 after the crisis. The other correlations that also increase are Indonesia, Japan, Malaysia, Singapore and Thailand. The only correlation that decreases after the crisis is between the Philippines and U.S. markets, from 0.016 to 0.0.These results could be good implications for portfolio management and financial risk analysis. We will examine the results from the plots and copula in the next section to see if there is anything interesting.

2. Empirical Results

Non-Parametric Plots

We are interested in the changes of dependence structure before and after the U.S. crisis in 2008, so our datawere divided into two sub groups as mentioned above.The K-plots and Chi-plots were generated to detect the relationship between the U.S. stock market and the other stock markets (Hong Kong, Indonesia, Japan, Malaysia, the Philippines, Singapore and Thailand). The results are reported in Figures 2 to 8, in which panel A is the structure before the crisis, panel B is after the crisis and panel C is for the whole sample. In each panel, part 1 (i.e., A1) is the K-plot and part 2 (i.e., A2) is the Chi-plot.

The plots for the U.S. and Hong Kong stock markets are in Figure 2. In the first part of all panels, the plotted line in the K-plot departs a distance from the diagonal line from both tails, indicating the presence of tail dependence. We use the Chi-plots in part 2 of all panels to get details of tail dependence for the pair. Before the crisis, in panel A2, we can see that all points are outside the control lines in the tail plots.

However, the tails exhibit the same pattern, so it is likely that there is no strong tail dependency for this pair before the crisis. After the crisis, in panel B2, the left tail and right tail display different patterns.

This shows the presence of the left tail dependence, since almost the dots are outside the control lines in the left tail plot, whereas a number of dots are within the control lines in the right tail plot.For the whole sample, we see the same result as that after the crisis with left tail dependence.Therefore, it is likely that the dependence structure between the U.S. and Hong Kong stock markets changed after the U.S. crisis in 2008.

Figure 3 presents the plots for the U.S. and Indonesian stock markets. In part 1 of all panels for the K-plots, there possibly exists tail dependence since all the plotted lines depart from the diagonal.In the Chi-plot of panel A2, the plots for both tails exhibit the same pattern, indicating no tail dependence before the crisis for this pair. In panel B2, after the crisis, the left tail plot is different from the right tail plot. There is no point plotted within the control lines in the left tail plot, indicating strong left tail dependence whereas a number of points within the control lines in the right tail plot, showing no right tail dependence.For the whole sample, we can see the presence of left tail dependence since the patterns for both tails are different, and almost no point is within the control lines in the left tail plot. So, in this case, there is likely a change in structure dependence between the two stock markets before and after the crisis.

We also detect a change in dependence structure for the U.S. and Singapore markets and for the U.S. and Thai markets (Figures7 and 8, respectively). For the U.S. and Singapore markets, the K-plots indicate tail dependence, but the Chi-plots indicate that there was no explicit tail dependence before the crisis and that there is left tail dependence after the crisis (no point is within the control lines of the left tail plot (panel B2, Figure 7). For the whole sample, there is left tail dependence between these two markets. Similarly, we can detect left tail dependence after the crisis for the U.S. and Thai markets, but there is no tail dependence before the crisis.

In contrast, there is no change in dependence structure between the U.S. stock market and the stock markets of Japan, Malaysia and the Philippines.The plots for the U.S. and Japan are shown in Figure 4. The K-plots indicate that both tails may have the same pattern in the two sub samples. The Chi-plots confirm that there is no difference in the patterns of the left and right tails before, after and for the whole period between these two stock markets. Therefore, the dependence structure between the U.S. and Japanese stock marketsdid not change after the crisis. We find the same results for the U.S. and Malaysia (Figure 5), and the U.S. and the Philippines (Figure 6).

The Copula Analysis

As mentioned in the Methods, our datawere divided into sub groups and filtered via GARCH(1,1) to obtain i.i.d data. The data are then modeled using the empirical distribution and fitted via the three copula functions, Clayton, Gumbel and Normal. The Clayton copula is able to capture left tail dependence, which indicates that two variables are likely to crash during the crisis; and that the Gumbel copula is able to capture right tail dependence, which shows that two variables are likely to boom together.The Normal copula does not show both tail dependencies.The copula results are reported in Table 3; all copulas passed the goodness of fit test mentioned.

In Table 3, the copula results for the U.S. and Hong Kong stock markets are presented in three smaller sections: before the crisis (B), after the crisis (A) and the whole examined period (W).Before the crisis, as can be seen, the best copula for the dependence structure between the U.S. and Hong Kong stock markets is the Normal copula, since its likelihood value is largest.

However, after the crisis, the best fitted copula for the dependence structure is the Clayton copula with thelargest likelihood value, indicating that the U.S. and Hong Kong stock markets are likely to go down together. This is also the case for these two stock markets when the whole sample data are examined; the best fitted copula is the Clayton copula. Explicitly, the dependence structure between these two markets changed after the U.S. crisis in 2008 from no tail dependence before to left tail dependence after the crisis. The result is consistent with the plot method results.

Like the above case, the dependence structure between the U.S. stock market and the stock markets of Indonesia, Singapore and Thailand also changed after the US crisis in 2008. The best copula for these three pairs is the Normal copula before the crisis and after the crisis the Clayton copula, indicating left tail dependence after the crisis. Interestingly, for the whole sample, the dependence structure of the pairs U.S. and Indonesia and U.S. and Singapore follows the Clayton copula like the U.S.-Hong Kong pair, but the US-Thailand pair follows the Normal copula, i.e., no tail dependence. This perhaps because the U.S.-Thailand pair shows weak left tail dependence with the Clayton copula,a parameter of 0.385 after the crisis compared with parameters of the Clayton copula for the U.S.-Hong Kong, U.S.-Indonesia, and U.S.-Singapore pairs of 0.7313, 0.532 and 0.6275, respectively. These results are consistent with the plot method results.The copula results revealthat the stock markets of Indonesia, Singapore, and Thailand are likely to go down with the U.S. stock market during amarket downturn, especially after the 2008 U.S. crisis. This also indicates that there is a considerable influence of information from the U.S. stock market to these three stock markets.

Interestingly, we did not detect any dependence structure change in the pairs U.S.-Japan, U.S.-Malaysia and U.S.-Philippines, since the best fitted copula for these three pairs is the Normal copula forthe two sub-groups and the whole period.The Normal copula does not show tail dependence, but we can detect an increase in its parameter after the crisis. The parameter for the U.S.-Japan pair increases from 0.4319 before the crisis to 0.5498 after the crisis; that of the U.S.-Malaysia pair from 0.38 to 0.449; and that of the U.S.-Philippines pair from 0.417 to 0.5266. This also indicates an increasing degree of association between the U.S. market and the three stock markets after the 2008 crisis.

In summary, we did not detect any change in dependence structure and tail dependence between the U.S. stock market and the stock markets of Japan, Malaysia and the Philippines, although the association of these market pairs becomes stronger after the 2008 US crisis. In the linear correlation in Table 2, it is likely that a diversification benefit can be achieved when investing between these seven examined markets and the U.S. market since they show low linear correlation.

However, U.S. investors might not gain a diversification benefit when investing in the stock markets of Hong Kong, Indonesia, Singapore and Thailand. The reason is that these market pairs show left tail dependence after the US crisis, which indicates the possibility of crashing together between these markets, even though the correlations between the U.S. market and these four stock markets are weak (see Table 2).These results show the usefulness of the copula method, which can provide richer information than linear correlation and plot methods.

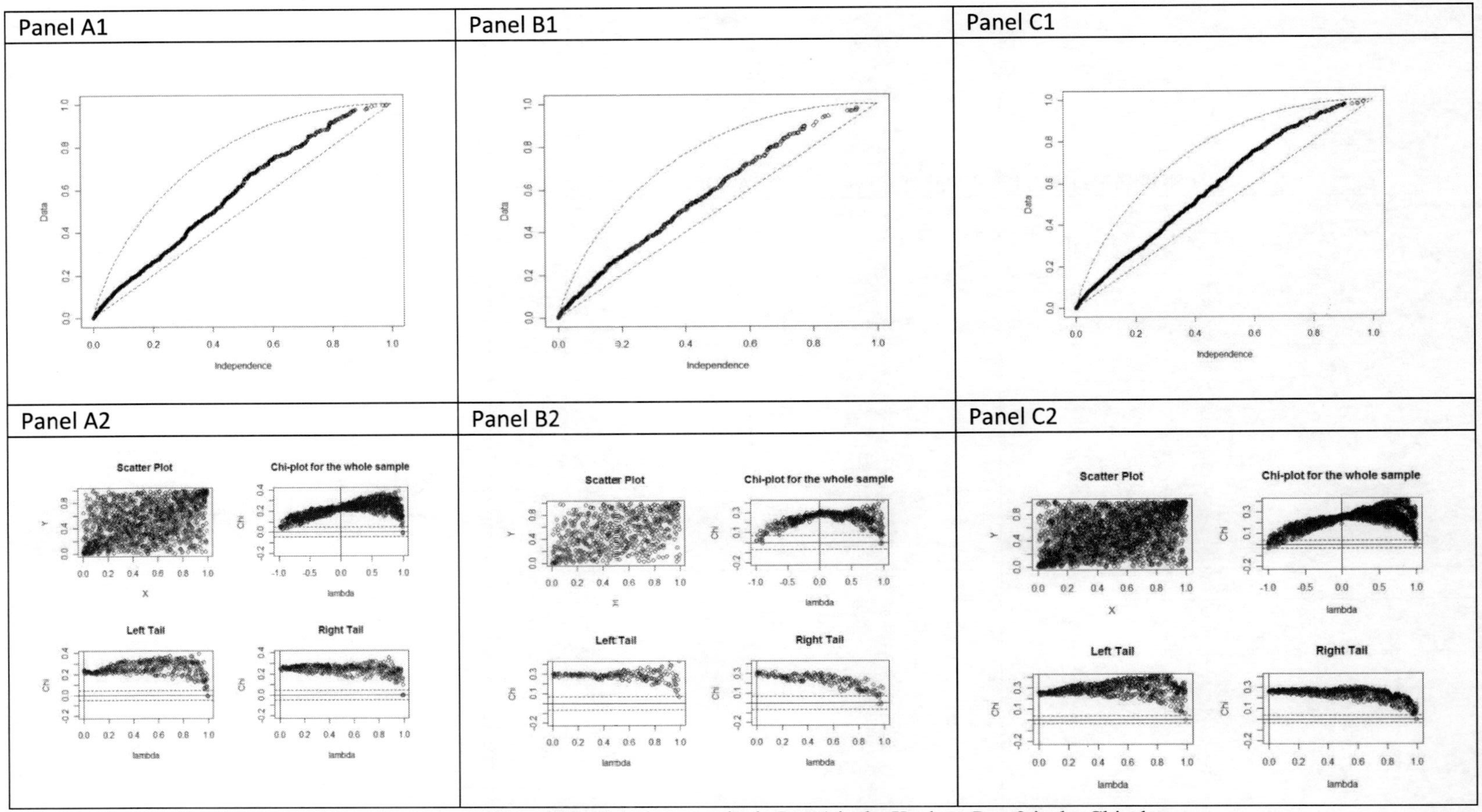

Notes:Panel A, B, C is for before, after the crisis and the whole period, respectively,Part 1 is the K-plots, Part 2 is the Chi-plots.

Figure 2. The US and Hong Kong stock marketsfrom January 2003 to November 2011.

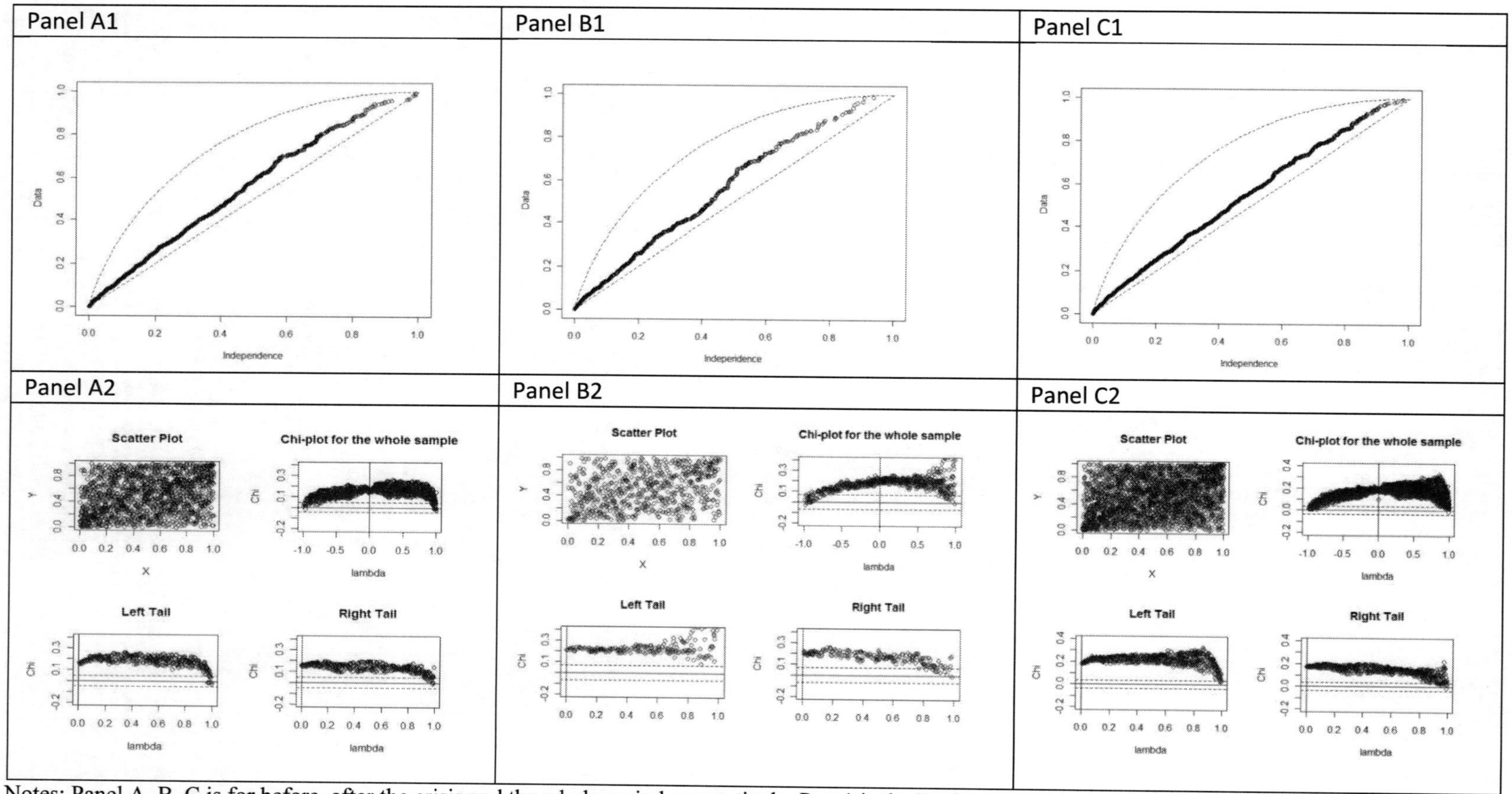

Notes: Panel A, B, C is for before, after the crisis and the whole period, respectively, Part 1 is the K-plots, Part 2 is the Chi-plots.

Figure 3. The US and Indonesia stock marketsfrom January 2003 to November 2011.

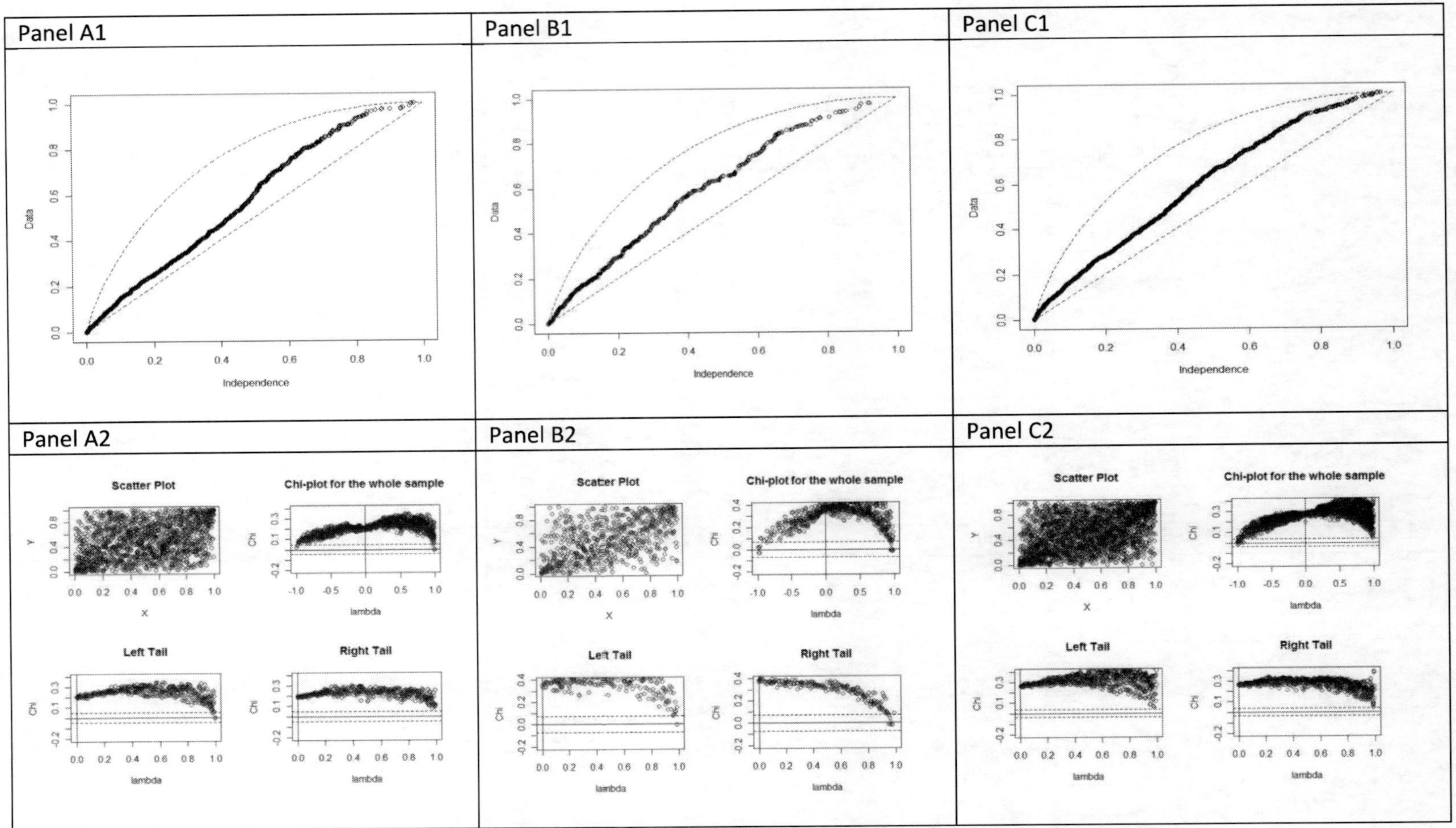

Notes: Panel A, B, C is for before, after the crisis and the whole period, respectively, Part 1 is the K-plots, Part 2 is the Chi-plots.

Figure 4. The US and Japan stock marketsfrom January 2003 to November 2011.

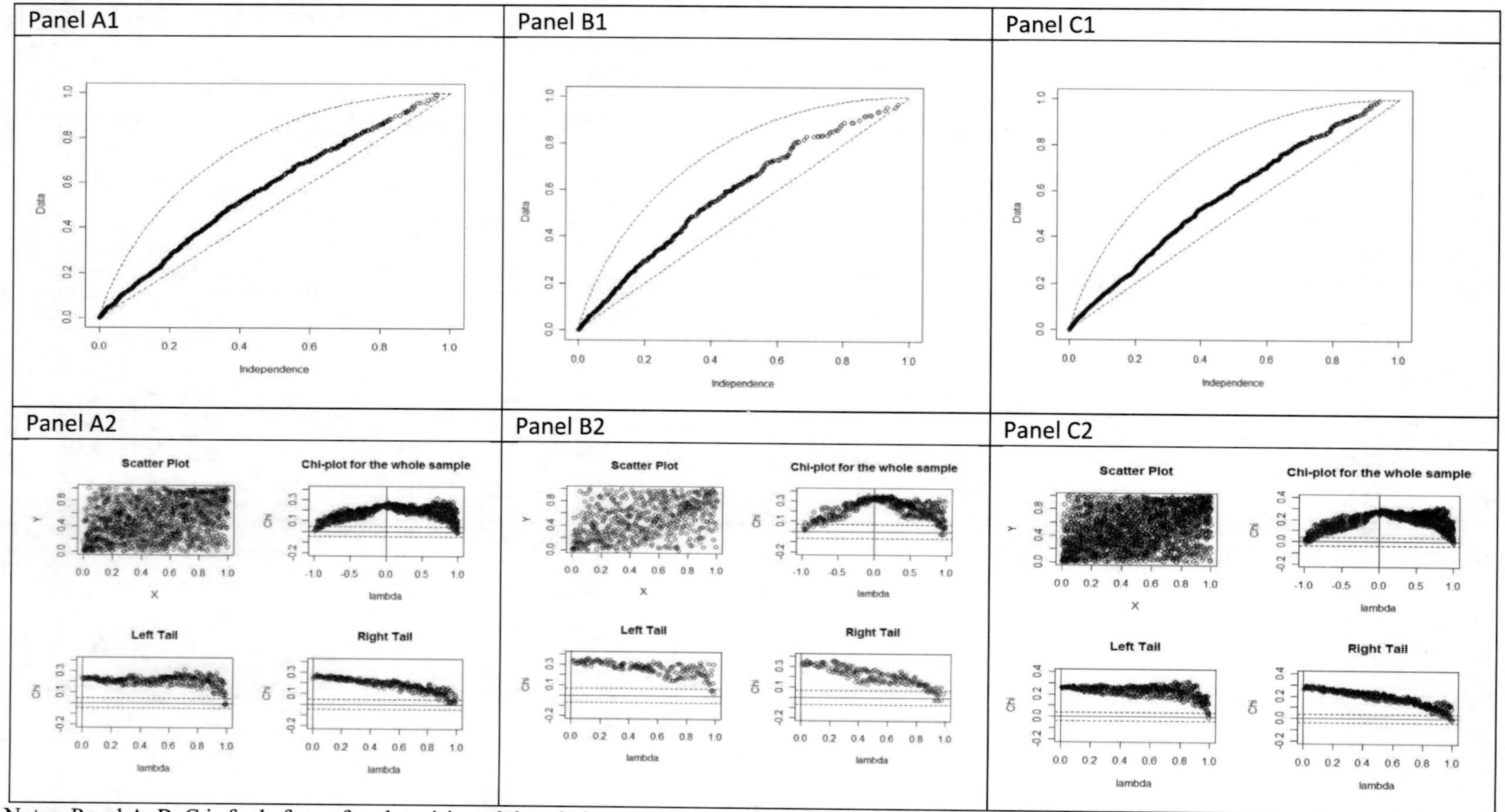

Notes: Panel A, B, C is for before, after the crisis and the whole period, respectively, Part 1 is the K-plots, Part 2 is the Chi-plots.

Figure 5. The US and Malaysia stock marketsfrom January 2003 to November 2011.

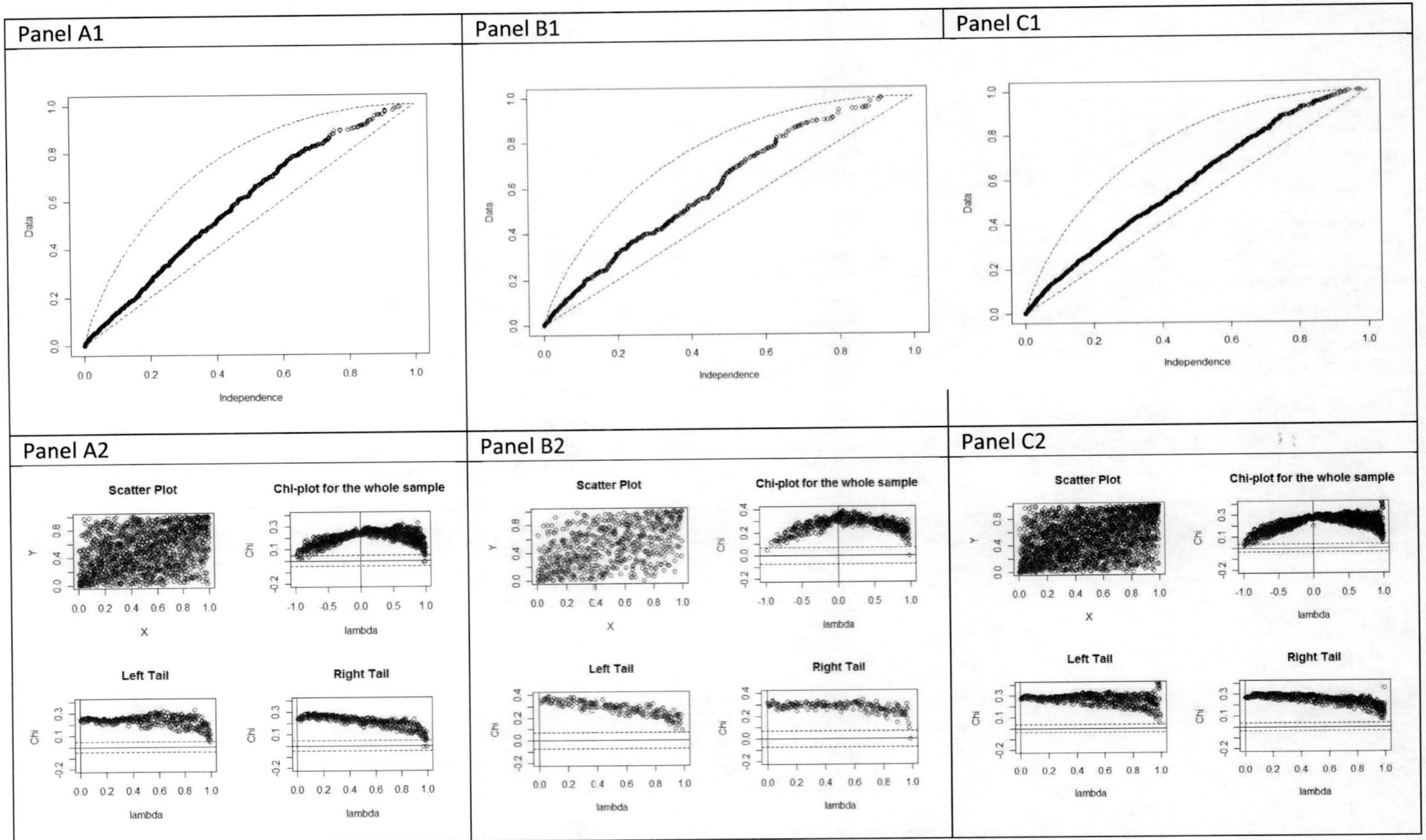

Notes: Panel A, B, C is for before, after the crisis and the whole period, respectively, Part 1 is the K-plots, Part 2 is the Chi-plots.

Figure 6. The US and Philippines stock marketsfrom January 2003 to November 2011.

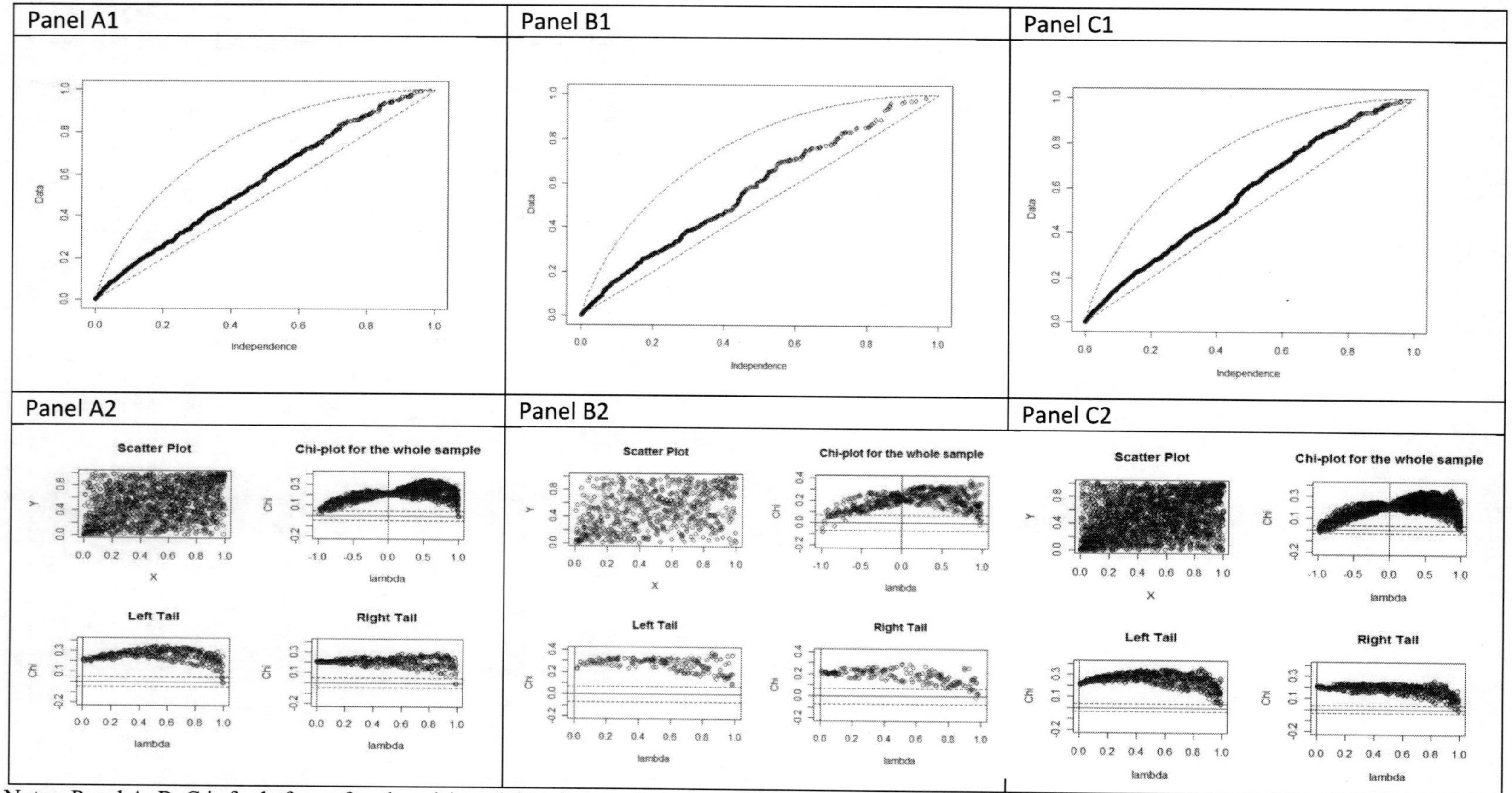

Notes: Panel A, B, C is for before, after the crisis and the whole period, respectively, Part 1 is the K-plots, Part 2 is the Chi-plots.

Figure 7. The US and Singapore stock marketsfrom January 2003 to November 2011.

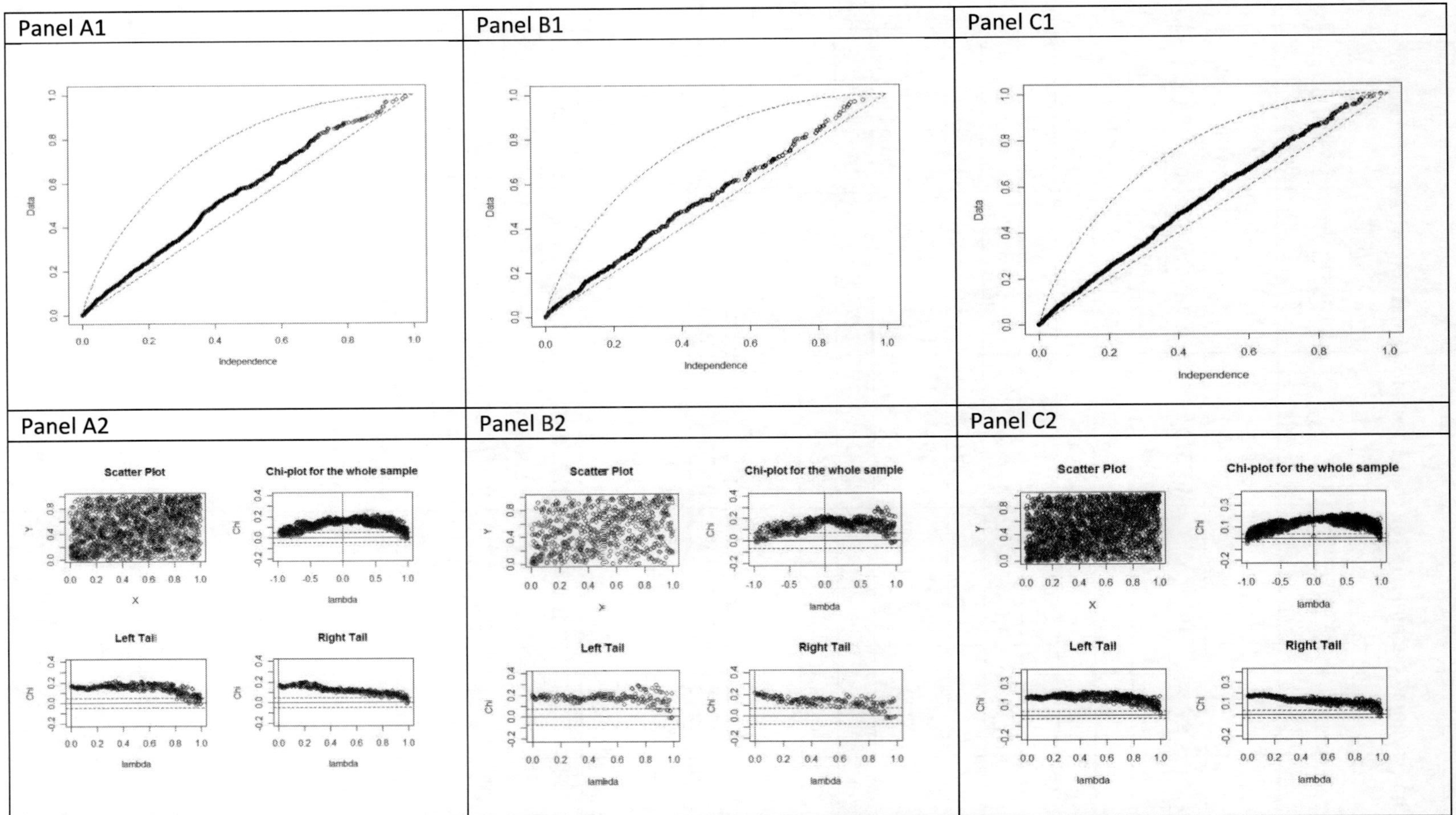

Notes: Panel A, B, C is for before, after the crisis and the whole period, respectively, Part 1 is the K-plots, Part 2 is the Chi-plots.

Figure 8. The US and Thailand stock marketsfrom January 2003 to November 2011.

Table 3. The estimated parameters for countries' stock markets with the US market

Country		Parameter	Clayton	Gumbel	Normal
Hong Kong	B	θ	0.6175	1.367	**0.4353**
		SE	0.045	0.028	0.0197
		LL	130.989	147.786	148.46
	A	θ	**0.7313**	1.392	0.4677
		SE	0.069	0.042	0.028
		LL	77.0319	66.675	76.938
	W	θ	**0.6949**	1.3763	0.4271
		SE	0.037	0.022	0.0158
		LL	244.293	230.1651	226.789
Indonesia	B	θ	0.3971	1.206	**0.0307**
		SE	0.0395	0.0233	0.023
		LL	67.312	57.613	69.854
	A	θ	**0.532**	1.2645	0.3531
		SE	0.064	0.038	0.033
		LL	47.474	36.82	41.459
	W	θ	**0.4676**	1.23	0.3279
		SE	0.0329	0.0192	0.0178
		LL	139.0956	108.146	128.005
Japan	B	θ	0.5792	1.3389	**0.4319**
		SE	0.0434	0.0268	0.0198
		LL	122.5493	131.156	145.748
	A	θ	0.9564	1.5421	**0.5498**
		SE	0.0778	0.0482	0.0242
		LL	108.5099	104.1325	113.3078
	W	θ	0.7989	1.4558	**0.4975**
		SE	0.0384	0.0238	0.0142
		LL	307.002	313.57	320.481
Malaysia	B	θ	0.5147	1.2815	**0.3803**
		SE	0.042	0.025	0.0212
		LL	101.95	92.277	110.2742
	A	θ	0.6715	1.3723	**0.449**
		SE	0.067	0.042	0.029
		LL	67.55	58.527	70.1933
	W	θ	0.5598	1.3024	**0.392**
		SE	0.0343	0.0208	0.0166
		LL	181.85	159.355	187.912

Country		Parameter	Clayton	Gumbel	Normal
Philippines	B	θ	0.5647	1.3226	**0.4171**
		SE	0.0432	0.0264	0.0203
		LL	116.63	116.31	134.96
	A	θ	0.7357	1.4702	**0.5266**
		SE	0.069	0.045	0.025
		LL	78.1311	92.6121	102.08
	W	θ	0.6695	1.3987	**0.4722**
		SE	0.0358	0.0225	0.0148
		LL	242.3454	261.78	284.33
Singapore	B	θ	0.5911	1.332	**0.41442**
		SE	0.044	0.0268	0.02
		LL	124.57	127.6896	132.9565
	A	θ	**0.6275**	1.3257	0.3984
		SE	0.067	0.04	0.031
		LL	59.99	50.3199	53.629
	W	θ	**0.5769**	1.3003	0.3716
		SE	0.0352	0.0208	0.017
		LL	187.22	164.06	167.354
Thailand	B	θ	0.3023	1.166	**0.2577**
		SE	0.038	0.022	0.024
		LL	41.037	39.024	48.448
	A	θ	**0.385**	1.1925	0.2871
		SE	0.0596	0.035	0.0353
		LL	27.73	22.0459	26.729
	W	θ	0.3392	1.1795	**0.2636**
		SE	0.031	0.018	0.0189
		LL	80.064	73.682	80.9699

Notes: B is Before, A is after the crisis, W is the whole sample. SE is standard deviation LL is log likelihood. All copula passed p-value goodness of fit test. Bold numbers is the parameter of the best fitted copula for each period.

CONCLUSION

This chapter examines the changes of dependencc structure between the U.S. stock market and seven other stock markets before and after the U.S. sub-prime mortgage crisis in 2008. By applying non-parametric methods, we found that there are changes in tail dependence in all market pairs before and after the crisis. Three copulas, Clayton, Gumbel and Normal, were applied. The copula results reveal that the dependence structure between the U.S. market and the stock markets of Hong Kong, Indonesia, Singapore and Thailand changed after the U.S. crisis. Particularly, these stock markets show left tail dependence with the U.S. stock market after the crisis but there was no tail dependence before the crisis. Therefore, the benefits of diversification between the U.S. market and those four stock markets may not be achieved, since these markets are likely to go down together. By contrast, we found no changes in dependence structure between the stock markets of Japan, Malaysia and the Philippines and the U.S. market after the crisis, but the associations between the U.S. stock market and those three markets increased.

These results, not previously reported in the literature to the best of our knowledge, provide evidence in favour of using copula, since the method provides more information on the relationship between variables. More importantly, our findings also have important implications for risk managers and hedging strategists in U.S. stock markets as well as the other examined stock markets. Investors or managers in these markets need to consider the dependence structure when making investment decisions since the structure shows the possibility of crashing or booming together, thus indicating if diversification gains can be significant.

ACKNOWLEDGMENTS

Special thanks to Professor Genest Christian, McGill University and faculty of commerce, Lincoln University, New Zealand for research support.

REFERENCES

Arouri, M. E. H., Bellalah, M., Nguyen, D. K., (2010). The comovements in international stock markets: new evidence from Latin American emerging countries. *Applied Economics Letters,* 17, 1323-1328.

Bhatti, M. I., Nguyen, C., (2012). Diversification evidence from international equity markets using extreme values and stochastic copulas.*Journal of International Financial Markets, Institution and Money,* 22, 622-646.

Chang, C. L., Hsueh, P. L., (2013). Dynamics of dependence between real estate and stock markets of emerging countries in Asia.*International Research Journal of Finance and Economics,* 103, 110-130.

Égert, B., Kočenda, E., (2011). Time-varying synchronization of European stock markets. *Empirical Economics,* 40(2), 393-407.

Fisher,N.I., Switzer P., (1985). Chi-plots of assessing of dependence.*Biometrika,* 72, 253-265.

Fisher,N.I., Switzer P., (2001). Graphical assessment of dependence: Is a picture worth 100 tests?*American Statistician,* 55(3), 233-239.

Genest, C., Boies, J.C., (2003). Detecting dependence with Kendall plots.*The American Statistician,* 57(4), 275-284.

Graham, M., Kiviaho, J., Nikkinen, J., (2012a). Integration of 22 emerging stock markets: A three-dimensional analysis. *Global Finance Journal,* 23(1), 34-47.

Graham, M., Kivihaho, J., Nikkinen, J., Omran, M., (2012b). Global and regional co-movement of the Mena stock markets: New evidence using wavelet squared coherency. *Journal of Economics and Business,* 65, 86-100.

Gupta, R., Guidi, F., (2012). Cointegration relationship and time varying co-movements among Indian and Asian developed stock markets. *International Review of Financial Analysis,* 21, 10-22.

Harrison, B., Moore, W., (2010). Stock market co-movement in the Caribbean.Economic Issues 15(1), 1.

Kiviaho, J., Nikkinen, J., Piljak, V., Rothovius, T., (2012). The co-movement dynamics of European frontier stock markets.*European Financial Management,* DOI: 10.1111/j.1468-036X.2012.00646.x.

Korkmaz, T., Çevik, E. T., Atukeren, E., (2012). Return and volatility spillovers among CIVETS stock markets. *Emerging Markets Review,* 13(2), 230-252.

Lee, C., Shie, F. S., Chang, C. Y., (2012). How close a relationship does a capital market have with other such markets? The case of Taiwan from the Asian financial crisis. *Pacific Basin Finance Journal,* 20, 349-362.

Lin, C. H. (2012). The comovement between exchange rates and stock prices in the Asian emerging markets. *International Review of Economics & Finance,* 22, 161-172.

Liu, L., Wan, J., (2012). The relationships between Shanghai stock market and CNY/USD exchange rate: New evidence based on cross-correlation analysis, structural cointegration and nonlinear causality test. *Physica A: Statistical Mechanics and its Applications,* 39, 6051-6059.

Luo, W., Brooks, R. D., Silvapulle, P., (2011). Effects of the open policy on the dependence between the Chinese 'A'stock market and other equity markets: An industry sector perspective. *Journal of International Financial Markets, Institutions and Money,* 21, 49-74.

Mishra, R. K., (2010). Stock market integration and volatility spillover: India and its major Asian counterparts. *Research in International Business and Finance,* 24, 235-251.

Nawawi, A., Azmi, N. N. K., Fadzil, F. J. M,. (2010). Therelationships of real estate and stock markets in Asia. Paper presented at the 6th IMT-FT Conference on Mathematics, Statistics and its Applications.

Nelsen, R.B., (2006).An introduction to copulas. Springer-Verlag, New York.

Nguyen, C., Bhatti, M. I., (2012). Copula modelingdependency between oil prices and stock markets: Evidence from China and Vietnam.*Journal of International Financial Markets, Institution and Money,* 22, 758-773.

Nieh, C. C., Yang, C. H., Kao, Y. S., (2012). Who has more influence on Asian stock markets around the subprime mortgage crisis–the US or China? *Applied Economics Letters,* 19, 329-335.

Prokhorov, A., (2008). A goodness-of-fit test for copulas. MPRA Paper No. 9998, online at http://mpra.ub.uni-muenchen.de/9998.

Rua, A., Nunes, L. C., (2009). International comovement of stock market returns: A wavelet analysis. *Journal of Empirical Finance,* 16, 632-639.

Wang, Y. C., Wu, J., Lai, Y., (2013). A revisit to the dependence structure between stock and foreign exchange markets: A dependence-switching copula approach. *Journal of Banking and Finance,* 37, 1706-1719.

In: Stock Markets
Editors: F. Petroni, F. Prattico and G. D'Amico
ISBN: 978-1-62808-751-2

Chapter 7

DIVERSIFICATION MEASURES FOR PORTFOLIO SELECTION

*Gianni Pola**
Quantitative Research, Amundi, Paris, France

Abstract

The recent crisis poses serious doubts on the effectiveness of diversification to reduce draw-downs in balanced portfolios: "diversification failed when it was mostly needed" was the leitmotif of many institutional investors after 2008. Nevertheless recent portfolio construction schemes, like risk parity and maximum diversification, make of diversification the kernel of asset allocation. While most approaches diversify on asset classes' level, the new challenge in asset allocation suggests diversifying on fundamental factors that are believed to be the main drivers of asset price dynamics. In the present work we firstly review the main approaches to analyse portfolio concentration and diversification, and then we show how to get optimally diversified asset allocation from a practical point of view. Factors approach can be divided in statistical-based methods, mainly based on principal component analysis, and more fundamental approaches (economic scenario methods) which ex-ante identify factors in terms of macroeconomic and market stress indicators. In this work we review main techniques

- to evaluate portfolio risk concentration (Herfindahl index, Lorentz curves, Gini coefficient),
- to measure risk distribution within the asset-class space (marginal contribution to risk, and entropy-based diversification measure)
- and within the principal components' space (Meucci 2009).

Moreover we briefly review the economic scenario methods. We conclude discussing implications in terms of portfolio constructions focussing mainly on two diversification measures: (1) the entropy-based diversification metric of a scaled function of the marginal-contributions-to-risk, and (2) the difference between the weighted sum of volatilities of each position and the portfolio total volatility.

*E-mail address: gianni.pola@amundi.com

Keywords: portfolio diversification, entropy, asset allocation, risk parity, diversification across macroeconomic scenarios

AMS Subject Classification: 62-07, 65K10, 90C30

1. Introduction

The recent crisis poses serious doubts on the effectiveness of diversification to reduce drawdowns in balanced portfolios: "*diversification failed when it was mostly needed*" was the leitmotif of many investors after 2008. In "The Battle for Investment Survival" [10], G. M. Loeb claimed that "*Diversification might be necessary where no intelligent supervision is likely. Otherwise, it is an admission of not knowing what to do*". Hence diversification is not an issue for the intelligent investor who is able to forecast markets return. However the bear market in equities in the last decade, and the consequent poor performance in pension funds and diversified allocations, again calls into question the predictability of asset risk premia, and the effect of incorrect assumptions in the portfolio selection process.

In [23] we claimed that today it is particularly difficult to estimate reasonable risk premia because:

- many financial variables are in an uncharted region, never reached going back many decades, and more than a century in some cases: whether they would revert to the mean or they would stabilise to new levels is not clear (e.g. Euro peripherals' bond market);
- the rising of macroeconomic volatility makes it difficult the application of equilibrium-based approaches;
- moreover the recent unconventional monetary policy of central banks may move the risk premia to unexpected figures in the future.

The uniqueness of the level reached by many financial variables should at least convince us to lower our confidence on predictability of assert risk premia.

In the eighties and nineties, Jobson and Korkie [13], Best and Grauer [2], Chopra and Ziemba[4] demonstrated that the sub-optimality due to estimation risk can be dramatic. This evidence led researchers and practitioners to investigate more robust portfolio construction schemes which can alleviate the estimation risk in the portfolio construction process: the most popular approaches were developed within Bayesian methods (e.g. the Black & Litterman model [3]) and Robust Asset Allocation models (e.g. [18]). In the last decade the financial industry moved even further, designing investment processes that can completely neglect assumptions on expected returns (see [29]). The most popular were the Minimum Variance, the Maximum Diversification, and the Risk Parity (see [5], [17] and [6]): these approaches allow the investor to make allocation according (only) to a risk model. Recently the need for diversification led the financial industry to explore new directions (see [11]), thus complementing traditional asset classes (bonds and equities) with commodities, real estate, investment styles (value, trend, carry, volatilities), and factors (growth, inflation, illiquidity, and tail risks).

The diversification approaches can be divided in two main groups: the *statistical methods* that define portfolio diversification according to portfolio weights or risk contribution, and the *economic scenario methods* that reinterpret financial markets according to a factor approach. In this chapter we discuss

- statistical methods: the Herfindahl index, the Lorentz curve, the Gini coefficient, the entropy-based diversification measure in portfolio weights and in risk contribution (assets and principal portfolios), the naive $1/vol$ rule, the maximum diversification metric, and a generalization of Herdindahl index, the Lorentz curve, and the Gini coefficient to risk contribution.
- economic scenario methods: the DAMS index.

The aim of this chapter is to review main diversification measures, to discuss them in practical applications to single-period portfolio optimization, to analyse implications in terms of portfolio rebalancing in multi-period investments, and finally to address the metric robustness versus estimation risk.

Implications of estimation risk to portfolio diversification is even more relevant in uncertain market conditions. We found that main instability in portfolio construction comes from the correlation estimation: the impact of estimation error in correlation is particularly severe in low-medium correlated investment universe as e.g. for diversified allocation that includes nominal bonds, inflation-linked bonds, equities, commodities, volatility, and dynamic strategies. We conclude the chapter pointing out main pitfalls in the correlation measure, providing a more robust metric within the Information Theory (see [7]), and concluding with some remarks from the DAMS approach (see [22]).

This chapter is organized as follows. Section 2 sets the notations and recall preliminary results. In section 3 we present main diversification measures. In section 4 we show some empirical results in a single-period investment, implications in terms of portfolio rebalancing, and finally we perform a Montecarlo experiment to evaluate the robustness of the diversification measures. In section 5 we briefly review the main cons in the correlation coefficient, and introduce the Kulback-Leibler pseudo-distance. Section 6 includes some conclusive remarks. The Appendix briefly reviews main analytical properties of the Kullback-Leibler pseudo-distance.

2. Fixing the Notation and Preliminary Results

Let us consider an investment universe made up of N risky assets. We indicate by $\{\mu_i\}_{i=1,\ldots,N}$ and $\{\sigma_i\}_{i=1,\ldots,N}$ respectively the asset expected returns and volatilities; let μ and σ be the N-by-1 vectors of asset expected returns and volatilities. Let ρ_{ij} stand for the element (i,j) of the correlation matrix. The covariance matrix Σ is given by $\Sigma_{ij} = \rho_{ij}\sigma_i\sigma_j$; Σ corresponds to a symmetric N-by-N matrix that is semidefinite positive.

In the following we indicate by $\{w_i\}_{i=1,\ldots,N}$ a set of portfolio weights; w refers to an N-by-1 vector. Portfolio expected return and volatility are given by:

$$\begin{aligned}\mu_p(w) &= \mu' w,\\ \sigma_p(w) &= (w'\Sigma w)^{1/2}.\end{aligned}$$

The shorthand notations for $\mu_p(w)$ and $\sigma_p(w)$ are resp. μ_w and σ_w. The *marginal risk* of asset i is defined as

$$\theta_i(w) = \frac{\partial \sigma_w}{\partial w_i}.$$

The *risk contribution* of asset i is defined as

$$\eta_i(w) = w_i \frac{\partial \sigma_w}{\partial w_i}.$$

It can be verified easily that

$$\sum_{i=1}^{N} \eta_i(w) = \sigma_w.$$

Finally we define the *relative* or *scaled marginal risk* $\tilde{\theta}_i(w)$ as

$$\tilde{\theta}_i(w) = \frac{1}{\sigma_i} \frac{\partial \sigma_w}{\partial w_i}.$$

As detailed in [8], the most popular forecast-free portfolio construction schemes can be expressed in terms of the above mentioned quantities:

- Equally Weighted portfolio (EW): $w_i = w_j$ for all $i, j = 1, \ldots, N$;
- Minimum Variance portfolio (MV): $\theta_i = \theta_j$ for all $i, j = 1, \ldots, N$;
- Risk Parity (RP) or Equally Risk Contribution portfolio: $\eta_i = \eta_j$ for all $i, j = 1, \ldots, N$;
- Most Diversified portfolio: $\tilde{\theta}_i = \tilde{\theta}_j$ for all $i, j = 1, \ldots, N$.

As reported in [16], the volatilities of the above mentioned portfolio schemes satisfy a precise hierarchy:

$$\sigma_{MV} \le \sigma_{RP} \le \sigma_{EW}, \tag{1}$$

σ_{MV}, σ_{RP}, and σ_{EW} representing (resp.) the volatility of the Minimum Variance, the Risk Parity, and the Equally Weighted portfolios.

In uncorrelated markets the variance of a portfolio is addictive in the variances of each asset: individual assets constitute additive sources of risk. Correlation among assets breaks this property introducing some mixed terms in portfolio variance. Indeed it is always possible to determine uncorrelated sources of risk. The principal component analysis (PCA) allows us to find independent directions: the PCA decomposition of Σ is given by

$$\Sigma = E \Lambda E',$$

E being the eigenvectors matrix, and Λ a diagonal matrix containing the eigenvalues $\{\lambda_i\}_{i=1,\ldots,N}$, s. t. $\lambda_1 \ge \lambda_2 \ge \lambda_3 \ge \ldots \ge \lambda_N$. The portfolio weights w can be projected in the eigenvector space through the eigenvectors matrix, as follows (see [21]):

$$\tilde{w} = E^{-1} w.$$

Hence the portfolio can be equivalently described in the asset space according to $\{w, \Sigma\}$ or in the eigenvector space according to $\{\tilde{w}, \Lambda\}$. The benefit of PCA is that usually few factors explain most of the full portfolio variance.

3. Portfolio Diversification Measures

This section is devoted to illustrate main metrics for portfolio diversification. Diversification can be defined according to

- **portfolio weights**: in this case the metric depends only on portfolio weights, and thus it is not affected by estimation risk (see sections 3.1, 3.2, 3.3, and 3.4 below);
- **asset risk**: usually the metrics are a function of the covariance matrix; estimation risk is crucial in this case (see sections 3.5, 3.6, 3.7, 3.8, 3.9, 3.10 and 3.11 below);
- **asset polarization towards fundamental factors**: estimation risk is not a relevant issue in this case (see section 3.12).

In the following sections we review the main techniques of each class. We present the results with respect to a portfolio allocation that fulfils the long-only and budget constraints (i.e. portfolio weights are positive and sum up to 1). However metrics in sections 3.1, 3.5, 3.6, 3.7, 3.8, 3.9, 3.10 and 3.11 can be easily generalized to the case of a benchmark allocation, i.e. portfolio weights no more positive, and that sum up to 0 (e.g. see [19]).

The diversification measure should be chosen according to the investment universe: as it will be clearer in the following, the diversification metrics in the portfolio weights are not appropriate to quantify diversification in diversified investment universe, as they consider all assets as equivalent (e.g. a short term bond is equivalent to commodity). On the other way round equity portfolio can be well described by diversification measures in portfolio weights. The number of assets for each investment type (e.g. nominal bond, equity, commodity) is relevant as well for most of the diversification measures, with the only exception for the entropy-based diversification metric in the principal component risk contribution and the DAMS approach that determine diversification of the relevant factors in the investment universe.

3.1. Herfindahl Index (D_{Herf})

The *Herfindahl index* is defined as

$$D_{Herf} = w'w,$$

D_{Herf} is bounded between $1/N$ and 1: the lower bound corresponds to maximally diversified portfolios, whereas the upper bound indicates high concentration. Usually D_{Herf} less then 0.01 indicates a well diversified portfolio, whereas D_{Herf} greater then 0.25 indicates high concentration. In portfolio construction it is preferable to consider a related quantity, as follows

$$\tilde{D}_{Herf} = 1 - w'w.$$

In fact $\tilde{D}_{Herf}$ is an increasing function of portfolio diversification.

3.2. Lorentz Curve ($\mathcal{L}$)

In economics the *Lorentz curve* represents the cumulative distribution function of the empirical probability distribution of wealth: this concept has been further developed in [8] to build a diversification measure. The Lorentz curve $\mathcal{L}$ is a function of portfolio weights w, and it is defined in the interval $[0,1]$. Let $\{w_{i;s}\}_{i=1,\ldots,N}$ represent the portfolio weights that are ordered in non-increasing order (i.e. $w_{1;s} \geq w_{2;s} \geq \ldots \geq w_{N;s}$). The Lorentz curve is defined for each i ranging from 0 to N as

$$\mathcal{L}(i) = \sum_{h=1}^{i} w_{i;s}.$$

The definition above leads to $\mathcal{L}(0) = 0$ and $\mathcal{L}(N) = 1$. The Lorentz curve is usually expressed in terms of the percentage of the population: the x-axis is rescaled from $[0,N]$ to $[0,1]$; we label it as $\mathcal{L}(x)$. The graphical shape of the Lorentz curve corresponds to a concave non-decreasing function. The portfolio is maximally diversified when the Lorentz curve converges to a line connecting points $(0,0)$ and $(1,1)$; the higher is the curvature of $\mathcal{L}$, the more concentrated is the portfolio. In Fig. 1 we report the Lorentz curves for some equity indices:

- The left panel shows that the Eurostoxx 50 is more diversified than the S&P 500, the Nasdaq 100, and the Hang Seng.
- The right panel provides an evaluation of the S&P 500 diversification in 2013, in August 2000 (before the bursting of the tech bubble), and in August 2007 (before the subprime crisis): the plot confirms that the tech crisis was profoundly different from the subprime crisis; the tech bubble modified strongly the index composition, thus reducing the index diversification.

The Lorentz curve is scarcely used in portfolio optimization because it is not a scalar quantity. Indeed it can be a useful tool to represent portfolio diversification in credit portfolios.

3.3. The Gini Coefficient ($\mathcal{G}$)

The *Gini coefficient* is a synthetic index quantifying the distance of the Lorenz curve from the diagonal line that expresses maximal diversification (see [8] for more details). It is 1 in case of maximal concentration, and 0 in case of maximal diversification. It is defined as

$$\mathcal{G} = 2\int_0^1 \mathcal{L}_{pwc}(x)dx - 1, \tag{2}$$

$\mathcal{L}_{pwc}(x)$ representing a piecewise continuous function obtained from $\mathcal{L}(x)$ through linear interpolation. We computed the Gini coefficients for the indices in Fig. 1 (left panel): EuroStoxx 50 (0.15), S&P 500 (0.29), Nasdaq 100 (0.29), and the Hang Seng (0.26). The Gini coefficients for the S&P 500 in 2000, 2008 and 2013 are (resp.) 0.35, 0.30, and 0.29 (see Fig. 1; right panel).

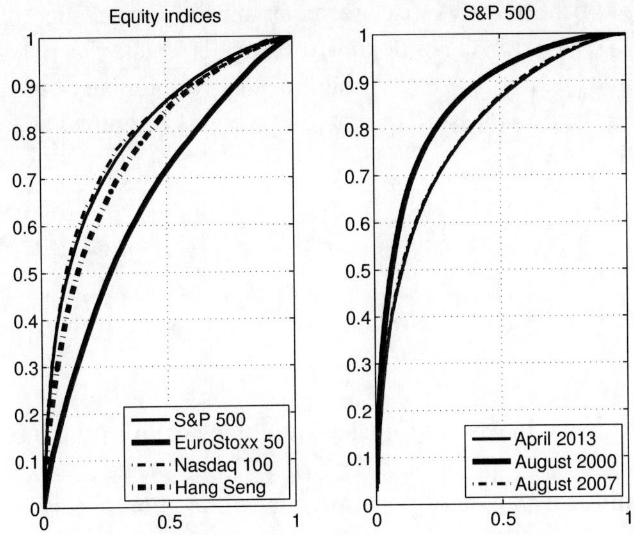

Figure 1. Left panel plots the Lorentz curves for some equity indices (market capitalization at 30/04/2013). Right panel plots the Lorentz curves of S&P 500 on market capitalization at 30/04/2013, 30/08/2000 and 30/08/2007.

3.4. Entropy-based Diversification Measure in Portfolio Weights (H_w)

Entropy is widely used in Physics to assess the degree of randomness of a physical system (see [9]). The *Shannon Entropy* is a functional of the probability of the system state.

Let us suppose that the system can be described by N states. Let $\{p_i\}_{i=1,\ldots,N}$ be the probability of each state. (We remark that p_i are positive numbers that sum up to 1.) The Shannon entropy is defined as:

$$H = -\sum_{i=1}^{N} p_i \log p_i,$$

log indicating the natural logarithm. It can be proven easily that H is always greater then 0, and

- H is maximal ($H_{max} = \log N$) for $p_i = 1/N$ for all $i = 1, \ldots, N$: in this case it is not possible to predict the future evolution of the physical system; all states are equally likely.

- H is minimal ($H_{min} = 0$) for $p_j = 1$ in correspondence of state j and 0 otherwise ($p_i = 0$ for all $i \neq j$): in this case the future evolution of the system is known and the physical system is not stochastic.

The *average number of relevant states*[1] is defined as

$$\mathcal{N}_H[H] = \exp(H).$$

[1]It can be proven easily that if $p_i = 1/M$ for each $i = 1, \ldots, M \leq N$, $\mathcal{N}_H[H] = M$. This analytical result motivates the definition. Meucci in [19] introduced an analogous definition.

Entropy-based diversification measures are based on the formal identification of portfolio weights $\{w_i\}_{i=1,\ldots,N}$ with the probability of system state $\{p_i\}_{i=1,\ldots,N}$ (see [1]), in fact $\{w_i\}_{i=1,\ldots,N}$ and $\{p_i\}_{i=1,\ldots,N}$ correspond to positive numbers that sum up to 1. The entropy-based diversification measure in portfolio weights is defined as follows

$$H_w = -\sum_{i=1}^{N} w_i \log w_i.$$

The average number of relevant states is interpreted here as the average number of relevant portfolio weights:

- $\mathcal{N}_H[H_w]$ is maximal in case of Equally Weighted portfolio and it is equal to N;
- $\mathcal{N}_H[H_w]$ is minimal in case of portfolio concentrated on one asset and it is equal to 1.

We move in the next sections to portfolio diversification measures in the risk space.

3.5. The Entropy-based Diversification Measure in Asset Risk Contribution (H_w^{risk})

In the previous paragraph we reviewed the entropy-based diversification measure in portfolio weights. We illustrate in the following a further generalization aiming to describe the diversification in the distribution of risk contributions across assets. The risk contribution is not a positive quantity and it does not sum up to one. We define the *rescaled risk contribution* as

$$\tilde{\eta}_i(w) = \frac{|\eta_i(w)|}{\sum_i |\eta_i(w)|}.$$

The entropy-based diversification measure in asset risk contribution corresponds to

$$H_w^{risk} = -\sum_{i=1}^{N} \tilde{\eta}_i(w) \log \tilde{\eta}_i(w).$$

The average number of relevant states is interpreted here as the average number of relevant risk contributions:

- $\mathcal{N}_H[H_w^{risk}]$ is maximal in case of Risk Parity portfolio and it is equal to N;
- $\mathcal{N}_H[H_w^{risk}]$ is minimal in case of portfolio risk concentrated on one asset and it is equal to 1.

H_w^{risk} is related to the naive approach of $1/vol$ portfolio solution (see next section): they lead to the same solution in case of constant correlation.

3.6. The 1/vol Rule ($D_{1/vol}$)

Among the Risk Parity portfolio construction schemes the most popular among practitioners consists in building portfolios inverse proportional to asset volatility. The portfolio weights are given in this case by:

$$w_{i;1/vol} = \frac{\frac{1}{\sigma_i}}{\sum_{j=1}^{N} \frac{1}{\sigma_j}}.$$

This solution maximizes H_w^{risk} in case of constant correlations, hence we define $D_{1/vol} = H_w^{risk}\jmath_{\{\rho_{ij}=0\}\forall ij}$.

3.7. The Herfindahl Index Revisited

The Herfindahl index is a function of portfolio weights. The generalization to risk contribution is achieved replacing the portfolio weights w with the rescaled risk contribution $\tilde{\eta}$, as follows

$$\tilde{D}_{Herf}^{risk} = 1 - \tilde{\eta}'\tilde{\eta}.$$

Some authors (see [19]) prefer a different definition:

$$\tilde{D}_{Herf}^{risk} = 1 - w'Cw,$$

C being the correlation matrix.

3.8. The Lorentz Curve Revisited ($\mathcal{L}^{risk}$)

The generalization to take into account risk contribution is given replacing the portfolio weights w with the rescaled risk contribution $\tilde{\eta}$. Because of possible negative correlation, the Lorentz curve $\mathcal{L}^{risk}$ is no more non-decreasing.

3.9. The Gini Coefficient Revisited ($\mathcal{G}^{risk}$)

The generalization of the Gini coefficient is given replacing $\mathcal{L}^{risk}$ in Eq. (2). We label it as $\mathcal{G}^{risk}$. Because of possible negative correlation $\mathcal{G}^{risk}$ can be greater than 1.

3.10. The Entropy-based Diversification Measure in Principal Component Risk Contribution (H_{pcs}^{risk})

In this section we introduce the entropy-based diversification measure in principal component risk contribution (see [19] for more details). The *variance concentration curve* is defined as follows:

$$\nu_i = \tilde{w}_i^2 \lambda_i,$$

ν_i representing the variance due to the portfolio projection on the i-th principal component. The portfolio variance is addictive in ν_i, as in the uncorrelated case, and it can be expressed as $\sigma_w^2 = \sum_{i=1}^{N} \nu_i$. The *diversification distribution* is given normalizing the variance concentration curve with the portfolio variance, as follows:

$$p_i = \frac{\nu_i}{\sigma_w^2}.$$

In [19] Meucci presents a further generalization through a conditional principal component analysis that fulfills specific constraints that are expressed in terms of a linear equation.

As eigenvectors related to the smallest eigenvalues are not relevant, as reported by the random matrix theory (see [27]), it is convenient to consider a rescaled diversification distribution obtained including only the most relevant eigenvectors:

$$\tilde{p}_i = \frac{p_i}{\sum_{i=1}^{K} p_i}.$$

K can be chosen in practice requiring that the most relevant eigenvectors explain a given portion of the full portfolio variance (e.g. 95%, 99%). The entropy-based diversification measure reads in this case as:

$$H_{pcs}^{risk} = -\sum_{i=1}^{K} \tilde{p}_i \log \tilde{p}_i.$$

The average number of relevant states $\mathcal{N}_H[H_{pcs}^{risk}]$ is interpreted here as the average number of relevant principal component risk contributions, hence it represents the number of portfolio independent bet. A different approach for entropy-based diversification measure in terms of principal portfolios can be found in [28].

3.11. The Diversification Measure in Most Diversified Portfolios (D_{MD})

In this section we briefly introduce the diversification measure that is related to the Most Diversified portfolio (see [5]); this strategy is sometimes referred in literature as Maximum Sharpe ratio portfolio (see [17]).

From a geometric point of view, the Most Diversified portfolio corresponds to the tangency portfolio in a standard mean-variance plane (see [8]) under the hypothesis of linear dependency between asset risk premia and asset volatility. The Sharpe ratio (see [30]) quantifies the efficiency of an index-or-strategy: it corresponds to the excess return over risk-free per unit volatility; let μ_{rf} be the risk-free rate. In the linear hypothesis for asset risk premia, expected returns can be written as:

$$\mu_i = \mu_{rf} + s\sigma_i, \tag{3}$$

s corresponding to the (constant) Sharpe ratio. The portfolio Sharpe ratio s_w is given by:

$$s_w = \frac{\sum_{i=1}^{N} \mu_i w_i - \mu_{rf}}{\sigma_w}.$$

Hypothesis in Eq. (3) modifies the equation above as follows:

$$s_w = s\frac{\sum_{i=1}^{N} \sigma_i w_i}{\sigma_w}.$$

The equation above is reported in literature as a diversification measure: it corresponds to the ratio of the linear combination of asset volatilities to the portfolio volatility. The diversification measure is defined as follows

$$D_{MD} = \frac{\sum_{i=1}^{N} \sigma_i w_i}{\sigma_w}.$$

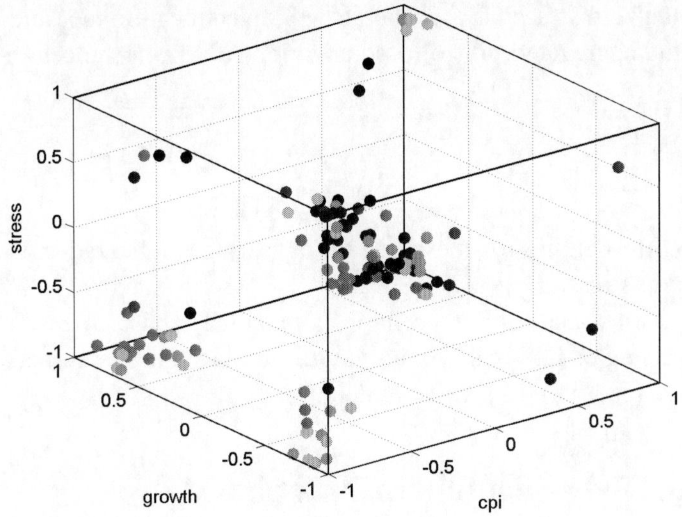

Figure 2. Exhibit taken from [22]. The scatter plot shows the polarization of 139 risky assets in the US to three factors (inflation, growth, and market stress). Polarization indicates the attitude of assets to perform well in rising or falling scenarios (see [22] for more details).

If asset correlation is 1, $D_{MD} = 1$, and thus D_{MD} does not depend on portfolio weights. In highly correlated markets D_{MD} might be ill-defined for portfolio optimization purposes.

3.12. Diversification Across Macroeconomic Scenarios (D_{DAMS})

A novel approach in Strategic Asset Allocation consists in looking at asset classes as vehicles of fundamental factors. According to this method, fundamental factors govern the majority of asset class dynamics, and hence asset allocation should be rephrased in terms of risk allocation of fundamental factors. In [22] we follow this research line proposing a new approach to build more robust Strategic Asset Allocation. The key principia is that *asset price dynamics can be largely explained in terms of changes in expectations of macroeconomic variables and market stress*: stocks move not because of low or high growth but mainly because growth is above or below expectations.

The most relevant factors to determining asset prices are inflation, growth, and market stress. As factors' changes are more relevant than the levels themselves, we define *rising* or *falling* scenarios according to acceleration or deceleration of fundamental factors. Financial markets polarize quite clearly when stimulated by a specific factor. They behave as electron spin in a magnetic field: they polarize towards rising (spin up) or falling (spin down) scenarios. Asset polarization is quantified by the polarization coefficients $\{P_i\}_{i=1,2,3}$: P is defined in the interval $[-1, 1]$, being equal to 1 (resp. -1) in case of asset preferring rising (resp. falling) scenarios (see [22] for more details). Assets can be represented by a scatter plot of the polarization coefficients in correspondence to the three factors: assets are represented as spots in a three-dimensional cube, geometric proximity among spots indicating macroeconomic similarity among assets (see Fig. 2).

According to DAMS (see [22]) the portfolio is well diversified if it is blend versus the macroeconomic and stress scenarios. The DAMS diversification measure is a function of the distance of the aggregated portfolio polarization spot from the centre of the cube, as follows

$$D_{DAMS} = 1 - \frac{2}{\sqrt{3}}\sqrt{\sum_{i=1}^{3}\left(jP_i(w)j - \frac{1}{2}\right)^2},$$

$\{P_i(w)\}_{i=1,2,3}$ corresponding to the portfolio aggregated polarization towards inflation, growth, and market stress. D_{DAMS} is equal to 1 in case of maximally diversification (diversification across macroeconomic scenario is maximal) and 0 in case of concentration towards specific rising or falling scenarios (portfolio placed in the corners of Fig. 2). We refer the interested reader to [22] for more details.

4. Portfolio Diversification in Practice

In this section we provide a portfolio analysis to point out main features of some of the diversification measures reviewed in the previous section.

We considered an investment universe in the US made up of $N = 9$ assets, as follows[2]

- **nominal bonds**: Barclays US Aggregate Treasury (B1), Barclays US Aggregate Corporate (B2), Barclays US Corporate High Yield (B3);
- **equities**: S&P 500 (E1), Russell 2000 (E2), Msci World (E3);
- **commodities**: Gold (C1), Crude Oil WTI (C2), Industrial Metals (C3).

Series are from 29/07/1983 to 29/03/2013; frequency is monthly.

4.1. Enhancing Diversification in Single-period Investment

In this section we clarify the relation between volatility and diversification. We present the results in the mean-variance settings. Asset expected returns and covariance matrix are set as follows:

- Expected returns are set according to a normative approach: we assume that each asset would deliver in the future the same Sharpe ratio (0.25); this figure is coherent with the long term historical average for the equity and bond markets. As detailed in [23], even if this approach presents several limitations, it remains appealing in building strategic asset allocation because it allows to get well diversified portfolios (see section 3.11). Risk-free is set according to the US 3-months Treasury bill at 30/04/2013.
- Covariance matrix is estimated according to a standard EWMA (last three years half life). The risk model to compute the covariance matrix is crucial in the evaluation of

[2]Bloomberg codes are (resp.) luattruu index, luactruu index, lf98truu index, sptr index, ru20intr index, ndduwi index, golds comdty, uscrwtic index, and crb metl index.

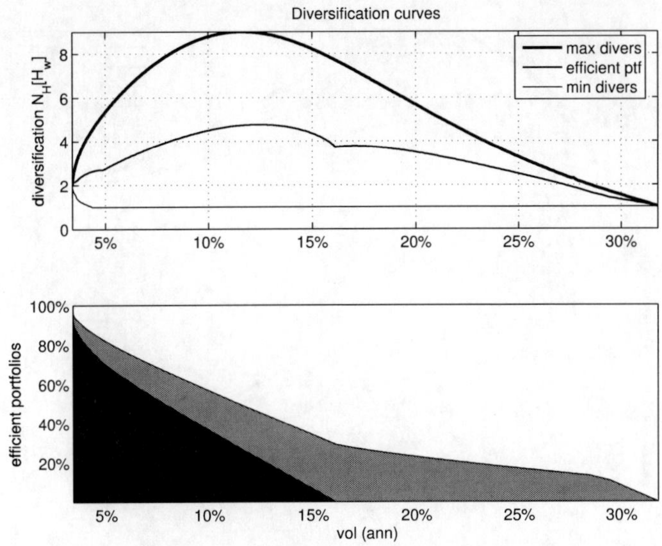

Figure 3. Top panel reports the diversification index $\mathcal{N}_H[H_w]$ as a function of portfolio volatility: the diversification curves refer to the efficient portfolios, and to the maximum and minimum diversification ones. Bottom panel reports the composition of the efficient portfolios.

portfolio diversification[3]. In the present work we do not discuss the implications of the risk model to portfolio diversification.

We define the *diversification curves* that express the relationship between a diversification measure and the portfolio volatility. Portfolio diversification depends primarily on the asset universe, the specific metric used to represent diversification, and the portfolio target volatility, as e.g.

- diversification is scarce around a volatility target that is far from the assets average volatility (diversification metric H_w);
- in strongly correlated markets it is difficult to achieve a good degree of diversification on risk contribution of principle components (diversification metric H_{pcs}^{risk});
- given an investment universe in the corner of the cube in Fig. (2), available diversification across macroeconomic scenarios is very limited (diversification metric D_{DAMS}).

We computed the efficient frontier including the long-only and budget constraints. Fig. 3 (lower panel) reports the asset allocation of the efficient portfolios. The Markowitz optimizer prefers commodities to equity: the average correlation between nominal bonds and commodities (0.13) is lower than that one between nominal bonds and equity (0.21).

[3]In [26] we compared the sample estimator to the Tikhonov method (see [20]) and to the Shrinkage approach (see [18]) in building diversified allocation. We found that the Tikhonov model leads to more diversified allocations.

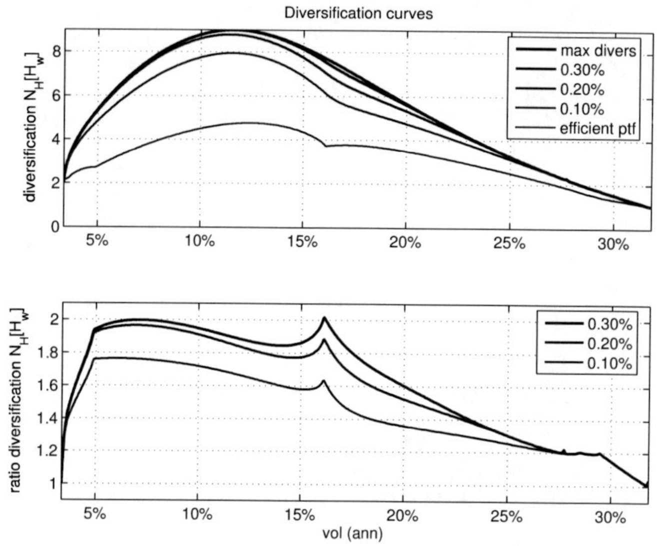

Figure 4. Top panels report the diversification curves for the efficient portfolios, the maximum achievable diversification, and constrained optimizations obtained with a penalty in terms of expected return (0.10%, 0.20%, and 0.30%). Bottom panel reports the ratio of the diversification curves with respect to that one of the efficient portfolios.

We quantified the maximum and minimum available diversification in the investment universe: the diversification curves correspond to the relevant numbers of portfolio weights $\mathcal{N}_H[H_w]$ as a function of the volatility (see upper panel Fig. 3). The diversification curves have been obtained maximizing (or minimizing) $\mathcal{N}_H[H_w]$ according to specific volatility constraints (long-only and budget constraints are included as well). Main findings are:

- the available diversification is maximal in correspondence of a volatility target of 11.63%, corresponding to the volatility of an Equally Weighted portfolio[4]. The shape of the curve depends on assets volatility and correlations.

- efficient portfolios deliver (about) half of the available diversification as expressed by the diversification curve: the maximal diversification corresponds to 4.77 that is half of the available diversification in the investment universe (9 assets).

Then we focus on a measurement of the required mean-variance inefficiency needed to enhance portfolio diversification. In Fig. 4 we consider a double optimization algorithm:

- we firstly optimize according to the standard mean-variance algorithm, $\mu_{eff}(\sigma)$ representing the efficient frontier in the mean-variance plane;

[4]In case of the diversification measure H_w^{risk}, the maximal diversification peak corresponds to the volatility of the Risk Parity portfolio. As a consequence of Ineq. (1), the maximal diversification peak in portfolio weights (H_w) is achieved on a higher volatility target than the peak corresponding to diversification in asset risk contributions (H_w^{risk}).

Table 1. The table reports the optimal allocations obtained maximizing H_w, $D_{1/vol}$, H_w^{risk}, H_{pcs}^{risk}, and D_{MD}, s.t. the long-only and budget constraints

Asset	port $\mathrm{H_w}$	port $\mathrm{D_{1/vol}}$	port $\mathrm{H_w^{risk}}$	port $\mathrm{H_{pcs}^{risk}}$	port $\mathrm{D_{MD}}$
B1	11.11%	28.95%	23.22%	75.17%	76.93%
B2	11.11%	21.65%	23.28%	6.74%	0.00%
B3	11.11%	11.93%	11.96%	6.99%	5.18%
E1	11.11%	7.92%	7.80%	0.00%	0.00%
E2	11.11%	5.91%	6.39%	9.90%	7.91%
E3	11.11%	7.30%	6.76%	0.00%	0.00%
C1	11.11%	6.78%	9.21%	0.88%	1.22%
C2	11.11%	3.98%	4.90%	0.00%	4.01%
C3	11.11%	5.59%	6.49%	0.32%	4.75%
return	4.23%	2.95%	3.14%	1.79%	2.14%
volatility	11.64%	7.06%	7.68%	3.67%	3.86%
Sharpe ratio	0.35	0.40	0.40	0.46	0.53
return MV	4.55%	3.27%	3.45%	2.02%	2.14%
$\mathrm{H_w}$	9.00	7.20	7.64	2.39	2.42
$\mathrm{H_w^{risk}}$	7.32	8.23	8.34	3.12	4.61
$\mathrm{H_{pcs}^{risk}}$	1.25	1.99	1.86	5.00	2.35
$\mathrm{D_{MD}}$	1.42	1.61	1.58	1.84	2.12

- for each volatility target σ_t, we consider the class of portfolios characterized by the risk-return pair $(\mu_{eff}(\sigma_t) - \Delta\mu, \sigma_t)$, $\Delta\mu > 0$ representing a penalty in terms of expected returns;

- given the set of mean-variance sub-optimal portfolios as expressed by $(\mu_{eff}(\sigma_t) - \Delta\mu, \sigma_t)$, we optimize with respect to H_w according to the long-only and budget constraints. In Fig. 4 we present the results of this exercise in correspondence of penalties equal to 0.10%, 0.20% and 0.30%. In Fig. 4 (upper panel) we report the diversification curves for each penalty, and compare them to the mean-variance diversification and the maximal available diversification. A small penalty (0.10%) is able to provide a higher degree of diversification, and hence to obtain more robust mean-variance solutions. A penalty of 0.30% permits to reach the maximal available diversification. In Fig. 4 (lower panel) we report the ratio of the diversification curves to that one of the efficient portfolios. It is evident that a penalty of 0.20% permits to achieve a ratio greater than 1.6 for almost of the whole risk spectrum.

The analysis presented in this section can be generalized to other diversification measures (see [26]).

4.2. Comparing Optimally Diversified Portfolios Across Different Diversification Metrics

In this section we present the optimally diversified portfolios according to diversification measures H_w, $D_{1/vol}$, H_w^{risk}, H_{pcs}^{risk}, and D_{MD}; in the portfolio optimization we included the long-only and budget constraints. In Tab. 1 we report the main results: for each portfolios we show the expected return, volatility, Sharpe ratio, the performance of the mean-variance solution that shares same volatility (return MV), and the figures for the four diversification measures. Each portfolio correctly maximizes its own objective function. Main results are:

- **Diversification measure** H_w. The optimal solution corresponds to the Equally Weighted portfolio. The portfolio is mean-variance inefficient, the inefficiency in terms of expected returns corresponding to 0.32%. H_w is maximal and equal to 9. Diversification in the asset risk contribution is good ($H_w^{risk} = 7.32$), whereas the portfolio is concentrated in term of risk contribution of principal portfolios ($H_{pcs}^{risk} = 1.25$). The portfolio volatility corresponds to the peak in the maximal diversification curve in Fig. 3.

- **Diversification measure** $D_{1/vol}$. The portfolio is highly diversified in asset risk contribution ($H_w^{risk} = 8.23$), and well diversified in portfolio weights ($H_w = 7.20$), whereas it is concentrated in terms of principal portfolios ($H_{pcs}^{risk} = 1.99$).

- **Diversification measure** H_w^{risk}. The portfolio is highly diversified in asset risk contribution ($H_w^{risk} = 8.34$), and well diversified in portfolio weights ($H_w = 7.64$), whereas it is concentrated in terms of principal portfolios ($H_{pcs}^{risk} = 1.86$). Imperfect correlation among assets reduce allocation in nominal bond in favour of commodities, as it is clear comparing the portfolio with previous one.

- **Diversification measure** H_{pcs}^{risk}. We selected only the first five principal components, they account for 97.37% of the full variance. The portfolio is maximally diversified ($H_{pcs}^{risk} = 5$). The portfolio looks poorly diversified in the asset space ($H_w = 2.39$ and $H_w^{risk} = 3.12$). The portfolio volatility is markedly lower than in the previous portfolios.

- **Diversification measure** D_{MD}. The portfolio correctly delivers the highest Sharpe ratio (0.53), and it is mean-variance efficient (see section 3.11). The portfolio is modestly diversified in portfolio weights ($H_w = 2.42$) and risk contribution ($H_w^{risk} = 4.61$ and $H_{pcs}^{risk} = 2.35$). Volatility is slightly higher than that one of the previous portfolio.

We point out that the entropy-based diversification measure on principal component risk contribution leads to portfolio that is concentrated in the asset space. Similarly the portfolio obtained maximizing the entropy-based diversification measure in the asset risk contribution is concentrated in the principal component space.

4.3. Analysing Implications in Terms of Portfolio Rebalancing in Multi-period Investments

In this section we face the problem of portfolio rebalancing. We consider $D_{1/vol}$, H^{risk}_{asset}, H^{risk}_{pcs}, and D_{MD}. The historical simulations presented in this section are out of sample: each allocation at time k is determined according to a sample estimation of the covariance matrix on 36-months rolling windows ending at time k; time-series are monthly. As in the previous section, the optimization is subjected to the long-only and budget constraints.

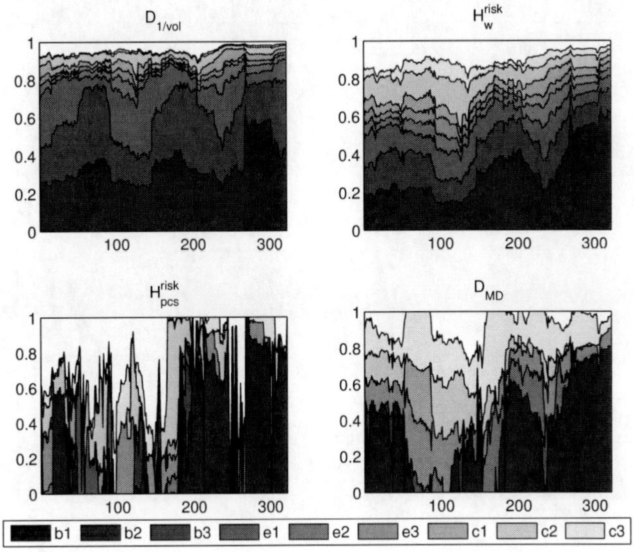

Figure 5. Back testing of diversification measures $D_{1/vol}$, H^{risk}_{w}, H^{risk}_{pcs}, and D_{MD}; series are from 29/07/1986 to 29/03/2013. Portfolios are optimized on a monthly basis; covariance estimation is historical on 36-months rolling basis. Back testing is out-of-sample. The plots report the optimal allocations.

Fig. 5 reports the asset allocations as a function of time. At first glance, it is evident that $D_{1/vol}$ and H^{risk}_{w} provide more stable allocations; H^{risk}_{pcs} and D_{MD} deliver unstable allocations over time: as we will see in the next section the estimation risk in correlation poses severe limitations in the practical application of these portfolio construction schemes. Moreover we should stress that high portfolio turn-over is costly in practical implementations of dynamic strategies. In Fig. 6 we report the back testing of the four strategies: we plot the gross cumulative performance; we included also the cumulative performance net of trading costs. We assume that the strategy can be implemented through liquid derivatives, thus cost hypothesis corresponds to 0.15% for 100% portfolio turn-over. The best performers are $D_{1/vol}$ and H^{risk}_{w}; the worst is H^{risk}_{pcs}. The average annual trading cost for $D_{1/vol}$, H^{risk}_{w}, H^{risk}_{pcs}, and D_{MD} corresponds to $0.08\%, 0.07\%, 0.55\%$ and 0.25%.

In Tab. (2) we report the correlation matrix among the simulated strategies in this section. Figures show that the strategies provide diversified approaches for portfolio diversification.

Table 2. The table reports the correlation matrix among portfolios obtained maximizing $D_{1/vol}$, H_w^{risk}, H_{pcs}^{risk}, and D_{MD} in a back testing from 29/07/1986 to 29/03/2013 (see Fig. 6)

	port $\mathbf{D_{1/vol}}$	port $\mathbf{H_w^{risk}}$	port $\mathbf{H_{pcs}^{risk}}$	port $\mathbf{D_{MD}}$
port $\mathbf{D_{1/vol}}$	1	0.8701	0.5352	0.4316
port $\mathbf{H_w}^{risk}$	0.8701	1	0.6878	0.7062
port $\mathbf{H_{pcs}^{risk}}$	0.5352	0.6878	1	0.5344
port $\mathbf{D_{MD}}$	0.4316	0.7062	0.5344	1

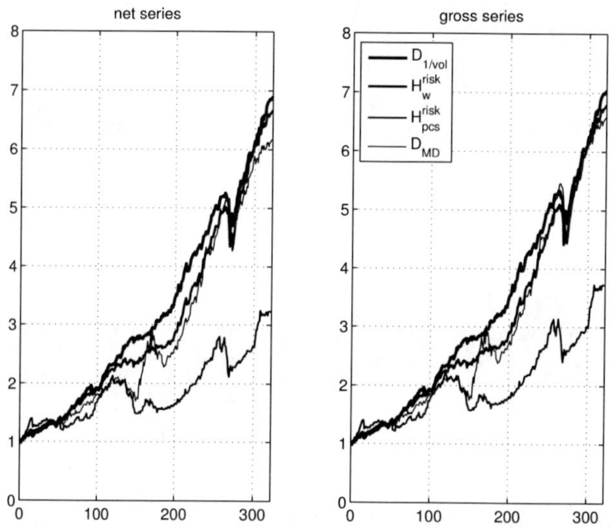

Figure 6. Back testing of diversification measures $D_{1/vol}$, H_w^{risk}, H_{pcs}^{risk}, and D_{MD}; series are from 29/07/1986 to 29/03/2013. Portfolios are optimized on a monthly basis; covariance estimation is historical on 36-months rolling basis. Back testing is out-of-sample. The plots report the cumulative performance; performances are gross and net of trading costs.

4.4. Testing Robustness of Optimally-diversified Portfolios to Estimation Risk

Our aim in this section is to evaluate robustness of diversification metrics $D_{1/vol}$, H_w^{risk}, H_{pcs}^{risk} and D_{MD} to estimation risk in the covariance matrix. We performed a Montecarlo experiment. We consider 10 assets, and we modelled them according to a multivariate gaussian distribution. The true unknown covariance matrix is composed as follows: volatilities are 1%, 2%, 3%, ..., and 10%, correlations are constant across all pairs and equal to 0.30 (weak correlation) and 0.90 (high correlation). The weak correlation hypothesis represents a diversified investment universe[5] (as e.g. nominal bonds, inflation-linked bonds, equities, commodities, volatility, and dynamic strategies), while the strong correlation settings refers

[5]The average correlation of assets in sections 4.1, 4.2, and 4.3 is 0.31.

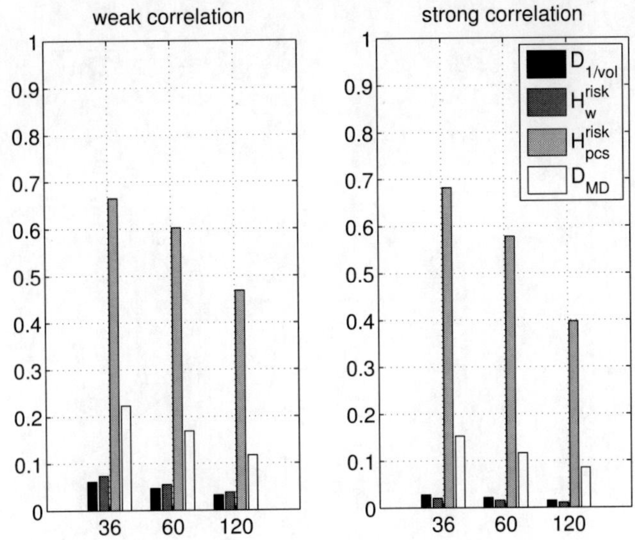

Figure 7. Average turn-over between the true portfolio and the estimated optimal ones. The two subplots refer to 0.30 correlation hypothesis (weak), and 0.90 (strong). Each subplot reports the average turn-over for four different portfolio construction schemes ($D_{1/vol}$, H_w^{risk}, H_{pcs}^{risk} and D_{MD}) and three different sample size (36, 60 and 120-months).

to an investment universe of correlated assets (e.g. equity portfolios). Estimation errors are generated simulating time-series according to different sample size: 36, 60, and 120 months; each configuration is simulated 10000 times. The impact of estimation risk is measured in terms of portfolio turn-over between the estimated optimal portfolios (obtained from the sample covariance matrix) and the true one (obtained from the true covariance matrix). Fig. 7 plots the average turn-over for the different parameters configuration: left (resp. right) panel refers to the weak (resp. strong) correlation hypothesis. Main results are

- $D_{1/vol}$ and H_w^{risk} are the most robust metrics; H_{pcs}^{risk} shows high instability;
- increasing the data sample size reduces the impact of estimation risk;
- increasing the average correlation reduces the impact of estimation risk (i.e. the strong correlation assumption leads to more stable allocations than those obtained in the weak correlation hypothesis).

Fig. 7 shows clearly that estimation risk poses severe constraints in practical implementation. In Fig. 8 we decompose the estimation risk within instability in volatilities and correlation. We consider the weak correlation hypothesis. In order to measure estimation risk in volatilities, volatility are estimated from simulated series, correlation corresponds to the true one; conversely in order to quantify estimation risk in correlation, correlation is estimated from simulated series and volatilities correspond to the true ones. Main findings are:

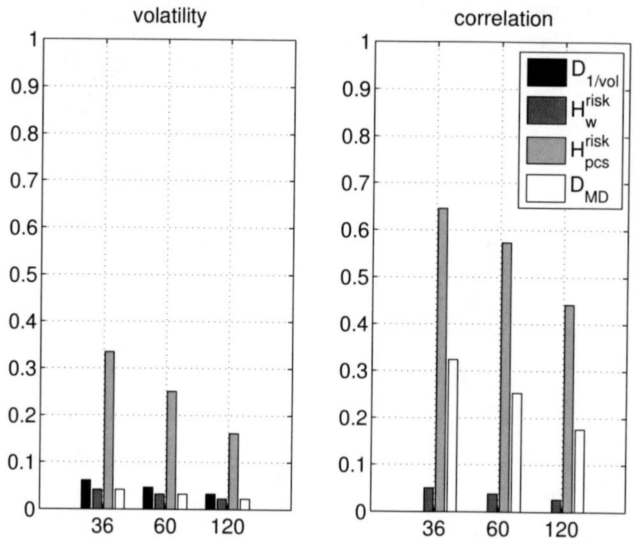

Figure 8. Average turn-over between the true portfolio and the estimated optimal ones. In the two subplots we separate the effect of estimation risk in volatility and correlation. Each subplot reports the average turn-over for four different portfolio construction schemes ($D_{1/vol}$, H_w^{risk}, H_{pcs}^{risk} and D_{MD}) and three different sample size (36, 60 and 120-months).

- **Diversification measure** $D_{1/vol}$: as portfolio construction depends only on volatility estimates, errors with respect to movement in correlation are zero;
- **Diversification measure** H_w^{risk}: errors due to estimation risk in volatilities and correlation are comparable;
- **Diversification measure** H_{pcs}^{risk}: dispersion in estimated portfolios is mainly explained in terms of estimation risk of correlation;
- **Diversification measure** D_{MD}: dispersion in estimated portfolios is mainly explained in terms of estimation risk of correlation.

Main results from this section and the previous one are: $D_{1/vol}$ and H_w^{risk} provide robust solutions to portfolio construction; H_{pcs}^{risk} is highly sensitive to correlation estimation risk, and thus it provides unstable allocations over time; D_{MD} is less sensitive than H_{pcs}^{risk}, but still noisy and still mainly impacted by estimation risk in correlation.

5. Measuring Dependency among Assets: From the Correlation Coefficient to the Kullback-Leibler Pseudo-distance

In the previous section we see that estimation risk in correlation poses severe limitations in the practical implementation of some entropy-based diversification measures. Moreover the notions of diversification and dependency among assets are closely related. We conclude this chapter briefly discussing main pitfalls in the correlation coefficient, then introducing the Kullback-Leibler pseudo-distance, and finally briefly reinterpreting the notion of asset dependency according to the DAMS approach.

The standard Pearson's r or correlation coefficient is defined as follows:

$$\rho = \frac{E\left[(x-\mu_x)(y-\mu_y)\right]}{\sigma_x \sigma_y}, \tag{4}$$

where $E[...]$ indicates the usual expectation operator, μ_x and μ_y stand for the expected values of x and y, and σ_x and σ_y for the standard deviations. While the correlation coefficient is widely used, there are some pitfalls and considerations that should be pointed out:

- the correlation reflects the noisiness and direction of a linear relationship, but not the *slope* which is better described by the *asset beta* (see [12]);
- the correlation approximates non-linear dependency between variables in terms of a linear relationship;
- as proven in [15], the statement according to which positive (resp. negative) correlated assets tend to rise together is flawed (see Fig. 9): correlation does not refer to trend; the drift is cleaned up as described in Eq. (4);
- correlation measures can even fail in identifying deterministic relationship between variables: let x be a random variables uniformly distributed between -1 and $+1$, and let $y = x^2$; even if x and y are deterministically related, the correlation coefficient is zero;
- the correlation does not take into account higher order terms like $x^2y, xy^2, x^2y^2, ...$;
- the correlation quantifies the dependency between two variable, but it cannot be generalized to describe relationship among more numerous variables.

A more robust approach to measure dependency among assets can be found within the Information Theory (see [7]): two variables are independent if and only if the joint probability equals the product of marginal distributions[6], i.e. $P(x,y) = P(x)P(y)$. The *Kullback-Leibler pseudo-distance* (KL pseudo-distance in the following) quantifies the distance between two probability distributions: it permits one to measure the distance between $P(x,y)$ and $P(x)P(y)$, and thus to evaluate the degree of dependency between random variables x and y. The KL pseudo-distance is defined (see [7]) as follows:

$$D\left(P(x,y)\|P(x)P(y)\right) = \sum_{x,y} P(x,y) \log \frac{P(x,y)}{P(x)P(y)}. \tag{5}$$

It can be proven that the KL pseudo-distance is always greater than zero, and equal to zero if and only if $P(x,y) = P(x)P(y)$: any dependency between x and y is certainly to increase

[6]If variables are Gaussian distributed variables are independent if and only if correlations are zero.

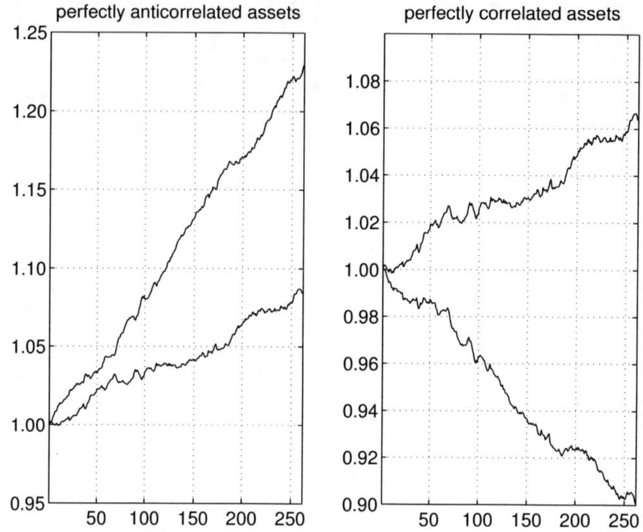

Figure 9. Exhibit redrawn from [15]. Left (resp. right) panel plots two synthetic assets with correlation coefficient equal to -1 (resp. $+1$).

the KL pseudo-distance. This property motivates why this measure is called distance[7]. The generalization of the KL pseudo-distance to more random variables is straightforward:

$$D\left(P(x_1,\ldots,x_N)\|\prod_{i=1}^{N}P(x_i)\right) = \sum_{x_1,\ldots,x_N} P(x_1,\ldots,x_N)\log\frac{P(x_1,\ldots,x_N)}{\prod_{i=1}^{N}P(x_i)}. \tag{6}$$

In the Appendix we briefly review some analytical properties of the KL pseudo-distance, and we briefly discuss the estimation problem. The KL pseudo-distance provides some improvements with respect to the correlation coefficient, in fact:

- it permits to detect non-linear relationship among variables;
- the KL pseudo-distance between two deterministically related variables is maximal, and equal to the entropy of the variables (see Appendix);
- it correctly interprets dependency between assets in Fig. 9;
- as shown in Eq. (6), the KL pseudo-distance is able to describe dependency among more than two variables.

Fig. 10 offers a comparison between the KL pseudo-distance and the correlation for a data set including the S&P 500 and the US Treasury 10-yr bond since December 1953. We considered 36-months rolling windows; Fig. 10 corresponds to a scatter plot of the two quantities. The KL pseudo-distance is computed on the sign of returns: the asset return space is described according to two symbols ($+1$, and -1). Confidence level bands have

[7]However it should be stressed that this measure is not symmetric. There are several ways to get a symmetric KL pseudo-distance (see [7]).

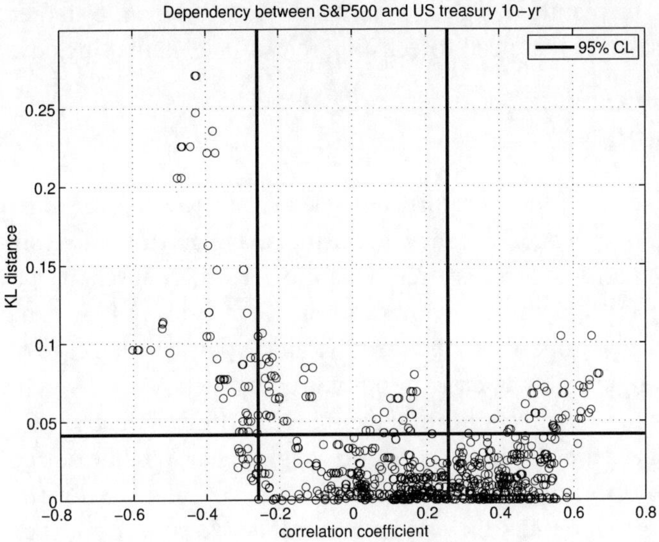

Figure 10. Scatter plot of the correlation coefficient vs the KL pseudo-distance. The black bands refer to 95% confidence level. Assets are S&P 500 and US Treasury 10-yr, database is from Schiller, time-series are monthly and from December 1953. Each point has been evaluated in rolling windows of 36 observations.

been computed numerically[8]. The plot shows clearly that there are many observations in the lowest right box: these observations would be (wrongly) interpreted, according to the correlation coefficient, as historical periods characterized by a positive trend between the S&P 500 and the US Treasury 10-yr bond; the KL pseudo-distance demonstrates that their relationship is not significant.

We conclude briefly discussing how the notion of correlation changes according to the DAMS approach (see section 3.12). According to DAMS, correlation itself is driven by factors dynamics. Assets placed in opposite corners in Fig. 2 are named *dual*: they present opposite polarizations. In [22] we show that according to this interpretation:

- dual assets present negative correlation that is stable over time (e.g. nominal bonds and commodities),
- assets in the same corners present positive correlation, that is stable over time (e.g. gold miners stocks and commodities),
- pairs of assets, which cannot be classified as in the previous items, present mixed correlation pattern that is not stable over time, and should tend to zero in the long run (e.g. nominal bonds and equity).

According to DAMS, correlation itself is a meaningless quantity, hence Strategic Asset

[8]We simulated uncorrelated gaussian random variables with a probability of positive performance equal to 0.60; this figure is coherent with historical estimates for the S&P 500 and the US Treasury 10-yr bond since December 1953.

Allocation should be mainly designed in terms of factors dynamics rather than on standard mean-variance packages that need forecasting returns and estimating covariance matrix.

6. Conclusion

Diversification is a useful tool for portfolio selection in presence of high uncertainty in financial markets. The recent crisis renewed the interest in portfolio diversification as demonstrated by the popularity in forecast-free portfolio construction schemes as Minimum Variance, Risk Parity and Maximum Diversification. Kaya et al. in [14] demonstrated that the Risk Parity approach is superior to the mean-variance portfolios in case of high uncertainty on asset expected figures and in case of leptokurtic markets.

We reviewed the main diversification metrics in portfolio selection. They can be divided in diversification measures (1) in the portfolio weights and (2) in the risk contribution (either in the asset space or in the principal component space), and (3) a metric derived from a factor approach. Among them the estimation risk is a key issue for the second class: we investigated in details robustness and efficacy of these diversification models. Main results coming from our analysis are:

- the simple entropy measure in portfolio weights (H_w) is very efficient in producing well diversified portfolios when coupled with the standard mean-variance model: we show that a small penalty in terms of expected return (about 0.20%) is enough to leave the optimizer to produce more robust allocations; moreover this metric does not suffer from estimation risk;
- the entropy-based diversification measure in asset risk contribution (H_w^{risk}) produces diversified allocations that are stable over time; estimation risk is small and well balanced between volatility and correlation; the optimal portfolios looked in the principal component space is quite concentrated;
- the entropy-based diversification measure in risk contribution of principal portfolios (H_{pcs}^{risk}) produces concentrated allocations in the asset space, that are unstable over time; estimation risk is very large and mainly due to correlation instability; estimation risk is even more severe in case of more diversified investment universe (small correlation among assets increases the dispersion of simulated portfolios around the true one);
- the diversification measure in Most Diversified portfolio (D_{MD}) produces concentrated allocations in the asset space; portfolios are unstable over time, estimation risk is large and mainly due to correlation instability; as in the previous case estimation risk is more severe in case of more diversified investment universe.

The applications presented in this chapter should be considered for illustrating purposes. The views expressed are those of the author and do not necessarily correspond to those of AMUNDI.

Acknowledgments

I would like to thank Ali Zerrad for his contribution in the analysis presented in section 4.4

Appendix

In the Appendix we report some analytical properties of the Kullback-Leibler pseudo-distance. Eq. (5) can be rearranged as

$$D\left(P(x,y)\|P(x)P(y)\right) = H(x) + H(y) - H(x,y), \tag{7}$$

where $H(x)$, $H(y)$ and $H(x,y)$ stand respectively for the Shannon Entropy of x, y, and the joint variable (x,y). This representation allows one to write down the following inequality:

$$D\left(P(x,y)\|P(x)P(y)\right) \leq max\left(H(x), H(y)\right), \tag{8}$$

the equality holding if and only if x and y are deterministically related. The second consequence of Eq. (7) is that it permits one to re-write the KL pseudo-distance as:

$$D\left(P(x,y)\|P(x)P(y)\right) = \log\left(\frac{N_x N_y}{N_{xy}}\right), \tag{9}$$

where N_x, N_y and N_{xy} are respectively the average number of relevant states of $P(x)$, $P(y)$, and $P(x,y)$.

We move now to briefly discussing the estimation problem in Eq. (6). For the sake of simplicity let us assume that random variables x_i can take only two values ($+1$ and -1). In this case the dimension of the asset response space is 2^N. Let $N = 4$. If we require at least 30 observations (on average) for each state, we need a sample size of $30 \cdot 2^4 = 480$, which is equivalent to 40 years of monthly observations. This simple evaluation clarifies why measuring the KL pseudo-distance might be sometimes difficult in practice; evaluating pair-wise dependency can be more efficient in case of short data sample (in this case we can lower 40 years of monthly observations to 10 years; i.e. $30 \cdot 2^2 = 120$). Nevertheless it is worth pointing out that there is a vast literature which faced the sampling problem of the KL pseudo-distance: many contributions can be found within the field of Computational Neuroscience, where the KL pseudo-distance has been extensively used to study neural coding of sensory information (see [31] [25] [24]).

References

[1] A. K. Bera and S. Y. Park. Optimal portfolio diversification using maximum entropy. *Econometric Reviews*, 27(4–6):484–512, 2008.

[2] M. J. Best and R. R. Grauer. On the sensitivity of mean-variance-efficient portfolios to changes in asset means: some analytical and computational results. *Review of Financial Studies*, 4:315–342, 1991.

[3] F. Black and R. Litterman. Asset Allocation: Combining Investors Views with Market Equilibrium. *Fixed Income Research Goldman Sachs*, 1990.

[4] V. Chopra and W. T. Ziemba. The effects of errors in means, variances, and covariances on optimal portfolio choice. *The Journal of Portfolio Management*, pages 6–11, 1993.

[5] Y. Choueifaty and Y. Coignard. Towards Maximum Diversification. *The Journal of Portfolio Management*, 35(1), 2008.

[6] R. Clarke, H. De Silva, and S. Thorley. Risk Parity, Maximum Diversification, and Minimum Variance: An Analytical Perspective. *The Journal of Portfolio Management*, 39(3):39–53, 2013.

[7] T. M. Cover and J. A. Thomas. *Elements of Information Theory.* Wiley series in Telecommunications and Signal Processing, 1991.

[8] P. Demey, S. Maillard, and T. Roncalli. Risk-based indexation. *Lyxor white paper*, 2012.

[9] R. P. Feynman, R. B. Leighton, and M. Sands. *The Feynman Lectures on Physics.* Addison-Wesley Publishing Company, 1963.

[10] G. M.Loeb. *Battle for investment survival.* John Wiley & Sons, 2007.

[11] A. Ilmanen. *Expected returns. An Investor's Guide to Harvesting Market Rewards.* Wiley Finance, 2011.

[12] J. C.Hull. *Options, Futures and Other Derivatives.* Prentice Hall, 2000.

[13] J. D. Jobson and B. Korkie. Estimation for Markowitz efficient portfolios. *Journal of the American Statistical Association*, 75:544–554, 1980.

[14] H. Kaya and W Lee. Demystifying Risk Parity. *Neuberger Berman Working Paper*, 2012.

[15] F.S. Lhabitant. Correlation vs. Trends: A Common Misinterpretation. *EDHEC-Risk Institute Working Paper*, 2011.

[16] S. Maillard, T. Roncalli, and J. Teiletche. The Properties of Equally Weighted Risk Contribution Portfolios. *The Journal of Portfolio Management*, 36(4):60–70, 2010.

[17] L. Martellini. Toward the design of Better Equity Benchmarks. *The Journal of Portfolio Management*, 34(4):1–8, 2008.

[18] A. Meucci. *Risk and Asset Allocation.* Springer Verlag, 2007.

[19] A. Meucci. Managing Diversification. *Risk*, pages 74–79, 2009.

[20] S. Park and D. P. O'Leary. Portfolio selection using Tikhonov filtering to estimate the covariance matrix. *SIAM J. Financial Math.*, 1:932–961, 2010.

[21] M. H. Partovi and M. Caputo. Principal Portfolios: Recasting the efficient frontier. *Economic bullettin*, 7:1–10, 2004.

[22] G. Pola. Rethinking strategic asset allocation in terms of Diversification Across Macroecononomic Scenarios. *AMUNDI Special Focus*, 2013.

[23] G. Pola and S. de Laguiche. Unexpected Returns. Methodological considerations on Expected Returns in Uncertainty. *AMUNDI Working Paper WP-032-2012*, 2012.

[24] G. Pola, R. S. Petersen, A. Thiele, M. P. Young, and S. Panzeri. Data-Robust Tight Lower Bounds to the Information Carried by Spike Times of a Neuronal Population. *Neuronal Computation*, 17(9):1962–2005, 2005.

[25] G. Pola, S. R. Schultz, R. S. Petersen, and S. Panzeri. A practical guide to information analysis of spike-trains. In *Neuroscience Databases*, pages 139–154. Springer Verlag, 2002.

[26] G. Pola and A. Zerrad. Implications of Estimation Risk in Portfolio Diversification. *In preparation*, 2013.

[27] M. Potters, J. P. Bouchaud, and L. Laloux. Financial applications of random matrix theory: Old laces and new pieces. *Acta Physica Polonica B*, 9:2767–2784, 36.

[28] M. Rudin and J. S. Morgan. A portfolio diversification index. *The Journal of Portfolio Management*, 32:81–89.

[29] A. Russo. Low risk equity investments: empirical evidence, theories, and the AMUNDI experience of alternative beta strategies. *AMUNDI Working Paper WP-033-2013*, 2013.

[30] W. F. Sharpe. The Sharpe ratio. *The Journal of Portfolio Management*, 21(1):49–58.

[31] A. Treves and S. Panzeri. The Upward Bias in Measures of Information Derived from Limited Data Samples. *Neural Computation*, 7(2):399–407, 1995.

In: Stock Markets
Editors: F. Petroni, F. Prattico and G. D'Amico
ISBN: 978-1-62808-751-2

Chapter 8

OPTIMAL FISCAL POLICY IN A SIMPLE MACROECONOMIC CONTEXT

Luca Correani[1,*] ***Fabio Di Dio***[2,†] ***and Stefano Patri***[3,‡]
[1]Department of Economics and Management, Tuscia University, Viterbo, Italy
[2]Consip S.p.A., Macroeconomic Modelling Unit, Rome, Italy
[3]Department of Methods and Models for Economics, Territory and Finance
Sapienza University of Rome, Rome, Italy

Abstract

This article derives optimal fiscal rules within a stochastic model of Keynesian type in the context of Poole (1970) analysis. By using optimal control theory and applying the Hamilton-Jacoby-Bellman equation, we extend the original Poole results concerning the output stabilization properties of monetary policy to the case of fiscal policy. In particular, we look for the optimal setting of government expenditure and lump-sum taxation in the case that the fiscal authority wishes to keep the product close to a reference value and that the economy is assumed to be affected by stochastic disturbances of real and/or monetary type. According to the findings an expenditure rule is preferable to a taxation rule whatever the source of disturbances.

PACS 05.45-a, 52.35.Mw, 96.50.Fm

Keywords: Fiscal Policy, Poole model, Hamilton-Jacoby-Bellman equation

AMS Subject Classification: 49L, 90C, 93A

1. Introduction

In this paper we address a common question in economics, namely, how should a Ramsey-type authority conduct output stabilization policy. In particular, we analyze how the policy-maker can choose between public expenditure or lump-sum taxation as its optimal policy

*E-mail address: correani@unitus.it
†E-mail address: fabio.didio@consip.it
‡E-mail address: stefano.patri@uniroma1.it

instrument in a Poole-type model (Poole, 1970). In his pioneering study of the choice of the optimal monetary instrument, Poole has shown that the stochastic structure of the economy and the source of different disturbances would affect the choice of the optimal policy instrument. In particular, he compares a money supply rule to an interest rate rule and uses output variability as the sole evaluation criterion. He finds out that an interest rate rule is better than a money supply rule if shocks originate in money markets, whereas a money supply rule gets better results in a context where output shocks operate. The original analysis of Poole was conducted within a stochastic variant of the standard textbook IS-LM model and has exerted a significant influence on both the theoretical literature and the real-world monetary practice.

A natural question stemming from Poole basic insight is whether a similar problem arises in fiscal policy. In this case it might be possible to evaluate the effectiveness of fiscal policy in stabilizing output in a stochastic context.[1]

Interestingly, the extension of the original Poole contribution to fiscal policy remained relatively unexplored. In fact, no existing analyses from that contribution onwards explicitly take into account the relative effectiveness of fiscal instruments in the original Poole context: subsequent developments have somewhat broadened the range of issues that could be studied with this model, rather by enriching it with other elements (e.g, the supply side and the rational expectations), notably by incorporating the Poole insights within modern general equilibrium models.

But while Poole's analysis has been generalized in several directions, e.g. to include a variable price level, an output/output gap distinction, and interest rate feedback rules, these extensions mainly entail deep changes in the basic Poole's setup (introducing aggregate-supply side and policy-rule specifications), so the advent of the optimizing IS-LM equations does not allow any critical difference to Poole's results.

The major extension of the basic Poole model is by Canzoneri et al.(1983), who augment the closed-economy Poole analysis with rational expectations and imperfect information. They show that the results of the original Poole analysis with respect to liquidity as well as output demand shocks are exactly replicated. Recently, in a standard New-Keynesian model Collard and Dellas (2005) examine the properties of alternative targeting procedures in an economy that represents a general equilibrium rendition of Poole contribution. In their model, they obtain the original Poole results concerning output stabilization properties of money and interest rate when the degree of intertemporal substitution is 'sufficiently' low (see also Collard and Dellas 2000). Hoffmann and Kempa (2009) extend the original Poole analysis to a general two country open-economy context for a large economy and a small open economy. Their results for the large economy resemble those of the original Poole analysis whereas in the small economy scenario the results of the large economy continue to hold only for domestic shocks.

The present paper instead takes an alternative line with respect the current literature.

In fact, our discussion of fiscal policy effectiveness is based on the original IS-LM model where the intertemporal optimization and expectations do not play any role in accounting for aggregate economic activity. In fact, we deal with this issue in the original

[1]As a matter of fact, in the conclusion of his paper Poole (1970) states that: "*While the instrument problem has been analyzed as a monetary policy problem, it is worth pointing out that a similar problem arises in fiscal policy*".

Poole stochastic model as we extend the original results concerning the output stabilization properties of monetary policy to the case of fiscal policy. A central feature of our analysis is that optimal policy is derived in a highly stylized environment. A key advantage of this stylized approach is that it facilitates understanding the ways through which policy should respond to stabilize output as a consequence of a particular shock in isolation. Furthermore, the mathematical technique is enough general and flexible to take into account the nature of the shock both of real and monetary type.

In fact, the mathematical tool we use is the Hamilton-Jacoby-Bellman equation applied to the minimization of an integral operator whose variable is described by a controlled stochastic differential equation. This procedure is independent from the nature of the shock.

Finally, while policy results are generally drawn with numerical simulations we developed a mathematical technique for the effects to be computed analytically with an explicit solution that makes more transparent the mechanism at work.

We find two main results. Firstly, the source of economy disturbances affects the effectiveness of fiscal policy. Secondly, an optimal expenditure rule is preferable to a taxation rule.

The remainder of the paper is organized as follows. Section 2 is devoted to a brief description of the model setup and discusses how real and monetary uncertainty works. Section 3 describes how fiscal authority solves the optimal problem of fiscal policy and explores which instrument, public expenditure or lump-sum taxation, is the optimal one in that context. Section 4 concludes.

2. The Setup

Following Poole (1970), the problem of a benevolent Ramsey-type authority is to keep the current output near an established reference value denoted by Y_f. Moreover, it is assumed to have always access to the available policy instruments, that is lump-sum taxation and government expenditure.

The authority is increasingly worse-off the larger the deviations are from the reference value. This assumption translates in a quadratic expected loss function J of the type:

$$J = \mathbf{E}[(Y_T - Y_f)^2], \tag{1}$$

where $[0, T]$ is the time span over which we work, Y_T is the stochastic level of output at time T, Y_f is the deterministic reference value and $\mathbf{E}$ denotes the expectation with respect to the probability law of Y.

The traditional IS-LM model, properly augmented to include stochastic shocks of fiscal policy, is assumed to be the constraint for the authority.

Thus, the authority wishes to minimize this function (1) subject to the constraint imposed by a stochastic fixed-price IS-LM model in differential form[2]:

$$dY_t = dC_t + dI_t + dG_t, \tag{2}$$

[2] We get the model in differential form to take properly into account the uncertainty. In fact, in the case of the textbook formalization of IS-LM model, the fiscal uncertainty actually would not operate and, as consequence, the fiscal instruments would be basically equivalent in stabilizing output.

$$dC_t = c dY_t^D, \tag{3}$$

$$dY_t^D = dY_t - dT_t, \tag{4}$$

$$dI_t = \gamma dY_t^D - h dr_t + \lambda_1 u_t dB_t, \tag{5}$$

$$dM_t - dP_t = l_1 dY_t^D - l_2 dr_t + \lambda_2 u_t dB_t, \tag{6}$$

where the symbols are the usual ones and the equations are actually self-explanatory: in the order, they are the resource constraint of the economy (the ex-ante equality between investment and saving), consumption equation C_t and the investment equation I_t that are function of national disposable income Y_t^D (and also of the interest rate r_t for the investment), the demand for money equation (as a function of national disposable income and the interest rate as well), G_t represents the government expenditure; T_t is the lump-sum taxation; $0 < c < 1$ and $\gamma > 0$, represent the speed of adjustment in the goods market; $h > 0$, $l_1 > 0$, $l_2 > 0$ the speed of adjustment in the money market. In the following, we also assume that money supply and prices do not change ($dM_t = 0$ and $dP_t = 0$). Moreover, u_t represents the derivatives of the available instrument (public expenditure or taxation) with respect to time.

Furthermore, dB_t is a Brownian motion and actually the source of the system uncertainty.

It is worth remembering that a diffusion process is a continuous version of the random walk, which is a solution of a stochastic differential equation. It is a continuous-time Markov process with continuous sample paths.

In the case that the uncertainty is not present, the model collapses to the deterministic IS-LM model. In this case, the coefficients of dB_t in (5) and in (6) are assumed to be null.

As a result, the reduced form of the deterministic case boils down to $dY_t^* = \mu_i u_t^{(i)}$ where the control variable $u_t^{(i)}$ is the variation rate of the control variable and accordingly, μ_i is Keynesian multiplier associated to the fiscal instrument. The index i runs over G, T and in particular it is set to G if the instrument is the public expenditure, whereas it is T if the instrument is the taxation policy.

The keynesian multiplier will be

$$\mu_G = \frac{1}{1 - c - \gamma + h l_1 / l_2}, \tag{7}$$

if the control variable is the public expenditure, or

$$\mu_T = \frac{-c - \gamma + h l_1 / l_2}{1 - c - \gamma + h l_1 / l_2}, \tag{8}$$

when the control variable is taxation (see the appendix A for more details).

According to the usual stability conditions of the system, taxation multiplier must be negative, so that the following relationship must hold jointly:

$$-c - \gamma + \frac{h l_1}{l_2} < 0, \tag{9}$$

and

$$1 - c - \gamma + \frac{hl_1}{l_2} > 0. \tag{10}$$

Both these two conditions together entail to the following relationship:

$$0 < c + \gamma - \frac{hl_1}{l_2} < 1. \tag{11}$$

In the following analysis, we will first discuss the consequences of allowing for uncertainty, alternatively, from real or monetary market involving different effects in term of fiscal instrument effectiveness.

The first case corresponds essentially to the IS curve shifts due to stochastic disturbance if the real interest rate was not to change. The second case is when monetary disturbances make it impossible to fix the shape of the LM curve in order to stabilize the system.

Then, we extend our analysis to the case of disturbances of both real and monetary side.

In order to illustrate this point according to the source of stochastic disturbances, it is necessary to adopt a flexible and general approach which may be able to easily describe both cases. The description in this section is based on a general representation of the cases at work. In fact, the model here is flexible enough to allow for a joint representation of a IS-LM with stochastic disturbances in both real and monetary markets.

In fact, through simple calculus, it is possible to determine the reduced form of the model described above in the case that equation (5) is stochastic ($\lambda_1 \neq 0$) and equation (6) is deterministic ($\lambda_2 = 0$, the case that uncertainty stems from real market only: see appendix A for more details)[3]:

$$\begin{aligned} dY_t &= \mu_i \, u_t^{(i)} \, dt + \sigma \, u_t^{(i)} \, dB_t, \\ Y_0 &= y, \end{aligned} \tag{12}$$

where μ_i is the Keynesian multiplier associated to the policy instrument considered (public expenditure G or taxation T), u_t represents the derivatives of the instrument with respect to time and σ (with $\sigma \in \mathbb{R}$) denotes the diffusion coefficient that can assume different functional forms according to the nature of the disturbance (real disturbance, monetary disturbance or both). In this case of real disturbances we have

$$\sigma = \frac{\lambda_1}{1 - c - \gamma + hl_1/l_2}. \tag{13}$$

In the sequel, in order to simplify the mathematical notation, we set: $u_t^{(i)} \equiv u_t$ as the two indices vary according to the instrument used in the analysis.

Also, it is possible to pinpoint the reduced form of the model described above in the case that equation (6) is stochastic ($\lambda_2 \neq 0$) and equation (5) is deterministic ($\lambda_1 = 0$: the case that uncertainty stems from monetary market only: see appendix A for more details):

$$\begin{aligned} dY_t &= \mu_i \, u_t \, dt + \chi \, u_t \, dB_t, \\ Y_0 &= y. \end{aligned} \tag{14}$$

---

[3]This formulation is a special case of the more general controlled Itô diffusion of the type:

$$dY_t = \mu(Y_t, u_t) \, dt + \sigma(Y_t, u_t) \, dB_t, \quad \text{with } Y_0 = y,$$

where $\mu(Y_t, u_t) = \mu u_t$ and $\sigma(Y_t, u_t) = \sigma u_t$.

In this case with monetary shock, the diffusion coefficient is

$$\chi = \frac{-h\lambda_2/l_2}{1 - c - \gamma + hl_1/l_2}. \tag{15}$$

When real and monetary disturbances are simultaneous (i.e. $\lambda_1 \neq 0$ and $\lambda_2 \neq 0$), the equation describing the economy reads (see appendix A for more details):

$$\begin{cases} dY_t = \mu_i \, u_t \, dt + (\sigma + \chi) \, u_t \, dB_t, \\ Y_0 = y. \end{cases} \tag{16}$$

Now, we shortly illustrate some mathematical details underlying equation (16). These points ought be useful to better clarify the mathematical notation in the text but also to allow for the instruments we are going to use to solve the optimal control problem.

Since for every t we shall have a random control variable on which the random variable Y_t depends, we consider a probability space with filtration

$$(\Omega, \mathcal{F}, \{\mathcal{F}_t\}_{t \geq 0}, \mathbb{P}),$$

where the filtration $\mathcal{F}_t$ is the one generated by the standard 1-dimensional Brownian motion B and is augmented by $\mathbb{P}$-null sets, that is:

$$\mathcal{F}_t = \sigma\Big(B_s, \ 0 \leq s \leq t\Big) \cup \Big\{A \in \mathcal{F} \,|\, \mathbb{P}(A) = 0\Big\}, \qquad \forall \, t \geq 0. \tag{17}$$

Moreover, we suppose that Y_0 is an integrable random variable with law π_0 and measurable with respect to $\mathcal{F}_0$ representing the initial value of the current income: for sake of simplicity, we assume that income at the time 0 is deterministic so that: $Y_0 = y$, constant with $y > 0$.

The control variable $u_t = u(t, \omega)$ is taken in a given family $\mathcal{A}$ of admissible controls:

$$\begin{aligned} \mathcal{A} := \big\{ u_t = u_0(t, Y_t(\omega)) \text{ for some} \\ \text{Borel-measurable functions } u^0 : [0, T] \times \mathbb{R} \longrightarrow \mathbb{R} \big\} \, . \end{aligned} \tag{18}$$

For more technical details about (17) and (18) see Appendix C.

The value at time t of this functions depends only on the state of the system at this time. These are called Markov controls because with such a u the corresponding process Y_t becomes an Itô diffusion, in particular a Markov process.

We are now able to minimize the operator J given in (1) under (12) or, alternatevely, (14) or (16) as a constraint. To this aim, we use the Hamilton-Jacobi-Bellman (HJB) equation (see theorem 5 in the appendix B).

As usual in the dynamic programming literature we now let the controlled diffusion Y start at time s from level $y > 0$; that is:

$$\begin{cases} dY_t^{s,y} = \mu_i \, u_{t-s} \, dt + \tilde{\sigma} \, u_{t-s} \, dB_{t-s} \, , & \text{with} \quad s \leq t \leq T \\ \\ \text{sub} \qquad Y_s^{s,y} = y \, . \end{cases} \tag{19}$$

and the optimization problem now reads

$$\phi(s, y) = \inf_{u \in \mathcal{A}} \mathbf{E} \left[(Y_T^{s,y} - Y_f)^2 \right] . \tag{20}$$

To apply the HJB method, we have preliminarily to transform the mean value J, given in the (1), into the mean value of an integral by Dynkin's formula (see theorem 1 of the appendix B).

According to Dynkin's formula the mean value J, given in (1), reads:

$$J(s, y; u) = (y - Y_f)^2 + \mathbf{E}\left[\int_s^T [2\,\mu_i\, u_{t-s}\,(Y_t^{s,y} - Y_f) + \sigma^2 u_{t-s}^2]\,dt\right], \tag{21}$$

and by virtue of the invariance of the problem under time translation (that is, the problem homogeneous over time), we can rewrite J in the form

$$J(s, y; u) = (y - Y_f)^2 + \mathbf{E}\left[\int_0^{T-s} [2\,\mu_i\, u_t\,(Y_t - Y_f) + \sigma^2 u_t^2]\,dt\right], \tag{22}$$

and the optimization problem can be written in the form:

$$\begin{cases} \phi(s, y) := (y - Y_f)^2 + \inf\limits_{u\in\mathcal{A}} \mathbf{E}\left[\int_0^{T-s} [2\,\mu_i\, u_t\,(Y_t - Y_f) + \sigma^2 u_t^2]\,dt\right] \\ \text{sub} \qquad dY_t = \mu_i\, u_t\, dt + \tilde{\sigma}\, u_t\, dB_t, \qquad \text{with} \quad Y_0 = y\,. \end{cases} \tag{23}$$

where $\tilde{\sigma}$ denotes a suitable value of σ, i.e. χ or $\sigma + \chi$, according to the type of uncertainty the economy is assumed to affected. Therefore, we have simply denoted by Y_t the process $(Y_t^{0,y})_{t\le T}$.

3. Solving the Optimal Control Problem for the Authority

If we apply the HJB equation to the second term on the left hand side of the optimization problem in (23) we will obtain (for more details see appendix B):

$$\inf_{u\in\mathcal{A}}\left\{ [2\,\mu_i u\,(y - Y_f) + \tilde{\sigma}^2 u^2] + \left[\frac{\partial\phi}{\partial s} + \mu_i u\frac{\partial\phi}{\partial y} + \left(\frac{\tilde{\sigma}^2 u^2}{2}\right)\frac{\partial^2\phi}{\partial y^2}\right]\right\} = 0\,. \tag{24}$$

To find an optimal control, we now derive equation (24) with respect to u and obtain

$$u = \bar{u} = \frac{-2\mu_i(y - Y_f) - \mu_i\,\dfrac{\partial\phi}{\partial y}}{2\tilde{\sigma}^2 + \tilde{\sigma}^2\,\dfrac{\partial^2\phi}{\partial y^2}}. \tag{25}$$

Substituting (25) into (24) we then obtain the value function:

$$2\,\mu_i\bar{u}\,(y - Y_f) + \tilde{\sigma}^2\bar{u}^2 + \frac{\partial\phi}{\partial s} + \mu_i\bar{u}\frac{\partial\phi}{\partial y} + \left(\frac{\tilde{\sigma}^2\bar{u}^2}{2}\right)\frac{\partial^2\phi}{\partial y^2} = 0. \tag{26}$$

Let us try to find a solution $\phi(s, y)$ of (25) and (26) of the form

$$\phi(s, y) = (y - Y_f)^2\, g(s), \tag{27}$$

with $g(T) = 1$.

By substitution of (27) into (25), we obtain:

$$\bar{u}(s, y) = \frac{-\mu_i \, (y - Y_f)}{\tilde{\sigma}^2}, \tag{28}$$

that is the optimal Markov control

$$u(s, \omega) = \bar{u}(s, Y_s(\omega)) = \frac{-\mu_i \, (Y_s - Y_f)}{\tilde{\sigma}^2}, \tag{29}$$

which, as we can easily observe, belongs to the set $\mathcal{A}$ given in the (18).

Substituting (27) into (26), we obtain:

$$g'(s) - \frac{\mu_i^2}{\sigma^2} \, g(s) = \frac{\mu_i^2}{\tilde{\sigma}^2}, \tag{30}$$

with $g(T) = 1$, that is

$$g(s) = 2 \, \exp\left[\frac{\mu_i^2}{\tilde{\sigma}^2} \, (s - T)\right] - 1. \tag{31}$$

By substitution of (31) into (27) and then into (23), we finally obtain the value function

$$\phi(s, y) = 2 \, (y - Y_f)^2 \, \exp\left[\frac{\mu_i^2}{\tilde{\sigma}^2} \, (s - T)\right]. \tag{32}$$

If we substitute the solution u given in (29) into the dynamic (16), we obtain the linear geometric stochastic differential equation:

$$d\tilde{Y}_t = -\frac{\mu^2}{\tilde{\sigma}^2} \, \tilde{Y}_t - \frac{\mu}{\tilde{\sigma}} \, \tilde{Y}_t \, dB_t \, , \tag{33}$$

where we have set $\tilde{Y}_t = |Y_t - Y_f|$. By Îto's formula the solution of equation (33) is

$$\tilde{Y}_t = \tilde{Y}_0 \, e^{-\mu^2 t/(2\tilde{\sigma}^2)} e^{-\mu B_t/\tilde{\sigma}}, \tag{34}$$

where $\tilde{Y}_0 > 0$. [4]

It is worth remembering that our aim is basically to draw a comparison of the two fiscal instruments in term of their ability to keep the product as close as possible to the reference value. The presence of a random component in (33) makes the comparison impossibile, the

---

[4]It worth noticing that the mean value of the random variable $\tilde{Y}_t$ is

$$\begin{aligned} \mathbf{E}[Y_t - Y_f] &= \tilde{Y}_0 \, e^{-\mu^2 t/(2\tilde{\sigma}^2)} \mathbf{E}\left[e^{-\mu B_t/\tilde{\sigma}}\right] = \\ &= \tilde{Y}_0 \, e^{-\mu^2 t/(2\tilde{\sigma}^2)} \, \frac{1}{\sqrt{2\pi t}} \int_{-\infty}^{\infty} e^{-x^2/(2t) - \mu x/\tilde{\sigma}} \, dx = \tilde{Y}_0 \, , \end{aligned} \tag{35}$$

because the probability law of $\tilde{Y}_t$ is the one of the Brownian motion B_t whose density function is

$$f(x) = \frac{1}{\sqrt{2\pi t}} \, e^{-x^2/(2t)} \, . \tag{36}$$

outcome depending on the actual realization of stochastic disturbance. As we will see, a possibile comparison is allowed by using both the logarithm and the expectation function.

In fact, by taking logarithm on both sides we can rewrite (34) in the form:

$$\log \tilde{Y}_t = \log \tilde{Y}_0 - \frac{\mu^2 t}{2\sigma^2} - \frac{\mu B_t}{\sigma}, \tag{37}$$

where the first two terms are deterministic while the last term is stochastic.

Then, by taking the expectation on both sides we have:

$$\mathbf{E}[\log \tilde{Y}_t] = \log \tilde{Y}_0 - \frac{\mu^2 t}{2\sigma^2}. \tag{38}$$

it is worth noticing that in order to compare terms we can take into account that the function logarithm is increasing and then does not change the inequality relation between its arguments.

According to the instrument we can substitute for the IS-LM parameters in place of μ and $\tilde{\sigma}$. We can thus rewrite the optimal problem solution as

$$\mathbf{E}\left[\log \tilde{Y}_t\right] = \log \tilde{Y}_0 - \frac{t}{2\lambda_1^2}, \tag{39}$$

if the policy instrument is public expenditure, and:

$$\mathbf{E}\left[\log \tilde{Y}_t\right] = \log \tilde{Y}_0 - \frac{t\left(-c-\gamma+hl_1/l_2\right)^2}{2\lambda_1^2}, \tag{40}$$

if the policy instrument is taxation.

By following the same procedure we have the solution in the case that uncertainty is associated to the money market (i.e., $\lambda_1 = 0$):

$$\mathbf{E}\left[\log \tilde{Y}_t\right] = \log \tilde{Y}_0 - \frac{\mu_i^2 t}{2\chi^2}. \tag{41}$$

Accordingly, if public expenditure is the policy variable equation (41) reads (see notation reported in appendix A for more details):

$$\mathbf{E}\left[\log \tilde{Y}_t\right] = \log \tilde{Y}_0 - \frac{t}{2\left(h\lambda_2/l_2\right)^2}, \tag{42}$$

while if policy instrument is taxation (41) becomes:

$$\mathbf{E}\left[\log \tilde{Y}_t\right] = \log \tilde{Y}_0 - \frac{t\left(-c-\gamma+hl_1/l_2\right)^2}{2\left(h\lambda_2/l_2\right)^2}. \tag{43}$$

When shocks are simultaneous, the solution reads:

$$\mathbf{E}\left[\log \tilde{Y}_t\right] = \log \tilde{Y}_0 - \frac{\mu_i^2 t}{2\left(\chi+\tilde{\sigma}\right)^2}, \tag{44}$$

that after substitution becomes:

$$\mathbf{E}\left[\log \tilde{Y}_t\right] = \log \tilde{Y}_0 - \frac{t}{2\left(\lambda_1 - h\lambda_2/l_2\right)^2}, \tag{45}$$

when policy instrument is public expenditure, and:

$$\mathbf{E}\left[\log \tilde{Y}_t\right] = \log \tilde{Y}_0 - \frac{t\left(-c-\gamma+hl_1/l_2\right)^2}{2\left(\lambda_1 - h\lambda_2/l_2\right)^2}, \tag{46}$$

if the policy-maker opts for taxation.

Equations (38), (41) and (44) are the key findings of the paper.

They describe the optimal path of income gap generated by the policy instrument adopted and affected by the stochastic disturbances. First they allow us to check if the source of economy disturbances may affect the effectiveness of a given instrument. Then, they enable us to answer the question whether it is public expenditure or lump-sum taxation the most effective instrument to stabilize output if stochastic shocks operate.

For the first question, it is easy to check out the result drawn from the following proposition:

Proposition 1. *The source of stochastic disturbances does affect the effectiveness of each instrument in stabilizing output. In particular, the policy instrument (public expenditure or taxation) is more effective in stabilizing output if the following condition holds:*

$$h/\lambda_1 > l_2/\lambda_2. \tag{47}$$

Proof. Comparing equation (39) with (42) and equation (40) with (43) we find that shocks from real side of the model are conductive to lower variability if the following inequalities hold:

$$\log \tilde{Y}_0 - \frac{t}{2\lambda_1^2} < \log \tilde{Y}_0 - \frac{t}{2\left(h\frac{\lambda_2}{l_2}\right)^2}, \tag{48}$$

$$\log \tilde{Y}_0 - \frac{t\left(-c-\gamma+h\frac{l_1}{l_2}\right)^2}{2\lambda_1^2} < \log \tilde{Y}_0 - \frac{t\left(-c-\gamma+h\frac{l_1}{l_2}\right)^2}{2\left(h\frac{\lambda_2}{l_2}\right)^2}. \tag{49}$$

Conditions (48) and (49) boil down to condition (47). □

It is worth remembering that λ_1 and λ_2 are the two parameters associated to the diffusion of uncertainty that represent, respectively, the sensitiveness of investments and money demand with respect to disturbances, while h and l_2 are, respectively, the sensitiveness of investments and money demand with respect to the interest rate. Hence, the ratios h/λ_1, l_2/λ_2, are likely to be considered as a 'sensitiveness ratios' to uncertainty, i.e. a measure of how the system is able to attenuate possible stochastic disturbances by tuning the interest rate. According to this interpretation, condition (47) shows that the higher is the 'sensitiveness ratio' on the real side of the system the lower the conductivity of impulses associated to stochastic disturbances.

Now we can draw the comparison between instruments. This case involves the comparison between equations (39) with (40) and (42) with (43). The result can be summarized by the following proposition:

Proposition 2. *Public expenditure is more effective in stabilizing output than lump-sum taxation. Interestingly, this holds whatever the nature of the shock (if it is of real or monetary type or both).*

Proof. The proof is based on the following lines. First we draw a comparison between the two policy instruments to address which of them is better than other in the case the uncertainty comes alternatively, from real or monetary side. Then we analyse which instrument fares better in the case that both types of disturbances are at work.

By comparing the different specifications of income gap in (39) and (40) (the disturbance is only on the real side) we obtain that public expenditure is more effective than taxation if:

$$-\frac{t}{2\lambda_1^2} < -\frac{\left(-c-\gamma+hl_1/l_2\right)^2 t}{2\lambda_1^2}. \tag{50}$$

By the same criterion, comparison between (42) and (43) (the shock stems from monetary market only) shows that public expentiture is more effective than taxation if:

$$-\frac{t}{2\left(h\lambda_2/l_2\right)^2} < -\frac{\left(-c-\gamma+hl_1/l_2\right)^2 t}{2\left(h\lambda_2/l_2\right)^2}. \tag{51}$$

Finally, by comparing (45) and (46) (disturbances are both of real and monetary type), public expenditure is more effective than taxation if:

$$-\frac{t}{2\left(\lambda_1-h\lambda_2/l_2\right)^2} < -\frac{\left(-c-\gamma+hl_1/l_2\right)^2 t}{2\left(\lambda_1-h\lambda_2/l_2\right)^2}. \tag{52}$$

Conditions (50), (51) and (52) are basically equivalent and boil down to the following inequality:

$$-1 < c+\gamma-\frac{hl_1}{l_2} < 1\,. \tag{53}$$

Hence, if (53) holds then public expenditure is preferable to taxation. Interestingly, this condition always must hold as we assume the model stability condition (11).Thus, condition (53) entails that under the usual assumptions (notably the condition in equation (11)) public expenditure is the most effective instrument to stabilize the product near the reference value. □

4. Conclusion

This paper analyses the optimal stabilization policy in the Poole original context. We find that the effectiveness of fiscal policy is affected by the nature of economy disturbances whatever the instrument used. Furthermore, an optimal government expenditure rule is preferable to a taxation rule under the usual stability conditions. We developed a methodology which generates stochastic processes as closed form solutions. Plainly, this model is too simple to be taken as the basis policy evaluation. In fact, the assumptions and the corresponding mathematical conditions, together with the use of stochastic processes in continuous time, are likely to ensure the simplicity of the model and its resolvability in closed form. The same conditions, however, give rise to some limits on applicability of the obtained results. Nonetheless, the simple analysis here may be both of pedagogical value and useful to pin down the determinants of the product in the well-known (stochastic) IS-LM context. A promising development of this model might be the introduction of distortionary taxation, coupled with the extension to a more complicated environment with lagged responses to the disturbances and policy actions.

5. Appendix A

In this Appendix we basically develop the same model in the text by explicitly unveiling how the model parameters enter into the reduced form, according to the instrument and the source of uncertainty.

A more compact representation of it is not allowed in this case as a consequence of the flexible approach in use.

5.1. Real and Monetary Uncertainty: The Case of Public Expenditure

$$dY_t = dC_t + dI_t + dG_t, \tag{54}$$

$$dC_t = c\, dY_t^D, \tag{55}$$

$$dY_t^D = dY_t - dT_t, \tag{56}$$

$$dI_t = \gamma Y_t^D - h\, dr_t + \lambda_1\, u_t\, dB_t, \tag{57}$$

$$l_1 Y_t^D - l_2\, dr_t + \lambda_2\, u_t\, dB_t = 0, \tag{58}$$

where dB_t is a Brownian motion and, in this case, the source of the system uncertainty and u_t is the variation of the control variable.

Let us solve equation (58) in dr_t:

$$dr_t = \frac{\lambda_2}{l_2}\, u_t\, dB_t + \frac{l_1}{l_2}\, Y_t^D. \tag{59}$$

Then, by substituting it in the equation (57) and assuming that the control variable is the public expenditure $u_t = dG_t/dt$ we have:

$$dI_t = \frac{dG_t}{dt} dB_t \left(\lambda_1 - \frac{h\lambda_2}{l_2} \right) + Y_t^D \left(\gamma - \frac{hl_1}{l_2} \right). \tag{60}$$

Now we substitute the equations (60), (55) and (56) in (54):

$$dY_t = c dY_t^D + \frac{dG_t}{dt} dB_t \left(\lambda_1 - \frac{h\lambda_2}{l_2} \right) + dY_t^D \left(\gamma - \frac{hl_1}{l_2} \right) + dG_t, \tag{61}$$

and, given that $dT_t = 0$ we have:

$$dY_t \left(1 - c - \gamma + \frac{hl_1}{l_2} \right) = u_t\, dB_t + \left(\lambda_1 - \frac{h\lambda_2}{l_2} \right) + dG_t\,, \tag{62}$$

that can be written down in a more compact form:

$$dY_t = \frac{1}{1 - c - \gamma + hl_1/l_2} dG_t + \frac{1}{1 - c - \gamma + hl_1/l_2} \left(\lambda_1 - \frac{h\lambda_2}{l_2} \right) \frac{dG_t}{dt} dB_t\,. \tag{63}$$

Equation (63) is a particular form of equation (16) with:

$$\mu_i = \mu_G = \frac{1}{1-c-\gamma+hl_1/l_2}, \qquad \sigma + \chi = \frac{\lambda_1 - h\lambda_2/l_2}{1-c-\gamma+hl_1/l_2} \quad \text{and} \quad u_t = \frac{dG_t}{dt}\,. \tag{64}$$

5.2. Real and Monetary Uncertainty: The Case of Lump-sum Taxation

Now we assume $dG_t = 0$ and $u_t = \frac{dT_t}{dt}$. Repeatig the same procedure we obtain:

$$dY_t = \frac{-c - \gamma + hl_1/l_2}{1 - c - \gamma + hl_1/l_2} dT_t + \frac{\lambda_1 - h\lambda_2/l_2}{1 - c - \gamma + hl_1/l_2} \frac{dT_t}{dt} dB_t\,. \tag{65}$$

Equation (65) is a particular form of equation (12) with:

$$\mu_i = \mu_T = \frac{-c-\gamma+hl_1/l_2}{1-c-\gamma+hl_1/l_2}, \qquad \sigma + \chi = \frac{\lambda_1 - h\lambda_2/l_2}{1-c-\gamma+hl_1/l_2} \quad \text{and} \quad u_t = \frac{dT_t}{dt}\,. \tag{66}$$

5.3. Real Uncertainty: The Case of Public Expenditure

Let us assume $u_t = dG_t/dt$ and that uncertainty is on the real side, $\lambda_2 = 0$. Equation (63) becomes:

$$dY_t = \frac{1}{1 - c - \gamma + hl_1/l_2} dG_t + \frac{\lambda_1}{1 - c - \gamma + hl_1/l_2} \frac{dG_t}{dt} dB_t. \tag{67}$$

Equation (67) is a particular form of equation (12) with:

$$\mu_i = \mu_G = \frac{1}{1-c-\gamma+hl_1/l_2}, \qquad \sigma = \frac{\lambda_1}{1-c-\gamma+hl_1/l_2} \quad \text{and} \quad u_t = \frac{dG_t}{dt}\,. \tag{68}$$

5.4. Real Uncertainty: The Case of Lump-sum Taxation

Let us assume $u_t = dT_t/dt$, and that uncertainty is on the real side, $\lambda_2 = 0$. Equation (65) becomes:

$$dY_t = \frac{-c-\gamma+hl_1/l_2}{1-c-\gamma+hl_1/l_2}\,dT_t + \frac{\lambda_1}{1-c-\gamma+hl_1/l_2}\,\frac{dT_t}{dt}\,dB_t\,. \tag{69}$$

Equation (69) is a particular form of equation (12) with

$$\mu_i = \mu_T = \frac{-c-\gamma+hl_1/l_2}{1-c-\gamma+hl_1/l_2}, \quad \sigma = \frac{\lambda_1}{1-c-\gamma+hl_1/l_2} \quad \text{and} \quad u_t = \frac{dT_t}{dt}\,. \tag{70}$$

5.5. Monetary Uncertainty: The Case of Public Expenditure

Let us assume $u_t = dG_t/dt$ and that uncertainty is on the monetary side, $\lambda_1 = 0$. Equation (63) becomes:

$$dY_t = \frac{1}{1-c-\gamma+hl_1l_2}\,dG_t + \frac{-h\lambda_2/l_2}{1-c-\gamma+hl_1/l_2}\,\frac{dG_t}{dt}\,dB_t\,. \tag{71}$$

Equation (71) is a particular form of equation (14) with

$$\mu_i = \mu_G = \frac{1}{1-c-\gamma+hl_1/l_2}, \quad \chi = \frac{-h\lambda_2/l_2}{1-c-\gamma+hl_1/l_2} \quad \text{and} \quad u_t = \frac{dG_t}{dt}\,. \tag{72}$$

5.6. Monetary Uncertainty: The Case of Lump-sum Taxation

Let us assume $u_t = dT_t/dt$ and that uncertainty is on the monetary side, $\lambda_1 = 0$. Equation (65) becomes:

$$dY_t = \frac{-c-\gamma+hl_1/l_2}{1-c-\gamma+hl_1/l_2}\,dT_t + \frac{-h\lambda_2/l_2}{1-c-\gamma+hl_1/l_2}\,\frac{dT_t}{dt}\,dB_t\,. \tag{73}$$

Equation (73) is a particular form of equation (14) with

$$\mu_i = \mu_T = \frac{-c-\gamma+hl_1/l_2}{1-c-\gamma+hl_1/l_2}, \quad \chi = \frac{-h\lambda_2/l_2}{1-c-\gamma+hl_1/l_2} \quad \text{and} \quad u_t = \frac{dT_t}{dt}\,. \tag{74}$$

6. Appendix B

Remark. *There exists a unique solution for the controlled equation (12) and we refer the reader, for example, to Øksendal (2003) for the proof.*

For $\bar{Y} < Y_f$ let us define the exit time τ of the dynamics as

$$\tau := \inf\{t > 0 \mid Y_t > \bar{Y}\}.$$

Remark 3. *By virtue of well known results, the measurability of τ with respect to the σ-algebra $\mathcal{F}_t$ follows. Indeed, we have that τ is a stopping time.*

Theorem 4 (Dynkin's formula). *Let Y_t be the Itô diffusion*

$$dY_t = \mu(Y_t)\,dt + \sigma(Y_t)\,dB_t, \quad Y_0 = y,$$

and $f \in C_0^2(\mathbb{R})$. If τ is a stopping time with $\mathbf{E}[\tau] < +\infty$, then it yealds

$$\mathbf{E}[f(Y_\tau)] = f(y) + \mathbf{E}\left[\int_0^\tau Lf(Y_s)\,ds\right], \tag{75}$$

where

$$Lf(z) := \mu(z)\,\frac{df}{dz} + \frac{1}{2}\,[\sigma(z)]^2\,\frac{d^2 f}{dz^2}\,. \tag{76}$$

Theorem 5 (HJB equation). *Suppose that we have*

$$V(s,y) := \sup_{u_t \in \mathcal{A}} \mathbf{E}\left[\int_s^\tau f(Y_t, u_t)\,dt\right], \tag{77}$$

with

$$\begin{cases} dY_t = \mu(Y_t,\, u_t)\,dt + \sigma(Y_t,\, u_t)\,dB_t, \\ Y_0 = y\ . \end{cases}$$

Suppose that $V \in C^2(\mathbb{R}^+)$ satisfies

$$\mathbf{E}\left[|V(Y_\alpha)| + \int_0^\alpha |L^v V(Y_t)|\,dt\right] < +\infty,$$

for all bounded stopping times $\alpha < \tau$, for all $y \in \mathbb{R}$ and all $v \in \mathcal{A}$, where

$$(L^z V)(s,y) := \frac{\partial V(s,y)}{\partial s} + \mu(y,v)\frac{\partial V}{\partial y} + \frac{\sigma^2(y,v)}{2}\frac{\partial^2 V}{\partial y^2}.$$

Moreover, suppose that an optimal control u^* exists, then we have

$$\sup_{v \in \mathcal{A}} \{f(y,v) + (L^v V)(y)\} = 0, \tag{78}$$

and the supremum is obtained if it yialds $v = u_t^* = u^*(t)$, that is

$$f(y, u^*(t)) + (L^{u^*(t)} V)(y) = 0\,.$$

The theorem 5 also applies to the corresponding *minimum* problem

$$\phi(s,y) := \inf_{u_t \in \mathcal{A}} \mathbf{E}\left[\int_s^\tau f(Y_t, u_t)\,dt\right].$$

We have in fact

$$\phi(s,y) = -\sup_{u_t \in \mathcal{A}} \mathbf{E}\left[\int_s^{\mathcal{T}} - f(Y_t, u_t)\, dt\right],$$

from which, by replacing V with $-\phi$ and f with $-f$, it follows that the (78) in the theorem 2 becomes

$$\inf_{v \in \mathcal{A}} \{f(y,v) + (L^z \phi)(y)\} = 0. \tag{79}$$

For the details of the proof of these two theorems we remind the reader to Øksendal (2003).

Appendix C

Definition 1. Given a set Ω, a $\sigma - algebra$ $\mathcal{F}$ on Ω is a *family* $\mathcal{F}$ of subsets of Ω which fullfills the following properties:

(i) the empty set $\emptyset$ belongs to $\mathcal{F}$;

(ii) if $F \in \mathcal{F}$, then the complement $\bar{F}$ of F in Ω belongs to $\mathcal{F}$, too;

(iii) if $A_1, A_2, A_3, \dots \in \mathcal{F}$, then $A := \bigcup_{i=1}^{\infty} A_i \in \mathcal{F}$. □

Definition 2. The pair $(\Omega, \mathcal{F})$ is called a *measurable space.* □

Definition 3. A *probability measure* $\mathbb{P}$ on a measurable space $(\Omega, \mathcal{F})$ is a function $\mathbb{P} : \mathcal{F} \longrightarrow [0,1]$ such that

(i) $\mathbb{P}(\emptyset) = 0$ and $\mathbb{P}(\Omega) = 1$;

(ii) if $A_1, A_2, A_3, \dots \in \mathcal{F}$ and $A_i \cap A_j = \emptyset, \ \forall i \neq j$, then $\mathbb{P}\left(\bigcup_{i=1}^{\infty} A_i\right) = \sum_{i=1}^{\infty} \mathbb{P}(A_i)$.

□

Definition 4. The triple $(\Omega, \mathcal{F}, \mathbb{P})$ is called a *probability space.* It is called a *complete probability space* if $\mathcal{F}$ contains all subsets S of Ω with $\mathbb{P} - outer\ measure$ zero, where the $\mathbb{P} - outer\ measure$, denoted by $\mathbb{P}^*$, is defined as

$$\mathbb{P}^*(G) = \inf\left\{\mathbb{P}(F) : F \in \mathcal{F} \text{ and } G \subset F\right\}.$$ □

Definition 5. For a given *family* $\mathcal{G}$ of subsets of Ω, the $\sigma - algebra$ denoted by the symbol $\mathcal{F}_{\mathcal{G}}$ and defined as

$$\mathcal{F}_{\mathcal{G}} = \bigcap \left\{\mathcal{F} : \mathcal{F} \text{ is a } \sigma - algebra \text{ of } \Omega \text{ and } \mathcal{G} \subset \mathcal{F}\right\}$$

is called the $\sigma - algebra$ *generated by* $\mathcal{G}$. □

Definition 6. If Ω is a topological space (e.g. $\Omega = \mathbb{R}^n$) equipped with the topology $\mathcal{G}$ of all open subsets of Ω, then the $\sigma - algebra\ \mathcal{B} = \mathcal{F}_{\mathcal{G}}$ is called the *Borel* $\sigma - algebra$ on Ω and the elements $B \in \mathcal{B}$ are called *Borel sets*. □

Definition 7. Given the *measurable space* $(\Omega, \mathcal{F})$, the (increasing) family $\{\mathcal{M}_t\}_{t\geq 0}$ of $\sigma - algebras$ of Ω such that

$$\mathcal{M}_{t_1} \subset \mathcal{M}_{t_2} \subset \mathcal{F}, \qquad \forall\, 0 \leq t_1 < t_2,$$

is called a *filtration* on $(\Omega, \mathcal{F})$. □

Acknowledgments

We are grateful to Giorgio Ferrari, Giuseppe Garofalo and Luigi Ventura for their helpful suggestions and comments.

References

[1] Canzoneri, Matthew B. & Henderson, Dale W & Rogoff, Kenneth S, 1983, The Information Content of the Interest Rate and Optimal Monetary Policy, *The Quarterly Journal of Economics*, MIT Press, vol. 98(4), pages 545-66, November.

[2] Collard, Fabrice & Dellas, Harris, 2005, Poole in the New Keynesian model, *European Economic Review*, Elsevier, vol. 49(4), pages 887-907, May.

[3] Collard, Fabrice & Dellas, Harris & Ertz, Guy, 2000, Poole Revisited, *CEPR Discussion Papers* 2521, C.E.P.R. Discussion Papers.

[4] Hoffmann Mathias & Bernd Kempa, 2009, A Poole Analysis in the New Open Economy Macroeconomic Framework, *Review of International Economics*, Wiley Blackwell, vol. 17(5), pages 1074-1097, November.

[5] Øksendal Bernt, 2003, *Stochastic defferential equations*, 6th ed., Sringer Verlag.

[6] Poole, William, 1970, Optimal Choice of Monetary Policy Instruments in a Simple Stochastic Macro Model, *The Quarterly Journal of Economics*, MIT Press, vol. 84(2), pages 197-216, May.

In: Stock Markets
Editors: F. Petroni, F. Prattico and G. D'Amico
ISBN: 978-1-62808-751-2

Chapter 9

SEMI-MARKOV MODELS IN HIGH FREQUENCY FINANCE: A REVIEW

***Guglielmo D'Amico*[1,*] *Filippo Petroni*[2†] *and Flavio Prattico*[3,‡]**
[1]Dipartimento di Farmacia,
Università "G. D'Annunzio" di Chieti-Pescara, Chieti, Italy
[2]Dipartimento di Scienze Economiche e Aziendali,
Università degli studi di Cagliari, Cagliari, Italy
[3]Dipartimento Ingegneria Industriale, dell'Informazione e dell'Economia,
Università degli studi dell'Aquila, L'Aquila, Italy

Abstract

In this paper we describe three stochastic models based on a semi-Markov chains approach and its generalizations to study the high frequency price dynamics of traded stocks. The three models are: a simple semi-Markov chain model, an indexed semi-Markov chain model and a weighted indexed semi-Markov chain model. We show, through Monte Carlo simulations, that the models are able to reproduce important stylized facts of financial time series as the persistence of volatility. In particular, we analyzed high frequency data from the Italian stock market from the first of January 2007 until end of December 2010 and we apply to it the semi-Markov chain model and the indexed semi-Markov chain model. The last model, instead, is applied to data from Italian and German stock markets from January 1, 2007 until the end of December 2010.

Keywords: semi-Markov; High Frequency Finance; Monte Carlo simulation; autocorrelation function

1. Introduction

Semi-Markov chains (SMC) are a wide class of stochastic processes which generalize at the same time both Markov chains and renewal processes. The main advantage of SMC is

*E-mail address: g.damico@unich.it
†E-mail address: fpetroni@unica.it
‡E-mail address: flavio.prattico@univaq.it

that they allow the use of whatever type of waiting time distribution for modeling the time to have a transition from one state to another. On the contrary, Markovian models have constraints on the distribution of the waiting times in the states which should be necessarily represented by memoryless distributions (exponential or geometric for continuous and discrete time cases respectively). This major flexibility has a price to pay: the parameters to be estimated are more numerous.

SMC generalizes also non-Markovian models based on continuous time random walks extensively used in the econophysics community, see for example [18, 20]. SMC have been used to analyze financial data and to describe different problems ranging from credit rating data modeling [4] to the pricing of options [5, 21] as well as for wind energy modeling which shares similar problems with the modeling of financial data such as the strong persistence of data, see [10, 11, 12].

With the financial industry becoming fully computerized, the amount of recorded data, from daily close all the way down to tick-by-tick level, has exploded. Nowadays, such tick-by-tick high-frequency data are readily available for practitioners and researchers alike [13, 19]. It seemed then natural trying to verify the semi-Markov hypothesis of returns on high-frequency data, see [7]. In [7] we proposed a semi-Markov model showing its ability to reproduce some stylized empirical facts such for example the absence of autocorrelations in returns and the gain/loss asymmetry. In that paper we showed also that the autocorrelation in the square of returns is higher with respect to the Markov model. Unfortunately this autocorrelation was still too small compared to the empirical one. In order to overcome the problem of low autocorrelation, in another paper [8] we proposed an indexed semi-Markov model for price return. More precisely we assumed that the intraday returns (up to one minute frequency) are described by a discrete time homogeneous semi-Markov process where we introduced a memory index which takes into account the periods of different volatility in the market. It is well known that the market volatility is autocorrelated, then periods of high (low) volatility may persist for long time. We made the hypothesis that the kernel of the semi-Markov process depend on which level of volatility the market is at that time. It is to be remarked that the weighted memory index is a stochastic process which do depend on the same Markov Renewal Chain to which the semi-Markov chain is associated. Then, in our model, the high autocorrelation is obtained endogenously without introducing external or latent auxiliary stochastic processes. To improve further our previous results, in [9], we propose an exponentially weighted index.

The rest of the paper is organized as follows. Section 2 describes the semi-Markov models of financial returns. Section 3 presents the results of the three different models as applied to real financial data. Section 4 discusses some concluding remarks.

2. Financial Return Models

In this section we present the models used for modeling the financial returns. Particularly we show the SCM, the indexed semi-Markov chain (ISMC) and the weighted-indexed semi-Markov chain (WISMC).

2.1. The Semi-Markov Chain Model

We define a SMC with values in a finite state space $E = \{1, 2, ..., m\}$, see for example [16, 14]. Let $(\Omega, \mathbf{F}, P)$ be a probability space; we consider two sequences of random variables:

$$J_n : \Omega \to E; \quad T_n : \Omega \to \mathbb{N} \tag{1}$$

denoting the state and the time of the n-th transition of the system, respectively.

We assume that (J_n, T_n) is a Markov Renewal Process on the state space $E \times \mathbb{N}$ with kernel $Q_{ij}(t),\ i, j \in E, t \in \mathbb{N}$.

The kernel has the following probabilistic interpretation:

$$\begin{aligned} &P[J_{n+1} = j, T_{n+1} - T_n \le t | \sigma(J_h, T_h),\ h \le t,\ J_n = i] \\ &= P[J_{n+1} = j, T_{n+1} - T_n \le t | J_n = i] = Q_{ij}(t) \end{aligned} \tag{2}$$

and it results $p_{ij} = \lim_{t\to\infty} Q_{ij}(t);\ i, j \in E,\ t \in \mathbb{N}$ where $\mathbf{P} = (p_{ij})$ is the transition probability matrix of the embedded Markov chain J_n.

Furthermore, it is useful to introduce the probability to have next transition in state j at time t given the starting at time zero from state i

$$\begin{aligned} b_{ij}(t) &= P[J_{n+1} = j, T_{n+1} - T_n = t | J_n = i] \\ &= \begin{cases} Q_{ij}(t) - Q_{ij}(t-1) & \text{if } t > 0 \\ 0 & \text{if } t = 0 \end{cases} \end{aligned} \tag{3}$$

We define the distribution functions

$$H_i(t) = P[T_{n+1} - T_n \le t | J_n = i] = \sum_{j\in E} Q_{ij}(t) \tag{4}$$

representing the survival function in state i.

The Radon-Nikodym theorem assures for the existence of a function $G_{ij}(t)$ such that

$$\begin{aligned} G_{ij}(t) &= P\{T_{n+1} - T_n \le t | J_n = i, J_{n+1} = j\} \\ &= \begin{cases} \frac{Q_{ij}(t)}{p_{ij}} & \text{if } p_{ij} \ne 0 \\ 1 & \text{if } p_{ij} = 0 \end{cases} \end{aligned} \tag{5}$$

It denotes the waiting time distribution function in state i given that, with next transition, the process will be in the state j. The sojourn time distribution $G_{ij}(\cdot)$ can be any distribution function. We recover the discrete time Markov chain when the $G_{ij}(\cdot)$ are all geometrically distributed.

It is possible to define the SMC $Z(t)$ as

$$Z(t) = J_{N(t)},\quad \forall t \in \mathbb{N} \tag{6}$$

where $N(t) = \sup\{n \in \mathbb{N} : T_n \le t\}$. Then $Z(t)$ represents the state of the system for each waiting time. We denote the transition probabilities of the SMC by $\phi_{ij}(t) = P[Z(t) = j | Z(0) = i]$. They satisfy the following evolution equation:

$$\phi_{ij}(t) = \delta_{ij}(1 - H_i(t)) + \sum_{k\in E}\sum_{\tau=1}^{t} b_{ik}(\tau)\phi_{kj}(t-\tau). \tag{7}$$

To solve equation (7) there are well known algorithms in the SMC literature [1, 14].

At this point we introduce the discrete backward recurrence time process $B(t)$ linked to the SMC. For each time $t \in \mathbb{N}$ we define the following stochastic process:

$$B(t) = t - T_{N(t)}. \tag{8}$$

If the semi-Markov chain $Z(t)$ indicates the state of the system at time t, $B(t)$ indicates the time since the last jump.

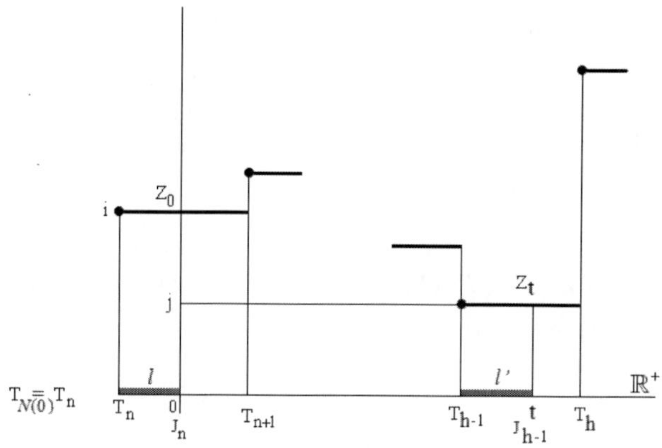

Figure 1. Trajectory of a SMC with backward times.

In Figure 1 we show a trajectory of a SMC. At time t the process $Z(t)$ is in the state J_{h-1} and the last transition occurred at time T_{h-1} then at time t the backward process holds $B(t) = t - T_{h-1}$.

The joint stochastic process $(Z(t), B(t), t \in \mathbb{N})$ with values in $E \times \mathbb{N}$ is a Markov process, see for example [16]. That is:

$$P[Z(T)=j, B(T) \leq v' | \sigma(Z(h), B(h)), h \leq t, Z(t)=i, B(t)=v]$$
$$= P[Z(T) = j, B(T) \leq v' | Z(t) = i, B(t) = v].$$

The SMC price model proposed by [7] assumes that the value of the asset under study is described by the time varying asset price $S(t)$. The time variable $t \in \{0, 1, \ldots, n\}$ where n is the number of considered unit periods.

The return at time t calculated over a time interval of length 1, is defined as

$$Z(t) = \frac{S(t+1) - S(t)}{S(t)}. \tag{9}$$

We assume that $Z(t)$ is a SMC with finite state space

$$E = \{-z_{min}\Delta, \ldots, -2\Delta, -\Delta, 0, \Delta, 2\Delta, \ldots, z_{max}\Delta\}$$

and kernel $\mathbf{Q} = (Q_{ij}(\gamma)), \forall i, j \in E$ and $\gamma \in \mathbb{N}$.

2.2. The Semi-Markov Model with Memory

In this subsection we propose a generalization of the SMC that is able to represent higher-order dependencies between successive observations of a state variable. One way to increase the memory of the process is by using high-order SMC as defined in [17]. Here we propose a more parsimonious model having the objective of defining a new model that appropriately describes empirical regularities of financial time series. To this end we extend the model described above allowing the possibility of reproducing long-term dependence in the square of stock returns. This model was advanced by [8] were a more complete treatment can be found.

Let $(\Omega, \mathbf{F}, P)$ be a probability space and consider the stochastic process

$$J_{-(m+1)}, J_{-m}, J_{-(m-1)}, ..., J_{-1}, J_0, J_1, ...$$

with a finite state space $E = \{1, 2, ..., S\}$. In our framework the random variable J_n describes the price return process at the n-th transition.

Let us consider the stochastic process

$$T_{-(m+1)}, T_{-m}, T_{-(m-1)}, ..., T_{-1}, T_0, T_1, ...$$

with values in $\mathbb{R}$. The random variable T_n describes the time in which the n-th transition of the price return process occurs.

Let us consider also the stochastic process

$$U_{-(m+1)}, U_{-m}, U_{-(m-1)}, ..., U_{-1}, U_0, U_1, ...$$

with values in $\mathbb{R}$. The random variable U_n describes the value of the index process at the n-th transition.

In reference [7] the process $\{U_n\}$ was defined as a reward accumulation process linked to the Markov Renewal Process $\{J_n, T_n\}$. In this paper we introduce a different index process U_n^m that is defined as follows:

$$U_n^m = \frac{1}{T_n - T_{n-(m+1)}} \sum_{k=0}^{m} \int_{T_{n-1-k}}^{T_{n-k}} f(J_{n-1-k}, s)ds, \tag{10}$$

where $f : E \times \mathbb{R} \to \mathbb{R}$ is a Borel measurable bounded function and $U^m_{-(m+1)}, ..., U_0^m$ are known and non-random.

The process U_n^m can be interpreted as a moving average of the accumulated reward process with the function f as a measure of the rate of reward per unit time.

The function f depends on the state of the system J_{n-1-k} and on the time s.

As an example you can think of the case in which $m = 1$ and $f(J_n, s) = (J_n)^2$. In this simple case we have that:

$$U_n^1 = \frac{1}{T_n - T_{n-2}} \left((J_{n-1})^2 \cdot (T_n - T_{n-1}) + (J_{n-2})^2 \cdot (T_{n-1} - T_{n-2}) \right), \tag{11}$$

which expresses a moving average of order $m + 1 = 2$ executed on the series of the square of returns with weights given by the fractions

$$\frac{T_n - T_{n-1}}{T_n - T_{n-2}}; \quad \frac{T_{n-1} - T_{n-2}}{T_n - T_{n-2}}. \tag{12}$$

It should be noted that the order of the moving average is on the number of transitions. As a consequence, the moving average is executed on time windows of variable length.

To construct an indexed model we have to specify a dependence structure between the variables. Toward this end we adopt the following assumption:

$$\begin{aligned} &P[J_{n+1}=j,\, T_{n+1}-T_n \le t | \sigma(J_h, T_h, U_h^m),\, h=-m,...,0,...,n, J_n=i, U_n^m=v] \\ &= P[J_{n+1}=j,\, T_{n+1}-T_n \le t | J_n=i, U_n^m=v] := Q_{ij}^m(v;t), \end{aligned} \tag{13}$$

where $\sigma(J_h, T_h, U_h^m)$, $h \le n$ is the natural filtration of the three-variate process.

The matrix of functions $\mathbf{Q}^m(v;t) = (Q_{ij}^m(v;t))_{i,j\in E}$ has a fundamental role in the theory we are going to expose. In recognition of its importance, we call it *indexed semi-Markov kernel.*

The joint process (J_n, T_n), which is embedded in the indexed semi-Markov kernel, depends on the moving average process U_n^m, the latter acts as a stochastic index. Moreover, the index process U_n^m depends on (J_n, T_n) through the functional relationship (10).

To describe the behavior of our model at whatever time t we need to define additional stochastic processes.

Given the three-dimensional process $\{J_n, T_n, U_n^m\}$ and the indexed semi-Markov kernel $\mathbf{Q}^m(v;t)$, we define by

$$\begin{aligned} &N(t) = \sup\{n \in \mathbb{N} : T_n \le t\}; \\ &Z(t) = J_{N(t)}; \\ &U^m(t) = \frac{1}{t - T_{(N(t)-\theta)-m}} \sum_{k=0}^{m} \int_{T_{(N(t)-\theta)-k}}^{t\wedge T_{(N(t)-\theta)+1-k}} f(J_{(N(t)-\theta)-k}, s)ds, \end{aligned} \tag{14}$$

where $T_{N(t)} \le t < T_{N(t)+1}$ and $\theta = 1_{\{t=T_{N(t)}\}}$.

The stochastic processes defined in (14) represent the number of transitions up to time t, the state of the system (price return) at time t and the value of the index process (moving average of function of price return) up to t, respectively. We refer to $Z(t)$ as an indexed semi-Markov process.

The process $U^m(t)$ is a generalization of the process U_n^m where time t can be a transition or a waiting time. It is simple to realize that if $\forall m$, if $t = T_n$ we have that $U^m(t) = U_n^m$.

Let

$$p_{ij}^m(v) := P[J_{n+1}=j | J_n=i, U_n^m=v].$$

be the transition probabilities of the embedded indexed Markov chain. It denotes the probability that the next transition is in state j given that at current time the process entered in state i and the index process is v. It is simple to realize that

$$p_{ij}^m(v) = \lim_{t\to\infty} Q_{ij}^m(v;t). \tag{15}$$

Let $H_i^m(v;\cdot)$ be the sojourn time cumulative distribution in state $i \in E$:

$$H_i^m(v;t) := P[T_{n+1}-T_n \le t | J_n=i,\, U_n^m=v] = \sum_{j\in E} Q_{ij}^m(v;t). \tag{16}$$

It expresses the probability to make a transition from state i with sojourn time less or equal to t given the indexed process is v.

The conditional waiting time distribution function G expresses the following probability:

$$G_{ij}^{m}(v;t) := P[T_{n+1} - T_n \leq t \mid J_n = i, J_{n+1} = j, U_n^m = v]. \tag{17}$$

It is simple to establish that

$$G_{ij}^{m}(v;t) = \begin{cases} \frac{Q_{ij}^{m}(v;t)}{p_{ij}^{m}(v)} & \text{if } p_{ij}^{m}(v) \neq 0 \\ 1 & \text{if } p_{ij}^{m}(v) = 0. \end{cases} \tag{18}$$

To properly assess the probabilistic behavior of the system, we introduce the transition probability function:

$$\phi_{(i_{-(m+1)},i_{-m},\dots i_0;j)}^{m}(t_{-(m+1)}, t_{-m}, \dots, t_0; t, V) :=$$
$$P[Z(t) = j, U^m(t) \leq V | J_0 = i_0, \dots, J_{-(m+1)} = i_{-(m+1)}, T_0 = t_0, \dots, T_{-(m+1)} = t_{-(m+1)}]. \tag{19}$$

In [8] it was shown that the transition probability function of the ISMC satisfies a renewal-type equation.

2.3. The Weighted-Indexed Semi-Markov Model

In this subsection we describe a further improvement of the SMC model described above, named Weighted-Indexed Semi-Markov Chain (WISMC) model which allows the possibility of reproducing long-term dependence in the square of stock returns in a very efficient way; this model was proposed and investigated by [9].

Let us assume that the value of the financial asset under study is described by the time varying asset price $S(t)$. The return at time t calculated over a time interval of lenght 1 is defined as $\frac{S(t+1)-S(t)}{S(t)}$. The return process changes value in time, then we denote by $\{J_n\}_{n\in\mathbb{N}}$ the stochastic process with finite state space $E = \{1, 2, \dots, s\}$ and describing the value of the return process at the n-th transition.

Let us consider the stochastic process $\{T_n\}_{n\in\mathbb{N}}$ with values in $\mathbb{N}$. The random variable T_n describes the time in which the n-th transition of the price return process occurs.

Let us consider also the stochastic process $\{U_n^\lambda\}_{n\in\mathbb{N}}$ with values in $\mathbb{R}$. The random variable U_n^λ describes the value of the index process at the n-th transition.

In reference [8] the process $\{U_n\}$ was defined as a reward accumulation process linked to the Markov Renewal Process $\{J_n, T_n\}$; in [8] the process $\{U_n\}$ was defined as a moving average of the reward process. Here, motivated by the application to financial returns, we consider a more flexible index process defined as follows:

$$U_n^\lambda = \sum_{k=0}^{n-1} \sum_{a=T_{n-1-k}}^{T_{n-k}-1} f(J_{n-1-k}, a, \lambda), \tag{20}$$

where $f : E \times \mathbb{N} \times \mathbb{R} \to \mathbb{R}$ is a Borel measurable bounded function and U_0^λ is known and non-random.

The process U_n^λ can be interpreted as an accumulated reward process with the function f as a measure of the weighted rate of reward per unit time. The function f depends on the current time a, on the state J_{n-1-k} visited at current time and on the parameter λ that represents the weight.
In next section a specific functional form of f will be selected in order to produce a real data application.

To construct the WISMC model we have to specify a dependence structure between the variables. Toward this end we adopt the following assumption:

$$\begin{aligned} &\mathbb{P}[J_{n+1}=j,\, T_{n+1}-T_n \le t|\sigma(J_h, T_h, U_h^\lambda),\, h=0,...,n,\, J_n=i, U_n^\lambda=v] \\ &=\mathbb{P}[J_{n+1}=j,\, T_{n+1}-T_n \le t|J_n=i, U_n^\lambda=v] := Q_{ij}^\lambda(v;t), \end{aligned} \tag{21}$$

where $\sigma(J_h, T_h, U_h^\lambda)$, $h \le n$ is the natural filtration of the three-variate process.

The matrix of functions $\mathbf{Q}^\lambda(v;t) = (Q_{ij}^\lambda(v;t))_{i,j\in E}$ has a fundamental role in the theory we are going to expose, in recognition of its importance, we call it *weighted-indexed semi-Markov kernel.*

The joint process (J_n, T_n) depends on the process U_n^λ, the latter acts as a stochastic index. Moreover, the index process U_n^λ depends on (J_n, T_n) through the functional relationship (20).

Observe that if

$$\mathbb{P}[J_{n+1}=j,\, T_{n+1}-T_n \le t|J_n=i, U_n^\lambda=v] = \mathbb{P}[J_{n+1}=j,\, T_{n+1}-T_n \le t|J_n=i]$$

for all values $v \in \mathbb{R}$ of the index process, then the weigthed indexed semi-Markov kernel degenerates in an ordinary semi-Markov kernel and the WISMC model becomes equivalent to classical semi-Markov chain model as presented for example in [14] and [2].

The triple of processes $\{J_n, T_n, U_n^\lambda\}$ describes the behaviour of the system only in correspondence of the transition times T_n. To describe the behavior of our model at whatever time t which can be a transition time or a waiting time, we need to define additional stochastic processes.

Given the three-dimensional process $\{J_n, T_n, U_n^\lambda\}$ and the weighted indexed semi-Markov kernel $\mathbf{Q}^\lambda(v;t)$, we define by

$$\begin{aligned} &N(t)=\sup\{n\in\mathbb{N} : T_n \le t\}; \\ &Z(t)=J_{N(t)}; \\ &U^\lambda(t)=\sum_{k=0}^{N(t)-1+\theta}\ \sum_{a=T_{N(t)+\theta-1-k}}^{(t\wedge T_{N(t)+\theta-k})-1} f(J_{N(t)+\theta-1-k}, a, \lambda), \end{aligned} \tag{22}$$

where $\theta = 1_{\{t>T_{N(t)}\}}$.

The stochastic processes defined in (22) represent the number of transitions up to time t, the state of the system (price return) at time t and the value of the index process (weighted moving average of function of price return) up to t, respectively. We refer to $Z(t)$ as a weighted indexed semi-Markov process.

The process $U^\lambda(t)$ is a generalization of the process U_n^λ where time t can be a transition or a waiting time. It is simple to realize that if $t = T_n$ we have that $U^\lambda(t) = U_n^\lambda$.

Let

$$p_{ij}^\lambda(v) := \mathbb{P}[J_{n+1} = j | J_n = i, U_n^\lambda = v],$$

be the transition probabilities of the embedded indexed Markov chain. It denotes the probability that the next transition is in state j given that at current time the process entered in state i and the index process is equal to v. It is simple to realize that

$$p_{ij}^\lambda(v) = \lim_{t\to\infty} Q_{ij}^\lambda(v;t). \tag{23}$$

Let $H_i^\lambda(v;\cdot)$ be the sojourn time cumulative distribution in state $i \in E$:

$$H_i^\lambda(v;t) := \mathbb{P}[T_{n+1} - T_n \leq t | J_n = i,\ U_n^\lambda = v] = \sum_{j\in E} Q_{ij}^\lambda(v;t). \tag{24}$$

It expresses the probability to make a transition from state i with sojourn time less or equal to t given the indexed process is v.

The conditional waiting time distribution function G expresses the following probability:

$$G_{ij}^\lambda(v;t) := \mathbb{P}[T_{n+1} - T_n \leq t \mid J_n = i, J_{n+1} = j, U_n^\lambda = v]. \tag{25}$$

It is simple to establish that

$$G_{ij}^\lambda(v;t) = \begin{cases} \frac{Q_{ij}^\lambda(v;t)}{p_{ij}^\lambda(v)} & \text{if } p_{ij}^\lambda(v) \neq 0 \\ 1 & \text{if } p_{ij}^\lambda(v) = 0. \end{cases} \tag{26}$$

3. Empirical Results

To check the validity of our models we perform a comparison of the behavior of real data returns and returns generated through Monte Carlo simulations based on the models. In this section we describe the database of real data used for the analysis, the method used to simulate synthetic returns time series and, at the end, we compare results from real and simulated data.

3.1. Database Description

The data we used to compare results between real data and the SMC model and the ISMC model are tick-by-tick quotes of indexes and stocks downloaded from *www.borsaitaliana.it* for the period January 2007-December 2010 (4 full years). The data have been re-sampled to have 1 minute frequency. Consider a single day (say day k with $1 \leq k \leq d$) where d is number of traded days in the time series. In our case we consider four years of trading (from the first of January 2007 corresponding to $d = 1076$). The market in Italy fixes the opening price at a random time in the first minute after 9 am, continuous trading starts immediately after and ends just before 5.25 pm, finally the closing price is fixed just after 5.30 pm. Therefore, let us define $S(t)$ as the price of the last trading before 9.01.00 am , $S(t+1)$ as the price of the last trading before 9.02.00 am and so on until

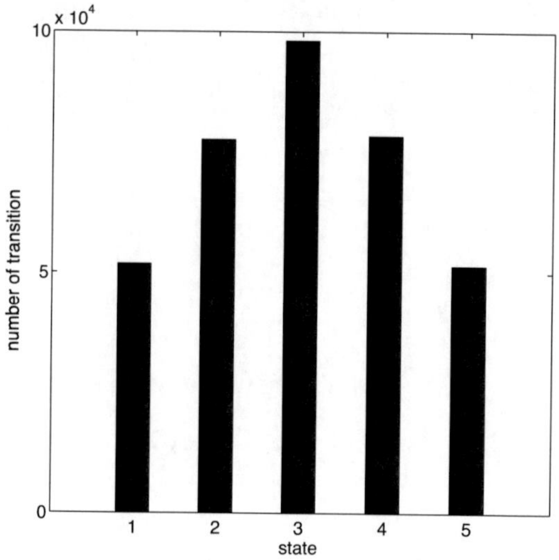

Figure 2. Number of transitions for the embedded Markov chain.

$S(nk)$ as the price of the last trading before 5.25.00 pm. If there are no transactions in the minute, the price remains unchanged (even in the case the title is suspended and reopened in the same day). Also define $S(nk+1)$ as the opening price and $S(nk)$ as the closing price. With this choice $n = 507$. There was a small difference before the 28th of September 2009 since continuous trading started at 9,05 am, and therefore prior of that date we have $n = 502$. Finally, if the title has a delay in opening or it closes in advance (suspended but not reopened), only the effective trading minutes are taken into account. In this case n will be smaller than 507. The number of returns analyzed is then roughly 508000 for each stock. We analyzed all the stocks in the FTSEMIB which are the 40 most capitalized stocks in the Italian stock market.

To be able to model returns as a SMC the state space has to be discretized. In the example shown we discretized returns into 5 states chosen to be symmetrical with respect to returns equal zero. Returns are in fact already discretized in real data due to the discretization of stock prices which is fixed by each stock exchange and depends on the value of the stock. Just to make an example, in the Italian stock market for stocks with value between 5.0001 and 10 euros the minimum variation is fixed to 0.005 euros (usually called tick). We then tried to remain as much as possible close to this discretization. In Figure 2 we show an example of the number of transition from state i to all other states for the embedded Markov chain.

For the WISMC model we choose 4 stocks from two databases of tick-by-tick quotes of real stocks from the Italian Stock Exchange ("Borsa Italiana") and the German Stock Exchange ("Deutsche Börse"). The chosen stocks are ENI and FIAT from the Italian database and Allianz and VolksWagen from the German database.The period used goes from January 2007 to December 2010 (4 full years). The data have been re-sampled to have 1 minute frequency. The number of returns analyzed is then roughly $500 * 10^3$ for each stock.

In these 4 examples, we discretized returns into 5 states chosen to be symmetrical with

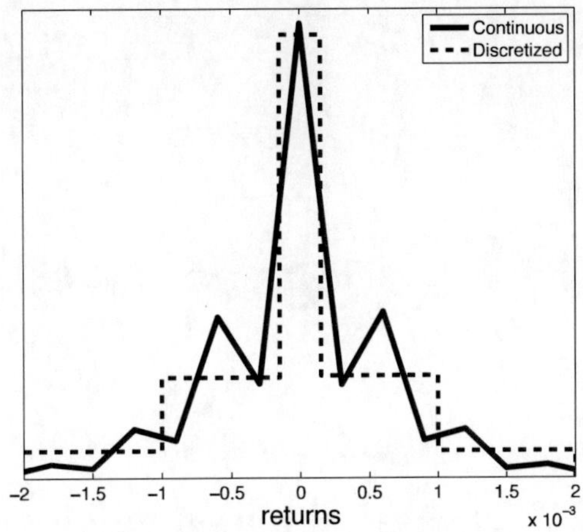

Figure 3. Discretization of returns.

respect to returns equal zero and to keep the shape of the distribution unchanged. Also in this case, returns are already discretized. In Figure 3 we show an example of the discretization of the returns of one of the analyzed stocks.

From the discretized returns we estimated the probabilities $\mathbf{P}$ and $G_{ij}(t)$ to generate a synthetic trajectory of the described models. For this aim we derive a Monte Carlo algorithm in order to simulate a trajectory of a given model in the time interval $[0, T]$. T is chosen such as the synthetic time series have the same length as the real one. The output of the algorithm consists in the successive visited states $\{J_0, J_1, ...\}$, the jump times $\{T_0, T_1, ...\}$ up to the time T.The follow algorithm is an example of Monte Carlo simulation for the semi-Markov model:

1) Set $n = 0$, $J_0 = i$, $T_0 = 0$, horizon time$= T$;
2) Sample J from $p_{J_n,\cdot}$ and set $J_{n+1} = J(\omega)$;
3) Sample W from $G_{J_n,J_{n+1}}(\cdot)$ and set $T_{n+1} = T_n + W(\omega)$;
4) If $T_{n+1} \geq T$ stop
   else set $n = n + 1$ and go to 2).

3.2. Results on the Autocorrelation Function

A very important feature of stock market data is that, while returns are uncorrelated and show an i.i.d. like behavior, their square or absolute values are long range correlated. It is very important that theoretical models of returns do reproduce this features. We then tested our models to check whether it is able to reproduce such behavior.

We remind the definition of the autocorrelation function: if Z indicates returns, the time lagged (τ) autocorrelation of the square of returns is defined as

$$\Sigma(\tau) = \frac{Cov(Z^2(t+\tau), Z^2(t))}{Var(Z^2(t))} \tag{27}$$

We estimated $\Sigma(\tau)$ for real data and for returns time series simulated with different models. The time lag τ was made to run from 1 minute up to 100 minutes. Note that to be able to

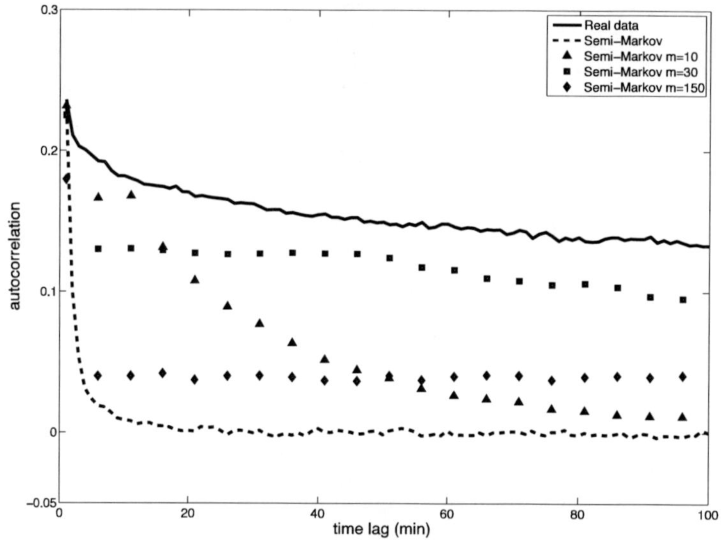

Figure 4. Autocorrelation functions of real data (solid line) and of 4 synthetic time series as described in the label.

compare results for $\Sigma(\tau)$ each simulated time series was generated with the same length as real data.

Results for the indexed semi-Markov model (few values of m), for real data and for a semi-Markov model without index are shown in Figure 4.

As expected, real data do show a long range correlation of volatility let us than analyze results for the synthetic time series. The simple semi-Markov model starts at the same value but the persistence is very short and after few time steps the autocorrelation decrease to zero. A very interesting behavior is instead shown by the semi-Markov models with memory index. If a small memory ($m = 10$ in the shown example) is used, the autocorrelation is already persistent but again decreases faster than real data. With a longer memory ($m = 30$) the autocorrelation remain high for a very long period and also its value is very close to that of real data. If m is increased further the autocorrelation drops again to small values. This behavior suggest the existence of an optimal memory m. In our opinion one can justify this behavior by saying that short memories are not enough to identify in which volatility status is the market, too long memories mix together different status and then much of the information is lost in the average. All this is shown in Figure 5 where the mean square error between each autocorrelation function of simulated time series and the autocorrelation function of the real data as a function of m is computed. It can be noticed that there exist an optimal value of the memory m that makes the autocorrelation of simulated data closer to that of real data.

For what regard the WISMC model, described in the section 2.3, this requires the specification of a function f in the definition of the weighted index U_n^λ in (20). Let us briefly remind that volatility of real market is long range positively autocorrelated and then clustered in time. This implies that, in the stock market, there are periods of high and low

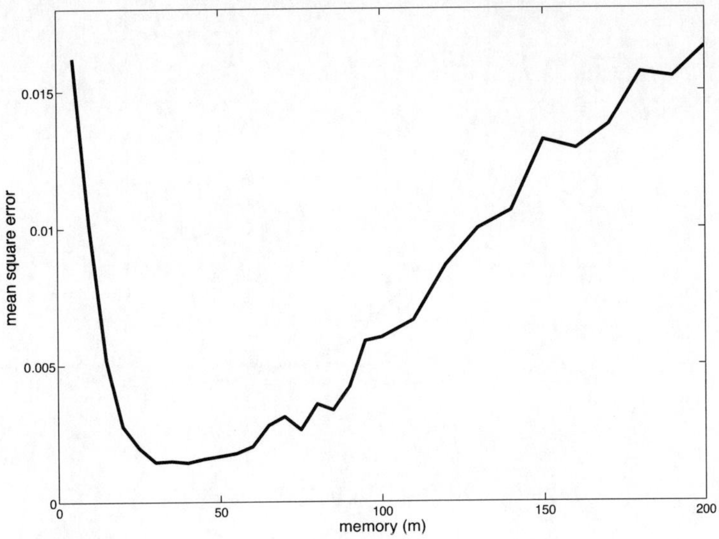

Figure 5. Mean square error between autocorrelation function of real data and synthetic data as a function of the memory value m.

volatility. Motivated by this empirical facts we suppose that also the transition probabilities depends on whether the market is in a high volatility period or in a low one. In contrast to the indexed semi-Markov model here we decided to use a more appropriate expression for f. We use an exponentially weighted moving average (EWMA) of the squares of returns which as the following expression:

$$f(J_{n-1-k}, a, \lambda) = \frac{\lambda^{T_n - a} J_{n-1-k}^2}{\sum_{k=0}^{n-1} \sum_{a=T_{n-1-k}}^{T_{n-k}-1} \lambda^{T_n - a}} \tag{28}$$

and consequently the index process becomes

$$U_n^\lambda = \sum_{k=0}^{n-1} \sum_{a=T_{n-1-k}}^{T_{n-k}-1} \left(\frac{\lambda^{T_n - a} J_{n-1-k}^2}{\sum_{k=0}^{n-1} \sum_{a=T_{n-1-k}}^{T_{n-k}-1} \lambda^{T_n - a}} \right). \tag{29}$$

The index U^λ was also discretized into 5 states of low, medium low, medium, medium high and high volatility. An example of the discretization used in the analysis is shown in Figure 6.

Given the presence of the parameter λ in the index function, we tested the autocorrelation behavior as a function of λ. Note that in the definition of the index variable the EWMA is performed over all the previous square of returns each with its weight. Before summing over all past returns we decided to check whether a better memory time m exists. For this reason we checked our model also against this other parameter. With this choice formula

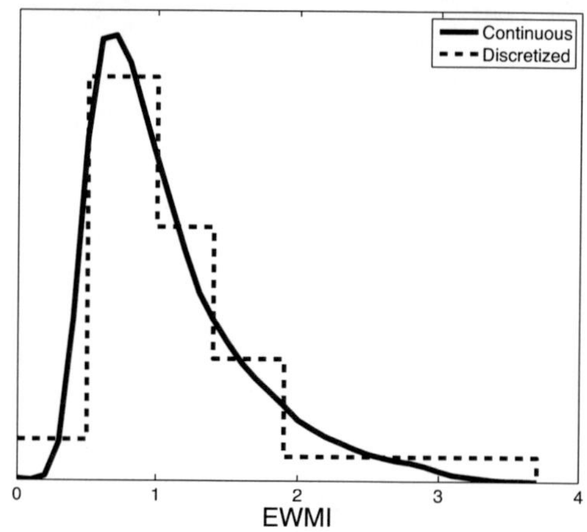

Figure 6. Discretization of index values.

(29) takes the form:

$$U_n^{\lambda}(m) = \sum_{k=n-m}^{n-1} \sum_{a=T_{n-1-k}}^{T_{n-k}-1} \left(\frac{\lambda^{T_n-a} J_{n-1-k}^2}{\sum_{k=n-m}^{n-1} \sum_{a=T_{n-1-k}}^{T_{n-k}-1} \lambda^{T_n-a}} \right). \tag{30}$$

In Figure 7 we show the mean square error between $\Sigma(\tau)$ obtained from real and simulated returns (using definition (30) for the index process) for the four stocks analyzed and for different m and λ. Let us make some considerations on the results shown in Figure 7: m should be chosen as big as possible and then definition (29) is appropriate as far as λ is chosen less than 1, in fact, in this last case definition (29) becomes equivalent to a moving average without weights and results presented in [8] hold for m. In Figure 8 we show again the mean square error but only as a function of the weights λ then using definition (29) for the index process. We can notice that the behavior is very similar for the different analyzed stocks even if the best value for λ is not the same for all of them. As it is possible to see the best values of λ for the stocks Fiat, Eni, Allianz and VolksWagen are 0.96, 0.97, 0.97 and 0.98, respectively.

The comparison between the autocorrelations for the best values of λ for each stock and real data is shown in Figure 9. This figure shows that real and synthetic data have almost the same autocorrelation function for the square of returns.

4. Concluding Remarks

We have modeled financial price changes through semi-Markov models. Our work is motivated by the existence in the market of periods of low and high volatility. The simple semi-Markov and the indexed semi-Markov models are able to capture almost all the correlation in the square of returns present in real data. The comparison between these two models shows that the ISMC model reproduce quite well the behavior of the market return thanks to the past volatility used as the memory index. We have shown that the time length

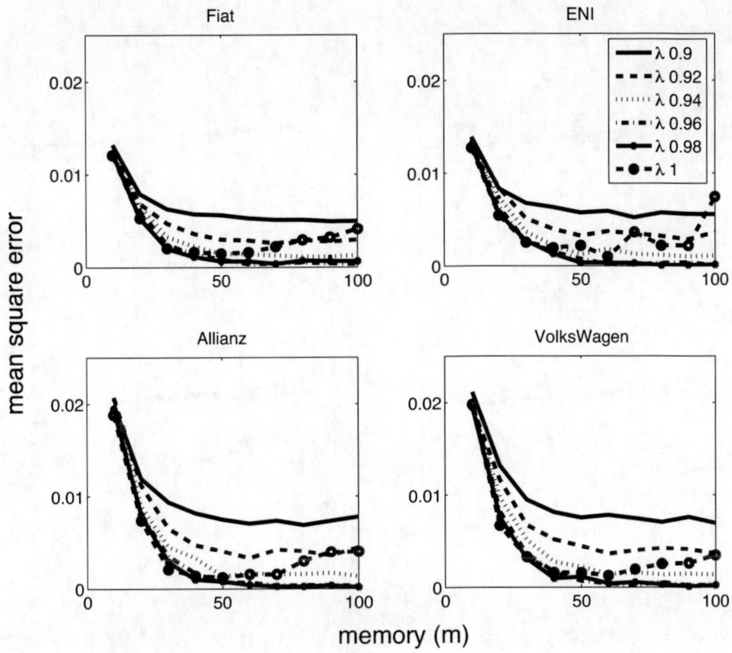

Figure 7. Mean square error between autocorrelation functions from real and simulated data as functions of m and for different values of λ.

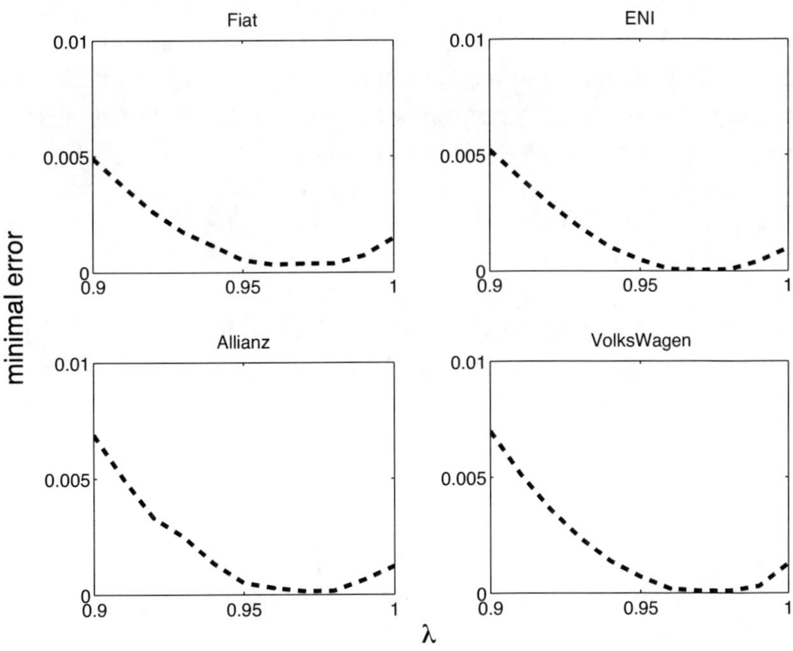

Figure 8. Mean square error between autocorrelation functions from real and simulated data as functions of λ.

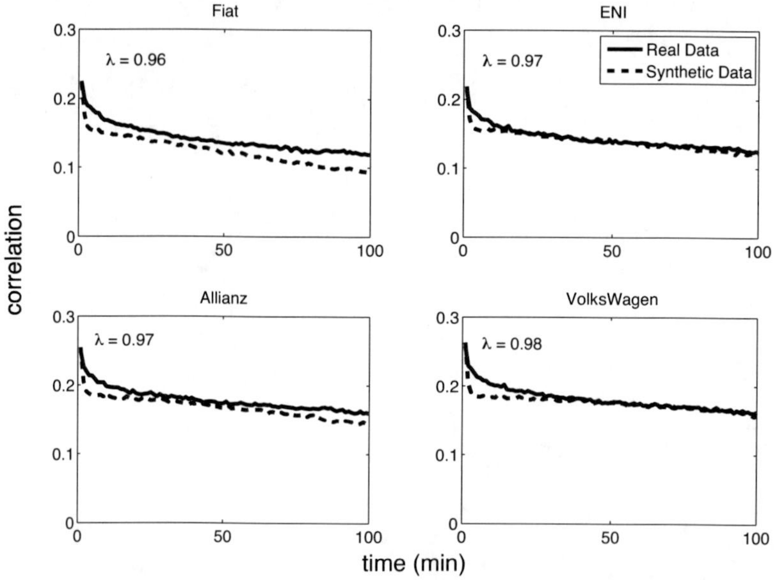

Figure 9. Autocorrelation functions of real data (solid line) and synthetic (dashed line) time series for the analyzed stocks.

of the memory does play a crucial role in reproducing the right autocorrelation persistence, indicating the existence of an optimal value.

The results presented for the WISMC model, instead, show that if the past volatility is used as an exponentially weighted index, the model is able to reproduce more correctly, than the ISMC model, the behavior of market returns. The returns generated by the model are uncorrelated while the square of returns present a long range correlation very similar to that of real data.

We have also shown, only for the WISMC model, by analyzing different stocks from different markets (Italian and German), that results do not depend on the particular stock chosen for the analysis even if the value of the weights may depends on the stock.

We stress that out models are very different from those of the ARCH/GARCH family. We do not model directly the volatility as a correlated process. We model returns and by considering the semi-Markov kernel and the semi-Markov kernel conditioned by a memory index and a weighted index the volatility correlation comes out freely.

References

[1] V. Barbu, M. Boussemart, N. Limnios. *Commun. Stat. Theory Method* 33 (2004) 2833.

[2] Barbu, V. and Limnios, N. (2008). *Semi-Markov Chains and Hidden Semi-Markov Models Toward Applications*. Springer-Verlag New York Inc.

[3] G. D'Amico, *Age-usage semi-Markov models*, *Applied Mathematical Modelling*, 35, (2011), 4354-4366.

[4] G. D'Amico, J. Janssen, R. Manca. Homogeneous semi-Markov reliability models for credit risk management, *Decisions in Economics and Finance*, 28, (2005), 79-93.

[5] G. D'Amico, J. Janssen, R. Manca. European and American options: The semi-Markov case, *Physica A*, 388, (2009), 3181-3194.

[6] G. D'Amico, J. Janssen, R. Manca. *Methodol Comput Appl Probab.* 12(2) (2010) 215.

[7] G. D'Amico, F. Petroni. *A semi-Markov model for price returns*, *Physica A* 2012, DOI: 10.1016/j.physa.2012.05.040.

[8] G. D'Amico, F. Petroni. *A semi-Markov model with memory for price changes*, *Journal of Statistical Mechanics: Theory and Experiment*, P12009, 2011

[9] G. D'Amico, F. Petroni. Weighted-indexed semi-Markov models for modeling financial returns." *Journal of Statistical Mechanics: Theory and Experiment* (2012) P07015.

[10] G. D'Amico, F. Petroni, F. Prattico. First and second order semi-Markov chains for wind speed modeling, *Physica A*, 392, (2013), 1194-1201.

[11] G. D'Amico, F. Petroni, F. Prattico. Reliability Measures of Second-Order Semi-Markov Chain Applied to Wind Energy Production, *Journal of Renewable Energy*, 2013, Article ID 368940, 6 pages.

[12] G. D'Amico, F. Petroni, F. Prattico. Wind speed modeled as an indexed semi-Markov process, *Environmetrics*, Article first published online: 24 MAY 2013, DOI: 10.1002/env.2215.

[13] D.M. Guillaume, M.M. Dacorogna, R.R. DavVe, J.A. MWuller, R.B. Olsen, O.V. Pictet. From the birds eye to the microscope: A survey of new stylized facts of the intra-daily foreign exchange markets, *Finance and Stochastics* 1, (1997), 95-129.

[14] J. Janssen and R. Manca, *Applied semi-Markov processes,* Springer, New York, 2006.

[15] M. H. Jensen, A. Johansen, F. Petroni, I. Simonsen. Inverse Statistics in the Foreign Exchange Market. *Physica A* 340, (2004) 678.

[16] N.Limnios, G. Opriçan, *Semi-Markov Processes and Reliability Modeling*, Birkhäuser, Boston. (2001).

[17] N. Limnios, G. Oprişan. An introduction to Semi-Markov Processes with Application to Reliability, In D.N. Shanbhag and C.R. Rao, eds., *Handbook of Statistics*, 21, (2003), 515-556.

[18] F. Mainardi, M. Raberto, R. Gorenflo, E. Scalas.*Fractional calculus and continuous-time finance II: The waiting-time distribution*, *Physica A*, 287, (2000), 468-481.

[19] F. Petroni, M. Serva. *Spot foreign exchange market and time series*, *The European Physical Journal B* 34, (2003), 495-500.

[20] M. Raberto, E. Scalas, F. Mainardi. *Waiting-times and returns in high-frequency financial data: An empirical study*, *Physica A* 314, (2002) 749-755.

[21] D.S. Silvestrov, F. Stenberg. *A pricing process with stochastic volatility controlled by a semi-Markov process*, *Communications in Statistics: Theory and Methods*, 33, (2004), 591-608.

[22] I. Simonsen. M.H. Jensen, A. Johansen, Optimal Investment Horizons, *Eur. Phys. J.* 27 (2002) 583.

In: Stock Markets
Editors: F. Petroni, F. Prattico and G. D'Amico
ISBN: 978-1-62808-751-2

Chapter 10

MULTIAGENT'S MODEL OF STOCK MARKET WITH P-ADIC DESCRIPTION OF PRICES

*V. Zharkov**
Institute of Natural Sciences, Perm State University, Perm, Russia

Abstract

A new multi-agent model of the stock market is formulated that contains four states in which the agents may be located. Next, the model is reformulated in the language of the functional integral containing fluctuations of prices and quantities of cash flows. It is shown that in the functional integral of that type description of the prices is given not by the real numbers as is made in many papers but the p-adic numbers. It is shown in the following simple examples extracted from the proposed theory that the p-adic description of prices gives good description of fractal behavior of the trends. The formula is given for the p-adic mapping of prices. Using this formula we obtain the main p-adic patterns which are the same as the patterns of Elliott wave theory, this fact allows us to give a rigorous mathematical proof of this theory. Our model is the only model that gives a strict point like description of the fractal behavior of prices. The developed approach opens the possibility to give the formulation of p-adic technical analysis of the stock market.

PACS: 89.65.Gh.

Keywords: Hubbard mode, Hubbard model, multiagents model, stock market, p-adic numbers

AMS Subject Classification: 20G42, 11D88

1. Introduction

Stock market is the complex dynamical system which consists an individual traders as basic elements. The most fundamental approach for modeling stock is to use the agents which simulate human traders. The second step is to derive the ensemble behavior of the whole market from the multi- agent trading processes. The main focus in the description of the

*E-mail address: vita@psu.ru

dynamics in the stock market in the recent years is to study ensemble of traders, their collective behavior through the production of prices of the traded assets. Many models was proposed. The most famous of them is the minority game, in which the traders can stay two states the state of selling and buying. In many papers analytical and numerical study was done on the properties of such models [1, 2, 22, 17, 18].

In this paper I consider the agents based approach to multifractal behavior of stock market. On the basis of the previously proposed agent-based model [23, 21] the new model with a fractal price behavior is built. I study the appearance of the p-adic description in the dynamics of prices in model. Efficient market hypothesis (EMH) is widely known since its inception by Samuelson in 1965 [17]. From the outset, it was criticized both for its useless in practical activities and from theoretical side pointing to the fact that some markets are predictable. EMH assumes that all information is taken into account in prices. According to Fama efficient market is a random walk such that the increment of prices satisfy the Gaussian distribution. The most significant drawback EMH is the most complete disregard for rare events or failures of large corrections.

EMH has far-reaching implications, which are discussed in majority of financial economics textbooks – investors are rational and homogeneous, financial returns are normally distributed, standard deviation is a meaningful measure of risk, there is a tradeoff between risk and return, and future returns are unpredictable. It is well known that capital markets comprise of various investors with very different investment horizons – from algorithmically-based market makers with the investment horizon of fractions of a second, through noise traders with the horizon of several minutes, technical traders with the horizons of days and weeks, and fundamental analysts with the monthly horizons to pension funds with the horizons of several years [18].

In this paper I am interested in the behavior of investors at various investment horizons as well as in scaling scheme of the market returns. My goal is to develop a model which takes into account different types of investors and their investment horizons. Note that the fractal shown in figure 2 different types of investors are marked with different depths of the fractal or the type of Elliott Waves [19]. Small investment periods are described by the fractal segment of the low level, average investment periods are represented by Elliott waves of type 1-2-3-4-5 and so on. The very nature of the fractal principle dictates for which there is a repetition of patterns in large scale in proportion. This discrete scale invariance gives us some principle by which we can predict the future movement of prices. Movement of future prices on large time scales should be similar to the movement of prices on a small scale. Scale invariance of fractals and Elliott waves give us a very simple principle of price forecasting. We need a more general mathematical scheme that will give us another mechanism that can be analyzed. Before we describe how to enter it we will give some procedure to draw figure in price - time in a multidimensional space. For example I can take the four-dimensional vector (open price, min, max, close price) and denote its as one point. Then on a more coarse-grained graph we have a point in four-dimensional space. To enter a three-dimensional space is necessary to take a coarse grid containing the three-vector of the form $(P(t_i), P(t_{i+1}), P(t_{i+2}))$, here $P(t)$ - price as function of the time. In a new functional integral approach proposed for the model, we find the regime with a deformed integration measure in which the standard integral is replaced with the Jackson integral. We indicate the relation to a p-adic functional integral. For the subsystems of traders orders and cash flow in the effective functional that results from the operator formulation of the Hubbard model [3], we find the two-parametric quantum derivative resulting in the appearance of the quantum $SU_{rq}(2)$ group. We establish the relation to the one-parametric quantum derivative and to the standard derivative.

This paper is devoted to justifying that a regime in which the studied macroscopic quantities are described by functions of a p-adic argument can arise in strongly correlated multielectron systems with strong multiagents interaction. We here justify the following scenario: p-adic numbers appear through a deformation of the integration measure depending on the deformation parameter q. The Jackson measure used when calculating macroscopic quantities appears in the functional integral in the strong correlation regime. In the case $q = 1/p$, where p is a prime, the Jackson integral becomes the p-adic integral [12]. We can therefore use functions of a p-adic argument to describe jumps in the Hubbard model. In particular, we here continue the investigation of the new formulation of the functional integral that we proposed in [10, 11]. Therefore, in what follows, we present a comparison with different versions of functional representations for creation-annihilation operators proposed in various papers. We show that the obtained expressions for supercoherent states result in more complex composite expressions for the operator symbols than those provided by the slave-boson and slave-roton approaches [8, 9]. The expressions for the creation-annihilation operators obtained here with various group reduction schemes in the Hubbard model first proposed in [10], result in all currently known formulations of the functional integral for systems with strong interaction. Moreover, as shown in [11], the proposed formulation allows studying various cohomologies of groups and supergroups and thus provides a controlled concretization and expansion of dynamical groups and symmetries spontaneously appearing when strengthening the interaction in multiagents systems. Our proposed representation for the effective functional and creation-annihilation operators is essentially nonlinear. This nonlinearity allows segregating those terms that provide quantum derivatives determining generators of the quantum algebra in expressions belonging to the universal enveloping algebra. In [6], we introduced the approximation in which radius vectors of vector fields were independent of the dynamical field coordinates. This assumption is equivalent to the approximation in which the values of the fields that correspond to the Casimir operators and to the invariants of the classical groups $SU(2)$ and $SU(1, 1)$ in our formulation are coordinate independent. Below, we demonstrate that these combinations determine two parameters of deformation of the quantum Lorentz group, which is the group of four-dimensional rotations. We treat the transition to the one-parameter quantum derivative in detail and show that the subsystems of traders orders and cash flow of the Hubbard model are described by deformed versions of nonlinear sigma models. We further calculate the part of the functional integral for the Hubbard model that results from expressions containing this quantum derivative. We realize our consideration on model contributions naturally present in the Hubbard model. We consider the limiting cases with respect to the deformation parameter and calculate the functional integral in these limit regimes. We calculate the effective functional following from the kinetic energy of the Hubbard model using supercoherent states containing no more than the first powers of fermionic fields. We fix the dynamical fields such that the residual expressions indicate the difference between our approach and other approaches in the literature. The main distinct feature of our representation is its nonlinearity, which allows introducing a two-parameter quantum derivative into the problem. When passing to a one-parameter quantum derivative, we obtain a deformed nonlinear sigma model in the auxiliary dimension determined by the scale factor. Further, by analogy with the diagram technique for atomic X-operators [10], we consider the integral of the scale factor linear in the quantum number. This integral determines the integration measure. Directly calculating the corresponding series, we show that in the limit case as the deformation parameter tends to zero, this series converges to the Jackson integral. Obtaining deformations of the integration measure when varying the deformation parameter is our main result. In the limit case of small q, the standard integral becomes the Jackson integral.

2. Mathematical Model of Agent Based Stock Market

This chapter is central to the search for the model of the stock market, showing fractal behavior. Below we show that we have formulated a model which can be reformulated in such a way that the effective functional gives us a p-adic description. Below we repeat parts of formulas, by presenting the material in a form that adopted in solid state physics. We briefly describe the general scheme for constructing the effective functional for the Hubbard model proposed in [6] and recently further developed, for example, in [11]. We begin with the Hubbard model written in terms of the standard creation-annihilation operators. We will take as a model the stock market model, written in terms of creation - destruction operators. This type of model is the standard representation for the Hubbard model [3] in the weak interaction limit.

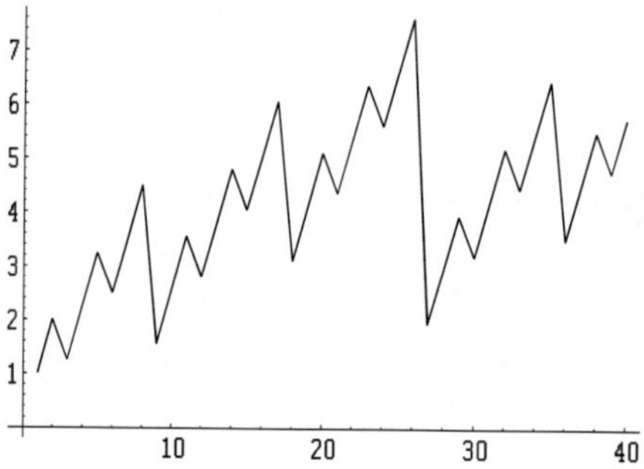

Figure 1. A subcritical wave for b < 1.

$$H = -W \sum_{ij\sigma} \alpha^{+}_{\sigma,i} \alpha_{\sigma,j} + U \sum_{i,\sigma} n_{\sigma,i} n_{-\sigma,i} - \mu \sum_{\sigma,i} n_{\sigma,i}, \quad (1)$$

where $\alpha^{+}_{\sigma,i}$, $\alpha_{\sigma,j}$ are the creation and annihilation operators, $n_{\sigma,i}$ is the electron density operator, W, U, μ are the respective width of the conductivity band, the one-site repulsion of two electrons, and the chemical potential, and σ determines the spin value. We sum over the indices i and j labeling the lattice sites. For instance, for a one-dimensional lattice, we have $N/2 < i < N/2$, where N is the total number of atoms. For electrons, we sum over the indices $\sigma = \pm 1/2$. In the weak correlation regime with a small on-site repulsion, we take the zeroth approximation for the kinetic energy and treat the repulsion perturbatively.

In the "atomic" approach with strong repulsion, we take a one-site contribution of the form

$$Un_{\sigma,i}n_{-\sigma,i} - \mu n_{\sigma,i}.$$

as the zeroth approximation. In what follows, we omit the index i in order to concentrate on the internal structure of the appearing fiber bundle. This term is diagonal in the "atomic" basis and has the eigenfunctions and eigenvalues ϵ:

$$|0\succ; |+\succ = \alpha_{\uparrow}^{+}|0\succ; |-\succ = \alpha_{\downarrow}^{+}|0\succ; |2\succ = \alpha_{\uparrow}^{+}\alpha_{\downarrow}^{+}|0\succ,$$

$$\epsilon_0 = 0, \epsilon_+ = -\mu, \epsilon_- = -\mu, \epsilon_2 = U - 2\mu.$$

We give a mathematical formulation of the market model consisting of a set of traders. The market consists of many traders marked the index i. Each trader may be in the following states: $|0\succ$;-state in which a trader has no money nor stock, $|+\succ = \alpha_{\uparrow}^{+}|0\succ$;-state in which a trader buys shares, $|-\succ = \alpha_{\downarrow}^{+}|0\succ$;-

state in which the trader sells the shares,

$|2\succ = \alpha_{\uparrow}^{+}\alpha_{\downarrow}^{+}|0\succ$-

state in which the trader holds shares of N.

General state in which the trader resides at any one time will be given to this function:

$\psi(i) = a_i \mid i0\rangle + b_i \mid i+\rangle + c_i \mid i-\rangle + d_i \mid i2\rangle$

here a_i, b_i, c_i, d_i - coefficients of general state. Since all of the state in which a trader can stay listed above us, the coefficients have the following restriction: $|\psi|^2 = a^2 + b^2 + c^2 + d^2 = 1$.

Problems of using of this type of functions are well known.The function of type a_i, d_i is symmetric in its coordinates (bosonic type), and the functions b_i, c_i is antisymmetric under the permutation of coordinates (fermion type). The general form of the functions $\mid G >$ given by (6), where the exponent is the expression $\sum_{mn} X^{mn}\phi_{mn}$, where the functions ϕ_{mn} are equal to components of the following expression$(\chi_k^*, \vec{h}, \vec{E})$. The supercoherent state (6) gives us the representation of a supergroup with a set of supergenerators X^{nm}.

We introduce the operators that take a trader out of $\mid i\succ$ in the state $\mid j\succ$.

The calculation of matrix elements for operators of general form $\alpha_{\sigma}^{+}, \alpha_{\sigma}$ in this basis leads to the following matrix representation:

For example, $\alpha_{\uparrow}^{+}$ will have the form:

$$\alpha_{\uparrow}^{+} = \begin{pmatrix} 0 & 0 & 0 & 0 \\ 1 & 0 & 0 & 0 \\ 0 & 0 & 0 & 0 \\ 0 & 0 & -1 & 0 \end{pmatrix} = X^{+0} - X^{2-}. \qquad (2)$$

It is seen that the operators α_{σ}^{+} contain two nonzero matrix elements. We introduce the operators $X^{rs}, r, s = 0, +, -, 2$ containing only one nonzero matrix element. Then we have the following expansion for the operators of creation - annihilation operators through Hubbard ones [10]:

$$\alpha_{\uparrow}^{+} = X^{+0} - X^{2-}, \alpha_{\downarrow}^{+} = X^{-0} + X^{2+}, \alpha_{\uparrow} = X^{0+} - X^{-2}, \alpha_{\downarrow} = X^{0-} + X^{+2}. \qquad (3)$$

Since the dimension of the basis we have is 4 and the creation operators are expressed in terms of matrix of $4*4$, we generally have a base of 16 operators.

We use this notation for this operator because it coincides with the γ_5 operator written in the chiral basis in quantum field theory (QFT). It also equals

$$\gamma_5 = (X^{00} - X^{22})^2 - (X^{++} - X^{--})^2.$$

Because we have a four-dimensional basis and the creation and annihilation operators are expressed as 4x4 matrices, we have a basis comprising 16 operators in the general case. From this set we remove the unity operators and the operators of the form

$$\gamma_5 = \begin{pmatrix} 1 & 0 & 0 & 0 \\ 0 & -1 & 0 & 0 \\ 0 & 0 & -1 & 0 \\ 0 & 0 & 0 & 1 \end{pmatrix}.$$

We can express the one-site Hubbard repulsion in terms this operator. Because we can express it in terms of other operators, we do not take it into account in what follows. The remaining operators on a site in the given basis can then be separated into the fermionic operators of the form

$$(X^{0+}, X^{0-}, X^{+0}, X^{-0}, X^{+2}, X^{-2}, X^{2+}, X^{2-}),$$

and the bosonic operators of the form

$$(X^{+-}, X^{-+}, X^{++} - X^{--}, X^{02}, X^{20}, X^{00} - X^{22}).$$

We omit the lattice index of these operators to indicate the possibility of obtaining generators of the global dynamical algebra. We can endow the Hubbard operators with the lattice index by taking N their copies, where N is the total number of lattice sites, and constituting the direct product from these copies. In terms of these operators, the Hubbard model becomes

$$H = U \sum_{i,r} X_i^{rr} - W \sum_{ij\alpha\beta} X_i^{-\alpha} X_j^{\beta} \tag{4}$$

Since the dimension of the basis we have is 4 and the creation operators are expressed in terms of matrix of $4*4$, we generally have a base of 16 operators.

Now we need to describe the operator describing the change in the market for buying and selling shares of the various traders.

We describe a term that can be called the kinetic energy of the market.

For example, the term $-W \sum_{ij\alpha\beta} X_i^{-\alpha} X_j^{\beta}$ describes the sale of the shares of traders $i$and traders j buying stocks. Other terms describe the various processes between trader i and trader j.

The potential energy of the market is equal to:

$$U \sum_{i,p} X_i^{pp} \tag{5}$$

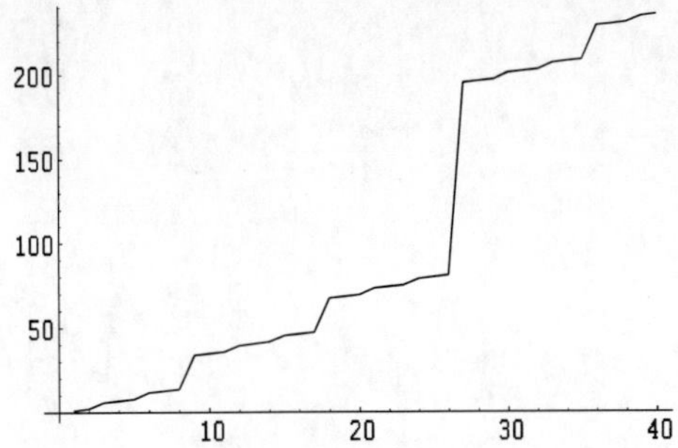

Figure 2. A supercritical wave for b > 1.

This term describes the total volume of shares at traders. The general solution of equation has the following form

$$| G >= \exp \begin{pmatrix} E_z & 0 & 0 & E^+ \\ \chi_1 & H_z & H^+ & 0 \\ \chi_2 & H^- & -H_z & 0 \\ E^- & -\chi_3 & \chi_4 & -E_z \end{pmatrix} | 0 > \tag{6}$$

If we substitute it in formula, we obtain an expression for the matrix elements as functions of the generalized phase (fields). We describe the local properties of market model by this function, which is equal to the supercoherent state.

In the exponent we have the dynamic fields that depend on the coordinates and time.

The electric field is given by the following three-dimensional vector type:

$$\vec{\mathbf{E}} = (E^+(x, y, z, t), E^-(x, y, zt), E^z(x, y, z, t)). \tag{7}$$

The magnetic field has three components, depending on the spatial and temporal coordinates

$$\vec{\mathbf{h}} = (h^+(x, y, z, t), h^-(x, y, z, t), h^z(x, y, z, t)). \tag{8}$$

Fermionic fields are given grassman valued functions of coordinates and time

$$\chi_k^*(x, y, z, t), \chi_k(x, y, z, t), k = 1, 2, 3, 4. \tag{9}$$

Expression (6) is the solution of the following problem: in the atomic basis, the site state is described by a wave function of the form

$$| G\,(i) >= a_i \mid i0\rangle + b_i \mid i+\rangle + c_i \mid i-\rangle + d_i \mid i2\rangle, \tag{10}$$

where a_i, b_i, c_i, d_i - are the coefficients of the atomic basis functions depending on the index i. We have the normalizing condition for the wave function

$$< G \mid G >^2 = a_i^2 + b_i^2 + c_i^2 + d_i^2 = 1.$$

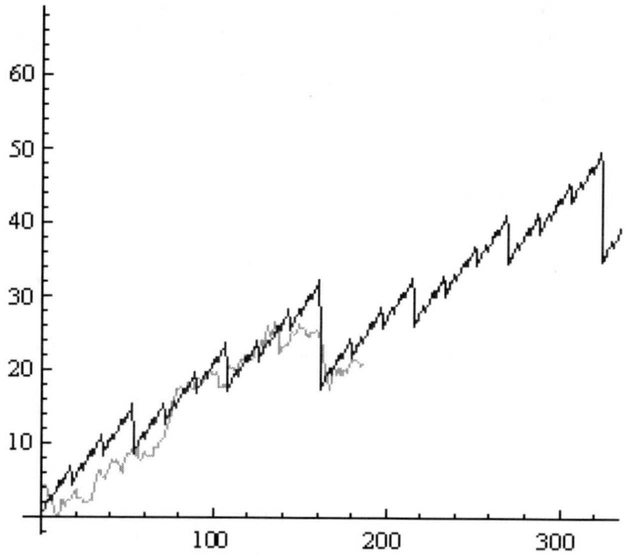

Figure 3. Fractal behavior of IBM stocks.

Supercoherent state (6) determines the supergroup representation with the set of supergenerators X^{nm}. We note that the expressions for the above supercoherent states were calculated exactly in [14]. As noted in [11], using computers and computer programs for working with supermatrices and superpoles, we can exactly calculate the functional itself. It is clear from [14] that the main distinction between our approach and the approaches in other papers is the nonlinear form of the supercoherent state expression. Below, we show that all the representations proposed in the literature for symbols of the creation-annihilation operators follow from our representation when the fields are fixed. We also show that it is the essentially nonlinear nature of the expressions in the supercoherent state, which are functions of electric and magnetic fields, that distinguishes our representation from the previously proposed functional integral representations for the Hubbard model. These nonlinear expressions contain quantum derivatives and, as a result, quantum groups. We use an absolutely different approach in this paper, and the discovery of quantum structures in the Hubbard model is therefore explainable.

The capital flow to market is given by the three-dimensional vector $\vec{E}$. The traders activity is described by three components of $\vec{h}$, depending on the spatial and temporal coordinates. Fermionic fields are given by odd grassmann's valued functions χ_j of the coordinates and time.

Next we use a functional formulation of many-electron systems, proposed in work [23, 21]. According to this approach, the evolution operator between initial and final states is given by the following functional integral with action, expressed through effective functional, which is calculated (4) using supercoherent state.

$$< G_f|e^{-iH(t_f-t_i)}|G_i >= \int_{|G_i>}^{|G_f>} D(G,G^*)e^{-iS[G,G^*]}; \qquad (11)$$

here the action is given by following expression:

$$S[G, G^*] = \int_{t_i}^{t_f} dt \int_V d^3r \frac{< G(r,t)|i\frac{\partial}{\partial t} - H|G(r,t>}{< G(r,t|G(r,t>} \tag{12}$$

Measure of functional integration is equal to:

$$D(G, G^*) = \prod_{t_i<t<t_f} \prod_r dG(r,t)^* dG(r,t) < G(r,t)|G(r,t) > \tag{13}$$

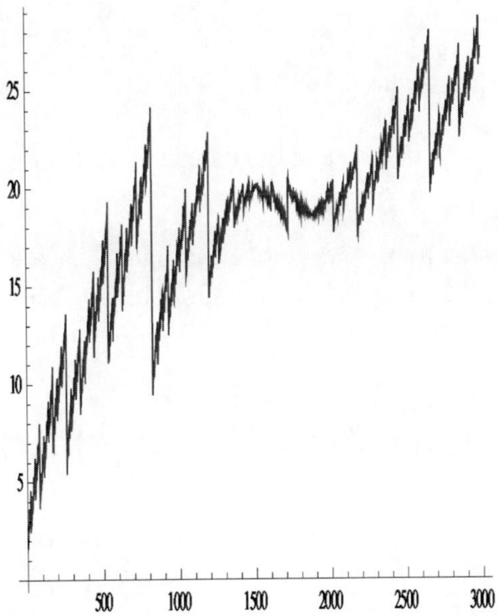

Figure 4. Nonstandard correction of Elliott impulse.

We give the reasons for using supercoherent states in the Hubbard model.

1) The first reason - is noted in numerous studies that there exist some kind of band-atomic particle duality in strongly correlated systems which, in regard to this matter is as follows. There are two alternative descriptions of the same system - one offers start of free gas and explore the Coulomb interaction as a perturbation, and the second is based on the limit of localized electrons and treats hopping as a perturbation. As far as we know, the only description that can interpolate between these two approaches is the functional approach based on supercoherent states.

2) The second reason is the lack of clarity with dynamical symmetry inherent to systems with strong interaction. As a consequence we have the uncertainty of the type of functional integral. In such circumstances, use of a common group ideology and supercoherent state is a reasonable and promising.

2.1. Definition of Supercoherent State

Thus, the state of the system is described by the following wave function, which depends on the coordinates x, y, z and time t.

$$\mid G >= exp \begin{bmatrix} E_z & 0 & 0 & E^+ \\ \chi_1^* & h_z & h^+ & 0 \\ \chi_2^* & h^- & -h_z & 0 \\ E^- & -\chi_3^* & \chi_4^* & -E_z \end{bmatrix} \mid 0 >, \tag{14}$$

$\mid G >$ acts on the space $(\mid 0 >, \mid + >, \mid - >, \mid 2 >)$ is a basis of "atomic" functions on which a coherent state is defined.

$$\mid G >= \begin{pmatrix} F\chi \\ Z(E) + 2B\chi_2\chi_1 \end{pmatrix},$$

here $F = (F_{ij}) = \begin{pmatrix} g_1^+ & g_1^- \\ g_3^+ & g_3- \end{pmatrix}$, and the index $i, j = 1, 2$; g coefficients are given in appendix $B = (0, b) + \rho(\psi)Z(\tau)E^-$.

We evaluate the expression for the supercoherent state to second order in the Grassmann fields. Next, we will compute this expression in Grassmann fields to the fourth degree. In this expression, $h^\dagger$ is the spinor representation of the magnetic vector, and $Z(\tau)$ - two-component spinor, equal to

$$Z = \begin{pmatrix} \cos(\tau) + \cos(\theta')\sin(\tau) \\ e^{i\varphi}\sin(\tau)\sin(\theta') \end{pmatrix},$$

$tg(\tau) = \frac{E\psi}{\psi'}$; $\rho = \sqrt{E^2\psi^2 + \psi'^2}$; prime means full derivative on α, $\psi = \frac{\delta(E^2K)}{\delta E^2}$; $b = \frac{\partial K}{\partial \alpha}$.

Introduce a special function

$$K = (ch(\alpha E)/E^2 - ch(\alpha h)/h^2)/(E^2 - h^2), \tag{15}$$

after calculations we should put α to unity.

We introduce the p, q-derivative

$$D_{pq}f(x) = (f(px) - f(qx))/((p-q)x). \tag{16}$$

Using it and the function $f(x) = ch(\sqrt{\alpha})/\alpha$, we write expression for the K in the form:

$$D_{E^2,h^2}f(\alpha) = (ch(\sqrt{\alpha}E)/(\alpha E^2) - ch(\sqrt{\alpha}h)/(\alpha h^2))/(\alpha(E^2 - h^2)) = K(\sqrt{\alpha})/\alpha^2. \tag{17}$$

We formulate a qualitative observation: expression for SCS can be described through D_{pq} and the usual derivatives. It is known that D_{pq} defines a two-parameter deformed oscillatory algebra. We consider several cases: a) $E_i = 0, h_i = 0$, then

$$\mid G >= \begin{pmatrix} 1 \\ \chi_1 \\ \chi_2 \\ 2\chi_2\chi_1 \end{pmatrix}$$

This expression coincides with the CS for fermionic operators b) $\chi_i = 0, h_i = 0$, $\mid G >= Z(E)$.

We calculate the symbols of vector operator ρ_1, ρ_2, ρ_3. Note that we have chosen a representation for CS selects the density of the ground state system. We also may to chose the magnetic (traders states) ground state, then we would have an expression for spin operators, with the operator ρ, if expressions replace E on h. In the future, a set of operators ρ_i we call the pseudospin (cash flow states), and S_i a spin.

$$\rho_3 \Rightarrow z_0^* z_0 - z_2^* z_2, \tag{18}$$

$$\rho^- \Rightarrow z_2^* z_0, \tag{19}$$

$$\rho^+ \Rightarrow z_0^* z_2. \tag{20}$$

A set of operators ρ_1, ρ_2, ρ_3 forms a algebra. It can be seen that the above expression for us ρ_i CS to become the SU (2) $E = i\pi/2, 3i\pi/2, ...$

In this case: $\rho_3 \Rightarrow cos(\theta), \rho^- \Rightarrow e^{i\phi} sin(\theta)$, $\rho^+ \Rightarrow e^{-i\phi} sin(\theta)$.

We see that E parametrizes the value of the Casimir operator and gives the magnitude pseudospin (spin). In the range of $0 < E < 1$ expression differ from CS for SU (2).

Calculating the symbols of spin operators, we have the following expression for the magnetic CS for the group SU (2): $S_q^+ = h^+ \frac{sh(h)}{h}(ch(h) + h_z \frac{sh(h)}{h}); S_q^- = h^- \frac{sh(h)}{h}(ch(h) - h_z \frac{sh(h)}{h}); S_q^z = ch^2(h) + \frac{sh^2(h)}{h^2}(h_z^2 - h^+ h^-)$.

Consider the symbols for the spin operators.

Replacing the values of vector operators on average in insulating phase α, we get:

$$S^+ = (1 - \alpha) S_q^+ + \alpha \chi_1^* \chi_2; \tag{21}$$

$$S^- = (1 - \alpha) S_q^- + \alpha \chi_2^* \chi_1; \tag{22}$$

$$S^z = (1 - \alpha) S_q^z + \alpha (\chi_1^* \chi_1 - \chi_2^* \chi_2). \tag{23}$$

This expression is very meaningful. It says that in the Hubbard model on the site contribution to the magnetic moment (price) given two terms: the first gives the spin density delocalized state (Gaussian fluctuation of price) and satisfies the linear $su(2)$ algebra, the second parametrizes localized contribution (fractal price) and defined representation of the group $SU(2)$. The originality of this model is the value of localized spin - it lies in the range from 0 to 1. Total spin is the sum of two components so that the total spin is 1/2. The same principle can be seen in the division of vector operators.

2.2. Evolution Operator

Below we give the procedure for obtaining of a functional integral for Hubbard model [6]. The functional representation is desirable especially for systems with strong interaction and the absence of small parameter. We use the coherent state for those supergroups that appear in strongly correlated systems. More specifically, our challenge will be to search for the group structure in strongly correlated systems which will describe their specificity. We take as a basis the following general group structure:

1) we unite the spatial coordinates with the times and will consider the four-dimensional space-time manifold as the base manifold on which a maximum possible conformal group act in the spinor representation,

2) electron operators describing the electronic degrees of freedom, complement the group to a supergroup, which should be superextensions of bosonic generators. This bosonic generators give the 4D rotation group

3) considering the spin (superspin) representation of supergroups, we construct super-coherent state that wil gives us the essentially nonlinear representation of the wave function, describing strongly correlated metal

3) using the calculated exact supercoherent state, we obtain nonlinear functional, describing an insulating and metallic phases.

Conventional coherent states [24] for simple Lie algebras widely used for the formulation of functional integral for Hamiltonians, in which variables have the generators of these algebras Lee. In the case of $SU(2)$ and $SU(1,1)$ group the group manifold is a sphere or a hyperboloid and is more complex space rather than a plane, which is the phase space for simple harmonic oscillator.

The amplitude of the transition between two states is defined by the following expression: $< Z_f|e^{-iH(t_f-t_i)}|Z_i >$. We need to get expression for the effective Lagrangian in the space of state $|Z>$. Evolution of a quantum system in time is defined by following operator:

$$U(t,t_0) = T_{ord}exp(-i\int_{t_0}^{t} H(\tau)d\tau);$$

if $t - t_0 = \delta t$ isa small quantity $\delta t << 1$, then

$$U(t_0+\delta t, t_0) = 1 - i\int_{t_0}^{t_0+\delta t} H(\tau)d\tau.$$

It follows that the symbol of the operator have a form

$$U(Z,Z^*|t_0+\delta t,t_0) = exp(-i\int_{t_0}^{t_0+\delta t} H(Z,Z^*|\tau)d\tau).$$

To find the symbol $U(Z,Z^*|t,t_0)$ divide the interval $[t_0,t]$ for N sites. Consider the matrix elements of evolution operator $exp(-iH(t_f-t_i)) < Z_f|$ between this states and $|Z_i>$ state. Factorize the operator $exp(-iH(t_f-t_i))\ by inserting unit \int d\mu(Z)|Z><Z| = 1$

$$< Z_f|exp(-iH(t_f-t_i))|Z_i >= \int \prod_{k=1}^{N} d\mu(Z_k) < Z_f|Z_N >$$

$$< Z_N|e^{-i\epsilon H}|Z_{N-1} > .... < Z_{k-1}|e^{-i\epsilon H}|Z_k > ... < Z_1|e^{-i\epsilon H}|Z_i >,$$

here $\epsilon = \frac{t_f-t_i}{N}$. To first order in this amount we can raise the expression for the Hamiltonian to the exponential argument

$$\frac{< Z_{k+1}|e^{-i\epsilon H}|Z_k >}{< Z_{k+1}|Z_k >} = \frac{< Z_{k+1}|(1-i\epsilon H)|Z_k >}{< Z_{k+1}|Z_k >} = e^{-i\epsilon\frac{<Z_{k+1}|H|Z_k>}{<Z_{k+1}|Z_k>}} + O(\epsilon^2). \quad (24)$$

We obtain the following representation:

$$< Z_f|e^{-iH(t_f-t_i)}|Z_i >= \lim_{N->\infty} \int \prod_{k=1}^{N} d\mu(Z_k) < Z_{k+1}|Z_k > e^{-i\epsilon \sum_{k=1}^{N} \frac{<Z_{k+1}|H|Z_k>}{<Z_{k+1}|Z_k>}}, \tag{25}$$

here $|Z_0 >= |Z_i >; < Z_{N+1}| =< Z_f|$.

Define the variation $|Z >$: $|\delta Z_{k+1} >= |Z_{k+1} > -|Z_k >$.

We have:

$$< Z_f|e^{-iH(t_f-t_i)}|Z_i >= \lim_{N->\infty} \int \prod_{k=1}^{N} [d\mu(Z_k) < Z_k|Z_k >] < Z_f|Z_N >$$

$$exp(\sum_{k=1}^{N} (Ln(1 - \frac{< Z_k|\delta Z_k >}{< Z_k|Z_k >}) - i\epsilon \frac{< Z_k|H|Z_{k-1} >}{< Z_k|Z_{k-1} >}).$$

Assuming that the main contribution gives the piecewise smooth trajectories we get:

$$\frac{d|Z >}{dt} = \frac{|\delta Z >}{\epsilon}.$$

Hold the first order in ϵ, we obtain

$$< Z_f|e^{-iH(t_f-t_i)}|Z_i >= \int_{|Z(t_i)>=|Z_i>}^{|Z(t_f)>=|Z_f>} D(Z, Z^*)e^{-iS[Z,Z^*]}; \tag{26}$$

$$S[Z, Z^*] = \int_{t_i}^{t_f} dt \int_V \mathbf{dr}(\frac{< Z(r, t|i\frac{\partial}{\partial t} - H|Z(r, t >}{< Z(r, t|Z(r, t >}$$
$$-i[Ln(< Z_f|Z(t_f) >) - Ln(< Z_i|Z(t_i) >)]).$$

Integration measure is given by the following expression:

$$D[Z, Z^*] = \prod_{t_i<t<t_f} \prod_r d\mu[Z(r, t)^*, Z(r, t)] < Z(r, t)|Z(r, t) > .$$

This expression will be for us in the future major representation for the Hubbard model.

The expression for the effective functional S governs the transition from the operator formulation in terms of the creation-annihilation operators and the Hubbard operators to the field theory formulation in terms of dynamical fields of the Bose and Fermi types. As shown in [11], the main point of this transition is the passage to the problem formulation in terms of the superbundle determined by a representation of the local supergroup of four-dimensional space rotations. In what follows, we need only the symbols of the creation and annihilation operators determined by the expressions $< G \mid \alpha_\sigma^+ \mid G >, < G \mid \alpha_\sigma \mid G >$. The general expressions for supercoherent states were calculated in [14]. Here, we take expressions for these states in the zeroth- and first-order approximations with respect to the Grassmann fields. We write the expressions for the coherent states and their conjugates in these approximations:

$$| G >= \begin{pmatrix} ch(E) + E_z\frac{sh(E)}{E} \\ a_1^+\chi_1 + a_2^+\chi_2 \\ a_1^-\chi_1 + a_2^-\chi_2 \\ E^-\frac{sh(E)}{E} \end{pmatrix}$$

$$< G |= (ch(E) - E_z\frac{sh(E)}{E}, (a_1^+)^*\chi_1^* + (a_2^+)^*\chi_2^*, (a_1^-)^*\chi_1^* + (a_2^-)^*\chi_2^*, -E^+\frac{sh(E)}{E})$$

The action of the operators on this state leads to the expressions

$$\alpha_\uparrow^+ \mid G >= \begin{pmatrix} 0 \\ ch(E) + E_z\frac{sh(E)}{E} \\ 0 \\ -a_1^-\chi_1 - a_2^-\chi_2 \end{pmatrix}, \alpha_\downarrow^+ \mid G >= \begin{pmatrix} 0 \\ 0 \\ ch(E) + E_z\frac{sh(E)}{E} \\ a_1^+\chi_1 + a_2^+\chi_2 \end{pmatrix}, \alpha_\uparrow \mid G >= \begin{pmatrix} a_1^+\chi_1 + a_2^+\chi_2 \\ 0 \\ -E^-\frac{sh(E)}{E} \\ 0 \end{pmatrix}, \alpha_\downarrow \mid G >= \begin{pmatrix} a_1^-\chi_1 + a_2^-\chi_2 \\ E^-\frac{sh(E)}{E} \\ 0 \\ 0 \end{pmatrix}.$$

The symbols for the creation and annihilation operators calculated on these states and written in the spinor form are

$$\begin{pmatrix} < G \mid \alpha_\downarrow^+ \mid G > \\ < G \mid \alpha_\uparrow^+ \mid G > \end{pmatrix} = E_{12}^{'} a_m\chi + \hat{E}_{11}A_m\chi^*,$$

$$\begin{pmatrix} < G \mid \alpha_\uparrow \mid G > \\ < G \mid \alpha_\downarrow \mid G > \end{pmatrix} = \hat{E}_{22}am\chi + E_{21}^{'}Am\chi^*. \tag{27}$$

Here, the 2x2 matrices $\hat{E}$ and $\hat{h}_i$ are

$$E_{12}^{'} = \hat{E}_{12}\begin{pmatrix} -1 & 0 \\ 0 & 1 \end{pmatrix}, E_{21}^{'} = \hat{E}_{21}\begin{pmatrix} -1 & 0 \\ 0 & 1 \end{pmatrix},$$

$$\begin{pmatrix} \hat{E}_{11} & \hat{E}_{12} \\ \hat{E}_{21} & \hat{E}_{22} \end{pmatrix} = \begin{pmatrix} ch(E) + E_z sh(e)/E & E^+ sh(E)/E \\ E^- sh(E)/E & ch(E) - E_z sh(E)/E \end{pmatrix}$$

$$a_m = f_3(ln(f_3/f_2))' + f_2((ln(f_2))' + E_z)\hat{h}_2.$$

$$\hat{h}_2 = \begin{pmatrix} (ln(f_2))' + h_z & h^+ \\ h^- & (ln(f_2))' - h_z \end{pmatrix}$$

$$\sigma = \begin{pmatrix} 0 & 1 \\ 1 & 0 \end{pmatrix}; A_m = \sigma a_m^*; \chi = (\chi_1, \chi_2)^T; \chi^* = (\chi_1^*, \chi^*)^T.$$

We recall the fields over which we integrate in the functional integral: the vectors $\vec{\mathbf{E}}$ and $\vec{\mathbf{h}}$ describing fluctuations of the respective electric and magnetic degrees of freedom and the

Grassmann fields χ_i. The combinations $E = \sqrt{E_z^2 + E^+E^-}, h = \sqrt{h_z^2 + h^+h^-}$, which are invariants of the two $SU(2)$ groups, also enter the supercoherent state. We here set them to be coordinate- and time-independent constants. These constants determine two deformation parameters in the quantum group problem. We now consider the coefficients f_2 and f_3. Expressions for these quantities are nonlinear in the above invariants. The method for calculating them exactly was developed in [14]. In the nonlinear representation of supercoherent states, we have four such coeficients:f, f_2, f_3, f_4. We describe the trick used to calculate these coefficients in [17]. We multiply the invariants E and h in the formulas by the scale factor x and subsequent show that we can obtain f, f_2, f_3, f_4 from f by taking derivatives with respect to x. At the end of the calculations we set the parameter x equal to unity. In the formulas presented above, such differentiations are marked by the prime. Expression (27) determines the representation for the creation-annihilation operators in the functional integral in terms of the three components of the vector $\vec{h}$. The representation depending on the vector $\vec{h}$ was proposed in [8]. We note that in the expressions there and also here, the local group is $SU(2) * SU(2)$. We consider particular cases of the above composite expressions for the creation-annihilation operators: 1) If $(E^+, E^-, E_z) = 0, (h^+, h^-, h_z) = 0$,then: $< G \mid \alpha_\sigma^+ \mid G >= \chi_\sigma^*, < G \mid \alpha_\sigma \mid G >= \chi_\sigma$ i.e., we obtain the holomorphic representation for the creation-annihilation operators. Substituting them in (1), we obtain the standard representation for ferminonic systems in terms of odd Grassmann-valued fields [7] 2) If $(h^+, h^-, h_z) = 0, (E^+, E^-, E_z) \neq 0$ then expression (27) generates the following

formulas for the functional symbols of the creation and annihilation operators:

$$\begin{pmatrix} < G \mid \alpha_\downarrow^+ \mid G > \\ < G \mid \alpha_\uparrow^+ \mid G > \end{pmatrix} = E'_{12} f_3 B\chi + \hat{E}_{11} f_3 B^* \sigma \chi^*, \tag{28}$$

$$\begin{pmatrix} < G \mid \alpha_\uparrow \mid G > \\ < G \mid \alpha_\downarrow \mid G > \end{pmatrix} = \hat{E}_{22} f_3 B\chi + E'_{21} f_3 B^* \sigma \chi^* \tag{29}$$

where $B = (ln(f_3))' + E_z$. Setting the expression for $/f_3$ equal to unity, we reduce these expressions to the slave-roton representation in [9].

3) If $(h^+, h^-, h_z) \neq 0, (E^+, E^-, E_z) = 0$, then expression (8) generates the following formulas for the functional symbols of the creation and annihilation operators[9]:

$$\begin{pmatrix} < G \mid \alpha_\downarrow^+ \mid G > \\ < G \mid \alpha_\uparrow^+ \mid G > \end{pmatrix} = \hat{E}_{11} A_m \chi^*, \tag{30}$$

$$\begin{pmatrix} < G \mid \alpha_\uparrow \mid G > \\ < G \mid \alpha_\downarrow \mid G > \end{pmatrix} = \hat{E}_{22} a_m \chi \tag{31}$$

$a_m = \hat{h}_3$, and in the logarithmic function is f_3, in this formula, we have $A_m = \sigma a_m^*$. We have thus shown that each representation for the creation-annihilation operators in the Hubbard model known to us is contained in some particular case of expression ((27) . We note that the main feature distinguishing our representation from those in the literature is the presence of the coefficients f_2 , f_3 f_4. Expressions for these coefficients were given in [14]. Below, we clarify the consequences of the presence of these coefficients.

3. Quantum Derivatives in the Hubbard Model

We see which functional results from the operator expression for the magnetic subsystem of the Hubbard model. Substituting expressions for the creation-annihilation operators in the expression for the kinetic energy, we obtain the functional

$$H = \sum_{ij} (f_4)^2 \begin{pmatrix} \chi_1^* \\ \chi_2^* \end{pmatrix}_i^T \begin{pmatrix} \chi_1 \\ \chi_2 \end{pmatrix}_j$$

We note that for $/f_4 = 1$, our representation coincides with the slave-roton representation used in many papers. Our aim is to study those terms in the functionals that are absent in the cited papers. We take the unit matrix as the matrix field $\hat{E}$, which indicates the independence on the space coordinates. We mentioned in the introduction that we want to obtain the expression for the coherent state for such $\hat{E}$. Because χ is a fermionic field, when passing to the momentum representation, we obtain a half-filled Fermi band over which we integrate to obtain the total number of fermions, i.e., a constant. We substitute this constant for the quadratic combination of fields $\chi_i^* \chi_j$. As the result, we obtain the expression for the effective functional at coinciding arguments $(i = j)$:

$$H = (f_4)^2 \tag{32}$$

where the coefficient f_4 is [11]: $f_4 = (Esh(E) - hsh(h))/(E^2 - h^2)$. This is precisely the factor that distinguishes our functional from the one in [8, 9]. At first glance, it is just a nonlinear coefficient. But...! We introduce the two-parameter derivative acting on a function $f(x)$ by the formula

$$D_{rq} f(x) = (f(rx) - f(qx))/((r - q)x)$$

.

It is known [13], that the three operators $(D_{rq}, x, x\frac{\partial}{\partial x})$ constitute the two-parameter quantum algebra $SU_{rq}(2)$ with the following commutation relations for the generators $(S^+, S^-, S_z) = (D_{rq}, x, x\frac{\partial}{\partial x})$:

$$[S_z, S^+] = S^+, [S_z, S^-] = -S^-, S^+S^- - \frac{r}{q} S^-S^+ = [2S_z]_{r,q}$$

We have the definition of the two-parameter quantum number [13]:

$$[X]_{rq} = \frac{q^X - r^{-X}}{q - r^{-1}}$$

Using the expression for D_{rq} we can rewrite the nonlinear coefficient f_4 in the form

$$D_{E^2,h^2}(x)(\sqrt{x} sh\sqrt{x}/x) = (E\sqrt{x} sh(\sqrt{x}E) - h\sqrt{x} sh(\sqrt{x}h))/(x(E^2 - h^2)).$$

We introduced the separate parameter x into the expression for f_4. The representation of this quantity in [14] implies that x determines the scale factor and is the dilaton field. We now show this. The complete set of fields in expression (6) for the supercoherent state and

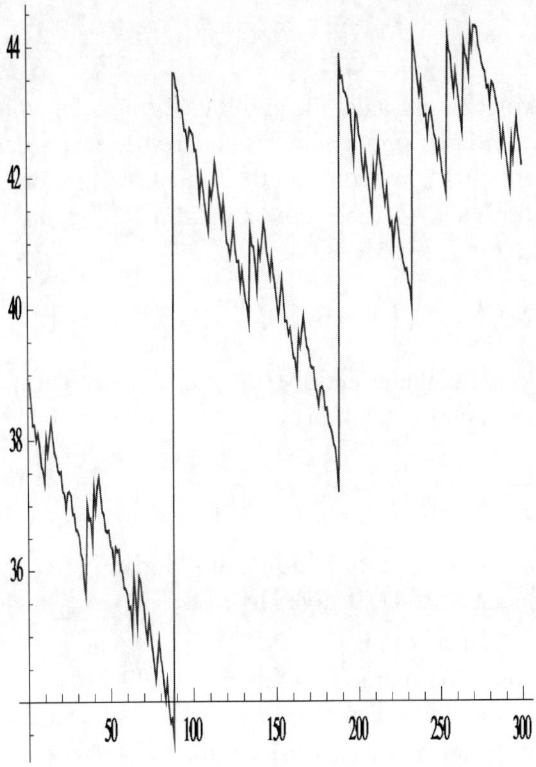

Figure 5. p-Adic description of triangle pattern in Elliott theory.

the functional integral integration measure is determined by the superalgebra whose matrix generators enter (6). It does not contain the dilation generator, whose matrix representation is γ_5 in the chiral representation related to the third diagonal term in (6). To take this term into account, we must calculate matrix (6) exactly with the full set of generators. Unfortunately, this problem is much harder than the problem solved in[14]. We introduce the scaling factor for the local fields $\vec{\mathbf{E}}$ and $\vec{\mathbf{h}}$ such that $\vec{\mathbf{E}}$"$- > \beta\vec{\mathbf{E}}, \vec{\mathbf{h}}$"$- > \beta\vec{\mathbf{h}}$ and pass to the primed fields. This factor can be a local x-dependent field $\beta(x)$, or a global x-independent field. We can introduce a functional integration over this field, and this field then enters the integration measure. Because fields of this type (of the dilation field in QFT) had never been previously discussed in the Hubbard model framework, we below concentrate on discussing possible qualitative effects resulting from taking this field into account. In this paper, we set the scaling factor independently of the coordinate x. We have already shown that the quantum derivatives act on precisely this variable. We note that $\beta(x)$, is replaced with x in formula (32) in order to introduce a unified notation for the entity of the extended space-time coordinates. Taking the scaling factor into account means passing to the $(d+l)$-dimensional space-time in the case of the d-dimensional initial space-time. Substituting the derivative D_{rq} in expression (32), we obtain the functional of the form

$$H = \sum_x (D_{rq}(x)f(x))^2 \tag{33}$$

where $f(x)$ is given by expression in the previous formula on which the derivative acts. The difference from the nonlinear sigma model is due to specific properties of the coordinate x, which defines the dilaton field. We consider the limit as rr $\rightarrow q$ or $E^2 \rightarrow 1/h^2$. It is clear that $D_{rq} \rightarrow D_q$ in this limit and becomes the one-parameter quantum derivative acting on functions by the formula

$$D_q f(x) = (f(qx) - f(q^{-1}x))/((q - q^{-1})x).$$

The commutation relations for the operators $((D_q, x, x\frac{\partial}{\partial x})$ constitute the quantum group $SU_q(2)$ [16] with the commutation relations

$$[S_z, S^+] = S^+, [S_z, S^-] = S^-, [S^+, S^-] = \frac{sh(S_z \ln(q))}{sh(\ln(q))}.$$

Letting $q \rightarrow 1$, we reduce the action of the quantum derivative D_q on arbitrary functions $f(x)$ to the action of the standard derivative [15], i.e., $D_q \rightarrow \frac{\partial}{\partial x}$. Replacing $D_q \rightarrow \frac{\partial}{\partial x}$, we obtain the standard nonlinear sigma model $(\frac{\partial f(x)}{\partial x})^2$. We note that f is a solution of the normalizing constraint condition on the coherent state, which customarily defines a vector field of unit length. Such a model describes a magnetic subsystem in a functional integral approach. On the operator level, it is the Heisenberg magnet in the Hubbard model. This magnet model is defined on the dilaton field and is one-dimensional. Returning to the general effective functional in the Hubbard model, we note that we have found a quantum symmetry and the way to introduce it into strongly correlated systems. It is especially important that subsequent contractions of quantum derivatives coincide with three levels of the tower of symmetries discovered in the Hubbard model in [10]. Formula (33), implies that in multielectron systems, we must study "quantum" magnets whose variables are generators of quantum Hopf algebras, not simple Lie algebras. We very briefly indicate the differences in the physical behaviors of such magnets. We here discuss only the behavior of the magnetic momenta and discuss more serious differences later. It is known that the Casimir operator $S_z^2 + S^+S^-$ of the group $SU(2)$ take the value: $S(S+1)$. The Casimir operator of the group $SU_q(2)$ is $S^+S^- + (\frac{sh(qS_z)}{q})^2$ and it is close to zero as $q- > 1$. In the physical language, this means that at the phase transition point at which a nonzero value of the parameter q appears, spin can arise smoothly with its value changing continuously from 0 to 1/2. This picture of the Mott-Hubbard-type metal-dielectric transition seems more natural compared with the phase transition scenario in which the spin instantly jumps from 0 (metal) to 1/2 (insulator of the Mott-Hubbard type). We now pass to studying a qualitative a behavior of a functional of type (33) using the functional integral.

4. The Jackson Integral

The above analysis of nonlinear expressions in the supercoherent state demonstrates that we can write complicated expressions in terms the action of the quantum derivative containing one or two deformation parameters. These derivatives act on functions of the variable, which was introduced in [14] as a purely technical tool ensuring a uniform form of writing expressions for f_2, f_3, f_4. The same variable was again used purely technically in [11] to calculate and write nonlinear expressions. In the preceding section, we showed that by taking the scaling factor into account, we obtain a model resembling a nonlinear sigma model but with quantum derivatives instead of the standard ones. In the limit where the one-parameter quantum derivative transforms into the standard derivative, we obtain the standard nonlinear sigma model. We thus qualitatively obtained a fact that is well known in the Hubbard model: the magnetic properties of the Mott-Hubbard dielectric at large values of the Hubbard repulsion U are described by the Heisenberg model with the exchange integral equal to W^2/U [3]. Below, we use the diagram technique for spin and Hubbard operators and also our diagram technique for constructing the "tower of symmetries" [[10]. When constructing the diagram technique for the Heisenberg model, we found the following trick useful. To the model action, which is quadratic in the spin operators, we add a term that is linear in the spin operators and proportional to S_z, the so-called Zeeman contribution. We then study the quadratic terms perturbatively. Summing the diagrams responsible for the local ordering results in a nonzero contribution to the magnetic field and ensures the possibility of calculating means over the ground state when setting the previously introduced field to zero. Our scheme and expression(33), imply that we encounter exactly the same situation. We cannot take (33), as the leading approximation in contrast to the case where we have the standard, not quantum, derivative. We must add a linear derivative and study how it affects calculating the ground state means. Below, we show that by deforming the derivative, we do not introduce new interaction types, as could be expected, but rather deform the functional integration measure, i.e., we change the type of the functional variable itself. In addition to the standard bosonic fields described by complex-valued functions and fermionic fields described by odd Grassmann-valued functions variables, fields with a nontraditional integration measure, for instance, taking values in the field of p-adic numbers, appear in the functional integral. The base of this field is determined by the means of the bosonic electric and magnetic fields, which provide the deformation parameters for the quantum groups. The standard scheme for studying functional integral (11) begins with the "zeroth" approximation obtained from an effective functional quadratic in either bosonic or fermionic variables, which reduces to Gaussian integrals over complex variables parameterized by momenta. We must be able to evaluate func-tionals containing quantum derivatives. For subsequent use, we briefly describe the scheme for constructing an effective functional using a holomorphic representation for creation and annihilation operators. To define an integral over trajectories completely, we must construct a functional series, which can then become a formal perturbation series. For this, we must know how to calculate integrals of the form

$$\int_0^c f(x)e^{-bx^2}dx = \sum_{i=0}^{\infty} \frac{f^{(n)}(0)}{n!} \int_0^c x^n e^{-bx^2}dx \tag{34}$$

for an arbitrary function $f(x)$. Clearly, we can exactly evaluate Gaussian integrals with power-law dependences, which allows standardly constructing a formal perturbation series. Using this, for each bosonic quantum system with a Lagrangian quadratic in the fields, we can set the complex numbers φ, φ^* into correspondence with the creation-annihilation operators $\beta_\sigma^+, \beta_\sigma$, satisfying the standard commutation relations. Each functional integral with a bosonic Lagrangian containing interactions of fields can then be constructed as a formal series in the interaction constant. To study effective functionals of type (33), we must replace the exponential in expression (34) as

$$\exp(b\varphi\varphi^*) \to \exp(bxD_q)$$

Because we replace the pair of operators $(x, \frac{\partial}{\partial x})$ with the holomorphic coordinates (φ, φ^*), we obtain our variant of quantization if we substitute the quantum derivative $D_q(x)$. for the standard one. Prom the definition of D_q, we have

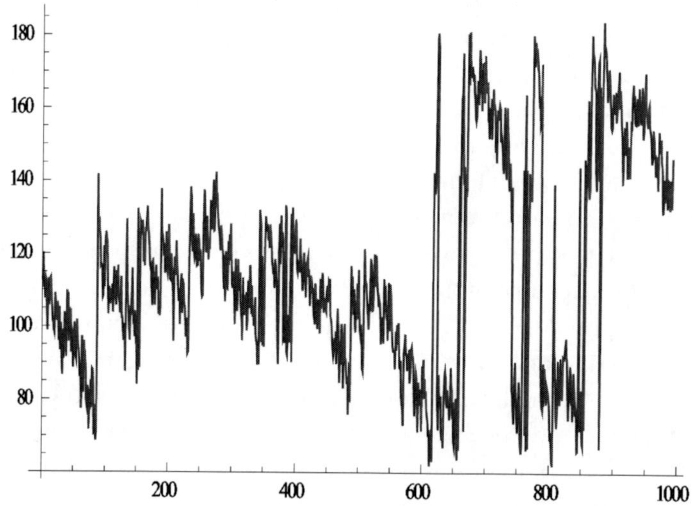

Figure 6. p-Adic random price signal.

$$D_q \to \frac{sh(\ln(q)x)}{sh(\ln(q))x} = \frac{[x]_q}{x}$$

Substituting this expression in the exponent results in the expression

$$\int_0^c f(x)e^{b[x]_q}dx \tag{35}$$

where $[x]_q = \frac{q^x - q^{-x}}{q - q^{-1}} = \frac{sh(x\ln(q))}{sh(\ln(q))}$. Calculating a functional integral containing general quantum derivatives D_{rq}, in a simpler case of the quantum derivative D_q, therefore requires calculating integrals of form (35), with arbitrary functions $f(x)$ of the variable x. We have thus described the scheme arising in the Hubbard model for contributions to the functional integral that contain quantum derivatives. Such integrals are always present in the general functional integral for the Hubbard model. To calculate (35), in the general form, we expand it in the Taylor series in the derivative Dq and expand the exponential $[x]_q$ in the series [15]:

$$\int_0^c f(x)e^{b[x]_q}dx = \sum_{m=0}^{\infty}\sum_{n=0}^{\infty} \frac{D_q^m(c)f(c)}{[m]_q!}\frac{b^n}{n!}\int_0^c (x-c)_q^m [x]_q^n dx \tag{36}$$

Here $(x-c)_q{}^m = (x-c)(x-qc)(x-q^2c).....(x-q^{m-1}c)$, and the quantum factorial

is

$$[n]_q! = [n]_q[n-1]_q....[2]_q[1]_q[0]_q$$

The constant c, which determines the limit scaling in the problem, arises in (36). We represent the action of an arbitrary power of D_q on $f(x)$ as a series,

$$D_q^{2n}(x)f(x) = \sum_{k=-n}^{n} d_{2k}^{2n}(q)f(q^{2k}x)$$

A similar formula describes the action of an odd power of the quantum derivative on a function; the summation then ranges odd powers. Integral (36) can then be expressed as a series in $f(cq^m)$ of the form (we present only the first terms of the series) $f(c)[I_0 + \frac{d_0^2}{[2]_q!}I_2 +$

$\frac{d_0^4}{[4]_q!}I_4 + \frac{d_0^6}{[6]_q!}I_6 + ...] + f(cq)[\frac{d_1^1}{[1]_q!}I_1 + \frac{d_1^3}{[3]_q!}I_3 + \frac{d_1^5}{[5]_q!}I_5 + ...] + f(cq^{-1})[\frac{d_{-1}^1}{[1]_q!}I_1 + \frac{d_{-1}^3}{[3]_q!}I_3 + \frac{d_{-1}^5}{[5]_q!}I_5 + ...] +$

$$f(cq^2)[\frac{d_2^2}{[2]_q!}I_2 + \frac{d_2^4}{[4]_q!}I_4 + \frac{d_2^6}{[6]_q!}I_6 + ...] + f(cq^{-2})[\frac{d_{-2}^2}{[2]_q!}I_2 + \frac{d_{-2}^4}{[4]_q!}I_4 + \frac{d_{-2}^6}{[6]_q!}I_6 + ...]$$

Here, the quantum number $[x]_q = \frac{q^x - q^{-x}}{q-q^{-1}}$ tend to x as $q -> 1$. We have the representation

$$I_n = \int_0^c (x-c)_q^m \exp(b[x]_q)dx$$

for the quantities I_n. These integrals reduce to integrals of the form $\int_0^c x^m \exp(b[x]_q)dx$ and can be evaluated as infinite series in b (the detailed scheme for calculating integrals of this type and detailed expressions for the series in these integrals will be published elsewhere). As a result, we have $I_n \approx 1$ as $q -> 0$. We present expressions for several quantum numbers: $[1]_q = \frac{q^1-q^{-1}}{q-q^{-1}} = 1$;

$[2]_q = \frac{q^2-q^{-2}}{q-q^{-1}} = q + q^{-1}$;

$[3]_q = \frac{q^3-q^{-3}}{q-q^{-1}} = q^2 + 1 + q^{-2}$ We note that (36) reduces to (34) as $q \to 1$. Expression (36) therefore contains a standard perturbative scheme for determining a functional integral. We consider the opposite limit $q << 1$. The expressions for quantum numbers and their factorials in this limit are $[1]_q \sim 1$, $[2]_q \sim q^{-1}$, $[3]_q \sim q^{-2}$, $[4]_q \sim q^{-3}$, $[5]_q \sim q^{-4}$, $[n]_q \sim q^{-(n-1)}$ for the general term.

Expressions for the factorials for $q << 1$, are: $[1]_q! = 1$, $[2]_q! \sim q^{-1}$, $[3]_q! \sim q^{-3}$,

$[4]_q! \sim q^{-6}$, $[5]_q! \sim q^{-10}$, and: $[n]_q! \sim \frac{1}{q^{n-1}}\frac{1}{q^{n-2}}...\frac{1}{q^2}\frac{1}{q}$ for the general term. Polynomials in the small-q regime are:$p_1^1 = -q$; $p_2^2 = q$; $p_3^3 = 1$; $p_4^4 = 1/q^2$; $p_5^5 = -1/q^5$; $p_6^6 = 1/q^6$. Substituting these expressions for $q << 1$ in formula (36), we obtain the series

$$\int_0^c f(x)e^{b[x]_q}dx \sim f(c) + f(cq)q + f(cq^2)q^2 + f(cq^3)q^3 + f(cq^4)q^4 + f(cq^5)q^5 + ..$$

We find that expression (36) becomes the Jackson integral [15] in the leading approximation in q. It is known [12], that for $q = \frac{1}{p}$, where p is a prime, the Jackson integral becomes the p-adic integral.

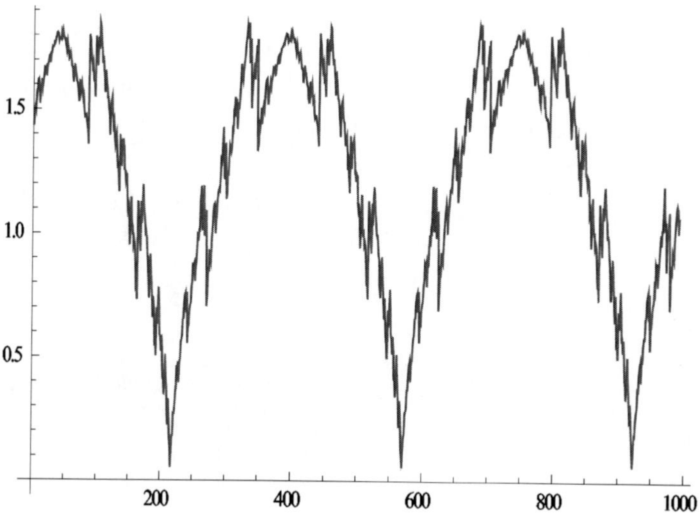

Figure 7. p-Adic description of sin() function.

5. Elliott Waves Theory

We have shown the existence of the regime described by the functional integral with the Jackson measure and deformation parameter q in the Hubbard model. At $q = 1/p$, in accordance with [12], this regime is described by the p-adic integral. To demonstrate the features of this approach, we consider some facts about p-adic numbers.

When dealing with natural numbers, if we take p to be a fixed prime number, then any positive integer can be written as a base p expansion in the form

$\sum_{i=0}^{n} a_i p^i$

where the a_i are integers in $\{0, p-1\}$. Using this approach to extending description to the rationals is to use sums of the form:

$\pm \sum_{i=-\infty}^{n} a_i p^i$.

With p-adic numbers, on the other hand, we choose to extend the base p expansions in a different way. Because in the p-adic world high positive powers of p are small and high negative powers are large, we consider infinite sums of the form:

$\sum_{i=k}^{\infty} a_i p^i$

where k is some (not necessarily positive) integer. With this approach we obtain the p-adic expansions of the p-adic numbers. Those p-adic numbers for which $a_i = 0$ for all $i < 0$ are also called the p-adic integers.

We briefly describe the necessary other information concerning p-adic numbers: p is a prime; an arbitrary rational number r admits the representation $r = p^{\nu}\frac{m}{n}$ where n and m are coprime to p. The p-adic norm of a rational number is $\mid r \mid_p = p^{-\nu}$, $\mid 0 \mid_0 = 0$. The field of the p-adic numbers Q_p is the completion of the field of rational numbers Q with respect to the p-adic norm.

As proposed in [4, 5], we describe the prices by the function $f_b(r) = \sum_0^N a_k p^{bk}$; $a_k = (0, 1, ..., p-1); k \in Z$. The coefficients a_k are here equal to the coefficients in the p-adic number representation defined by the series rr $= \sum_0^N a_k p^k$; $a_k = (0, 1, ..., p-1); k \in Z$.

We take $p = 3$. The numerical modeling of this function for $b = 0.5$ and $b = 1.5$ is shown in the figures. On the ordinate, we have integers presented as series for r. The coefficients in $f_b(r)$ are taken from the p-adic expansion for these numbers. The result for $f_b(r)$ is presented on the axis OY. We set $b = 0.5$ in Fig. 1 and $b = 1.5$ in Fig. 2.

Elliott observed waves of different levels throughout the unfolding of a trend in a given time frame. There are certain patterns, significant price ratios and time ratios in the waves. The theory can be summarized in a few basic principles:

(1) Action of a trend is followed by reaction of retracement.

(2) There are five waves in the direction of the main trend, usually labeled as waves 1, 2, 3, 4, 5, followed by three corrective waves, called waves a, b, c. Waves 2 and 4 are corrective to waves 1 and 3, and waves b and c are corrective to wave a and b respectively. Such a sequence of waves is also called a 5-3 move.

(3) A 5-3 move of 8 waves completes a cycle, which then becomes 2 subdivision of the next higher 5-3 move. This is the key characteristic of a fractal as we know today.

(4) The underlying 5-3 move pattern tends to remain constant, though the price range and time span of each wave may vary.

Diagonal

Also known as the Diagonal Triangle (leading diagonal and ends on the diagonal). Diagonal is a common 5-wave motive wave, labeled 1-2-3-4-5 that moves with a big trend. Diagonals move within two channel lines bounding drawn from wave 1 to wave 3, and from wave 2 to wave 4.

Zigzag (ZZ):

Zigzag - a 3-wave pattern, labeled ABC, generally moving against the larger trend. This is one of the most common corrective Elliott patterns.

Flat (FL)

A flat is a model of three waves labeled ABC, which generally move sideways. This corrective, counter-trend and very common Elliott pattern.

The triangle (triangle convergent (CT) and expanding triangle (ET)):

The triangle is a normal corrective pattern with 5 waves, labeled ABCDE, which move against the trend. Triangles move within two channel lines drawn from wave A to wave C, and from wave to wave B D. The triangle pattern is converging or diverging depending converge or diverge line of the channel.

In author paper [21] it was shown that a multi-agent model which is proposed in this paper leads to the p-adic description of price series. And this description perfectly describes fractals. The advantage of the p-adic description of fractals is that the fractal behavior of prices is defined locally. We describe fractals as pointwise. This description gives an exact match with the theory of Elliott patterns, which means rigorous mathematical basis of this theory by p-adic mathematics. Below we give some examples of application of p-adic functions to the price series. In fig.1 I give the p-adic impulse pattern of Elliott theory. In fig.2 I give alternative stepwise wave.

Below (fig.3) the graphs of IBM shares are shown. The second curve shows the procedure a p-adic interpolation of real data. Different time scales are used. The second curve shows the real data. It is seen that qualitatively, the p-adic functions well describe the real data. We also see that the p-adic functions give a good description of the patterns that appear in the theory of Elliott waves. In this theory, the emergence of trend is associated with the pattern, which is called a triangle. Triangle defines the behavior of volatility in time. When the volatility tend to zero, in this point the new trend appears. In fig.5 a triangle is shown. It can be described if we take the number field base equal to a rational number. In fig. 4 I show an alternative correction after an impulse Elliott wave containing five small pulses. In fig. 6 I show that the p-adic functions can give a signal that looks like random, right signal is made up of deep irregular fluctuations. In fig. 7 I construct a p-adic function of the sin(). It can be seen that the harmonic function acts as an envelope for the fractal behavior.

6. Conclusion

We have shown that the regime described by the p-adic functional integral exists in the functional integral for the Hubbard model. Finally, we stress that the functional integral in the Hubbard model, as shown in this paper, can be successfully reformulated in terms of both the standard and the Jackson integral and that the latter can be reduced to the p-adic integral in a particular case. We have the impression, supported by the comparison with experimental prices data that in the strong correlation regime, the description of multi-electron systems is invariant under the choice of the number field. We can begin with either a p-adic or real number description. It seems plausible that this situation can be clarified if an exact analytic calculation of coefficients in expressions (36) would be possible. Because our main regimes were $q- > 1$ and $q- > 0$, it seems plausible that we should study the crossover regime from the p-adic to the standard perturbation series based on Gaussian integration in more detail if we will be able to calculate series (36) more exactly. This regime would clarify an interesting question: which order parameter appears in the system upon the introduction of the p-adic description whose distinct feature is the appearance of fractal behavior in physical quantities?

We have shown that the proposed model of the stock market that contains a lot of traders leads to two regimes: 1) a p-adic regime, describing the fractal behavior of prices [19, 21], and 2) fluctuation mode behavior of prices with a Gaussian distribution .

References

[1] Challet D., Zhang Y., (1997), *Physica* A 246, 407-418.

[2] LuxT., MarchesiM., (1999), Scaling and Criticality in a Stochastic Multi-Agent Model of a Financial Market, in *Nature*, 397, 498.

[3] Hubbard J., (1963), *Proc.Roy.*, Soc. 276 A, 238.

[4] Zharkov V. (2011), *9th Int. Symp. on Crystalline Organic Metals, Superconductors and Ferromagnets*. Sep. 25-30, Poznan.

[5] Zharkov V. *Physica status solidi*, Proceeding of ISCOM 2011, arXiv:cond-mat/1111.6476

[6] Zharkov V.M.,(1984), *Theor. Math. Phys.*, 60, 902-907; (1991),86, 181-188. arXiv:cond-mat/9612033.

[7] Konopleva N.P. Popov V.N.,(2000), Gauge Fields [in Russian], Editorial URSS, Moscow; English transl., Harwood Academic, Chur (1981).

[8] Hermele M. (2007),*Phys.Rev.*, B.V.76, 035125, arxiv:cond-mat/0701134.

[9] Ki-seok Kim. (2006), *Phys. Rev. Lett.*, 97, 136402.arXiv:cond-mat/0603473, Ki-Seok Kim, Jung Hoon Han. arXiv:cond-mat/0605266, Ki-Seok Kim.(2007), *Phys.Rev.*, B 75, 245105, arXiv:cond-mat/0609415.

[10] Zharkov V.M.,(1992), New functional representation for Hubbard model, coherent state, and tower of algebras, *Theor. Math. Phys.*, 90, 49-54; arXiv:cond-mat/9612033vl (1996).

[11] Zharkov V.M., Kirchanov V.S.,(2011), *Theor. Math. Phys.*, 166, 210-223.

[12] Vladimirov V.S., Volovich I.V., Zelenov E.I., (1994), *p-Adic Analysis and Mathematical Physics* [in Russian], Nauka, Moscow; English transl. (Series Sov. East Eur. Math., Vol. 10), World Scientific, Singapore (1994).

[13] Chakrabarti R., Jagannathan R., (1991), *J. Phys. A. Math. Gen.* 24, L711-7718,arXiv.org:cond-mat/0202313.

[14] Zharkov V.M., Kirchanov V.S., *New path integral representation for Hubbard model: I. Supercoherent state*, arXiv: cond-mat/1002.3043, *New path integral representation for Hubbard model: II. Spinless case*, arXiv: cond-mat/1006.1511.

[15] Kac V.,Cheung P.(2002), *Quantum calculus*, Springer.

[16] Chari V., Pressley A. (1994), *A guide to quantum group*, Cambridge University Press.

[17] Samuelson P. (1965), Proof that properly anticipated prices fluctuate randomly. *Industrial management Review*, 6(2),41-49.

[18] Kristoufek L., *Fractal market Hypothesis and Global financial crices*, aRxiv:1203.4979.

[19] Frost A., Pretcher R.,(2011), *Elliott wave principle: Key to market behavior.*

[20] Sornette D.,(2006), *Critical phenomena in natural science*, Springer.

[21] Zharkov V. (2012), *Adelic theory of stock market, Market risk and financial Market modeling*, Springer.

[22] Coolen ACC., (2005), *The Mathematical theory of minority games - statistical mechanics of interacting agents*, Oxford University Press.

[23] Zharkov V., (2009), p-adic approximation of stock market prices Bulletin of Perm University, *Information systems and Technologies*, 9 (35), 25-29.

[24] Perelomov A., (1986), *Generalized coherent states and their applications*, Springer, Berlin.

In: Stock Markets
Editors: F. Petroni, F. Prattico and G. D'Amico
ISBN: 978-1-62808-751-2

Chapter 11

A NON-HOMOGENEOUS SEMI-MARKOV APPROACH TO FINANCIAL CHOICES

Gianfranco Corradi*[1]*, Giovanna De Medici*[1]*,
***Jacques Janssen*[2] *and Raimondo Manca*[1*]**
[1]MEMOTEF, Università di Roma "La Sapienza," Roma, Italy
Universitè Libre de Bruxelles, Tubize, Belgium

ABSTRACT

In the choices made over the time about different sums to invest, the preference relation and the related indifference relation are of great interest in the development of the deterministic finance theory.

In a previous paper we demonstrated how it is possible to address this kind of problem in a stochastic environment by means of Semi-Markov processes. In this paper, we will enhance the previous results, giving greater weight to the non-homogeneous case, which, in spite of its greater difficulty, seems to be a more natural approach to the problem.

In this paper some new results on the numerical solution of this kind of process will also be presented. Furthermore, an applicative example will be given.

1. INTRODUCTION

As noted in a previous paper (Janssen, Manca, De Medici 1995) the evaluation of financial operations in a deterministic environment was studied and, in our opinion, fully solved.

The theory of financial operation evaluation can be seen as a particular case of individual decision making. It can be faced either in the deterministic case or in the stochastic environment by means of the preference based approach. In the deterministic case this approach permits introducing the theory from an axiomatic point of view (Volpe di Prignano

[*] Corresponding Author address: Email: raimondo.manca@uniroma1.it

(1985), Janssen et al. (2009)) and each financial problem can be addressed starting from this approach. More precisely, the axiomatization permits obtaining, once we have to face a particular problem, formulas that could be useful to solve it.

We also think that the stochastic approach possibly allows a general axiomatization, but this problem will be further studied in a future work. However, in this paper, as in the previous one (Janssen, Manca & De Medici (1995)), we take the first steps in this topic.

It is important to point out that these kinds of problems are, in a more general environment, typical microeconomic problems (see for example Mas-Colell, Whinston & Green (1995)). In this environment, they become a deterministic case rather than a stochastic one.

In this paper we will detail how the microeconomic approach is related to the axiomatic finance theory. We will also explain how it is a central problem, in the stochastic environment, to be able to forecast the probability distribution (lottery) as a function of the state and the times of financial operation and, in this way, to evaluate the expected utility form of the operation. To forecast the probability distribution, the "discrete time non-homogeneous semi-Markov processes" (DTNHSMP) will be used, which were introduced in Janssen & De Dominicis (1984), Janssen & Manca (2007). We will also present the numerical solution to these special kinds of processes as given in De Dominicis & Manca (1984), giving some new results for DTNHSMP in the numerical solution of the transient case, i.e. with a finite horizon. Finally, we will present an applicative example that will solve the process and then present results that can be achieved by implementing DTNHSMP.

The financial literature has already addressed the problem of considering the development of financial operations over time using stochastic processes, but only in particular cases.

So there are, in addition to the two fundamental papers by Black & Scholes (1973) on option pricing and by Vasicek (1977) on stochastic interest rate, many other papers that were written but, fundamentally the theory was developed only for application in a particular problem, sometimes to evaluate derivatives, other times to forecast the evolution of interest rates, but never, to the authors' knowledge, to give a general framework to evaluate any kind of financial operation. Also , a number of very interesting papers written in the last years, such as those by Buhlmann (1992), (1994) and Norberg (1995), treat particular cases and are not useful to address the problem of evaluating any kind of financial operation.

So we can say that none of these papers have tackled the problem of constructing an axiomatic theory of financial operation evaluation in a stochastic environment. Our approach is quite general and permits application in any financial problem and also in the derivative evaluation, for example Janssen, Manca & Di Biase (1997) and (1998).

2. Deterministic Environment

Fundamentally, the mathematics of finance is based on the study of preference between dated sums, where a dated sum is a couple of real numbers i.e.:

$$(S,t), S,t \in \Re \tag{2.1}$$

where S is a sum and t a time.

Given a people and an epoch we have:

$$(S',t') \preceq (S'',t'') \tag{2.2}$$

if the people prefer to have S'' at time t'' instead of S' at time t', then we say that the dated sum *(S, t)* is strictly preferred to (S',t'), and we denote:

$$(S',t') \prec (S'',t'') \tag{2.3}$$

in the case that it is verified that:

$$(S',t') \preceq (S'',t'') \tag{2.4}$$

and that it is not verified that:

$$(S'',t'') \preceq (S',t') \tag{2.5}$$

Furthermore, in the case that it is verified that:

$$(S',t') \preceq (S'',t'') \text{ and } (S',t') \preceq (S'',t'') \tag{2.6}$$

we say that the dated sums (S',t') and (S'',t'') are indifferent, and we denote:

$$(S',t') \approx (S'',t'') \tag{2.7}$$

In general we suppose that, for our individual, the following holds:

$$(S,t') \prec (S,t'') \text{ iff } \begin{cases} t' > t'' & S > 0 \\ t' < t'' & S < 0 \end{cases} \tag{2.8}$$

$$(S',t) \prec (S'',t);\ S' < S'' \tag{2.9}$$

The preference order relation that we defined is supposed to be complete and transitive (Duffie, (1988)). In this way, given a people and a given instant, (2.7) defines a so-called indifference relation $\Re$ on dated sums. So, we say that:

$$(S',t')\ \Re\ (S'',t'') \text{ iff } (S',t') \approx (S'',t'') \ . \tag{2.10}$$

As a further remark, we point out that, in the hypothesis of completeness and transitivity of the preference relation, the related indifference relation is reflexive, symmetric and transitive, i.e. an equivalence (Mas-Colell, Whinstone & Greene, (1995)). As already known (Volpe di Prignano, (1985)), in this case the interest law related to the indifference relation is the compound law.

Considering the dynamic time development, the indifference relation can change, depending on the evolution of the money utility function of the people that we are considering. In the same way that two different people will, usually, have different indifference relations.

This is a static approach to the theory of the preference between dated sums, but we can also study this phenomenon from a dynamic point of view. In fact, given t', t'' and S', for the given assumptions, then we have that $\exists! S''$ and (2.7) hold. For this reason we can define the following three variable functions:

$$S'' = \varphi(t', t'', S') \tag{2.11}$$

This function gives, for each triple, the only sum that satisfies (2.7).

It is clear that this is a continuous approach to the problem; in fact, all three variables and also the result are continuous. It is possible to discretize the sums and, in this way, to obtain:

$$E = \{S_1, S_2, \ldots, S_n\}, \tag{2.12}$$

which is the set of possible sums. Everything remains the same, except that (2.11) represents a three variable function in which one of the parameters and the function can assume a finite number of values.

Furthermore, we can suppose that $t \in \aleph$ and, in this case, (2.11) represent a three variable discrete function.

3. The Stochastic Environment

If the two dated sums are fixed "a priori", then the people who would like to exchange are working in a deterministic environment; but, usually a person, who has a sum at a given time and would like to invest this sum for a given period, doesn't know what amount he will consequently receive from a given type of investment. However it is reasonable to suppose that the given person will know, at time t'', the interval within the sum can change, i.e. in discrete environment if we have (S', t') then at time t'' we can have:

$$E \in \{S_1, S_2, \cdots, S_m\}, \tag{3.1}$$

where S_1 is the minimum value at time t'' that the sum S can assume and S_m is the maximum value and the possible values belong to $[S_1, S_m]$.

In this way we can consider E as the set of possible outcomes of a random variable (r.v.). If we work according to the static approach, we have to construct the distribution probability

$$P = \{p_1, p_2, \cdots, p_m\} \tag{3.2}$$

of this r.v..

Once we know (3.1) and (3.2) it is possible to evaluate the operation at time t'' by means of:.

$$\overline{S} = \sum_{i=1}^{m} p_i S_i , \tag{3.3}$$

which gives the expected value of our r.v. and:

$$\sigma(S) = \sqrt{\sum_{i=1}^{m} p_i (S_i - \overline{S})^2} \tag{3.4}$$

represents its variability.

With this information (expected value and riskiness) the person can decide whether to perform the investment or not.

Also in the stochastic approach we can study the dynamic development of the phenomenon. In this case the model can be constructed once we know the variation of the sums, since the information will depend on the probability distribution that we are going to construct. For this reason (2.11) can be seen as a distribution that depends on the three variables; the sum S' at time t', the time t'', and the other variable S'' that represents the outcomes of the r.v.. We can describe the probability distribution of this r.v. in the following way:

$$p(S', S'', t', t'') = P\left[S(t'') = S'' \middle| S(t') = S'\right] \tag{3.5}$$

where:

$$S', S'' \in S \text{ and } t', t'' \in \aleph \tag{3.6}$$

Once we have computed (3.5) we can also have, for the dynamic case, the expected value and the riskiness of the financial operation.

It is important to consider that, in a stochastic environment, considering the financial operations prior to the epoch of contract is meaningless: This is the reason why the times are positive in (3.6). Further observation reveals that (3.5) can be considered as a stochastic process.

Moreover, it should be pointed out that, usually, when a person decides to invest an amount of money, the time when the operation will end, as well as the sum, is unknown. For this reason we can also consider the disinvesting time as a r.v.. This fact implies that, to study the problem correctly, we should also consider the time t'' as a r.v., therefore we need a bidimensional stochastic process that will be able to consider all the described aspects.

4. The Stochastic Process Approach in the Discrete Time Case

It is clear that when we deal with the dynamic stochastic approach to our problem we are defining a stochastic process that studies the evolution of the sums during the time of the contract duration. In our definitions we follow the approach given in Cynlar (1975) and in Janssen & Manca (2006).

As we previously noted, in the real word, we are not interested in the continuous state approach, in fact if we invest, for example, 1000 US $ (a relatively small sum) an outcome rounded at most to the nearest cent provides enough information, we are not interested in the smaller decimals. This is the main reason prompting utilization of a finite state space. Another recent paper described the advantages of working with a discrete state space (Buhlmann, (1994)).

Furthermore, from an applicative point of view, it makes sense to also consider discretized time. Depending on the kind of investment, we are perhaps interested in knowing the results after an hour or a day or maybe a year, but certainly not instant after instant.

Therefore, for the sake of applicability, it is sensible in this situation to work in a discrete time and discrete state space environment.

Let:

$$E = \{S_1, S_2, \ldots, S_m\} \tag{4.1}$$

the discrete state space and:

$$t \in \aleph \tag{4.2}$$

Now we need to define DTNHSMP with a finite state space.

If X_n represents the value of the sum at transition n, it is usual to assume that the stochastic process

$$(X_n, n \geq 0) \tag{4.3}$$

is a non-homogeneous Markov process where the transition probability function at time t is:

$$P_s = p_{ij(s)}, \tag{4.4}$$

which represents the embedded Markov chain in the DTNHSMP. This gives the probability to go from state i to state j at time s, where state k represents the sum $S_k \in E$.

Clearly this approach is not satisfactory because the time of change can no longer be considered another r.v. We can improve this basic presentation with the introduction of

$$(T_n, n \geq 0) \tag{4.5}$$

where T_n represents the time at transition n and thus we get a random sum that runs in the time i.e. a r.v.. We can now introduce the two dimensional stochastic process

$$((X_n, T_n), n \geq 0) \tag{4.6}$$

where clearly:

$$0 \leq T_0 \leq T_1 \leq \ldots \leq T_n \leq \ldots \tag{4.7}$$

T_0 represents the time of the first investment of the sum.

The $(X - T)$ process is called a discrete time non-homogeneous Markov renewal process.

The basic reason for building the evolution model is that the $(X - T)$ process satisfies the assumption of additive non-homogeneous semi-Markovianity as defined in Janssen & De Dominicis (1984). This means that for all $n>0$, we have:

$$P\left[X_{n+1} = j, T_{n+1} \leq t \middle| X_\nu, T_\nu, \nu \leq n-1, X_n = i, T_n = s\right] =$$

$$= P\left[X_{n+1} = j, T_{n+1} \leq t \middle| X_n = i, T_n = s\right] \tag{4.8}$$

with of course $s<t$.

Property (4.8) is simply a two-dimensional Markov condition for the $(X - T)$ process.

The associated non-homogeneous semi-Markov matrix kernel $\mathbf{Q}$ is defined as a four variable function whose general element is given by:

$$Q_{ij(st)} = P\left[X_{n+1} - j, T_{n+1} \leq t \middle| X_n = i, T_n = s\right]. \tag{4.9}$$

Now it is possible to express (4.3) in the following way:

$$p_{ij(s)} = P\left[X_{n+1} = j \middle| X_n = i, T_n = s\right] \tag{4.10}$$

and so with relation (4.9):

$$p_{ij(s)} = Q_{ij(s,\infty)} \tag{4.11}$$

For the sequel we also need to introduce the following probabilities:

$$H_{i(st)} = P\left[T_{n+1} \leq t \middle| X_n = i, T_n = s\right], \tag{4.12}$$

knowing that at time s we have the sum S_i, (4.12) gives the probability of a transition before or at time t.

Of course we also have:

$$H_{i(st)} = \sum_{j \in E} Q_{ij(st)} \tag{4.13}$$

$$H_{i(s\infty)} = 1 \tag{4.14}$$

Another interesting r.v. is the sojourn time in one of the states after a transition in this state. For example, if at time s the r.v. sum has the value S_i, then the probability that this sum becomes S_j before t will be represented by the function

$$G_{ij(st)} = P\left[T_{n+1} \le t \middle| X_n = i, X_{n+1} = j, T_n = s\right] \tag{4.15}$$

From basic DTNHSMP results (Janssen & De Dominicis (1984)), we can write:

$$Q_{ij(st)} = G_{ij(st)} p_{ij(s)}. \tag{4.16}$$

To write the evolution equations in the discrete case, it is necessary to define the following values:

$$b_{ij(st)} = P[X_{n+1} = j, T_{n+1} = t | X_n = i, T_n = s]. \tag{4.17}$$

Therefore, we immediately get:

$$b_{ij(st)} = \begin{cases} 0, & s \ge t \\ Q_{ij(st)} - Q_{ij(st-1)} & s < t \end{cases} \tag{4.18}$$

and conversely:

$$Q_{ij(st)} = \sum_{h=s}^{t} b_{ij(sh)}. \tag{4.19}$$

Now we can define the associated non-homogeneous semi-Markov process Z as

$$Z = (Z_t, t \in \aleph) \tag{4.20}$$

representing the situation at time t of the dated sum.

The transition probabilities of the Z-process are defined in the following way:

$$P_{ij(st)} = P\left[Z_t = j \middle| Z_s = i\right]. \tag{4.21}$$

The evolution equations of the Z-process are:

$$P_{ij(st)} = \delta_{ij}(1 - H_{i(st)}) + \sum_{h=1}^{m}\sum_{\theta=s}^{t} b_{ih(s\theta)} P_{hj(\theta t)} \cdot \qquad (4.22)$$

where δ_{ij} is the Kronecker symbol. Expressed this way, the first part of the right side in (4.22) represents the probability of remaining in the state i and is not equal to zero iff i is equal to j. Furthermore, the second part indicates the probability of staying at time t in the state j once the system reaches state i at time s and there is at least one transition between s and t.

We would like to highlight that Z_t is a process in which the state is a couple of sums and times and (4.22) represents the probability that we were looking for at the end of the previous paragraph.

5. The Numerical Solution

The equation (4.22) in block matrix form can be written in the following way:

$$\mathbf{P}_{(s,t)} = \mathbf{D}_{(s,t)} + \sum_{\theta=s}^{t} \mathbf{B}_{(s,\theta)} \mathbf{P}_{(q,t)} \qquad (5.1)$$

where,

$$D_{i,j(s,t)} = \delta_{ij}(1 - H_{i(st)}) . \qquad (5.2)$$

Each element of (5.9) is an m-order square matrix; furthermore $\mathbf{D}_{(st)}$ is a diagonal matrix and results:

$$\mathbf{D}_{(ss)} = \mathbf{I}_m \qquad (5.3)$$

and if s>t then all the blocks are zero.

From (5.1) we obtain:

$$\mathbf{P}_{(st)} - \sum_{\theta=s}^{t} \mathbf{B}_{(sq)} \mathbf{P}_{(qt)} = \mathbf{D}_{(st)} , \qquad (5.4)$$

which can be written as:

$$\begin{bmatrix} \mathbf{I} & -\mathbf{B}_{(0,1)} & -\mathbf{B}_{(0,2)} & -\mathbf{B}_{(0,3)} & \cdots \\ \mathbf{0} & \mathbf{I} & -\mathbf{B}_{(1,2)} & -\mathbf{B}_{(1,3)} & \cdots \\ \mathbf{0} & \mathbf{0} & \mathbf{I} & -\mathbf{B}_{(2,3)} & \cdots \\ \mathbf{0} & \mathbf{0} & \mathbf{0} & \mathbf{I} & \cdots \\ \vdots & \vdots & \vdots & \vdots & \ddots \end{bmatrix} * \begin{bmatrix} \mathbf{P}_{(0,0)} & \mathbf{P}_{(0,1)} & \mathbf{P}_{(0,2)} & \mathbf{P}_{(0,3)} & \cdots \\ \mathbf{0} & \mathbf{P}_{(1,1)} & \mathbf{P}_{(1,2)} & \mathbf{P}_{(1,3)} & \cdots \\ \mathbf{0} & \mathbf{0} & \mathbf{P}_{(2,2)} & \mathbf{P}_{(2,3)} & \cdots \\ \mathbf{0} & \mathbf{0} & \mathbf{0} & \mathbf{P}_{(3,3)} & \cdots \\ \vdots & \vdots & \vdots & \vdots & \ddots \end{bmatrix} = \begin{bmatrix} \mathbf{D}_{(0,0)} & \mathbf{D}_{(0,1)} & \mathbf{D}_{(0,2)} & \mathbf{D}_{(0,3)} & \cdots \\ \mathbf{0} & \mathbf{D}_{(1,1)} & \mathbf{D}_{(1,2)} & \mathbf{D}_{(1,3)} & \cdots \\ \mathbf{0} & \mathbf{0} & \mathbf{D}_{(2,2)} & \mathbf{D}_{(2,3)} & \cdots \\ \mathbf{0} & \mathbf{0} & \mathbf{0} & \mathbf{D}_{(3,3)} & \cdots \\ \vdots & \vdots & \vdots & \vdots & \ddots \end{bmatrix} \quad (5.5)$$

To devise the solution for the evolution equation, it is necessary to solve an infinite order linear system. This system results in one solution. This result was proven in De Dominicis & Manca (1984), generalizing results given in Riesz (1913).

The solution can be obtained by means of the truncation method demonstrated in Riesz (1913), which can be described in the following way:

a) solution of the system for the first n equation and the first n unknown;
b) solution of the system given by the first $n+1$ equation and unknown;
c) the first n components obtained in b) are compared with the solution obtained in a), if the corresponding components of the two solutions differ by less then a fixed ε, then the iterative **process** is stopped, otherwise

$$n+1 \rightarrow n \quad (5.6)$$

is posed and the procedure is iterated starting with another time from a).

In our case, this algorithm can be applied without problems; the only difference is that, at each step, it is necessary to add a new row and a new column of order m square matrices that form the (5.5) system. If there are n rows and n columns in the previous step, then the new iteration should give *2n+1 m*-order square matrices more for each three matrices in (4.12) but, as can be seen, n of these blocks for all the three matrices are null matrices and do not contribute to the solution. For this reason, for each step the number of equations and unknowns increases according to $m^2(n+1)$.

Suppose that we have to solve the system up to the time n, which means

$$\begin{bmatrix} \mathbf{I} & -\mathbf{B}_{(0,1)} & -\mathbf{B}_{(0,2)} & \cdots & -\mathbf{B}_{(0,n)} \\ \mathbf{0} & \mathbf{I} & -\mathbf{B}_{(1,2)} & \cdots & -\mathbf{B}_{(1,n)} \\ \mathbf{0} & \mathbf{0} & \mathbf{I} & \cdots & -\mathbf{B}_{(2,n)} \\ \vdots & \vdots & \vdots & \ddots & \vdots \\ \mathbf{0} & \mathbf{0} & \mathbf{0} & \cdots & \mathbf{I} \end{bmatrix} * \begin{bmatrix} \mathbf{P}_{(0,0)} & \mathbf{P}_{(0,1)} & \mathbf{P}_{(0,2)} & \cdots & \mathbf{P}_{(0,n)} \\ \mathbf{0} & \mathbf{P}_{(1,1)} & \mathbf{P}_{(1,2)} & \cdots & \mathbf{P}_{(1,n)} \\ \mathbf{0} & \mathbf{0} & \mathbf{P}_{(2,2)} & \cdots & \mathbf{P}_{(2,n)} \\ \vdots & \vdots & \vdots & \ddots & \vdots \\ \mathbf{0} & \mathbf{0} & \mathbf{0} & \cdots & \mathbf{P}_{(n,n)} \end{bmatrix} = \begin{bmatrix} \mathbf{D}_{(0,0)} & \mathbf{D}_{(0,1)} & \mathbf{D}_{(0,2)} & \cdots & \mathbf{D}_{(0,n)} \\ \mathbf{0} & \mathbf{D}_{(1,1)} & \mathbf{D}_{(1,2)} & \cdots & \mathbf{D}_{(1,n)} \\ \mathbf{0} & \mathbf{0} & \mathbf{D}_{(2,2)} & \cdots & \mathbf{D}_{(2,n)} \\ \vdots & \vdots & \vdots & \ddots & \vdots \\ \mathbf{0} & \mathbf{0} & \mathbf{0} & \cdots & \mathbf{D}_{(n,n)} \end{bmatrix} \quad (5.7)$$

This is enough to determine the solution because of the upper triangularity of the coefficient matrix, which allows applying the "backward substitution". Furthermore, the blocks on the main diagonal of the coefficient matrix are identity m-order matrices, however we do not need an m-order matrix inversion.

So, to find the solution at step n, it is only necessary to determine products and sums of m-order matrices.

To carry out the iterative step, it is necessary to solve the following system:

$$\begin{bmatrix} \mathbf{I} & -\mathbf{B}_{(0,1)} & \cdots & -\mathbf{B}_{(0,n)} & -\mathbf{B}_{(0,n+1)} \\ \mathbf{0} & \mathbf{I} & \cdots & -\mathbf{B}_{(1,n)} & -\mathbf{B}_{(1,n+1)} \\ \vdots & \vdots & \ddots & \vdots & \vdots \\ \mathbf{0} & \mathbf{0} & \cdots & \mathbf{I} & -\mathbf{B}_{(n,n+1)} \\ \mathbf{0} & \mathbf{0} & \cdots & \mathbf{0} & \mathbf{I} \end{bmatrix} * \begin{bmatrix} \mathbf{P}_{(0,0)} & \mathbf{P}_{(0,1)} & \cdots & \mathbf{P}_{(0,n)} & \mathbf{P}_{(0,n+1)} \\ \mathbf{0} & \mathbf{P}_{(1,1)} & \cdots & \mathbf{P}_{(1,n)} & \mathbf{P}_{(1,n+1)} \\ \vdots & \vdots & \ddots & \vdots & \vdots \\ \mathbf{0} & \mathbf{0} & \cdots & \mathbf{P}_{(n,n)} & \mathbf{P}_{(n,n+1)} \\ \mathbf{0} & \mathbf{0} & \cdots & \mathbf{0} & \mathbf{P}_{(n+1,n+1)} \end{bmatrix} =$$

$$\begin{bmatrix} \mathbf{D}_{(0,0)} & \mathbf{D}_{(0,1)} & \cdots & \mathbf{D}_{(0,n)} & \mathbf{D}_{(0,n+1)} \\ \mathbf{0} & \mathbf{D}_{(1,1)} & \cdots & \mathbf{D}_{(1,n)} & \mathbf{D}_{(1,n+1)} \\ \vdots & \vdots & \ddots & \vdots & \vdots \\ \mathbf{0} & \mathbf{0} & \cdots & \mathbf{D}_{(n,n)} & \mathbf{D}_{(n,n+1)} \\ \mathbf{0} & \mathbf{0} & \cdots & \mathbf{0} & \mathbf{D}_{(n+1,n+1)} \end{bmatrix} \tag{5.8}$$

Now we compute the nth column blocks of the matrix **P** of the equation (5.8). Taking into account (5.3), we get:

$$\begin{aligned} \mathbf{P}_{(n,n)}^{(n+1)} &= \mathbf{I} \\ \mathbf{P}_{(n-1,n)}^{(n+1)} &= \mathbf{D}_{(n-1,n)} + \mathbf{B}_{(n-1,n)} \mathbf{P}_{(n,n)}^{(n+1)} \\ &\vdots \\ \mathbf{P}_{(0,n)}^{(n+1)} &= \mathbf{D}_{(0,n)} + \sum_{r=1}^{n} \mathbf{B}_{(0,r)} \mathbf{P}_{(r,n)}^{(n+1)} \end{aligned} \tag{5.9}$$

We put $(n+1)$ as the superscript to signify that (5.9) represents the solutions of the $n+1^{\text{th}}$ step.

From (5.7) and (5.8) it results that the nth column of the (5.7) system is the same as the nth column of the (5.8) system, in this way we have proved the following:

Proposition 5.1 The system (5.5) can be solved by means of the truncation method without applying any iterative process.

This proposition assumes a relevant importance in the DTNHSMP application. In fact, it is clear that, in general, we are interested in finite horizon time forecasting. Furthermore, usually in the non-homogeneous case, it is not possible to manage the asymptotic behavior of this kind of processes. For these reasons, we are interested in solving the DTNHSMP in the applications in the transient case, i.e. in a finite time horizon. However, from proposition 5.1 it results that the transient solution for a given time horizon n corresponds to the first n block matrix of the system (5.5) solution.

The only difficulty in the solution of the transient case can descend from the orders of the matrix and of its blocks. But the algorithms to determine the solutions are very simple and fast. In fact, as previously mentioned, the coefficient matrix is an upper triangular block matrix in which the blocks in the main diagonal are unitary matrices and no matrix inversions are necessary.

The real problem stems from the evaluation of the embedded non-homogeneous Markov chain and the construction of the increasing functions $G_{ij(st)}, t = s, \dots, \infty$. For these tasks it is necessary to use statistical instruments and to construct a "scenario" that permits good utilization of the really powerful tool that we defined.

3. A Numerical Example

To numerically illustrate the proposed model, let us suppose that we are interested in the dynamic evaluation of an asset whose possible values are restricted to the following:

maximum value: state 11 = 20000
intermediate values: state 10 = 19000
state 9 = 18000
state 8 = 17000
state 7 = 16000
state 6 = 15000
state 5 = 14000
state 4 = 13000
state 3 = 12000
state 2 = 11000
minimum value state 1 = 10000.

We postulate up to a two year time horizon. The period posed is a month; in this way we have 11 states and 25 time periods from 0 up to 24.

To derive results we constructed a "Mathematica" program able to solve DTNHSMP.

Table 1. Transition probabilities at time 0

Transition matrix at time 1

	1	2	3	4	5	6	7	8	9	10	11
1	0.11508	0.20508	0.14877	0.09085	0.14684	0.05159	0.09679	0.02471	0.06910	0.01889	0.03230
2	0.15206	0.09237	0.13678	0.13723	0.06661	0.11994	0.10249	0.08070	0.04632	0.05414	0.01137
3	0.07502	0.15543	0.14136	0.10637	0.10817	0.11317	0.10061	0.04767	0.06021	0.04038	0.05163
4	0.10872	0.10830	0.13336	0.13617	0.09829	0.12676	0.10225	0.09837	0.05348	0.01936	0.01494
5	0.05490	0.06953	0.13980	0.10085	0.10465	0.14711	0.09293	0.08720	0.07695	0.06856	0.05753
6	0.07324	0.06784	0.08721	0.11715	0.13471	0.10833	0.08661	0.11907	0.05819	0.07480	0.07285
7	0.06188	0.07998	0.07084	0.08985	0.12023	0.11738	0.08538	0.12760	0.09594	0.06549	0.08543
8	0.02267	0.08570	0.06623	0.07473	0.11365	0.07335	0.12893	0.15199	0.12141	0.07739	0.08396
9	0.00447	0.04391	0.03405	0.06250	0.09829	0.13953	0.10114	0.15492	0.12453	0.09594	0.14071
10	0.01608	0.03288	0.05960	0.07166	0.10436	0.07105	0.07170	0.13814	0.13613	0.13948	0.15893
11	0.02216	0.01298	0.03665	0.02343	0.06396	0.12807	0.15198	0.11846	0.11281	0.14591	0.18360

To apply the semi-Markov processes, it is necessary to evaluate:

1) the transition matrix $\mathbf{P}_{(s)}$, embedded Markov chain in DTNHSMP;
2) the matrix $\mathbf{G}_{(s,t)}$, waiting time distribution functions (d.f.).

The corresponding values can be obtained by means of observation of real data, in this example we filled up both matrices with pseudorandom numbers.

The matrix $\mathbf{P}_{(s)}$ is formed by 25 square matrices each one of order 11. Each of these matrices represents the transition probabilities at time *s*. Filling up these matrices we supposed that the transition probabilities are bigger in the three mean diagonals and they decrease moving away from them. The transition probability matrix at time 1 is reported in the Table 1:

The matrix $\mathbf{G}_{(s,t)}$ is formed by 25×25 square matrices each one of order 11. It is an upper triangular block matrix. It results that:

$$G_{ij(s,t)} > 0 \text{ if } s < t, \;\; i, j \in \{1,\ldots,11\}, \; s \in \{0,\ldots,23\} \tag{6.1}$$

Table 2. D.F. of waiting time in a fixed state given the arrival state

1.2		2.5	
0.0686693	0 - 1,	0.048234	1 - 2
0.0869034	0 - 2,	0.0517992	1 - 3
0.125819	0 - 3,	0.103144	1 - 4
0.173014	0 - 4,	0.109809	1 - 5
0.177101	0 - 5,	0.172370	1 - 6
0.239573	0 - 6,	0.239397	1 - 7
0.271002	0 - 7,	0.286419	1 - 8
0.325844	0 - 8,	0.351679	1 - 9
0.394935	0 - 9,	0.400787	1 - 10
0.445495	0 - 10,	0.470971	1 - 11
0.513563	0 - 11,	0.504282	1 - 12
0.558356	0 - 12,	0.519115	1 - 13
0.602921	0 - 13,	0.541922	1 - 14
0.620377	0 - 14,	0.545760	1 - 15
0.645842	0 - 15,	0.562321	1 - 16
0.665479	0 - 16,	0.610480	1 - 17
0.715788	0 - 17,	0.645973	1 - 18
0.731454	0 - 18,	0.653449	1 - 19
0.781820	0 - 19,	0.726265	1 - 20
0.820131	0 - 20,	0.733316	1 - 21
0.882271	0 - 21,	0.812839	1 - 22
0.898686	0 - 22,	0.888162	1 - 23
0.917190	0 - 23,	0.926003	1 - 24.
0.972981	0 - 24.		

The 25×25 elements of the $\mathbf{H}_{(s,t)}$ are 11 component vectors, as results from (4.13).

Table 3. Expected asset values at period 24

Expected asset value at time 24											
	1	2	3	4	5	6	7	8	9	10	11
1	13888	14221	14476	14526	14799	15120	15142	15547	15687	15943	15923
2	13888	14324	14400	14602	14811	14955	15245	15526	15607	15923	16033
3	13900	14167	14187	14753	14650	14898	15191	15497	15461	15918	16287
4	13699	13949	14331	14415	14781	14916	15216	15562	15830	16133	16267
5	13656	14157	14346	14390	14706	15010	15266	15536	15822	15918	16344
6	13760	13742	14151	14442	14700	14962	15277	15584	15843	16230	16267
7	13467	13914	14093	14472	14627	14916	15314	15708	15803	16454	16436
8	13492	13762	14065	14301	14674	15219	15256	15666	15929	16336	16702
9	13190	13776	14153	14151	14759	15117	15374	15763	16096	16469	16641
10	13324	13649	13972	14264	14552	15101	15416	15846	16264	16422	16694
11	13478	13535	13816	14245	14615	14963	15468	15756	16080	16452	16737
12	13207	13408	13865	14206	14656	15126	15475	15787	16148	16434	17001
13	13134	13399	13773	14189	14555	14988	15309	15673	16295	16440	17007
14	12956	13366	13917	14179	14508	14809	15528	15819	16227	16483	16862
15	12982	13287	13610	14323	14574	15085	15484	15835	16420	16765	17064
16	12982	13613	13828	14169	14541	14911	15420	15832	16384	16625	17011
17	12800	13077	13726	14042	14508	15056	15447	15848	16351	16912	17444
18	12791	13316	13748	14065	14481	15149	15473	16107	16294	16887	17183
19	12878	13115	13524	14193	14480	15120	15555	15847	16314	16976	17501
20	12907	13181	13656	13766	14462	15196	15636	16158	16348	16901	17627
21	12658	13024	13647	14010	14572	14972	15623	16060	16631	17046	17410
22	12589	12893	13572	14039	14476	14899	15512	15952	16672	17181	17378
23	12525	12834	13298	13820	14278	15160	15643	16085	16795	17271	17783
24	12273	12708	12790	13600	14370	14978	15574	16273	16721	17398	17985

Table 4. Expected asset present values at period 24

Expected asset present value at time 24											
	1	2	3	4	5	6	7	8	9	10	11
1	12597	12899	13130	13176	13424	13714	13734	14102	14229	14460	14442
2	12648	13045	13114	13299	13489	13620	13884	14140	14214	14502	14602
3	12710	12954	12973	13491	13396	13623	13891	14171	14138	14556	14893
4	12578	12808	13158	13235	13572	13695	13971	14288	14535	14813	14936
5	12589	13051	13225	13266	13557	13838	14074	14323	14587	14675	15067
6	12737	12721	13099	13369	13607	13850	14141	14425	14665	15023	15058
7	12517	12932	13099	13450	13595	13863	14234	14600	14688	15293	15276
8	12591	12843	13125	13346	13694	14202	14237	14620	14865	15245	15586
9	12359	12908	13261	13259	13829	14165	14406	14770	15083	15432	15593
10	12536	12842	13145	13420	13691	14208	14504	14908	15302	15451	15706
11	12732	12786	13052	13457	13806	14135	14612	14884	15190	15542	15811
12	12527	12717	13151	13474	13902	14347	14678	14974	15317	15588	16125
13	12508	12761	13117	13514	13862	14275	14580	14927	15519	15657	16197
14	12389	12781	13309	13559	13873	14161	14849	15127	15517	15762	16124
15	12465	12758	13068	13752	13994	14484	14867	15204	15765	16097	16384
16	12515	13124	13332	13659	14019	14375	14866	15263	15795	16027	16400
17	12391	12659	13286	13592	14044	14574	14952	15341	15828	16371	16885
18	12433	12942	13362	13670	14075	14724	15039	15655	15837	16413	16701
19	12568	12799	13198	13851	14131	14755	15181	15465	15921	16567	17079
20	12648	12915	13381	13489	14171	14890	15321	15833	16019	16561	17272
21	12454	12814	13427	13784	14337	14730	15371	15801	16362	16771	17129
22	12436	12737	13408	13869	14300	14719	15323	15759	16469	16973	17167
23	12424	12730	13191	13708	14163	15038	15517	15955	16659	17131	17639
24	12223	12656	12738	13545	14312	14917	15511	16207	16653	17328	17912

Table 5. Asset values standard deviations at period 24

Asset values standard deviations at time 24											
	1	2	3	4	5	6	7	8	9	10	11
1	2945	2932	2936	2808	2935	2831	2842	2883	2958	2943	3028
2	3031	3012	2919	2820	2796	2835	2859	2851	2862	2986	3018
3	3112	2988	2861	2826	2811	2859	2790	2910	2973	2995	3016
4	3101	2959	2931	2832	2752	2711	2841	2750	2832	2946	3083
5	3032	2987	2892	2782	2759	2808	2827	2819	2935	3013	3049
6	3005	2976	2862	2735	2731	2770	2744	2746	2898	2964	3078
7	3101	2973	2862	2744	2635	2724	2643	2712	2897	2842	3068
8	3111	2940	2805	2713	2659	2685	2721	2713	2782	2898	3040
9	3007	2949	2863	2659	2718	2630	2669	2675	2801	2877	3065
10	3123	2940	2783	2720	2613	2579	2623	2637	2686	2917	3037
11	3162	2932	2741	2595	2605	2685	2568	2636	2858	2939	3084
12	3149	2824	2768	2612	2561	2562	2565	2732	2808	3008	2972
13	3072	2861	2687	2609	2578	2556	2527	2660	2710	2936	3010
14	2983	2877	2805	2606	2510	2524	2584	2622	2749	2918	3061
15	3014	2775	2581	2680	2539	2541	2562	2653	2663	2827	3026
16	3071	2924	2757	2534	2474	2538	2489	2528	2681	2885	3089
17	2930	2723	2597	2523	2501	2360	2562	2553	2696	2806	2898
18	3012	2811	2758	2546	2427	2424	2391	2527	2783	2662	3022
19	3114	2751	2614	2601	2351	2441	2444	2527	2718	2804	2850
20	3086	2838	2705	2413	2503	2458	2340	2493	2656	2811	2820
21	2958	2800	2653	2582	2369	2471	2418	2590	2605	2641	2995
22	2967	2622	2476	2402	2393	2408	2275	2472	2486	2658	2954
23	2895	2543	2507	2230	2301	2405	2377	2441	2399	2542	2838
24	2806	2462	2020	2290	2157	2296	2298	2249	2307	2350	2679

Once (4.22) is solved, we can then obtain the following probability distributions:

$$P_{i,1(s,t)},\ldots,P_{i,11(s,t)} \text{ with } i\in\{1,\ldots,11\} \text{ and } s\in\{0,\ldots,24\},\ s\le t\,.$$

Now it is possible to compute for each *i, s ,t* of the (6.2) the asset mean values and related standard deviations.

It must also be considered that we are working in the transient case, with a 24 month horizon time, therefore we consider all of these d.f. to be trimmed at the last period.

An example of the increasing d.f. is reported in Table 2. The increasing d.f. are more precisely reported in the transition from state 1 to state 2 starting at time 0, as well as from state 2 to state 5 starting at time 1; the second index representing the time of change, the difference between the two times represents the waiting time in the starting state.

After the construction of the embedded Markov chain and the distribution functions, we were then able to apply the DTNHSMP.

In the first step we obtain the matrix $\mathbf{Q}_{(s,t)}$, after this we can compute the matrix $\mathbf{B}_{(s,t)}$. The next step is to obtain the matrix $\mathbf{H}_{(s,t)}$. Finally, we can solve the evolution equation (4.22).

In Tables 3 and 4 the expected asset values and the related present values are given, respectively. The rows represent the time period and the columns represent the starting state. The values at period 24, starting from month 0 up to month 23, are given in the first table. In the second table, the same values discounted at the starting time are given. The monthly rate of interest is equivalent to 5% per year, which means about .00407412. In Tables 5 and 6, the standard deviations are given relative to the elements of Tables 3 and 4, respectively.

Tables 7 and 8 present, as in Table 3 and 4, the expected asset values and the related present values, respectively. This time the values are given at time period 23 starting from month 0 up to month 22. Tables 9 and 10 give the standard deviations relative to the elements of Tables 7 and 8, respectively.

Table 6. Asset present value standard deviations at Period 24

Asset present values standard deviations at period 24											
	1	2	3	4	5	6	7	8	9	10	11
1	2671	2659	2663	2547	2662	2567	2578	2615	2683	2669	2746
2	2761	2743	2659	2568	2546	2582	2604	2597	2606	2720	2749
3	2846	2732	2616	2584	2570	2614	2551	2661	2719	2739	2758
4	2847	2717	2691	2600	2527	2489	2609	2525	2600	2705	2831
5	2795	2753	2666	2565	2544	2589	2606	2599	2705	2778	2811
6	2782	2754	2650	2532	2528	2564	2540	2541	2683	2744	2849
7	2882	2764	2660	2550	2449	2532	2457	2520	2693	2642	2852
8	2904	2743	2618	2532	2481	2505	2540	2532	2596	2704	2837
9	2818	2763	2683	2492	2547	2464	2501	2506	2625	2696	2872
10	2939	2766	2618	2559	2458	2426	2468	2481	2527	2744	2857
11	2987	2769	2589	2452	2461	2536	2426	2490	2700	2777	2913
12	2987	2678	2626	2478	2429	2430	2433	2591	2663	2853	2819
13	2926	2725	2559	2485	2455	2434	2407	2533	2580	2796	2867
14	2852	2751	2683	2492	2400	2414	2471	2507	2628	2790	2928
15	2894	2664	2479	2573	2437	2440	2460	2548	2557	2715	2905
16	2960	2819	2658	2442	2385	2447	2400	2437	2584	2781	2978
17	2837	2636	2514	2442	2421	2285	2480	2471	2609	2716	2805
18	2927	2732	2680	2474	2359	2356	2324	2456	2705	2587	2937
19	3039	2685	2551	2539	2294	2382	2385	2466	2652	2737	2781
20	3024	2780	2650	2365	2453	2409	2293	2443	2602	2754	2763
21	2911	2755	2610	2541	2331	2431	2379	2548	2563	2598	2946
22	2931	2591	2446	2373	2364	2379	2247	2442	2456	2626	2918
23	2871	2523	2487	2212	2283	2386	2358	2421	2379	2521	2815
24	2795	2452	2012	2281	2148	2286	2289	2240	2297	2340	2668

Table 7. Expected asset values at period 23

Expected asset values at period 23											
	1	2	3	4	5	6	7	8	9	10	11
1	13495	13989	14310	14388	14778	15097	15207	15679	15835	16212	16188
2	13534	14085	14218	14489	14729	14948	15337	15668	15797	16162	16349
3	13613	13895	13935	14574	14555	14929	15227	15599	15635	16239	16591
4	13422	13714	14143	14306	14700	14891	15306	15712	16046	16404	16514
5	13287	13884	14182	14236	14638	15037	15339	15709	16026	16176	16676
6	13365	13468	13957	14256	14624	14981	15323	15669	16045	16531	16624
7	13104	13665	13857	14296	14513	14926	15414	15806	15968	16730	16861
8	13160	13523	13864	14113	14579	15223	15269	15771	16159	16648	17085
9	12853	13427	13964	13973	14718	15087	15457	15955	16299	16788	17000
10	12940	13332	13741	14138	14504	15138	15467	16010	16491	16674	17061
11	13040	13234	13563	14087	14575	14966	15543	15903	16267	16709	17170
12	12794	13081	13602	14078	14544	15176	15534	15864	16316	16697	17407
13	12759	13126	13516	14026	14407	14952	15380	15883	16538	16762	17379
14	12576	13023	13583	13984	14419	14808	15625	15973	16491	16848	17320
15	12517	12840	13237	14117	14452	15143	15585	15998	16673	17187	17522
16	12510	13197	13511	13996	14406	14917	15468	16028	16615	17013	17429
17	12296	12657	13446	13875	14490	15056	15528	16036	16719	17299	17949
18	12253	12828	13406	13933	14436	15031	15577	16250	16681	17301	17839
19	12200	12679	13200	13913	14343	14987	15614	16056	16624	17460	18178
20	12079	12587	13178	13619	14463	15122	15754	16305	16914	17518	18255
21	11752	12631	13149	13661	14437	14830	15582	16168	17083	17723	18165
22	11625	11908	12937	13665	14326	15058	15711	16234	17372	17806	18320
23	11530	11687	12612	13294	14247	15008	15775	16386	17593	18283	18954

Table 8. Expected asset present values at period 23

Expected asset present values at period 23											
	1	2	3	4	5	6	7	8	9	10	11
1	12291	12740	13032	13104	13458	13749	13849	14279	14421	14765	14743
2	12376	12880	13001	13249	13468	13669	14025	14328	14445	14779	14950
3	12499	12758	12794	13381	13364	13708	13981	14323	14356	14910	15233
4	12374	12643	13038	13189	13552	13728	14110	14485	14793	15123	15224
5	12299	12852	13128	13178	13550	13919	14199	14541	14835	14973	15437
6	12422	12518	12972	13250	13592	13924	14242	14563	14913	15364	15451
7	12229	12752	12931	13341	13543	13929	14384	14750	14901	15612	15735
8	12331	12671	12991	13224	13661	14264	14308	14778	15141	15599	16009
9	12092	12632	13138	13146	13847	14194	14542	15011	15335	15795	15994
10	12224	12594	12981	13356	13702	14300	14611	15124	15578	15752	16117
11	12368	12553	12865	13362	13824	14196	14743	15084	15429	15848	16286
12	12185	12458	12955	13407	13852	14453	14794	15109	15539	15902	16578
13	12201	12551	12925	13413	13777	14298	14707	15188	15815	16029	16619
14	12075	12504	13042	13426	13845	14218	15002	15336	15833	16177	16630
15	12068	12379	12762	13610	13933	14599	15025	15423	16074	16569	16892
16	12110	12774	13078	13548	13945	14439	14973	15515	16084	16468	16871
17	11951	12302	13069	13485	14083	14633	15092	15586	16250	16814	17446
18	11957	12519	13083	13597	14088	14669	15201	15858	16279	16884	17409
19	11955	12424	12935	13633	14055	14685	15299	15733	16290	17109	17812
20	11884	12384	12966	13399	14230	14878	15500	16042	16641	17235	17961
21	11609	12478	12989	13495	14262	14651	15393	15972	16876	17509	17945
22	11531	11811	12833	13554	14210	14936	15584	16103	17232	17662	18172
23	11483	11639	12561	13240	14189	14947	15711	16320	17522	18209	18877

Table 9. Asset value standard deviations at period 23

Expected asset present values at period 23											
	1	2	3	4	5	6	7	8	9	10	11
1	2938	2887	2889	2730	2863	2735	2741	2834	2923	2916	3028
2	3018	3010	2869	2751	2722	2800	2780	2789	2804	2954	3031
3	3089	2979	2786	2759	2744	2772	2726	2855	2942	2973	2974
4	3066	2921	2884	2737	2694	2614	2773	2684	2763	2876	3071
5	3005	2954	2844	2678	2684	2730	2742	2744	2874	2974	3012
6	2992	2938	2788	2654	2677	2647	2640	2683	2821	2926	3073
7	3046	2940	2799	2673	2554	2648	2565	2610	2873	2749	3031
8	3044	2876	2719	2633	2534	2563	2692	2591	2679	2810	2970
9	2929	2896	2804	2546	2616	2523	2575	2581	2704	2777	2998
10	3068	2856	2714	2635	2534	2458	2503	2546	2563	2862	2964
11	3149	2833	2641	2475	2449	2537	2391	2539	2782	2873	3022
12	3066	2710	2633	2497	2405	2485	2499	2601	2720	2968	2865
13	2947	2741	2563	2478	2457	2413	2400	2514	2567	2893	2865
14	2852	2787	2639	2424	2387	2397	2473	2518	2644	2839	2955
15	2894	2620	2386	2575	2337	2361	2458	2436	2467	2683	2860
16	2972	2808	2678	2428	2338	2343	2351	2386	2525	2717	3002
17	2729	2520	2406	2356	2296	2189	2434	2405	2534	2610	2728
18	2841	2646	2541	2406	2112	2256	2230	2296	2629	2471	2849
19	2926	2586	2345	2330	2128	2236	2206	2273	2556	2593	2545
20	2793	2623	2332	2044	2051	2102	2092	2229	2336	2553	2510
21	2632	2665	2394	2052	2099	2097	1970	2321	2275	2280	2771
22	2521	2078	2143	2084	1906	2068	1820	2134	1774	2297	2569
23	2496	1902	1721	1532	1810	1591	1334	1838	1690	1940	2144

In Tables 11 and 12 there are, as in previous tables, expected asset values and related present values, respectively, but this time the starting period is always 0 and the evaluation period goes from 1 up to 24. As can be seen, the last two rows of matrices 11 and 12 are equal to the first row of Tables 1,5 and 2,6, respectively.

Table 10. Asset present value standard deviations at Period 23

Expected asset present value standard deviations at period 23

	1	2	3	4	5	6	7	8	9	10	11
1	2676	2630	2632	2486	2607	2491	2496	2581	2662	2656	2758
2	2760	2753	2624	2515	2489	2561	2542	2550	2564	2701	2771
3	2837	2735	2558	2533	2520	2546	2503	2621	2701	2730	2731
4	2827	2693	2658	2523	2483	2409	2556	2475	2547	2652	2831
5	2782	2735	2632	2479	2484	2527	2538	2540	2660	2753	2788
6	2781	2730	2592	2467	2488	2460	2453	2494	2622	2720	2856
7	2843	2744	2612	2495	2384	2471	2394	2436	2681	2566	2829
8	2853	2695	2548	2467	2374	2402	2522	2427	2510	2633	2783
9	2756	2724	2638	2396	2461	2373	2423	2428	2544	2613	2821
10	2898	2698	2563	2489	2394	2322	2364	2405	2421	2704	2800
11	2987	2688	2505	2348	2323	2406	2268	2408	2638	2725	2867
12	2920	2581	2507	2378	2291	2366	2380	2477	2591	2827	2728
13	2818	2621	2451	2370	2350	2307	2295	2404	2455	2767	2740
14	2739	2676	2534	2328	2292	2302	2374	2418	2539	2726	2838
15	2790	2526	2300	2483	2253	2276	2369	2349	2379	2586	2757
16	2877	2718	2592	2351	2263	2268	2276	2310	2444	2630	2906
17	2653	2450	2338	2290	2232	2128	2366	2338	2463	2537	2652
18	2773	2582	2480	2348	2061	2201	2176	2240	2566	2411	2780
19	2867	2534	2298	2283	2085	2191	2162	2227	2505	2540	2494
20	2748	2581	2295	2011	2018	2068	2058	2193	2298	2512	2469
21	2600	2633	2365	2027	2074	2072	1946	2293	2247	2252	2737
22	2501	2061	2126	2067	1890	2052	1805	2117	1760	2278	2549
23	2486	1895	1714	1526	1802	1584	1329	1831	1683	1933	2135

Table 11. Expected asset values from the period 1 up to the period 24 starting at time 0

Expected asset values from the period 1 up to the period 24 starting at time 0											
	1	2	3	4	5	6	7	8	9	10	11
2	10113	11108	12064	13034	14009	14984	15983	17006	17916	18860	19902
3	10272	11215	12139	13089	14009	14997	15980	16950	17867	18769	19745
4	10370	11337	12245	13150	14002	15008	15901	16897	17794	18711	19536
5	10429	11478	12302	13148	14025	14985	15899	16837	17720	18595	19410
6	10588	11618	12410	13188	14066	14994	15835	16792	17609	18500	19231
7	10708	11756	12462	13242	14098	14988	15772	16758	17558	18411	19057
8	10815	11863	12525	13275	14115	15020	15767	16702	17453	18294	18912
9	10904	11998	12616	13347	14176	15002	15747	16666	17372	18192	18752
10	11034	12104	12693	13422	14186	15034	15694	16614	17278	18081	18581
11	11170	12209	12794	13456	14216	15010	15644	16552	17197	17986	18403
12	11323	12318	12835	13493	14234	15054	15606	16554	17108	17868	18262
13	11445	12410	12929	13545	14244	15054	15584	16526	17013	17804	18100
14	11600	12518	12999	13585	14298	15064	15559	16456	16914	17669	17954
15	11795	12650	13100	13659	14348	15080	15539	16387	16840	17559	17811
16	11936	12764	13228	13729	14377	15086	15511	16326	16772	17427	17657
17	12076	12892	13368	13796	14418	15065	15447	16262	16707	17322	17479
18	12219	12987	13504	13841	14428	15042	15416	16174	16601	17187	17294
19	12418	13149	13626	13923	14475	15041	15372	16129	16489	17054	17126
20	12603	13329	13754	14022	14549	15042	15349	16035	16389	16909	16937
21	12806	13474	13882	14092	14572	15038	15302	15946	16252	16754	16769
22	12995	13631	14014	14171	14613	15057	15270	15868	16100	16580	16569
23	13210	13797	14143	14272	14684	15061	15204	15762	15973	16388	16379
24	13495	13989	14310	14388	14778	15097	15207	15679	15835	16212	16188

Table 12. Expected asset present values from the period 1 up to the period 24 starting at time 0

Expected asset present value standard deviations at period 23											
	1	2	3	4	5	6	7	8	9	10	11
2	10072	11063	12015	12981	13952	14923	15918	16937	17843	18784	19821
3	10188	11124	12041	12983	13895	14876	15851	16813	17722	18617	19585
4	10244	11200	12096	12991	13832	14826	15709	16692	17578	18484	19299
5	10261	11293	12103	12936	13799	14744	15643	16565	17434	18295	19096
6	10375	11384	12160	12923	13783	14692	15517	16454	17254	18128	18844
7	10450	11473	12161	12922	13759	14627	15392	16354	17135	17968	18598
8	10512	11531	12174	12903	13719	14599	15324	16234	16964	17781	18381
9	10555	11614	12212	12920	13722	14522	15243	16132	16816	17610	18152
10	10638	11669	12237	12940	13676	14494	15130	16017	16657	17432	17913
11	10725	11723	12284	12920	13650	14412	15021	15893	16512	17270	17669
12	10828	11779	12274	12903	13611	14396	14923	15830	16360	17086	17463
13	10900	11819	12313	12900	13566	14337	14842	15739	16203	16956	17238
14	11003	11874	12329	12886	13562	14288	14758	15609	16043	16759	17029
15	11142	11950	12375	12904	13554	14246	14679	15480	15909	16587	16825
16	11229	12009	12445	12916	13526	14193	14593	15360	15779	16395	16613
17	11315	12080	12526	12927	13510	14117	14474	15237	15655	16231	16378
18	11403	12120	12603	12917	13465	14037	14386	15094	15492	16039	16139
19	11541	12221	12665	12940	13454	13979	14287	14991	15326	15851	15917
20	11666	12338	12732	12979	13467	13924	14208	14843	15171	15652	15677
21	11806	12422	12798	12992	13434	13864	14107	14700	14982	15445	15459
22	11932	12515	12867	13011	13417	13824	14020	14569	14782	15223	15213
23	12079	12616	12933	13051	13428	13773	13903	14414	14606	14986	14978
24	12291	12740	13032	13104	13458	13749	13849	14279	14421	14765	14743

Finally, in Tables 13 and 14 the standard deviations related to Tables 11 and 12 are reported, respectively.

Table 13. Asset value standard deviations from the period 1 up to the period 24 starting at time 0

Asset value standard deviations from the period 23 1 up to the period 24 starting at time 0											
	1	2	3	4	5	6	7	8	9	10	11
2	752	700	552	498	633	526	416	534	709	821	669
3	1146	1017	911	760	820	799	665	871	917	1086	1100
4	1286	1235	1172	932	940	910	913	1072	1138	1218	1473
5	1393	1439	1295	1042	1086	1051	1002	1209	1326	1427	1640
6	1603	1645	1479	1151	1294	1136	1215	1329	1517	1564	1867
7	1733	1801	1571	1296	1445	1239	1356	1469	1628	1669	2063
8	1855	1918	1687	1416	1572	1390	1417	1627	1781	1822	2190
9	1933	2035	1801	1541	1713	1464	1510	1746	1881	1917	2303
10	2043	2106	1885	1656	1799	1568	1649	1830	2016	2009	2417
11	2145	2187	1987	1733	1924	1694	1771	1949	2132	2099	2523
12	2253	2276	2045	1832	2027	1787	1878	2017	2211	2179	2608
13	2349	2345	2143	1913	2098	1872	1952	2106	2275	2251	2675
14	2426	2425	2211	1987	2196	1950	2037	2170	2350	2336	2728
15	2528	2494	2309	2091	2298	2031	2119	2232	2426	2400	2775
16	2601	2543	2400	2175	2369	2124	2189	2288	2496	2452	2833
17	2646	2595	2490	2265	2433	2193	2291	2338	2547	2539	2881
18	2698	2648	2561	2329	2513	2272	2349	2432	2597	2600	2917
19	2734	2701	2644	2408	2581	2347	2426	2491	2681	2668	2957
20	2788	2741	2707	2460	2644	2417	2469	2574	2724	2739	2984
21	2831	2776	2759	2536	2701	2494	2545	2633	2801	2790	3000
22	2882	2806	2810	2594	2775	2577	2626	2697	2846	2829	3019
23	2902	2833	2864	2667	2818	2657	2688	2771	2898	2879	3026
24	2938	2887	2889	2730	2863	2735	2741	2834	2923	2916	3028

Table 14. Asset present value standard deviations from the period 1 up to the period 24 starting at time 0

Asset present value standard deviations from the period 23 1 up to the period 24 starting at time 0											
	1	2	3	4	5	6	7	8	9	10	11
2	749	697	550	496	631	524	414	532	706	817	666
3	1136	1009	904	754	814	793	659	864	909	1077	1091
4	1270	1220	1157	921	929	899	902	1059	1125	1204	1456
5	1370	1416	1274	1025	1068	1034	986	1190	1305	1404	1613

Asset present value standard deviations from the period 23 1 up to the period 24 starting at time 0

	1	2	3	4	5	6	7	8	9	10	11
6	1571	1612	1449	1128	1268	1114	1190	1302	1487	1533	1829
7	1691	1758	1533	1265	1410	1210	1323	1434	1588	1629	2014
8	1803	1864	1640	1377	1528	1351	1377	1582	1731	1771	2129
9	1871	1970	1743	1492	1658	1418	1462	1690	1821	1856	2229
10	1969	2030	1818	1596	1734	1511	1589	1765	1944	1937	2330
11	2060	2100	1908	1664	1847	1627	1700	1872	2047	2016	2423
12	2155	2176	1955	1752	1938	1709	1796	1929	2114	2083	2494
13	2237	2233	2041	1822	1998	1783	1859	2006	2167	2144	2548
14	2301	2300	2098	1885	2083	1850	1932	2058	2229	2216	2588
15	2388	2356	2181	1975	2171	1918	2002	2109	2292	2267	2622
16	2447	2392	2258	2046	2229	1998	2060	2153	2349	2307	2665
17	2479	2432	2333	2122	2280	2055	2147	2191	2387	2379	2700
18	2518	2471	2390	2174	2345	2120	2192	2269	2423	2426	2722
19	2541	2511	2457	2238	2398	2181	2255	2315	2492	2479	2748
20	2581	2538	2506	2277	2448	2237	2285	2383	2521	2536	2762
21	2610	2559	2543	2338	2490	2299	2346	2428	2582	2572	2765
22	2646	2576	2580	2382	2548	2366	2411	2476	2613	2598	2772
23	2654	2591	2619	2439	2577	2430	2458	2534	2650	2633	2767
24	2676	2630	2632	2486	2607	2491	2496	2581	2662	2656	2758

CONCLUSION

In this paper we demonstrated how it is possible to apply DTNHSMP to evaluate a financial operation, which we think is an important step towards applying these kinds of processes to real world finance problems.

We also gave a numerical example illustrating the great number of data that can be obtained by solving the non-homogeneous semi-Markov processes. In the paper a DTNHSMP numerical solution is also reported. The proposition shows that the solution in the transient case also gives the general solution of the process in the considered horizon time.

The proposed approach can also be useful for the development of an axiomatic theory of financial exchange in a stochastic environment, but in order to investigate this aspect it is necessary to study the non-homogeneous semi-Markov process with continuous time and continuous state space. Furthermore, extending these kinds of processes could be used to extend the continuous time continuous state space Markov processes (diffusion processes) used in the evaluation of financial instruments.

The authors are also working on applying the model to a real problem, which takes into account the necessity to collect data specific to the DTNHSMP in order to apply the model in the financial environment.

References

Black F. & Scholes M. (1973), The Pricing of Options and Cooperate Liabilities. *Journal of Political Economy* 81, p. 637-659.

Buhlmann H., (1992), Stochastic Discounting, *Insurance, Mathematics and Economics* 11, p.113-127.

Buhlmann H., (1994), Continous and Discrete Models in Finance, in particular for Stochastic Interest Rate, *Rivista AMASES* 17, p. 3-20.

Cynlar E. (1975) . *Introduction to stochastic processes.* Prentice Hall, NY.

De Dominicis R. & Manca R. (1984), An algorithmic approach to non-homogeneous semi-Markov processes, *Communications in statistics, Simulation and computation.* 13, p. 113-127

Duffiapplie D. (1988), *Security Markets Stochastic Models*, Academic Press.

Janssen J. & De Dominicis R. (1984), Finite non-homogeneous semi-Markov processes. *Insurance: Mathematics and Economics*. 3 p. 157-165.

Janssen J., Manca R. (2006) Applied semi-Markov Processes (with J. Janssen) Springer Verlag, New York.

Janssen J., Manca R (2007).Semi-Markov risk models for Finance, Insurance and Reliability. Springer.

Janssen J., Manca R., Volpe di Prignano E. (2009) Mathematical Finance. Deterministic and stochastic models.Iste-Wiley.

Janssen J., Manca R. & De Medici G. (1996), Financial Operation Evaluation: a Semi-Markov Approach, *Proc. of the V AFIR Symposium* vol. 3 bis, CESIAF, Brussels.

Janssen J., Manca R. & Di Biase G. (1997), Markov and Semi-Markov Option Pricing Models with Arbitrage Possibility. *Applied Stochastic Models and Data Analysis* 13, p. 103-113.

Janssen J., Manca R. & Di Biase G. (1998), Non Homogeneous Markov and Semi-Markov Models for Pricing Derivative products. Submitted to *ASTIN 98 Conference.*

Mas-Colell A., Whinston M.D. & Green J. R. (1995), *Microeconomic Theory.* Oxford University Press.

Norberg R. (1995), A Time-Continous Markov Chain Interest Model with Applications to Insurance. *Applied Stochastic Models and Data Analysis* 11, p. 245-256.

Riesz F. (1913), *Les systemes d'equations lineaires a une infinite' d'inconnues*. Gauthier-Villar Paris.

Vasicek O. (1977), An Equilibrium Characterization of the Term structurte. *Journal of Financial Economics* 5, p. 177-188.

Volpe di Prignano E. (1985), *Manuale di Matematica Finanziaria*, ESI Napoli.

INDEX

T

V

W